Nature in the History of Economic Thought

From antiquity to our own time those interested in political economy have with almost no exceptions regarded the natural physical environment as a resource meant for human use. Focusing on the period 1600–1850, and paying particular attention to major figures including Adam Smith, T.R. Malthus, David Ricardo and J.S. Mill, this book provides a detailed overview of the intellectual history of the economic consideration of nature from antiquity to modern times. It shows how even someone like Mill, who was clearly influenced by romantic notions regarding the spiritual need for contact with pristine nature, ultimately regarded it as an economic resource. Building on existing scholarship, this study demonstrates how the rise of modern sensitivity to nature, from the late eighteenth century in particular, was in fact a dialectical reaction to the growing distance of modern urban civilization from the natural environment. As such, the book offers an unprecedentedly detailed overview of the intellectual history of economic considerations of nature, whilst underlining how the history of this topic has been remarkably consistent.

Nathaniel Wolloch is a Fellow at the Minerva Humanities Center, Tel Aviv University, specializing in European intellectual history. He is the author of *Subjugated Animals: Animals and Anthropocentrism in Early Modern European Culture* (2006), and *History and Nature in the Enlightenment: Praise of the Mastery of Nature in Eighteenth-Century Historical Literature* (2011).

Nature in the History of Economic Thought

How natural resources became an economic concept

Nathaniel Wolloch

Routledge
Taylor & Francis Group
LONDON AND NEW YORK

First published 2017
by Routledge
2 Park Square, Milton Park, Abingdon, Oxon OX14 4RN

and by Routledge
711 Third Avenue, New York, NY 10017

First issued in paperback 2018

Routledge is an imprint of the Taylor & Francis Group, an informa business

British Library Cataloguing-in-Publication Data
A catalogue record for this book is available from the British Library

Library of Congress Cataloging-in-Publication Data

Names: Wolloch, Nathaniel, author.
Title: Nature in the history of economic thought: how natural resources became an economic concept / Nathaniel Wolloch.
Description: Abingdon, Oxon; New York, NY: Routledge, 2017. | Includes bibliographical references.
Identifiers: LCCN 2016021683
Subjects: LCSH: Economics—History. | Nature—Economic aspects—History. | Natural resources—History.
Classification: LCC HB75 .W787 2017 | DDC 333.701—dc23
LC record available at https://lccn.loc.gov/2016021683

ISBN 13: 978-1-138-32988-1 (pbk)
ISBN 13: 978-1-138-69149-0 (hbk)

Typeset in Times
by codeMantra

To my parents, Dina and Amatzia Wolloch

Contents

Preface

Business news and news regarding the environment have both become a ubiquitous part of our lives. Turning on our televisions, we have come to expect news about global warming, or about environmental hazards and disasters. As for economic topics, these receive their very own broadcast networks and dominate much of primetime newscasts. For most of human history, however, this was not the case. People have always been preoccupied with their material condition, and particularly in early societies were well-aware of their ineluctable and often dangerous dependence on their natural surroundings. Yet they had no substantive reflexive awareness of these issues, or at least have left us very little evidence of such interests. They were much more preoccupied with their immediate familial and social relations, with their dependency on monarchs or other despotic rulers, with religious rites and of course with the harsh realities of daily life in the pre-industrial age. With material and cultural progress, however, they became increasingly interested in thinking about their existence, both individual and collective. Gradually, this led to the development of various intellectual and artistic achievements. Among these was an increasing interest in what modern terminology would define as social and economic conditions. At the same time, philosophical and scientific advances led to increasing interest in the natural world and human beings' mutual interaction with it. It was only a matter of time before these two interests were combined, and people became interested in the place that nature played in social and economic development.

This book is concerned with how the discussion of this topic emerged and developed in the history of political-economic thought. I use the term "political economy" here in the sense in which it was used till the late nineteenth century, conceiving economics as integrated with broad social, political and cultural developments. At the outset it should be made clear not just what this book is about, but what it is not about. It is not about the history of economic thought in general, let alone about economic history. It is not about concepts such as natural law or natural rights, but strictly about nature as a physical resource. Yet it is also not about environmental philosophy or environmental history strictly defined (though perhaps it should be considered an integral part of the latter), nor about the history of specific technologies of utilizing nature, nor about the history of specific types or cases of natural-resource management. While these topics surface at times throughout the discussion, this is primarily a study in intellectual history. Much of the following pages will be concerned with the nineteenth century, yet little attention will be given to the wide range of attitudes toward nature that emerged in this period, not least to romantic art, and even less to scientific developments, most significantly the Darwinian revolution. The focus here is very precise – this is a book about how the economic consideration of nature emerged as an intellectual concept. This might seem initially an esoteric scholarly exercise, and indeed some passages below will probably prove difficult reading to all but specialists. Nevertheless, I believe that without detailing the development of this idea, we cannot truly understand how the modern debate about the environment has emerged. Given that the use of natural resources, and the theorizing of this use, developed in tandem, we might say that without understanding the intellectual history of this theorizing we cannot really comprehend the human-nature relationship in general. Whether one believes in the need to enhance the use of natural resources, or in the need to curb this use for environmental or social reasons, an understanding of this history is absolutely necessary.

Surprisingly, very few scholars have attempted a broad yet thorough intellectual-history study of this topic. The existing literature either presents general overviews, or else more detailed studies of specific chapters in this history. Among the many valuable studies in either of these veins I have found works by Margaret Schabas, Richard Grove and Fredrik Jonsson particularly significant and helpful. These will be considered below in the appropriate places. I should state in advance that despite criticizing some of their interpretations, I have found their work indispensable and of very high quality. At this point I will only mention my main departure from their respective interpretations. Like most historians, they search for moments of change. In my opinion, however, the history of economic considerations of nature was one of consistent development of one main theme – the emphasis on the ineluctable need to maximize the use of natural resources and thus further human development. As the following pages will document in detail, despite the many changes in the history of economic thought, and in the way this theme was considered, this basic assumption remained constantly evident, mutatis mutandis. This is a history of continuity rather than change.

This book could have been much lengthier had my scholarly abilities been greater. As a scholar primarily of the Enlightenment, I have centered mainly on the economic thought of the seventeenth, eighteenth and nineteenth centuries, and particularly on classical political economy. Some attention, nevertheless, has been given both to earlier and to later economic thought. This seemed necessary both to enable a proper understanding of the roots of classical political economy on the one hand, and of its significant influence on modern economic thought on the other. It was also essential for making a reasonable claim that the history of economic thought in general, not just classical political economy, has persisted in a fundamentally similar consideration of nature. Readers will, however, hopefully accept the fact that I am not an expert on either these earlier or later periods.

The book is arranged into three parts, divided along thematic and sometimes chronological lines. Detailed attention has been devoted to major figures such as

Adam Smith, David Ricardo, T. R. Malthus and J. S. Mill, but many other figures, some well-known, others less so, receive attention, at times quite detailed. The chapters of the first part outline major developments in the economic thought of antiquity, the Middle Ages, the Renaissance and in seventeenth-century mercantilism. The chapters of the second part center on how the Enlightenment legacy influenced the development of political-economic thought, not least regarding such topics as historical progress and the issue of population. They consider major developments in eighteenth-century economic thought such as Physiocracy, and particularly the constitutive contribution of Adam Smith, but also the significant influence which these developments had on nineteenth-century thought. This part, in sum, examines the ideological foundations of the classical political-economic emphasis on the use of natural resources. The next and final part examines the more prescriptive aspects of the economic consideration of nature – how political economists discussed the use of natural resources, most prominently agriculture, but in other ways as well, and what policy measures they recommended to enhance the efficiency of this use. Finally, in the Epilogue, I discuss some central developments in modern economic considerations of nature, both in the nineteenth century (socialism and neoclassicism) and in the twentieth century. While I am perhaps biased toward my own field of study, I think that the emphasis of classical political economy is a justified one. On the one hand the classicists crystalized earlier economic notions in an unprecedented systematic form, and on the other they created the foundations for modern economic thought. This is particularly clear when it comes to the history of attitudes toward nature.

This book is in many ways a sequel to my previous book, *History and Nature in the Enlightenment: Praise of the Mastery of Nature in Eighteenth-Century Historical Literature*. Shortly after finishing this earlier study it became clear to me that the analytical observations of Enlightenment historians were subsequently, indeed almost immediately, transferred into the nascent field of political economy, yet this time not just as observations, but also as policy prescriptions. This was to have profound implications for the development of the human relationship with the natural environment in modern times. In a proleptic vein I would like to address a criticism which a few of the reviewers of *History and Nature in the Enlightenment* have raised in recent years, and which one of the reviewers of the present manuscript has also expressed. These scholars have objected to what they see as the restricted thematic focus of these books. They point to the fact that attitudes toward nature were not confined to the historiographical, or to the economic, realms, and that scientific, literary and philosophical perspectives developed different considerations of nature. My outlines of the development of the historiographical and the economic outlooks praising the use of natural resources therefore seem to them one-dimensional and limited. However, nowhere have I claimed that these books present a comprehensive outline of the development of attitudes toward nature. In both books I have made it abundantly clear that other considerations, not least romantic sensitivity toward nature, were also significant. Yet these other considerations of nature have received much more attention from scholars over the years, to the detriment of a truly comprehensive historical understanding. Perhaps some of these scholars feel an encroachment on their interpretative perspectives, I'm not sure. Nevertheless, the history of such topics as the historiographical and the economic consideration of nature also needs to be told, and this is the aim of these books.

Furthermore, some scholars might mistake my focus on historical views which often indiscriminately advocated the use of nature, as somehow an agreement with these outlooks. Yet this is far from true. My aim is to further a better knowledge of the history of attitudes toward nature. I do not consider it part of the task of historians to utilize the historiographical platform as a forum for political or ethical advocacy. That is not to say that I aim for any Rankean "objectivity." As a historian of Enlightenment historiography I sympathize with the need for an ethical motivation behind the writing of history. Yet the historian's views, in my opinion, should be insinuated, mainly by a proper presentation of historical information and interpretation of sources, rather than brought to center stage. The latter approach is the province of philosophers, not historians, and this is particularly true when considering environmental issues. Most environmental historians (in the broad sense of historians of the human interaction with, and attitude toward, nature) are no doubt motivated by what might be termed, rather broadly, a "pro-environmental" outlook. In my earlier studies, particularly on the history of attitudes toward animals, I also let this ethical outlook underline my historical research in a rather overt manner. In recent years, however, I have come to realize that this does more harm than good in terms of proper historical research, and historians can make their best contribution by informing public and philosophical debates rather than participating in them directly (qua historians; as human beings, of course, they have as much right, and indeed duty, to participate in these debates). I should admit that I have also come to a more moderate view of environmental topics, and it seems to me that unfettered extremes, whether in favor of industrial use of natural resources, or in favor of environmental and conservation policies, are both practically and philosophically unproductive. The challenge is finding the proper balance between them.

I would like to thank one of the reviewers of the manuscript for some very constructive suggestions. The team at Routledge also deserve thanks for their efficiency and amiability. I would also like to mention my friends and colleagues in both the Eighteenth-Century Scottish Studies Society, and the Mediterranean Society for the Study of the Scottish Enlightenment. Conversations with them in recent years have often helped the formation of my ideas on the topics discussed in this book.

As always my greatest debt is to my family. As a small, very small, token of gratitude, this book is dedicated to my parents.

List of abbreviations

EET *Early English Tracts on Commerce*, ed. J. R. McCulloch (Cambridge: Cambridge University Press, 1970 [1856]).

EPP T. R. Malthus, *An Essay on the Principle of Population*, ed. Patricia James, 2 vols. (Cambridge: Cambridge University Press, 1989).

LPE Dugald Stewart, *Lectures on Political Economy*, ed. Sir William Hamilton, 2 vols. [Vols. VIII–IX of *The Collected Works of Dugald Stewart*] (Edinburgh: Thomas Constable, and London: Hamilton, Adams, and Co., 1855–56; reprint Bristol: Thoemmes Press, 1994).

MPPE John Stuart Mill, *Principles of Political Economy, with Some of Their Applications to Social Philosophy*, ed. J. M. Robson, Introduction by V. W. Bladen, 2 vols. [Vols. II–III of *The Collected Works of John Stuart Mill*] (Toronto: University of Toronto Press, and London: Routledge & Kegan Paul, 1965).

OSPE Nassau W. Senior, *An Outline of the Science of Political Economy* (London: W. Clowes and Sons, 1836; reprint New York: Augustus M. Kelley, 1965).

RPPE David Ricardo, *On the Principles of Political Economy and Taxation* [Vol. I of *The Works and Correspondence of David Ricardo*], ed. Piero Sraffa, with the collaboration of M. H. Dobb (Cambridge: Cambridge University Press, 1951).

SPPO James Steuart, *An Inquiry into the Principles of Political Oeconomy*, 3 vols. (Dublin: James Williams and Richard Moncrieffe, 1770; reprint London: Thoemmes Press, and Tokyo: Kinokuniya Company, 1992).

STPE Jean-Baptiste Say, *A Treatise on Political Economy, Or the Production, Distribution and Consumption of Wealth*, trans. C. R. Prinsep, Introduction translated by Clement C. Biddle (Philadelphia: Claxton, Remsen & Haffelfinger, 1880; reprint New York: Augustus M. Kelley, 1971).

WN Adam Smith, *An Inquiry into the Nature and Causes of the Wealth of Nations*, eds. R. H. Campbell, A. S. Skinner, and W. B. Todd, 2 vols. (Oxford: Clarendon Press, 1976).

Part I

Attitudes toward nature from antiquity to mercantilism

1 From antiquity to the Renaissance

A consistent and systematic body of economic theorizing only emerged, at the earliest, with seventeenth-century mercantilism. Nevertheless, earlier economic ideas were often original and influential. While our attention here will be primarily with classical political economy, we therefore need to devote at least some, if far from comprehensive, attention to classical and medieval sources, and their attitude toward nature. The view of nature that emerged in the seventeenth century inherited these earlier notions, and specifically their anthropocentric cosmology, with its consideration of nature as primarily a resource meant for human use.[1] By the eighteenth century nascent political-economic thought developed these earlier notions and incorporated them within a more systematic economic philosophy.

Greek *Oikonomia*

Two main roots combined to establish the predominant Western view of nature – the one biblical cosmology, the other classical philosophy. Modern critics have often viewed the biblical outlook, specifically as developed in the book of *Genesis*, as the source of Western civilization's anthropocentric, and often destructive, attitude toward nature.[2] Whether one accepts this criticism or not, it remains clear that biblical cosmology did play a vital role in substantiating the view of nature as meant for human use. Yet the classical heritage also played an equally significant role in this context. Platonic and Aristotelian cosmology lay the foundations of what in the early modern era came to be known as the Great Chain of Being, the idea that all life forms were arranged in a continuous chain from the least to the most developed, with each link including all the qualities of the former, with an additional new one of its own. While the angels and God stood above and apart from this chain, in the terrestrial realm its superior and ultimate manifestation were human beings.[3] By the early modern era, both the religious and the classical cosmologies had become intertwined, serving as a forceful anthropocentric *Weltanschauung* affecting many aspects of the cultural attitude toward nature, not least the development of the economic concept of natural resources.[4]

Two examples, Aristotle and Xenophon, will serve to demonstrate how early ideas of political economy already manifested the notion that nature was first and foremost a resource meant for human cultivation. Both philosophers, at this early stage of Western historical development, already developed the idea of managing natural resources efficiently for human use.[5] Scholars are divided as to whether the Greek debates on political economy qualify as economic analysis in the modern sense, but for our purposes we can assume as much, since as regards the perception of nature as an economic resource, it is already possible to see manifestations of the more sophisticated outlooks of subsequent eras.[6] At the center of Greek political economy stood the concept of *oikonomia*, essentially the management of the economy of the household, which, when transposed to the larger setting of society in general, formed the etymological root of the notion of political economy, and eventually modern economics. Greek economic thought considered nature as capable of satisfying all human needs without encountering any scarcity. The art of *oikonomia* consisted in managing the excess that nature made possible, in order to generate surplus produce. The prudential challenge this raised was to use this surplus for the benefit of one's friends or the polis, without succumbing to immoral and unnecessary consumption.[7]

Aristotle differentiated between various forms of the production of subsistence, including shepherds, husbandmen, brigands, fishermen and hunters. At times one encountered those employed in more than one of these occupations. This was not yet a type of stadial perception of human progress, which would become ubiquitous in eighteenth-century thought. Nevertheless, there were early vestiges here of similar types of observations relating forms of food production, based on utilization of natural resources, to social arrangements. *Oikonomia* for Aristotle was concerned less with the mere acquisition of inanimate things, and more with the political and social relations among free people as this related, among other things, to such acquisition. In this respect it was also relevant that in considering *oikonomia*, he also differentiated between those who produced their food, and those who obtained it by exchange and retail trade. The former were honorable occupations, the latter, in his opinion, dishonorable and unnatural, a form of profiting at other people's expense (in the Enlightenment this critical view of commerce would be reversed).[8] The useful aspects of acquiring wealth included, first, knowledge of livestock and husbandry, but in addition also less praiseworthy things such as exchange, commerce, usury and service for hire. In between, in terms of its morality, was the form of wealth acquisition that was partly natural, concerned with utilizing nature, specifically land, for the acquisition of things other than food, for example, timber and mining.[9] Aristotle nevertheless considered those occupied in the material aspects of providing the necessaries of life, no matter if they produced food or traded for it, as less vital to society compared with those concerned with the higher tasks of military, political and juridical administration.[10] In making such observations he was far from realizing the connection between material progress and higher cultural developments, which would become such a mainstay of eighteenth-century thought.

Elsewhere, however, he seemed somewhat more cognizant of the need for a proper material basis underlining a state's existence. In this respect the natural qualities of the state's territory were particularly noteworthy, most significantly the quality of the soil and the possibility of an outlet to the sea.[11] Aristotle favored agriculture over other occupations. An agricultural society was the population most amenable to democratic life, followed by a shepherding society. Other democracies, composed of artisans, traders or laborers, were inferior, since these occupations provided no room for excellence.[12] Aristotle praised the acquisition of wealth as part of household management, concerned as it was with obtaining the necessary amounts of food. Yet he condemned the acquisition of superfluous wealth. The acquisition of wealth was part of *oikonomia*, thus of social-political life, so long as it was concerned with production, not with retail and trade. Positive production was based on what nature provided human beings as sources of food. It was at this point that the human task of managing the household began, which in other words meant rationally utilizing natural resources, so as to create the material wealth necessary for the existence of human society. Wealth in this respect was first and foremost food. Aristotle viewed nature as the source providing means of life, and the art of acquiring wealth of this type as a natural occupation.[13] The later idea of economic surplus production as the mainstay of trade and progress was still not recognized in his outlook, and neither was the idea of economic growth. Socratic philosophers such as Aristotle preferred discussing the stationary state of economic existence rather than a situation of growth. Aristotle emphasized adaptation and management in regard to the things nature conferred to human beings, rather than innovation and transformation. The Socratic outlook centered on improving the community's quality of life rather than on social evolution, substantive historical change or the increased control of natural resources.[14] It is therefore not surprising that Aristotle, though from a distinctly non-Malthusian perspective, emphasized the importance of limiting the nation's population.[15]

It should however be emphasized that his logic on this point was far removed from any environmental logic in the modern sense. There was no conception in Aristotle of a limit to natural resources, or of the worth of nature removed from the human context. His cosmological outlook was distinctly anthropocentric, viewing nature as existing for human use. Just as plants existed for the sake of animals, so did animals (and thus plants also) exist for the sake of human beings. This notion of a scale of beings crowned by humanity was evinced when he wrote, "Now if nature makes nothing incomplete, and nothing in vain, the inference must be that she has made all animals for the sake of man."[16]

A similar outlook was shared by Xenophon, whose notion of household management, *oikonomia*, was later to inspire John Ruskin's political economy.[17] Like Aristotle, he shared the preference of managing natural resources rather than transforming them, and evinced a preference for agriculture, regarding it as the mother of all other arts.[18] He was well aware of the relationship between the natural environment and a state's development. He noted how the natural properties of the country in Attica enabled the Athenian inhabitants to obtain food entirely from their own soil, which according to Xenophon was the best means of doing so. The land and sea were abundantly provided with all that human beings needed, from food to stone and silver, and the situation of Athens afforded international trade.[19] Anticipating the view that would become common in Western thought until the countering influence of Malthus, Xenophon, in contrast with Aristotle, regarded a growing population as a positive situation. The same positive estimate pertained to proper cultivation of land, and Xenophon regarded husbandry as a noble pursuit fit even for kings.[20] Land could be considered wealth only when properly utilized to support its owner.[21] Xenophon repeatedly praised agriculture. It provided both food and luxuries, and improved the character of those engaged in it, as well as their military abilities. It had social and other virtues, supported other arts, and moreover, was the pleasantest of occupations. "For when husbandry flourishes, all the other arts are in good fettle; but whenever the land is compelled to lie waste, the other arts of landsmen and mariners alike well-nigh perish."[22] Here in a nutshell was already evident the outlook which would become predominant in the history of economic thought, viewing nature as primarily a resource meant for human cultivation, and considering uncultivated nature as a waste.

Medieval economic views

The combination of the biblical and classical anthropocentric cosmologies became increasingly evident in the Middle Ages, with the pivotal role in this development played by St. Thomas Aquinas, who famously integrated Aristotelianism within the canon of Christian scholasticism. Medieval Christian economic discussions were often concerned with topics such as usury. Nevertheless, they also addressed other economic issues.[23] Aquinas in particular perceived human beings as divinely created by nature both as political and as social beings, thus encompassing both economic and spiritual aspects of human behavior which emerged in the social setting.[24] He repeatedly emphasized the cosmological-religious domination of human beings over nature. Both due to their rationality, and to divine ordinance, nature was meant for their use.[25] External things were not in themselves possessed by human beings, and were only subject to divine command. Yet as far as their use was concerned, human beings had a natural dominion over them, since with the aid of their reason and will, they could utilize such natural things for their advantage. In this respect possession of external things was natural to human beings. In other words, for Aquinas it was the utilization of material nature which validated human cosmological supremacy over it. Here Aquinas evinced a basic preconception of Locke's later labor theory of value. This was also evident when he further emphasized that only in society could individuals devote their attention to their respective occupations.[26] Aquinas did not outline a full labor theory of value in Locke's later sense, yet he did recognize that investment of labor, as occurred in cultivating land, conferred proprietary rights. He may thus have played a part in pointing the way for the subsequent development of the labor theory of value.[27]

After discussing the divinely ordained dominion of human beings over nature based on the book of *Genesis*, Aquinas made an analogy between the creation of the world, and the duties of a king when establishing a city or kingdom. This could only be done based on the use of things which already existed in nature. The king needed to choose a location which was healthy, fertile and easily defended. Internal locations in the city also had to take consideration of the needs and occupations of the various inhabitants.[28] In other words, if only implicitly, Aquinas outlined a philosophy which emphasized human material and social progress based on the proper utilization of natural resources, including the basic role that division of labor played in this process. He was less modern, and more akin to his Greek predecessors, when he claimed that self-sufficiency in providing food was preferable to relying on commerce, which he regarded as advancing public immorality. On the other hand he seemed surprisingly more modern when he claimed that cities should be established in places which were pleasant in terms of their natural beauty, since people could not survive long without pleasure, even though such enjoyment was not to be indulged in excessive manner, otherwise it became morally corrupting.[29]

Aquinas demonstrated how in the scholastic outlook, in contrast with the Socratic, the view of humanity as adjusting itself to the forces of nature was replaced by that of human beings as molders of the physical world.[30] This fundamental change was the result of the coupling of the classical and the biblical outlooks, and was evident in the economic views of other medieval philosophers, for example, John Duns Scotus.[31] Without using the modern term "economy," Scotus, relying on St. Augustine, claimed that the economic value of material things was not in themselves, but rather emerged from their utility for human beings.[32] Before the Fall private property had not existed since people only used what they needed. After the Fall, due to the inequality in powers, vices and virtues, positive law was required to regulate the division of what people needed, thus making private property necessary.[33] This outlook was in line with the common Christian religious consideration of material culture as a necessary evil. According to the resulting laws, anything unclaimed went to the first occupant, and in this way human beings were dispersed over the earth. When the owners of immovable property, however, made no use of it, this property was considered abandoned, in which case whoever occupied it had to become its rightful owner in the interest of the state, to avoid legal battles over its ownership.[34] Like Aquinas, Scotus's views evinced a pre-Lockean conception of value and property.

Late medieval economic discussions continued to retain a distinct notion of divine intervention in all things, economic life included. In the fourteenth century Nicolas Oresme could still claim that Providence had made sure that gold and silver would not be too plentiful, and the attempts of alchemists to produce them would fail, since it would have been inexpedient had the material of money been too plentiful.[35] Yet, as Joel Kaye has claimed, Oresme was a key figure in the late medieval shift in natural philosophy toward such things as quantification and geometrical representation, which was influenced by the experience and understanding of the rapid monetization of the European marketplace and society.[36] By the advent of the early modern period, in any event, the religious attitude toward nature would become eclipsed by the growing empiricism of the Renaissance. What remained more ostensible was the contribution of medieval thought to the idea of historical development, not least in the economic field. In large part this was due to the teleological component of Christian thought, with its emphasis on the advent of the end of history and the Last Judgment, an idea which of course had been absent from the Socratic worldview. While the religious component of this idea remained less in force in modern economic thought, the notion of material and social development and progress was to become increasingly significant for political-economic debates.

Renaissance and pre-mercantilist economic ideas

Historians often allude to a secularizing process which European civilization underwent from the end of the Middle Ages. It is important to remember, however, that this process, though evident and at times with dramatic cultural and intellectual consequences, was essentially relative. At no point in the history of Western civilization, including our own, have secular notions remained unchallenged by persistent religious ideas, the latter often predominating even in contexts considered as significantly secular. As we pass from medieval to early modern and modern economic discourses, it is easy to assume that religious ideas became increasingly irrelevant. This, however, would be a mistake, not least regarding the economic consideration of natural resources. Political-economic discourses, even when not mentioning this explicitly, by and large accepted the anthropocentric legacy of the biblical and classical outlooks. The history of the economic consideration of nature from the early modern era to our own time thus developed under the persistent shadow of this outlook, which regarded nature as first and foremost a resource meant for human use. How exactly this use was to be defined, and within which cultural, economic and social limits, was however a more changeable set of ideas, which enabled significant transformations in attitudes toward nature. Nevertheless, at this early stage of our discussion, we can already state that *grosso modo*, the tale of the economic consideration of nature was essentially a linear one of increasing emphasis on the utilization of natural resources. A more "environmental" consideration of nature, in the modern sense of ecological economics, entered the stage only at a very late point, and its influence, as we shall see toward the end of our discussion, has been far from decisive.

Coming back to the early modern era, *prima facie*, explicit references to divine intervention became scarce in economic literature. An interesting example was Nicholas Copernicus's *Essay on the Coinage of Money*, a surprising work for those used to consider him primarily for his revolutionary contributions to the history of science and astronomy. In this short essay Copernicus evinced slight, though not insignificant, recognition of the material basis for economic development. He mentioned barren soil as one of the potential causes which debilitated kingdoms, even though he did not devote it particular attention.[37] Commenting on the bad effects of debased coin, he noted how cheap money fostered laziness more than it helped the poor, raising the price of food and other products. A rise in the value of money would not truly burden tenants, since in response to the rise in the price of land, they would raise the prices of their agricultural produce and their livestock.[38] Copernicus may not have devoted detailed attention to the utilization of natural resources, yet he was clearly aware of the connection between what in modern terms would be called monetary policy, and the conditions necessary for such utilization.

The year after the death of Copernicus in 1543 saw the birth of the Italian author Giovanni Botero, with whose work we encounter for the first time a systematic economic outlook in the modern sense.[39] Not surprisingly, this outlook also included discussions of aspects of the human-nature economic relationship which will concern us in the following pages, including the cultivation of natural resources, and the issue of population. Machiavelli's humanistic emphasis on the importance of martial virtue in the pursuit of greatness was replaced from the late sixteenth century by a growing emphasis, specifically by Botero, on economic and commercial means to achieve state greatness. This preceded the subsequent eighteenth-century similar emphasis, though without the latter's promotion of self-interest. Botero also had great influence on English seventeenth-century thought, and its promotion of colonialism as an expression of the pursuit of state greatness through economic and commercial means.[40]

Botero claimed that the arts of war and peace were to no avail without eloquence, which in itself required a knowledge of the works of nature underlining human efforts. "Nothing awakens the intellect, illumines the judgment and rouses the mind to great things more than a knowledge… of the order of nature." Here Botero followed with a long list of astronomical, physical, spiritual, botanical, zoological, climatic and other natural phenomena, all from which the ruler "may derive wisdom in the administration of the state and greatness of spirit."[41] A prince also needed to know the natural characteristics of his country so he could "amend it by art and industry." The rulers of China were particularly praiseworthy in this respect.[42] Botero duly recognized the significance of natural resources, human, animal, mineral and water, as a source of revenue for a prince.[43] He emphasized the importance of cultivating natural resources through agriculture and other means. He agreed with the common theory that a fertile climate encouraged idleness, and a barren one industry.[44] This notion, of the inverse relation between a country's fertility, or lack thereof, and cultural decline or progress, was to become commonplace in the eighteenth and nineteenth centuries, and has even been termed the "natural resources curse."[45] We shall repeatedly encounter it throughout our discussion.

Nevertheless, Botero did not always follow this line of argument. He noted how the fact that a city enjoyed fertile natural surroundings did not ensure its greatness, since in such a situation its inhabitants might make do with their local produce, without necessarily aspiring to trade and profit beyond their immediate necessities. A natural location amenable to trade could, however, supply the basis for unifying the inhabitants beyond mere natural existence. Botero still did not recognize the subsequent economic concept of surplus, but he did claim that only in such conditions were a city's inhabitants possessed with more produce than required for immediate consumption. In such a situation they did not need to emigrate or turn to other cities, while on the other hand they could attract merchants from abroad who would trade for this excess local produce. He was not yet a thorough mercantilist, but he did recognize a distinct concept of rivalry between different city-states.[46] There were aspects of a country's natural qualities, other than its fertility, which could enhance progress. Botero noted that the rarity of navigable rivers in Italy prevented its cities from becoming larger and more populous. He claimed that God had created water not only as a necessary element, but mainly as a means for transporting products and connecting different countries, so that human beings, when finding themselves in need of each other's respective products, would mutually trade and thus become a community, leading to the growth of human love and unity. This was a reason for praising the construction of canals.[47]

Like almost all commentators on political-economic issues before the late nineteenth century, Botero particularly emphasized the significance of cultivating land. Agriculture had both material and social benefits. Labor in agriculture, although also in mechanical trades, prompted people to concentrate on their work and keep their distance from higher things such as state and government. Encouraging such occupations was a good means of keeping them pacific and easy to control. In this spirit Romulus had allowed the Romans to labor only in agriculture or war, thus turning them into proper citizens.[48] Agriculture, and all forms of cultivation of the land, together with their ensuing products, were ultimately the basis of propagating population. Therefore it was incumbent upon the ruler to encourage agriculture, as well as all forms of public works such as clearing useless or superfluous forests, draining marshes and constructing canals. Botero also anticipated subsequent economic views regarding the wastefulness of leaving land uncultivated. "Land should not be used unprofitably or made into parks such as there are in plenty in England, where the people complain greatly since they have to go short of grain because of this."[49]

Botero accorded particular significance to enlarging a state's population. This was a source of strength, even though the qualities of the population also mattered, such as their valor, industriousness and willingness to work in agriculture and commerce. The larger the population, the more important it was to cultivate the soil to provide food and raw materials for industry. Botero perceived a mutual connection between the size of the population and the cultivation of natural resources, yet ultimately it was the former which preceded the latter. It was this which enabled the utilization of resources. A state with a large and industrious population would inevitably cultivate its natural resources and prosper. Given enough inhabitants, even were they not industrious, they would make prosperity possible, as well as strategic depth in wartime. "Where there are many people, the land must be well cultivated, and the land provides the foodstuffs necessary for life, and the raw materials for industry."[50] The number of inhabitants, however, was less important than taking proper advantage of their labor to create profit. This required that a city not only possess fertile soil, but also be situated in a properly accessible site, both by land and water, thus attracting foreign merchants. Even this was not enough, though, since it also had to be attractive in terms of its politics, economy, culture and religion.[51] A ruler might augment the number of his country's inhabitants, and thus his power, by encouraging propagation. This could be done either by encouraging marriage, or by promoting agriculture, the arts, education and the establishment of colonies, as well as the assimilation of new territories by alliances or conquest.[52]

The most important thing necessary for enhancing a state's population, wealth and power, was the industry of its inhabitants and the number of crafts in which they were employed. Art was "the rival of nature," and therefore it was necessary to determine what was more important, the fertility of the soil or human industry. Botero had no hesitation in choosing the latter. "Firstly, the products of the manual skill of man are more in number and of greater worth than the produce of nature, for nature provides the material and the object but the infinite variations of form are the result of the ingenuity and skill of man." Raw materials were secondary in importance compared with the products made from them, which were much more expensive than the raw materials. Examples included silk, iron implements, marble and timber. It was much more significant for a state to have inhabitants capable of working raw materials in various ways, than of owning those materials in themselves. This was another reason why not always the countries possessing the most natural resources were also the richest countries. "Nature gives a form to the raw materials and human industry imposes upon this natural composition an infinite variety of artificial forms; thus nature is to the craftsman what raw material is to the natural agent."[53] This differentiation between the natural and the artificial would subsequently resurface in greater detail in mercantilist thought, as would Botero's argument that a ruler needed to prevent the exportation of raw materials necessary for production. Expressing a common early modern notion, Botero viewed the quantity and quality of a state's inhabitants as the initial source of its ruler's power and wealth, since it was these which gave form to nature's products.

Botero, however, was sophisticated enough to recognize that a large population without the proper cultural setting might in fact lead to more harm than good. This pre-Malthusian caution has often been considered probably his most original contribution to political-economic thought. No doubt exaggerating, Joseph Schumpeter has gone so far as to claim that Botero's was "the only performance in the whole history of the theory of population to deserve any credit at all."[54] Botero claimed that a large population was useless in itself if the ability to feed, grow and educate children adequately was lacking. He was also presciently aware of environmental hazards, specifically the spread of disease and plagues, which resulted from crowded and filthy cities with unpurified air. Propagation therefore included not just generation, but also upbringing and support. There was a maximal limit of inhabitants beyond which they became an unhealthy burden to the state. In a healthy state this population remained steady for a lengthy period of time, with an outlet for growing numbers provided by newly-established colonies. Botero claimed that in the last three thousand years the number of members of the human race had been about the same. This view implied that he regarded the growth of one nation's population as coming at the expense of other nations, a rather idiosyncratic "balance of population" which one does not encounter in subsequent mercantilist literature.[55] In any event, he evinced a certain conception of unsustainable over-population, though in contrast to Schumpeter's view, nothing close to Malthus's later more realistic and sophisticated approach.

Botero's views on population were also related to his general views on progress, and specifically his support for the establishment of colonies, and more generally, his view of the civilizing influence which European colonization had on non-Europeans.[56] His historiographical philosophy perceived a point of greatness toward which cities grew. They then either remained stationary, or else declined. This was also the basis for his assumption that the world population in general was divinely ordained to remain static. The propensity for propagation remained constant, yet the actual growth of population, disregarding such disasters as war and famine, was also dependent on the accessibility of food which a city could either grow or import. The more a city became populous, the more acute this problem became, as the example of Rome had proved. Cities were ultimately forced to find outlets either by establishing colonies, or by conquests. Yet, as already noted, Botero claimed that these outlets also had their limit, which in global terms had been reached three millennia earlier, when "the world was replenished as full with people as it is at this present, for the fruits of the earth and the plenty of victual doth not suffice to feed a greater number."[57] This insistence on the static number of global population notwithstanding, Botero recognized, more than any other contemporaneous thinker, the connection between material and cultural progress and the cultivation of natural resources, not least for providing sustenance and thus fueling further progress. These points would later be developed in much greater detail and sophistication by political-economic thinkers from the mercantilists onward. Yet Botero's place as one of the earliest minds to have a clear conception of key economic issues cannot be doubted.

The country, however, which would see the development of political-economic thought more than any other, was England (and later of course Britain in general), where this intellectual development unsurprisingly went in tandem with its gradual rise to European and then world dominance. An interesting case of early mercantilist views in England was presented in a sixteenth-century treatise attributed to John Hales. Hales supported encouraging arable farming so that it would equal pasture. This meant that the government should enlarge the market for corn and limit the market for wool. He was therefore also in favor of limiting enclosures (though not abolishing them), and in favor of a freer market in grain.[58] Enclosures, claimed Hales, would not have been damaging to people's livelihood had the land been distributed among everyone, and each person would have cultivated his own land. Yet in reality, enclosures were reserved for the few, and were enforced, thus turning arable land into pasture. In such a situation, coupled with growing population, most inhabitants were left without a livelihood, and therefore the poverty and general dearth of the era were augmented.[59] Ameliorating this situation required a duties policy to make wool cheaper, and thus less profitable as an export commodity, or, conversely, and through similar tax policies, to make corn more expensive and thus profitable as an exportable commodity.[60] Hales regarded all elements of society – farmers, artisans, scholars, knights, merchants – as mutually dependent. As a result, the damage to land cultivation resulting from unequal enclosures was ultimately harmful to society in general, since it disturbed the balance between the profitability of various occupations, and the different types of uses of land. Furthermore, Hales was aware that the agricultural surplus of a good year could be preserved for subsequent scarce years, as well as be used for international trade.

He was cognizant of the need for trading with foreign nations to obtain products which insufficiently existed in England. Yet he already manifested the developing nascent mercantilist outlook of the positive balance of trade, claiming that imports should not exceed exports.[61]

While discussing enclosures, Hales also noted the importance of encouraging husbandry (in contrast with raising cattle on pasture), by preserving the profitability of agriculture. This could be achieved by affording farmers the greatest possible freedom to sell their produce as they saw fit, a policy which would encourage the economy in general. The moment the price of corn would rise, "yet that price would provoke everie man to set plowghe in the ground, to husband waste groundes, yea to turne the landes which be Inclosed from pasture to arable lande; for every man will the gladder folow that whearin they se the more proffit and gaines. And therby must nedes insue both greate plentie of corne, and also much treasure should be browght into this Realme by occasion therof; and besides that, plentie of all other victualles increased emonst vs."[62] The improved cultivation of land thus had an ameliorative influence on the economy in general. Hales claimed that in England, precisely because its soil was not particularly fertile and arable, this required more labor, which prompted industry and economic development. Conversely, more fertile soil, which did not require great effort to cultivate, would result in a smaller population, and would be occupied more by beasts than by human beings.[63] This of course was a version of the inverse relationship theory between climate and cultural progress which we have already encountered. Like Botero, Hales already recognized several key aspects of subsequent political-economic discourse.

2 Mercantilism and natural resources

Mercantilism in England and elsewhere

What in the sixteenth century were prescient examples of economic insight became in the following century a consistent (though not always systematic) body of mercantilist political-economic discourse, most prominently visible in England.[1] The essential component of mercantilist policy was the idea of promoting national interests, by definition at the expense of other nations – one nation's gain was another's loss (colonies being considered similar to other nations in this respect, to keep them subservient to the mother country). This became evident in the concept of the balance of trade, which had to remain positive, or in other words required maintaining more exports than imports. This conception of a balance of trade as a zero-sum game between nations rested on the assumption of the finiteness of general global resources.[2] The balance of trade policy usually needed to be enforced by government intervention, mainly in the form of duties, taxes and bounties, although occasionally mercantilists recognized that certain aspects of trade were best left free. Mercantilists of course were often more sophisticated than this, and many understood that depending on which products were considered, at times imports might be constructive. A common theme, for example, was that raw materials were better imported, while finished products manufactured from these materials should be exported, thus preserving the dependence of other counties or colonies on the manufacturing nation.[3] Some mercantilists emphasized the fact that bullion, gold and silver, constituted the real measure of wealth, and therefore the balance of trade was first and foremost in the precious metals. Yet other mercantilists recognized that the balance of trade applied to all manner of commodities and to the economy in general. Both approaches left much room to argue for the necessity of advancing the cultivation of the nation's natural resources, whether in themselves, or as resources ultimately translatable to bullion.[4] The ensuing prosperity would become evident not least in a growing population, which would enable devoting more labor to the cultivation of natural resources. Mercantilist writers attempted to reach the proper proportion of population. Some expressed apprehension regarding over-population, but most often the mercantilist outlook advocated increasing population to the utmost.[5] On these points a near-unanimity was discernable among a wide variety of mercantilist authors, many of them members of the merchant class which attained significant economic and political prominence in the seventeenth century, particularly in England. It also often seemed that the mercantilist policies were working. For example, the success in food production in England and Holland created surpluses, thus leading to the exchange of food as a commodity, and consequently also affecting the market in land.[6]

One further point needs to be emphasized to gain a proper understanding of the mercantilist emphasis on utilizing natural resources. This was the influence of the rising rational and mechanistic thought of the Scientific Revolution. Mercantilism attempted to explain social phenomena according to the new methodology of contemporary natural science.[7] Germano Maifreda has traced this process to Renaissance developments, and Joel Kaye has claimed that even earlier, in the late Middle Ages, it was in fact the monetization of the European economy which influenced the quantifying tendencies in natural philosophy.[8] In any event, by the seventeenth century it was from the new scientific praxis that political economy imbibed a distinct anthropocentric assumption about the subservience of nature to human needs, although both spheres of thought ultimately owed this cosmological outlook to the traditional biblical and classical heritage. One might tend intuitively to assume that biblical cosmology was particularly influential in the Middle Ages, yet in fact it became even more so during the Scientific Revolution when, through scientific progress, an attempt was made to recover humanity's prelapsarian control of nature.[9] This position was evident in Francis Bacon's influential commendations for the investigation of nature. In his view humanity had, with the Fall, lost its right over nature. This could only be recovered by toil, understood by Bacon and most scientifically minded contemporaries to mean science, and its resulting material advancement.[10] However, the religious influence on actual scientific praxis was increasingly marginalized, as a combination of rational and mathematical precision, coupled with growing attention to careful empirical investigations, laid the foundations of the modern scientific and technological utilization of nature which would reach its apogee with the advent of the Industrial Revolution. The influence of these scientific innovations on the political-economic consideration of natural resources was therefore of two sorts – first, regarding the increased tendency toward a rational and scientific approach to the discussion of practically any topic, social and economic issues included (what Hume later would term the "science of man"); and second, in considering nature as an object for human manipulation not just in the traditional religious cosmological view of domination, but in actual practical terms, based on the new scientific foundations. Thus, despite the seeming decline in direct religious preconditioning for considerations of nature, the traditional biblical and classical cosmology was subsumed within this new scientific outlook, leading to the development of the modern utilization of nature, as well as its theoretical and intellectual underpinnings in various fields, from natural science to political economy. As we will consider later, this has led some modern commentators to severely criticize the Scientific Revolution as a source for the modern uninhibited use of nature, a critique which ultimately indicts economics as much as the natural sciences. At this point, however, it is enough to say that whatever one thinks of this development, its actual influence cannot be doubted.

This influence can be seen repeatedly in considerations of natural resources, and related issues such as population, in the writings of various mercantilists, by and large extolling trade in general, and protectionist policies to further English interests in particular. For example, Lewes Roberts, who was a member of the East India Company and represented the Levant Company on a mission to Constantinople, favored the cultivation of land as one of the sources for producing tradable products. He considered nature strictly as a useable resource. It yielded both "natural commodities or wares," and "artificial commodities or wares." This differentiation between natural products, meaning raw materials, and artificial ones, meaning products based on manufactured use of such raw materials, was to be commonplace in mercantilist literature. It testified precisely to the influence of the Scientific Revolution, in favoring the utilization of nature, in manufactured "artificial" products, to uncultivated "natural" resources. According to Roberts the natural products which nature and the land yielded without cultivation, were useless to the nation when on the one hand there was no use for them, and on the other hand they were not utilized for commerce. "[T]hese excellencies which nature herein afforded them [the inhabitants of various countries such as the 'Kingdomes of India'], would be prejudiciall to them, and their ground over-laid with sundry (though otherwise) excellent trees, and exquisite Minerals, whose fruit or worth would thus not be requested nor sought after, neither by their neighbours, nor yet by forraigne Nations, where the same are wanting…" Even a country which possessed such commodities would not profit from them, since it would not, through commerce, receive in exchange for them those commodities which it lacked. "Againe, the earth, though notwithstanding it yeeldeth thus naturally the richest and most precious commodities of all others, and is properly the fountaine and mother of all the riches and abundance of the world… yet is it observable, and found true by daily experience in many countries, that the true search and inquisition thereof, in these our dayes, is by many too much neglected and omitted." Lewes accused both the English proprietors of land, and the tenant farmers, of concentrating on immediate profits rather than thinking of the longer term. They therefore neglected such things as cultivating and manuring barren tracts of land, or draining marshy bogs, things which received more attention in some other countries. Yet, according to Lewes, even when this was done, and the land was cultivated with care, it did not contribute to enriching the kingdom or estate without the benefit of commerce.[11]

Similar observations were made by Samuel Fortrey, who specifically addressed the need for a large population, and also approved of other types of cultivation beyond agriculture, such as mining, specifically recommending enclosures as a means for improving the land.[12] He claimed that a nation's riches consisted of two things – store and trade. The former was either natural or artificial. Natural store was itself divided into three types – agricultural produce (mainly land and cattle), mined minerals such as iron and lead and fishery produce. The artificial store consisted of manufactures, which in England meant mainly woolen products.

As for trade, it was either domestic or foreign. In all these fields, according to Fortrey, England was superior to other countries.[13] Noting the interdependence between increased cultivation and production on the one hand, and population on the other, he claimed that "People and plenty are commonly the begetters the one of the other, if rightly ordered."[14] He also repeated his call for greater industriousness in the cultivation of England's natural treasures, principally the cultivation of land (emphasizing the need for enclosures), mining and fishing.[15]

Yet another well-known mercantilist tract, *Britannia Languens, or a Discourse of Trade*, attributed to one William Petyt, reiterated similar themes.[16] Petyt noted that among the many positive results of a growing population was the improvement of the land itself. Foreign trade would encourage a rising population of those who labored in trade, and also encourage a rise in consumption and in the price of land. All these developments were described in effect as intertwined. Moreover, the rise in revenue from land would encourage a competition for purchasing it, and hence a rise in its value, and then "the very Earth must receive an inevitable *Improvement* by their Industrious numbers, whilst every one will be able and willing to possess and manure a greater or lesser part, according to his occasions; there is hardly any Land in *England* but may be improved to double the value, and very much to treble and more."[17] A rising population was significant, however, only if people would be employed not only in agriculture, but also in trade and manufactures.[18] Like many mercantilists, Petyt recognized that agriculture, manufactures and commerce were interdependent, despite the primary importance of agriculture. As for the natural advantages which England possessed over its rivals Holland and France, as far as economic development was concerned, "Our great *Wasts, and void Lands*, which are our present Grief and Scandal, may on the regulation of our Trade, prove highly beneficial to us, since they will afford present room for a vast Increase of People, whether Forreign Planters, or others."[19] Voicing views which would become common in subsequent political economy, he considered uncultivated nature as a waste, and discerned no perceptible limit to nature's munificence and the ability to enhance its cultivation.

Several mercantilists became particularly renowned for their economic theorizing. Among the earliest of these was Thomas Mun, who was also independently-minded, and in the early seventeenth century already evinced a nuanced approach more sophisticated than most contemporary mercantilists.[20] He favored a positive balance of trade, but he was not a bullionist, recognizing that the commodities it could purchase were more important than bullion in itself. He was also not in favor of government control of trade, regarding commercial factors more important than political ones.[21] On the issue of utilizing natural resources, however, he was more in line with the predominant approach. He also recognized the argument for the inverse relation between the quality of the climate, and cultural progress, and was even mentioned by Marx on this point.[22] The issue of utilizing natural resources was evidently significant for his economic system.[23] Mun claimed that "all men do know, that the riches or sufficiency of euery Kingdome, State, or Commonwealth, consisteth in the possession of those things, which are needfull for a ciuill life. This sufficiency is of two sorts: the one is naturall, and proceedeth of the Territorie it selfe: the other is artificiall, and dependeth on the industry of the Inhabitants." England possessed both assets, including "great plentie of naturall riches, both in the Sea for Fish, and on the Land for Wooll, Cattle, Corne, Lead, Tin, Iron, and many other things for Food, Rayment, & Munition; insomuch, that vpon strickt tearmes of need, this land may liue without the help of any other Nation." Nevertheless, Mun observed that in order "to liuve well" it was important to engage in trade, and specifically to exchange England's surplus produce with the produce of foreign nations. Industry therefore was important both in order to encourage commerce with foreign nations, and in order to promote the arts at home. When either of these failed, the commonwealth was impoverished.[24]

The population of England had in recent times grown considerably according to Mun, and therefore it was important that industry help compensate for the consumption and waste of both home commodities and foreign wares. Through industry and the arts, it was important to augment the production of wares which otherwise had to be imported, thus helping foreign nations at the expense of England. Mun's mercantilist position thus implied that growing population was not an unconditional benefit, and was even damaging, unless it was accompanied not only with growing consumption, but also with growing production and the avoidance of waste. This frugality, however, did not extend to the use of natural resources.[25]

The differentiation between natural and artificial wealth was also relevant to England's mercantile contest with Holland, its main trading rival in the seventeenth century, and the contest with which spurred many passages in English mercantilist works. England possessed abundant natural treasures, yet Mun was angry that the English of his time had become lazy and fond of pleasure, while neglecting to foster these natural treasures. The Dutch, on the other hand, were much more diligent, and thrived thanks to their industriousness, occasionally at England's expense, particularly by fishing in "His Majesties Seas."[26] Mun further addressed the difference between natural and artificial wealth when he discussed the use of natural substances. Iron ore, for example, when left in mines, was much less valuable compared with the products which could be manufactured from it. Similarly, one could compare fleece-wools with cloth. The proprietors of natural treasures were a minority compared with the people employed in various arts, who manufactured products from these natural materials. Therefore the employment of the multitudes contributed to augmenting the traffic and the wealth of the nation.[27] There was no room in Mun's outlook for anything other than an instrumental consideration of nature. Trees, therefore, were meant to be utilized and not merely looked at.[28] He opposed the claim that building vessels meant for trade with the East Indies was a waste of materials such as timber, because such ships were not also used for other purposes. Mun claimed that these ships were easily repaired and were therefore not wasteful, and furthermore, the East India Company helped the realm with provisions required for ship construction. This instrumental approach left no room for aesthetic appreciation of nature, let alone "environmental" considerations in the modern sense.[29]

Later in the century, the commendation of utilizing natural resources remained a bulwark of mercantilist doctrine. This was evident in the thought of one of the most innovative political economists of the era, William Petty, often credited with the early form of statistical data collection known as political arithmetic.[30] He was one of the prime examples of the mercantilist attempt to explain social phenomena along the lines of contemporary natural science.[31] Petty was a member of the Hartlib Circle which coalesced around the polymath Samuel Hartlib, and promoted a political-economic Baconian program of advancing humanity through scientific cooperation and advancement of natural knowledge, most notably agricultural improvements.[32] Given all this, it is not surprising that Petty was interested in furthering both the utilization of England's natural resources, and the concomitant augmentation of its population. Nevertheless, he was sophisticated enough to recognize that a simple quantitative growth of population was insufficient to promote prosperity. The absolute number of inhabitants was less important for prosperity than the ratio between population and land. Also significant were the qualities and situation of the land on the one hand, and the characteristics of the population on the other. Regarding the latter, such things as the relative occupations of various inhabitants were particularly significant, and influenced the way they cultivated the land and utilized it to create wealth.[33] Cultivating land and cultivating population were therefore intertwined.

Petty claimed that it was economically beneficial to populate a land to the utmost limit, so long as the land was able to supply enough food for the population.[34] He did not seem aware of the possibility of over-population. In the future, when London would have millions of inhabitants, this would not cause any problems of over-population, whether economic, physical or social.[35] According to Petty, the greater the labor expended in cultivating the land, the greater was its proportionate role, in relation to the land, in creating value. This highlighted the need to encourage population growth, properly educated for labor, since the value of land was proportionate to how many people it could feed. From this perspective, not settling as many people on land as possible was to waste it.[36] This highlighted the fact that with Petty, as with other mercantilists, one already encounters early notions of the desirability of economic progress, or in modern terms economic growth, which would become more pronounced in the eighteenth century. In particular, as we will see later on, the notion of agricultural surplus, and how it stimulated non-agricultural development, would become increasingly important, and vestiges of it were already visible in Petty's outlook.[37]

Petty was aware of the vital connection between a nation's natural resources and its cultural progress. He claimed that a small nation could thrive even more than a large one if it possessed the proper geographical and natural situation, and in particular, if the utilization of this natural situation, through labor, was pursued with greater diligence. Also of particular significance for enriching a country was naval transportation, another point on which Petty preceded later figures such as Adam Smith. Petty nevertheless did not particularly highlight agricultural production, noting that "There is much more to be gained by Manufacture than

Husbandry, and by Merchandize than Manufacture."[38] Utilization of land and animals was important, but manufactures and trade were even more so.

Among the later generation of mercantilists, one of those more aware of the significance of natural resources was Charles Davenant, who developed a commercial version of civic humanism, combining a classical republican outlook with an apprehensive acknowledgment of the inevitable need to encourage commerce. Yet despite recognizing the importance of commerce, Davenant remained aware of the importance of land cultivation. He also supported the slave trade, a position which of course would become increasingly criticized, not least on economic grounds, in the Enlightenment.[39] Like most mercantilists Davenant believed in the need for a growing population, though he did recognize that this was desirable only so long as the inhabitants labored, thus contributing to national wealth. This included not just agriculture, but also such things as mines and fisheries.[40]

According to Davenant, "The soil of no country is rich enough to attain a great mass of wealth, merely by the exchange and exportation of its own natural product." Therefore, England required the wealth it obtained by trading with other countries, while using the products it acquired from its colonies. In order to live beyond a mere subsistence level, it needed commodities beyond those native to its soil. Without trade the land and its products would be of little value.[41] This approach hinted at near-heresy from a mercantilist viewpoint, acknowledging the benefits of international trade, although Davenant remained a firm mercantilist in favoring English interests. Nevertheless, these mutual benefits were not least perceptible in relation to cultivating natural resources. "Wisdom is most commonly in the wrong, when it pretends to direct nature. The various products of different soils and countries is an indication, that providence intended they should be helpful to each other, and mutually supply the necessities of one another." It was therefore unnecessary to force the raising or manufacture of any product which was unsuited to the native soil or inhabitants' character in any particular country. Therefore, if England was not the undisputed leader in woolen manufactures, which were suited to its nature, this was solely the fault of its inhabitants. With the proper state-directed policy, England might become the richest and most powerful country in Europe, thanks to its natural resources and location.[42]

Among later mercantilists, the one most interested in the issue of natural resources was Josiah Child.[43] Child's sophisticated mercantilism accepted, at least up to a point, certain principles of economic and commercial liberty.[44] While repeating his insistent claims for lowering interest to encourage the English trade and economy, he asserted that this would also lead to raising the value of land and rent, since a lower interest rate would encourage investment in improving the land itself. More commerce would also enable foreigners to purchase land in England, thus further raising the land's value and improvement, as well as making more rivers navigable.[45] Lowering interest would also lead to a growth of population, which was a direct result of augmented trade and improved land. A trading nation had a greater ability to feed its inhabitants, which made marriage easier. Commerce also provided more employment, and thus obviated the need for emigration, and even occasionally encouraged immigration of foreigners who had not found sufficient work in their native countries.[46] A country's fertility could cause a growth in its population, and vice versa. A nation's wealth and the size of its population were intertwined. Furthermore, lowering interest would not only enhance trade and population, but these in themselves would eventually lead to liberty of conscience.[47] Child thus viewed material progress as leading to higher social, cultural and political progress, another point on which he evinced pre-Enlightenment notions.

In addition to lowering interest in general, Child also recommended lowering the rate of usury. One of the reasons for this was that it would encourage the preservation of wood and timber. The high rate of usury in England made the improvement of land disadvantageous for its owners, with the result that there was also less available work for agricultural laborers. In Holland, in contrast, loans were cheaper, and consequently one saw how there they kept the land safe from flooding, and cultivated it profitably. This happened because in Holland land was dear and money cheap, whereas in England, on the contrary, money was dear and land cheap.[48] Should England make the necessary changes, the value of its commodities would rise and perhaps even double. "Then would all the wet Lands in this Kingdom [England] soon be drained, the barren Lands mended by Marle, Sleech, Lime, Chalk, Sea-sand, and other means, which for their profit, mens [*sic*] industry would find out."[49] If, on the other hand, usury would not be limited, the opposite results would ensue, "and consequently all works of Industry and Charge, for improving of Lands, would be quite neglected and given over: We should only eat upon one another with Usury, have our Commodities from other Nations, let the Land grow barren and unmanured, and the whole State in short time come to beggary."[50] Child thus viewed the improved cultivation of natural resources, principally land, as an indicator of healthy economic circumstances. Intertwined with advanced trade and a growing population, and promoted by a low rate of interest and usury, all this led to, and was supported by, progressive social and political circumstances, ultimately conducted by a proper state policy.

In accordance with his mercantilist outlook, Child regarded colonies as profitable for the prosperity of the mother country. Colonial natural resources became part of the general economic fabric which promoted the prosperity of the colonies, and particularly the mother country itself. Child claimed that England's American colonies (or "plantations" as he termed them) did not cause a diminishing population in England itself. Among the reasons for this was the fact that land, no matter how fertile, would not enrich any country without sufficient laborers. Furthermore, depopulation in itself was an impoverishment of a nation, and nations were rich or poor not in accordance with the quality of their soil, but with the quantity of their population.[51] Those who left England would have done so in any case for various reasons. There was a tendency for the quantity of population and the amount of available employment to adjust to each other. Furthermore, the consumption of English products in the colonies encouraged work and population in England itself. If the proper conditions existed in the mother country, its colonies would enhance its employment and population. These conditions included a low interest rate and the preservation of liberty and property, which would encourage agriculture and manufacturing beyond basic subsistence level.[52] Like other mercantilists, Child regarded the government as ultimately responsible for creating these proper conditions for a nation's prosperity. The English exemplified this, since they were superior to the Spanish in cultivating their colonial lands, as well as in colonial population, due to the differences in culture and policy between both nations.[53]

Elsewhere, in a short essay titled "A Discourse of the Nature, Use and Advantages of Trade," Child yet again demonstrated his sophisticated mercantilist philosophy, evincing on occasion certain quasi-Enlightenment notions of progress, while reiterating his view of commerce as the prime promoter of the power and glory of a nation.[54] This attention to the importance of commerce was to be further emphasized, as we shall see, in the eighteenth century, particularly among Scottish Enlightenment philosophers, though based upon a different perspective from that of the mercantilists, one much more critical of governmental intervention in the economy.

While in this work Child did not yet propound a distinct stadial version of the development of society in the manner later detailed particularly in eighteenth-century Scotland, he already outlined a simpler, yet, for a seventeenth-century mercantilist, quite original type of history of human society, in a manner not dissimilar to other later and more sophisticated examples of eighteenth-century conjectural history. He described the initial state following the banishment from the Garden of Eden, when human beings remained content with the natural produce of the earth. Subsequently, however, as their numbers multiplied, some became the owners of land and acquired dominion over others. The need to provide food for growing numbers became acute. "And the various measures and methods of making all things subservient to Man's Use or Pleasure, are so many Providential circumstances of susteining [*sic*] those Millions of People, that might Starve for want, had they not opportunity of Ministring to those that abound in Plenty." Child thus evinced the common anthropocentric view of natural resources as intended first and foremost for promoting human prosperity. In any event, human beings subsequently began building cities, and established laws, government and trade. As they became increasingly dispersed over the globe, people discovered that other countries abounded in various products, and they began coveting what was least available in their own countries. They built ships to discover and investigate distant lands in search of such hidden treasures. They also began, each according to their respective abilities, to covet vainglorious products. Yet Child, again preceding the logic of eighteenth-century thought, this time regarding the unintended positive consequences of free trade, observed that such vainglorious behavior and fondness for multifarious products also led to beneficial consequences, both in regard to the ensuing arts and inventions, and in encouraging commerce.[55]

Moving from this outline of human cultural development, Child claimed that most of the English trade was based on the surplus that the tenants of land produced, so they could earn beyond the level of rent which they had to pay. Husbandry thus in effect served as the basis for the development of practically all other professions, and of economic activity in general. In this manner those who worked and improved the land, though they did not own it, contributed to general public prosperity.[56] With the aid of mutual commerce, the wealth of England as manifested in its surplus produce was transported to the remotest regions of the globe, preserved correspondence with humanity, "and tends to the civilizing the unsociable Tempers of many barbarous People." This mutual commerce, ultimately based on surplus agricultural produce, also enabled transporting some of the treasures of these "barbarous people" to England, and supported English navigation.[57] Child here promoted the notion, which would later gain increased credence among Enlightenment philosophers, that contact with superior European civilization would ultimately benefit indigenous colonial populations, and help expedite their cultural progress.

Reiterating his observation of the connection between population and economic prosperity, Child noted that there were many tracts of uncultivated land in England. It was therefore advisable to enlarge the population, so there would be enough laborers to work this land, thus supporting all the consequent beneficial economic advantages.[58] Interestingly, Child proved much less advanced in his social-economic thinking when he recommended supporting the cultivation of land by imposing taxes and excises not on the owners of land, but rather on agricultural laborers, since a tax imposed on many people, rather than on a small section of the public, was felt and upset to a lesser extent, since it was divided among more people.[59] This perspective was subsequently of course to become totally unacceptable. Nevertheless, in what related to the significance of cultivating natural resources for general prosperity, Child evinced the main aspects of mercantilist thought which would remain valid in subsequent classical political economy, even while the main tenets of mercantilist balance of trade and state-supported national predominance went out of fashion.

So far we have considered only English mercantilists, yet mercantilist economic policy was prevalent in most seventeenth-century European states, if on a lesser scale. A few examples will serve to demonstrate this fact. In France, one of the first political economists to develop mercantilist ideas in detail was Antoine de Montchrestien, commonly credited with inventing the term "political economy."[60] Montchrestien was clearly aware of the significance of cultivating natural resources to supply human wants.[61] Like other mercantilists, he differentiated between natural and artificial objects, in which human labor cultivated the former.[62] Agriculture held pride of place in cultivating nature. "It is necessary to work to get fed; and to feed so as to be able to work" ("Il faut travailler pour se nourrir; et se nourrir pour travailler"). Sustenance depended on agricultural labor, and like many other European savants, Montchrestien also praised it from a moral perspective. Agricultural laborers were significant for France, and therefore it was important to ameliorate their condition and lift them out of poverty.[63]

The Spanish mercantilist Jerónimo de Uztáriz shared the common mercantilist assumption that population and prosperity went hand in hand.[64] Noting the situation in Spain, he claimed that the fact that there were ample people willing to work as shepherds, "whose occupation is the most laborious and severe that can be imagined, exposed as they are to the rigours of heat, cold and wet, ill fed and worse cloathed, having the desert for a lodging, rocks for a pillow, and brutes for their companions, ever banished from all the conveniencies of life," meant that given the proper encouragement, there would be no lack in laborers in various more pleasant manufacturing professions. The depopulation encountered in some provinces of Spain was due to an improper policy which unduly taxed the common laboring population, thus playing into the hands of foreign nations who benefited from the commerce with Spain at her loss. Yet this policy could be amended and prosperity and population reanimated in Spain.[65] Due to its improper policies, Spain did not benefit from its overseas colonies like the Portuguese or the Dutch, and its commerce was inferior even to that of Genoa. Particularly noteworthy, according to Uztáriz, was the international trade of the Dutch, owing to the small number of sailors they employed on their ships, their low import and export duties, and the broad international reach of their trade. Like English contemporaries, he viewed the Dutch as prime rivals for mercantile supremacy, and indeed as rivals worthy of emulation. Their low duties made it profitable to import various foreign products to Holland, where their own population enjoyed these products, and foreigners found it advantageous to trade for them. This enabled the Dutch to thrive despite the natural disadvantages of their country, which was a small sandy stretch of land, a quarter of which was uncultivated, another quarter devoted to pasture, "the rest being water, or land that yields neither fruit, grass, trees, or any thing useful in life, some writers insist that their harvests cannot supply a fourth of their own consumption, the worst circumstance a people can labour under."[66] Uztáriz clearly regarded Holland as a prime example of how a proper commercial policy could enable a nation to prosper and overcome even disadvantageous natural circumstances.

As regards his own country, Uztáriz approved of the "vast and wonderful enterprise" of using Spanish timber for the construction of ships, timber which was cut down in the very heart of the Pyrenees and transported, through mountains and other obstacles, by roads and waterways, as far off as the Mediterranean.[67] Nature had been kind to Spain in affording it a good climate and all the necessaries for human life, depriving it only of unhealthful foods such as spices. These and various luxuries, which Uztáriz considered in conservative fashion as vain superfluities, were unnecessary in themselves, but were advantageous as articles for international trade, which therefore was to be encouraged by low import duties.[68] The situation was different regarding grain and other food products such as various fruits, oils and liquors (which perhaps unsurprisingly Uztáriz did not consider as unnecessary luxuries, although he did criticize their excessive consumption, approving the dilution of wine with water, and preferring producing them mainly for export). Grains were particularly important, subject to the vagaries of weather, and were sometimes plentiful and at other times scarce. Consequently, the policy regarding their exportation or importation, by raising or lowering duties, could range from encouragement to prohibition.[69] Uztáriz was evidently aware of the fluctuations in regard to the grain trade, which would subsequently instigate so much controversy among classical political economists. In any event he regarded trade, particularly in agricultural products, as an encouragement to enhanced cultivation. "[T]he more we facilitate the vent and exportation of any fruits or manufacture, so much the more we insure the cultivation and enlargement of them in those places, from whence they are exported."[70]

Given the significant attention that Dutch policies received in mercantilist literature, an example of a Dutch mercantilist seems necessary, even though, somewhat surprisingly, the Dutch, like most European countries, were less diligent in producing theoretical discussions of mercantilist policy than the English.[71] The most famous Dutch mercantilist was Pieter de la Court, even though his main work was for many years erroneously attributed to Holland's ill-fated Grand Pensionary Johan de Witt. De la Court was an original political economist, and approved of free trade policies more than most mercantilists. This was related to his professed republicanism and opposition to Orangist monarchism in Holland. While not a democrat in the full modern sense, he had distinct democratic inclinations by seventeenth-century standards, much more so than most mercantilist contemporaries. Yet he did evince a distinct mercantilism in his attempt to advance Dutch political and economic prominence.[72]

Holland's geography and climate, claimed de la Court, with its low ground and proximity to the sea, held many disadvantages, such as long winters, short seasons which necessitated careful cultivation, and not least the need for maintaining dykes against inundations. The country also lacked mines and mineral deposits, and had little fertile land, with its cultivable regions requiring frequent manuring. Even in times of peace, let alone in wartime, these conditions posed a challenge, since Holland was unable to feed its inhabitants with its own agricultural produce, and required its manufactures and commerce to do so.[73] Uztáriz's depiction of Holland's meager natural resources was therefore corroborated by de la Court's first-hand observations. Holland's prosperity was therefore obviously owing to the efficient use its inhabitants made of those natural resources they did possess. This was an implicit version of the theory regarding inverse relations between natural abundance and cultural progress. Not even an eighth of Holland's population, according to de la Court, could subsist on its own agricultural produce. Its natural disadvantages were, however, offset by the fact that Holland's proximity to the sea afforded it great advantages in its fisheries, particularly of herring and cod, though also in whaling, while its many rivers and canals facilitated inland commerce. Holland was superior in its fishing production to all other nations. Its free government supported this prosperity, but its cold climate also enhanced it, since it was easier to work in cold rather than warm weather. The Dutch also were toughened and inured to hard work by their simple diet, and by the impositions of their geographical disadvantages. To enable the continuance of this prosperity required maintaining the country's economic policies and the free government which enacted them, and therefore de la Court regarded the possibility of a monarchical government as the chief threat to the country.[74] While various mercantilists had supported free trade, at least within certain limits, this emphatic support for wide-ranging free trade, rather than government control, as the route to national prosperity, was uncommon for the seventeenth century.

Part of this advocacy for freedom of trade included support for low taxes. De la Court even opposed the monopolies of the professional guilds, as well as of the East and West Indies companies, which may have been necessary in founding Holland's colonial trade, but had become detrimental to its interests. Holland's international trade was flourishing, and with proper policies, not least if these would be reciprocated in other countries which could also lift restrictions on trade, it could become even more prosperous.[75] The dependence on the fishing industry and on manufactures, sea navigation and trade, was so significant, providing the livelihood of those laboring in other professions, that the government should impose no taxes on these occupations, unless in the most dire national circumstances. Manufactures might lead to the development of fisheries and trade, yet in Holland it seemed that the reverse process had been more effective, and that fisheries and trade had led to the development of many types of manufactures in which Holland excelled, not least the construction of ships, usually with foreign timber.[76]

Like most mercantilists de la Court supported the notion of a large population as a necessary condition and sign of prosperity, and he was perspicacious enough to recognize the dependence of population on subsistence, and thus on the proper economic foundation for producing or providing by other means, mainly trade, the necessary amounts of food. Holland's means of subsistence relied on its agriculture, but given the above-noted deficiencies, even more so on its fisheries, manufactures and trade. Its large population enabled farmers to thrive despite heavy taxes, since in contrast with farmers in other countries, they were able to sell almost all their produce for home consumption, thus forgoing the need to export it.[77] Evidently, given the proper economic policy, a small amount of arable land could have its benefits. What mattered was the use human beings made of nature, not nature in itself.

De la Court lamented the fact that Holland had not taken the opportunity of founding free colonies in the uncultivated lands it had discovered, which would have traded with the mother country and redounded to her prosperity. Commercial companies had been given the monopoly to found such colonies, under the assumption that the Dutch were fit only for trade, not for agriculture and planting colonies. These companies did not establish new colonies and their policies damaged the interests of Holland.[78] This criticism of the commercial colonial companies as guided by the interests of their merchant governors rather than the national interest, was later to be elaborated more systematically by Adam Smith. Yet for de la Court this did not amount to a full condemnation of mercantilist balance-of-trade philosophy. Only under dire necessity did people accept work in these monopolistic colonial companies. Yet given the proper policy, it would be the best and most diligent among the Dutch inhabitants who would be drawn to new colonies. They would then advance in manufactures and trade, but also, as de la Court emphasized, in cultivating the colonial lands as Dutch inhabitants had done in foreign colonies, where they

> have not only manured unfruitful unplanted lands, but also undertaken the chargeable and hazardous task of draining of fenlands. And it is observable,

> that in all the said places, their butter, cheese, fruits and product of the earth, are more desired, and esteemed than those of their neighbours. And if we farther observe, that no countries in the world, whether the land be for breeding or feeding, are so well ordered as those of our plain lands in *Holland*; and that no other boors or husbandmen do travel so many countries as ours do; we shall be convinced, that no nation under heaven is so fit for setting up new colonies, and manuring of ground as our people are.[79]

De la Court therefore regarded the Dutch as perfectly capable of agricultural labor. Nevertheless, there was less opportunity, due to its small amount of arable land, of doing so in Holland itself, than in new colonies, should the government enable their foundation by freeing the country's international trade from the monopoly of the commercial companies. Throughout, de la Court recognized the connection between a firm economic foundation based on proper policies enhancing the efficiency of utilizing a country's specific natural resources, and the ensuing general social and cultural progress.

To varying degrees, as we have seen, this consideration of natural resources was shared by many mercantilists. In emphasizing the durability of these ideas, it should be remembered that the emphasis put on classical political economy in studies of the history of economic thought, and not least on Smith's criticism of mercantilism, tends to belittle mercantilism as an antiquated political and economic philosophy best left to history books. Nevertheless, one should remember that mercantilist ideas, and not just about the importance of cultivating natural resources, have remained in force, and surface periodically, even in modern times, including the idea of a balance of trade.[80] The history of economic thought, as indeed of many other topics, is as much a tale of accumulating ideas and influences, as of paradigmatic shifts.

Locke and the agricultural argument

The most significant new argument regarding the economic significance of cultivating natural resources which would come out of mercantilist thought and influence later political-economic discussions originated, as so many other ideas of the early Enlightenment, in the thought of John Locke. While not always considered as strictly a mercantilist there is every reason to regard him as such, not least in connection with the idea of supporting England's economic progress at the expense of other nations.[81] For those used to consider Locke primarily as a key figure in the rise of empirical philosophy, and as an early proponent of Enlightenment notions of education, liberalism and tolerance, it might come as somewhat of a surprise that he was emphatically, and not always successfully, involved in the economic policy debates of late seventeenth-century England. He participated in a heated contemporaneous monetary debate, opposing the proposal to reduce the amount of silver in English coins. Acceptance of his position had negative immediate consequences, yet nevertheless set the basis for the modern gold standard notion. This happened, even though he erred in equating money with specie. This mistake drew considerable criticism from contemporaries, as did his less erroneous assertion that the value of gold and silver was different from that of other commodities. The latter were assessed according to their usefulness, not like the former according to their universal imaginary exchange value.[82]

Locke's thought was always anchored in an attempt to understand and ameliorate concrete social and political realities. He claimed that the human mind was less suited to abstract thinking regarding the meaning of the world, and to wide-ranging philosophical questions regarding nature. It was more suited for obtaining practical knowledge, with the help of which human beings utilized natural resources more efficiently, thus assisting human society in its advance beyond savage existence, and toward culture and progress. Therefore Locke favored preoccupation with natural history rather than with general theories about nature. All this pertained to the physical aspect of life, whereas the spiritual aspect was the province of belief in god and consequent religiously motivated behavior.[83] Economic issues, therefore, were squarely within the province of human understanding and control.

Locke's theories of property and justice recognized the significance of the need to utilize natural resources to ensure prosperity. A country with a population that properly utilized natural resources was preferable to a more fertile country whose inhabitants did not do so.[84] The only viable way for a nation to grow rich, he claimed, was through conquest and commerce, and only the latter was a true option for England. It was the use made of natural resources through industry and trade that enriched a nation, not the possession of resources in themselves. Thus England, which did not possess sufficient mines, was in a better position to prosper by trade, than countries with greater stocks of mines. Mines provided gold and silver, but working them wasted valuable labor. In true mercantilist fashion, Locke noted that what mattered was not cultivating mines to produce specie, but rather possessing a greater proportion of the valuable metals than other nations, and this was to be attained by trade, for which England's maritime power made her particularly suited.[85] It was therefore not the mere possession of natural resources that mattered, but rather what a nation did with them, in this case not even merely cultivating them, but utilizing them to enhance trade. This emphasis on the prime importance of trade was an aspect of mercantilism which was to remain in force in eighteenth-century political economy, other disagreements notwithstanding, and with the exception of the Physiocrats, with their preference of agriculture.

Interestingly enough, Locke, more than most subsequent classical political economists who thought that water only had value in use, and no value in exchange (due to its seemingly endless abundance), was already aware that water might become scarce and consequently expensive, although he still thought that air would remain free of such scarcity.[86] It seems that he had at least some conception of the finiteness of natural resources.[87] Yet he did not follow through with this idea to any ecological implications in the modern sense, which were very far from Locke's view of nature as ultimately a resource meant for human use. Indeed, he was a prime example of how the traditional anthropocentric biblical cosmology was subsumed within the new, more rational and scientific, view of nature as a resource meant for human cultivation. Locke openly accepted the divinely ordained human dominion over nature.[88] Like most seventeenth- and eighteenth-century political economists, he regarded cultivating nature and enhancing population as interconnected, and as a mercantilist he saw it as the distinct task of government policy to enhance both these objectives. A proper policy would also advance agriculture, and also motivate immigration rather than emigration. The only way to increase the profits of landholders was by drawing more money into the country. This would raise the price of both rent and agricultural products. Lowering rent, on the other hand, would deter not only foreign investment, but also the foreigners themselves from coming to England, while the "increase of people being the increase both of strength and riches."[89]

All this notwithstanding, Locke's most famous contribution to political-economic thought was his labor theory of value. While early notions of this concept were recognized before, it was Locke's version which proved the decisive one in promoting the idea that it was the investment of labor in cultivating natural resources which conferred economic value on them, and made them the objects of judicial proprietary rights.[90] This theory was developed in the famous remarks on nature in America in the fifth chapter, "Of Property," in Locke's most influential political work, the *Second Treatise of Government*, often considered the fountainhead of modern liberal political philosophy.[91] In terms of enhancing the modern consideration of nature as first and foremost a resource meant for human use, this was to prove one of the most important texts in political-economic literature.

According to Locke, labor invested nature with an additional quality making it useful to mankind, and turning it into property. He noted that "Nothing was made by God for Man to spoil or destroy."[92] Yet he did not perceive uncultivated nature as having any usefulness. Leaving nature in an uncultivated state was in fact almost a sin. Locke with this remark did not intend anything "ecological" in the modern sense, quite the contrary. His point was that human beings would only have an incentive to cultivate those natural resources which would yield, beyond the produce they consumed themselves, a surplus with which they could barter for other products. Only with the invention of money would this type of production reach a truly effective level, which would enable a maximal level of resource cultivation, based on the investment of labor. "[L]abour makes the far greatest part of the value of things we enjoy in this world: and the ground which produces the materials, is scarce to be reckoned in, as any, or, at most, but a very small part of it: so little, that even amongst us, land that is left wholly to nature, that hath no improvement of pasturage, tillage, or planting, is called, as indeed it is, waste; and we shall find the benefit of it amount to little more than nothing." The obvious conclusion was that the more labor was utilized in cultivating natural resources, the better; hence that the larger the population, the better. "This shows how much numbers of men are to be preferred to largeness of dominions; and that the increase of lands, and the right of employing of them, is the great art of government."[93] These ideas, as we have seen, were common in mercantilist literature. Yet Locke, in emphasizing the significance of labor as the constituent of value, invested these ideas with new meaning, making them more potent for subsequent political economy, when other aspects of mercantilist philosophy had been discarded.

These remarks were famously made using the example of America, and this played a leading part in supporting the nascent colonial enterprise. When Locke notably remarked that "in the beginning all the world was America," he meant just that, "in the beginning," or in other words, at the initial point of historical progress, the state of nature, when human beings began cultivating their natural surroundings.[94] As his eighteenth-century continuators would do to an even greater extent, Locke, based on the popular travel reports on the North American Indians, made conjectural-history assumptions which a priori supposed that the true project of utilizing the vast natural resources of America was only really begun by the European settlers. This prompted his use of the New World as the most tangible contemporary example of such a state of nature. The outlines of subsequent Enlightenment conjectural history regarding the rise of civilization, which we will discuss in detail later, were thus already evident in Locke's discussion of the emergence of property as a social, judicial and economic phenomenon. Moreover, the propensity for utilizing natural resources in itself also justified the colonial occupation of land. The indigenous Americans were liberally provided by nature with everything necessary for advancing as far as any other nation, "yet for want of improving it by labour, have not one hundredth part of the conveniences we enjoy: and a king of a large and fruitful territory there feeds, lodges, and is clad worse than a day-labourer in England."[95]

This of course ultimately justified the colonial dispossession of the American Indians, since if they did not make proper use of their natural resources, they lost their claim to them. Dispossession of something not properly cultivated was in fact no dispossession from this viewpoint. Locke's ideas were the most influential manifestation of the common early modern "agriculturalist argument" for possessing lands in the colonies, lands seemingly neglected by the natives. This argument was based on the ancient Roman principle of *res nullius*, or the similar notion of *vacuum domicilium*, according to which "empty things," primarily land, belonged to all mankind till they were made use of. Unused land was thus viewed as open for possession, an underlying assumption of Locke's claim for labor leading to proprietary possession.[96] This idea was to prove highly influential, both as a justification for colonial dispossession of indigenous inhabitants (and not necessarily for the purportedly benign intention of better cultivation), and more broadly, in providing new support for the traditional view of nature as above all a resource meant for human utilization. As we will see, the use of the labor theory of value to establish humanity's right over nature was to have a consistent place in subsequent political economy.

Forestry and the management of natural resources

Mercantilism may not have coalesced into a shared and coherent economic philosophy, yet most mercantilists did share basic assumptions. Underlining these was a growing emphasis on the use of rational and scientific principles to organize and control reality, be it physical nature, or political and social phenomena. Several broad tendencies in early modern culture came mutually into play to enhance this process – rational modes of philosophical inquiry, the empirical emphasis of the Scientific Revolution, and the gradual emergence of the modern nation-state, the latter related to a growing mechanism of centralized state bureaucracy. All this affected the human attitude toward nature, as increasing emphasis on national interests accorded growing attention to the management of natural resources. As we have seen, mercantilist authors, if haphazardly, became increasingly aware of this fact. In the seventeenth century burgeoning modern political-economic thought increasingly accorded attention to management of natural resources. These resources had of course been managed, intentionally or not, by human societies throughout millennia, yet not on the national scale which became increasingly predominant with the approach of modernity. Managing nature, in tandem with managing the economy and the state in general, increasingly assumed the guise of a professional science. Realization of the limited quantities of available resources, though not necessarily their finiteness, also became more evident. What today we would term as sustainability, was already a concept receiving increasing attention.[97] While political economists did not concern themselves with the strictly scientific aspects of this issue, they became increasingly aware of its economic significance from the seventeenth century onwards, and we will encounter this awareness many times in the following pages. A few remarks therefore seem in order concerning this issue, specifically regarding one of the most vital early modern natural resources, timber. In the seventeenth and eighteenth centuries forestry became a science meant to serve national interests, in close connection with mercantilist attempts at managing the economy in general. Since the Middle Ages agricultural improvements in general had enhanced the scientific basis of the cultivation of land.[98] Agriculture, particularly as the chief source of food production, would become, as we will see, one of the most central concerns of eighteenth- and nineteenth-century political economy. Yet other topics, not least forestry, were far from ignored.

The need to sustainably manage natural resources was particularly evident regarding forestry, since in the pre-modern world wood was a vital natural resource, the veritable fuel of material life, and consequently the one most heavily managed (and mismanaged).[99] In the early modern era, despite growing recognition of the consequences of deforestation, European countries did not react with a comprehensive forestry management policy similar to that which emerged at about the same time in Tokugawa Japan. Yet Britain did react by moving before other countries to a coal-based economy.[100] Elsewhere, from the Venetian Republic to Germany, a similar concern with forestry, intertwined with broad social and political developments, also emerged.[101] While forestry was not concerned with the natural environment for its own sake in our contemporary sense, by the eighteenth century there emerged increasing awareness of the impact of humanity on its natural environment. This entailed the need to manage natural resources responsibly. This pertained to wood as to other resources.[102] The famous Enlightenment naturalist the Comte de Buffon, for example, composed two detailed essays on forestry.[103] In Scotland, where Adam Smith was establishing the modern discipline of political economy, forest management and afforestation were emerging.[104] Later, forestry management policy in the British empire, mainly in India, was to influence the advance of forestry throughout the empire, and eventually the world, serving as a prime source of modern utilitarian environmentalism, beyond the romantic type of environmentalism which has come to predominate modern environmental thought.[105]

In discussing the theoretical debates of political economists, it is therefore important to remember that economic theory developed hand in hand with increasing material economic reality. As modern modes of wide-scale, and eventually national, economic production and distribution developed, the necessary theoretical underpinning developed as well. The practical and the theoretical sides of economic existence were interrelated and mutually reinforcing, laying the material foundations for the modern world. Nowhere was this more noticeable than in what concerned the human utilization of nature.

Late mercantilists

While the heyday of mercantilism was the seventeenth century, mercantilist notions remained influential in the following century. The eighteenth century is remembered as the time when classical political economy emerged, primarily with Adam Smith, but also with important predecessors such as David Hume on the one hand, or the Physiocrats on the other. Yet one has to remember that Smith wrote and published in the second half of the century. In general, the Enlightenment, in terms of political-economic theory, was an era of transition. The more novel ideas which emerged will concern us in the following chapters. Here we will address several figures who exemplified the persistence of mercantilism. This was particularly evident in France. Still under the thrall of the reign of Louis XIV, and the obviously mercantilist policies of Colbert, political economists of the first half of the eighteenth century, though already voicing new ideas, still maintained key mercantilist notions.

One such author was Jean-François Melon, whose essentially mercantilist opinions included such things as support for the slave trade.[106] Nevertheless, he also evinced more Enlightenment-type novel views, not least regarding the beneficial effects of luxury, and a generally optimistic view of human progress. Once sufficient people were employed in necessary occupations such as agriculture, manufactures and military work, claimed Melon, the superfluous population should work in producing luxuries, which were relative to the stage of development of different societies (luxury in one was a common product in another). Proper encouragement of luxury production prevented unemployment and idleness.[107] Melon was more modern than earlier mercantilists in rejecting the moral criticisms of luxury, and claiming it was the right of people to seek luxurious gratification even to their own ruin. This liberal attitude was emphasized further by the claim that it enhanced employment among the laboring class who produced these luxuries. Melon thus regarded luxury as both morally permissible, and as promoting economic development and population. He viewed large measures of both production and consumption as advantageous. "[A] greater Consumption cannot fail of being an Advantage, when the Earth produceth abundantly."[108] This was an early, if undeveloped, example of the subsequent notion of Say and Ricardo regarding the veritable impossibility of general gluts. It implied the assumption of the unlimited capacity of nature to support human progress.

Not surprisingly, Melon, like earlier mercantilists, although also like most subsequent Enlightenment political economists, supported the need for a large population.[109] Yet in addition to large numbers, the inhabitants needed to be industrious. "The Strength of a State, is not to be measured, by the Extent of its Territory, but by the Number of its Inhabitants, and the Usefulness of their Labour."[110] Therefore, from an economic viewpoint, the true measure was not the number of inhabitants in themselves, but the amount of produce which their labor created, both in cultivating natural resources, and in using natural raw materials for production. Making advances in agriculture or manufactures, or in other words augmenting the efficiency of labor, was thus tantamount to a growth of population, since less laborers were required for the same amount of work, and the remainder could be otherwise employed, either for more production, or else for the conquest of other countries.[111] Once a country was fully peopled, its manufactures supplied with all necessary workers, and all its land cultivated, the next step was to establish colonies, though Melon, in mercantilist fashion, emphasized the need to keep these in dependence on the mother country.[112]

Like the more sophisticated among earlier mercantilists, Melon entertained notions of freedom of trade, though not to the extent of later *laissez faire*. Commerce required liberty and protection. With most products the former was more important, though regarding corn (a synonym for grains in general till the late nineteenth century), because of its importance, this had to give way to at least some protection. Production of corn, and of food in general, was of the first necessity, and therefore had to precede production of less necessary items, as also of superfluous luxuries, their economic beneficial influence notwithstanding.[113] The equation of food production meant first and foremost cultivation of the land, agriculture. As would become increasingly evident in Enlightenment, and later classical, political economy, the production of basic foodstuffs was tantamount to cultivating the land. "To reclaim barren Lands, and make them profitable; is to conquer new Countries, without making any one Person Miserable." Peopling and cultivating new lands was a better way to conquer new territories than by conquest, with all the miseries of war, even if it seemed less illustrious to vulgar people.[114] The significance of growing population or the acquisition of new conquered lands notwithstanding, what ultimately mattered from an economic viewpoint was to what extent the population and the land were utilized to create more produce, more wealth. "Number of Inhabitants, Extent and Fertility of Soil, are useless in Countries, where the Lands remain uncultivated, through Sloth, or Discouragement."[115] The natural resources of a country, properly cultivated, were the true key to progress.

An Irish-French early eighteenth-century political economist who has received much more attention from scholars than Melon, was Richard Cantillon. Due to his systematic and abstract style of discussion he is often considered a harbinger of modern economic analysis. Scholars are divided on whether to view him as a supporter or critic of mercantilism. It seems best however to consider him a key transitional figure between mercantilism and classical political economy, evincing both types of economic perspective, and squarely within the confines of Enlightenment political economy, with its increasingly more sophisticated concept of economic growth.[116] Cantillon immediately began his important work *Essai sur la Nature du Commerce en Général* by noting that the cultivation of natural resources was the basis for human economics, writing – "The Land is the Source or Matter from whence all Wealth is produced. The Labour of man is the Form which produces it: and Wealth in itself is nothing but the Maintenance, Conveniencies, and Superfluities of Life." Land produced various plants, as well as mines and minerals, while rivers and seas supplied fish, all of which human labor transformed into wealth.[117] Land was therefore of prime economic significance. It has even been suggested that Cantillon formulated a land theory of value, measuring value by the amount of land, not labor as in labor theories of value.[118] In fact, he regarded the combination of both land and labor as determining economic value.[119] He was also aware of the significance of other types of natural-resource cultivation, such as mining, even if he did not consider them as vital as agriculture.[120]

Cantillon outlined various forms of human social organization. The private possession of land, often on unequal terms, was an inevitable part of human social development. Such inequality, he claimed, was evident both in nomadic and in sedentary societies.[121] Cantillon did not utilize the terminology of later Enlightenment stadial theory, yet he seemed aware of the crucial differentiation between nomadic and sedentary stages of progress, the latter exemplified in the adoption of an agricultural life. Farming was an absolutely necessary element of economic existence. As long as the land was even minimally fertile, it was necessary to have villagers living in its vicinity. Furthermore, the city was dependent on the country. It was the quantity of villages' agricultural produce which determined the size of adjacent market towns. City inhabitants were relatively less directly dependent on agricultural produce, yet ultimately all urban merchants and manufacturers relied on landlords, and so on the latter's agricultural produce. Only princes and proprietors of land lived independently, while all other social classes and laborers depended on agricultural production. Some laborers were able to accumulate capital and gain a certain level of independence, yet merchandise of various sorts was much more subject to accident and loss compared with the ownership of land. The proprietors' land would, however, remain useless if it was not cultivated. Therefore, while the proprietors did have greater power to direct economic activity for their own purposes, there was a mutual dependence between them and other social groups.[122] Cantillon's analysis implied that the dependence of urban manufactures on agriculture also entailed the opposite dependence, since the city provided the market for the country. This interdependence of agricultural and manufacturing production would later be emphasized further by Smith.

Nature in itself had no economic value if it was not cultivated. "Nature is altogether indifferent whether the Earth produce grass, trees, or grain, or maintains a large or small number of Vegetables, Animals, or Men."[123] In other words, the economic situation was not dependent on nature in itself but rather on how human beings utilized it. A nation of hunters such as the Iroquois would be able to support only a certain level of population, while a nation which devoted more attention to agriculture, such as the Chinese, would be able to support a greater population due to a more enhanced cultivation of land for the production of food. Cantillon was cautiously in favor of a large population, recognizing the connection between population and subsistence levels, and the significance of proper employment.[124] He noted that it was possible to cultivate natural resources, particularly land and animals, to the utmost level, accompanied by the maximal growth of population. "Experience shews that Trees, Plants and other Vegetables can be increased to any Quantity which the Extent of Ground laid out for them can support." Similarly, it was possible to multiply domestic animals such as horses, cattle and sheep, and the only limit to this multiplication was how much sustenance for these animals could be grown on the land. "It is not to be doubted that if all Land were devoted to the simple sustenance of Man the race would increase up to the number that the Land would support."[125]

China's population was the largest found in any country, due to the Chinese emphasis on maximal agricultural production. Yet Cantillon was also aware that this led to over-population and large-scale death, in times when there was not sufficient food for all this population. While not yet evincing a Malthusian type of worry over the ability of nature to sustain population, he was well aware that a large population was a benefit only in healthy economic circumstances, not least relying on efficient agricultural cultivation. The country with the smallest population, in comparison, was the interior of America, where savages made due with the life of hunters without cultivating land.[126] The situation of modern Europe was in general in between these two extremes, although different regions of the continent were dissimilarly developed. In general, Europe's situation also demonstrated how the size of the population depended on the level of food production. The European situation was further complicated by the transference of some of the economic activity in the direction of industrial production, mining and commerce, yet even this did not change the basic dependence of the population on food. A further complication resulted from the fact that the wealthier social classes chose to purchase luxuries, which in terms of the utilization of land for population were not the most efficient produce. The most efficient situation was that of minimal livelihood, when all agricultural production was utilized for enhancing population. Cantillon, however, was clearly aware that this did not happen in Europe's complicated reality. He also expressly avoided claiming what was the best option – maximal utilization of natural resources for population, even if this resulted in wide-scale poverty, or rather a smaller population living more at ease. Princes and proprietors of land could promote either possibility up to a point, but Cantillon implied that the wealthier social classes were unwilling to live at a level of bare subsistence.[127]

Like other eighteenth-century intellectuals Cantillon was preoccupied with questions of historical progress and decline. He outlined a general historical model of the rise and decline of states, which advanced till the stage when consumption of luxuries led to impoverishment. It was all but impossible to arrest this process, although occasionally it was possible to encourage resumption of growth and prosperity.[128] Nevertheless, an abundance of money in a state was generally a positive thing, so long as it enhanced consumption, and thus also led to greater cultivation of land.[129] Cantillon consistently emphasized the importance of maximizing agricultural production, yet only so long as this did not exceed the point where the production of food enabled a proper economic existence. To a certain extent this presaged Malthus's later outlook, although Cantillon was not comparably pessimistic, and seemed unaware that over-population was indeed a conceivable problem for Europe, or for humanity in general, with the exception of China. His was basically the confident outlook of the Enlightenment, seen through the lens of an innovative political economist whose observations on the connection between natural-resource cultivation and general economic prosperity heralded the more detailed analyses of subsequent classical political economy.

One other figure of late mercantilism should be mentioned here, the Scotsman Sir James Steuart. Eclipsed even in his time by the work of Adam Smith, Steuart's lengthy work on political economy, despite its prolixity, included many original observations, often evincing an international outlook not found even in Smith, the result of many years Steuart spent on the continent. His political economy straddled two approaches, on the one side traditional mercantilist notions, on the other many aspects of the more novel Enlightenment outlook. Here we will outline some of his views, specifically related to the material foundation of national prosperity, based on cultivation of natural resources. This will serve to round off the discussion of mercantilist attitudes toward nature. In the next chapter we will return to Steuart in relation to more novel eighteenth-century developments.[130]

According to Steuart the only thing which remained inconsumable was the surface of the earth, which was never lost and never ceased to be useful. One might change the face of the earth, yet it would always continue to exist. He distinguished between the intrinsic worth of consumable commodities, in other words the simple substance or production of nature, and the useful value, which meant the value of products resulting from modification by human effort.[131] This was reminiscent of Locke's labor theory of value. Steuart further claimed that all countries had unique natural advantages in respect of production meant for foreign trade. He disagreed with Montesquieu's view that climate influenced culture. In his opinion this happened only when other circumstances had no influence and climate was considered in isolation. Yet whenever climatic forces created political inconvenience this led to a desire to overcome them (a somewhat diluted version of the theory of inverse relation between natural conditions and cultural progress). Underlining this observation was Steuart's assumption that in most cases the statesman heading government would utilize every circumstance to promote his plans for the state. Furthermore, "If a nation then has formed a scheme of being long great and powerful by trade, she must first apply closely to the manufacturing every natural produce of the country." This required employing a sufficient number of laborers, otherwise the natural produce would end up being exported without yielding additional value from labor. In other words, inefficient utilization of nature was economically unprofitable. In this situation the state's natural advantages would essentially be lost. A situation in which cultural customs, work habits and government policy were all erroneous, was tantamount to the natural advantage's not having existed in the first place.[132]

Steuart noted that a state might find itself in an inferior commercial position vis-à-vis another state either due to the latter's superiority in working habits and political-economic policy, or due to its superiority in climate and situation, in which case there was no way to compete with it. Natural disadvantages such as remote location or barren soil prevented a state from adequately competing with other countries in foreign trade. In this situation it could only import additional wealth by passive trade, and the statesman could only encourage the circulation of existing wealth. When food and other necessaries were nature's gift to a state, it was necessary to discourage foreign competition for them. In such a situation the lowest possible price was preferable, since no industrious person would suffer as a consequence. Yet when effort was required to produce food, it was necessary to maintain a certain price level to support those who produced it.[133]

Steuart's views presupposed that there was something fixed in the natural situation of countries in terms of supporting their economies. When a country was forced to reduce exports only to articles of pure natural produce, it reached the lowest level of commerce while still remaining able to enjoy its natural advantages. With proper policy, these natural products in themselves could still be used as a basis for enhancing national wealth even when there was no more export. In this situation it was necessary to enhance the production of these natural products, use them frugally, and eventually when possible export the surplus in the most advantageous manner, though always making sure that sufficient subsistence remained for the local poor.[134] One of the related topics which Steuart considered was the issue of land taxes. He advocated taxing land in ways which encouraged agricultural improvements. Taxes were therefore not to be raised when the land was improved. Nevertheless, farmers were more at their ease in terms of taxation compared with all other classes in England. Since they lived on the fruits of the earth, they avoided many of the excises other classes were subject to. Therefore Steuart saw no problem imposing additional land tax on them rather than on the landowners. The latter did, however, tend to live beyond their means due to the expenses involved in maintaining their estates and upholding the traditional social estimation of their families. Steuart, though, avoided criticizing the landowners as Ricardo would later do.[135]

In computing the produce of the earth for the purpose of taxation, all the expenses incurred for such things as human and animal food had to be deducted. Only the net produce of the earth was taxable. In fact, the farmers produced a surplus which was necessary for them as for the economy in general. In Steuart's opinion the state needed to tax those who purchased the surplus agricultural produce, not those who produced it. The tax was on money, not on the produce itself, which had it been directly taxed, would have led to hunger among some of the population. When money rather than the produce was taxed, very few would end up starving, lacking either talent, industry or the ability to arouse the compassion of the charitably-disposed. All this had to do with proportional taxation. There was, however, also the matter of cumulative taxes such as tithes, which were unjustly imposed on all the produce of the land, not just the surplus. Steuart consequently opposed tithes on lands and their produce, though not land taxes in general.[136] Economic activity and policy issues such as taxation ultimately relied, according to Steuart, on recognition of the underlying dependence on nature. He thus compared taxes with the "taxes" imposed by nature, specifically in years of scarcity due to harsh climatic conditions or other natural circumstances. In such years the lower social classes exhibited the ability to make due with scant subsistence, and thus the lack of accommodating natural circumstances became a spur to industry.[137]

All this demonstrates the strengths and weaknesses of Steuart's approach. The tendency to go into great technical detail regarding issues such as taxation would become part and parcel of eighteenth-century political economy, yet Steuart's prolixity tended to obfuscate the clear systematic vision evinced by other Enlightenment authors. At times it seems that he was inconsistent. Were farmers to be taxed? Was there a strict inverse relation between natural circumstances and cultural progress? A consistent and systematic vision regarding these topics is absent in Steuart's analysis. Nevertheless, this was the result of fastidiousness rather than omission. Ultimately, Steuart presented an updated eighteenth-century version of the mercantilist aim of advancing national interests. The recognition of utilizing natural resources as a basis for prosperity was a vital part of this outlook which, as we will now see, was to receive a much more sophisticated intellectual underpinning in the Enlightenment, compared with the rudimentary observations of seventeenth-century mercantilism.

Part II

The Enlightenment roots of classical political economy

3 Pre-classical Enlightenment developments

By the turn of the eighteenth century increasing attention was being devoted to systematic discussions of economic issues in their general social, political, ethical and historical context. This generalizing approach was exemplified by the term "political economy," encompassing a wider vision of economic issues than the more modern term "economics." The latter came into fashion in the late nineteenth century with Alfred Marshall, at a time when economic analysis gained by increasing methodological and mathematical precision, but lost in terms of the ability to consider the relevance of broad cultural concerns to economic issues. In the eighteenth century, by comparison, political economy was not so much *integrated within* wide-ranging intellectual concerns, as it *emerged from* these concerns. It was no accident that Adam Smith was by profession a professor of moral philosophy, and was led as such to creating the basis for modern economic analysis (Joseph Schumpeter's criticism of his originality notwithstanding).[1] The increasing scholarly interest in Smith in recent years has in large part been devoted to recreating this broad context of economic debate. It is clear that if we are to understand the intellectual foundations of eighteenth-century political economy, it is vital to understand several key aspects of the Enlightenment *Weltanschauung*, specifically those related to the idea of historical progress, and the growing recognition that material progress was the basis for higher cultural development.[2] One aspect of this recognition was exemplified by increasing attention to the question of population, which as we have seen had already been recognized in basic form in the preceding century. Another, more original contribution of the Enlightenment, was a new and sophisticated theorizing of historical development, most notably evident in the idea that cultural progress was a stadial process. In this and the following three chapters we will discuss how these topics became evident in Enlightenment political economy, how they contributed to an increasingly more sophisticated discussion of natural resources, and how this intellectual legacy was maintained in subsequent classical political economy well into the nineteenth century. In the subsequent chapters we will discuss more direct ways in which natural resources were approached in the intellectual history of political economy.

Enlightenment stadial theory

One of the most crucial intellectual developments of the Enlightenment was an increasing interest in the historical development of human societies. Consideration of the history of European civilization on the one hand, and of non-European societies all over the world on the other, fueled the attempt to outline a universal theory of human development. The result was later termed by Dugald Stewart (appropriately in his biography of Adam Smith), as "conjectural history."[3] Basically, this was a type of early theoretical anthropology, an attempt to conjecture what the initial stages of human social development had been before historical documentation had begun. This type of inquiry became increasingly popular in the eighteenth century, constituting a pillar of many types of intellectual debate. For Rousseau, most famously in his *Discourse on Inequality*, conjectural history served to criticize the immorality of advanced civilization. Yet most Enlightenment philosophers did not share this criticism. Either they straightforwardly favored progress, or else they recognized its inevitability, while attempting to ameliorate its injustices and corruptions.

Conjectural history became of increasing interest most notably among Scottish Enlightenment savants. Given the crucial role that Scotland was to play in the rise of classical political economy, this seems far from fortuitous. The Scottish type of conjectural history specifically favored the idea that human societies developed in stages. This stadial outline usually emphasized four stages, what came to be known as the four-stages theory. The assumption was that given similar natural conditions, all human societies developed from an initial stage of existence based on hunting (what today we would term "hunting-gathering societies"), then to a pastoral stage based on shepherding, then, making the crucial shift from a nomadic to a sedentary existence, moving to an agricultural stage, and finally to the ultimate commercial mode of life. Throughout this lengthy process the changing manner of acquiring subsistence was a crucial factor. The production of food was of course based on cultivation of natural resources. Therefore, stadial theory evinced a consistent interest in how material progress, based on cultivation of these resources, laid the foundations for historical progress in general. This was a crucial contribution of the Enlightenment, most notably of the Scottish Enlightenment, to modern intellectual history. Ultimately, though of course in very different guise, it came into play even in the Marxist idea of dialectical materialism.[4]

The most significant version of stadial theory was outlined by Adam Smith, and preserved in notes taken during his lectures by one of his students. Smith claimed that as their numbers rose, human beings found a hunting-gathering existence tenuous, and began taming wild animals. Animal domestication usually preceded that of plants, and therefore shepherding in most cases preceded agriculture, when human beings would "naturally turn themselves to the cultivation of land and the raising of such plants and trees as produced nourishment fit for them." Agricultural life would eventually lead to further progress and eventually to trade. "When therefore a country is stored with all the flocks and herds it can support, the land cultivated so as to produce all the grain and other commodities necessary for our subsistence it can be brought to bear, or at least as much as supports the inhabitants when the superfluous products whether of nature or art are exported and other necessary ones brought into exchange, such a society has done all in its power towards its ease and convenience." Smith recognized, however, that while civilization was based on a command of nature, natural surroundings needed to be amenable to cultivation to begin with. "The soil must be improvable, otherwise there can be nothing from whence they might draw that which they should work up and improve. That must be the foundation of their labour and industry." This implied that societies would differ in their cultural achievements. Those developing in amenable surroundings had the possibility to attain the highest form of commercial existence, while others, devoid of such circumstances, might find themselves unable to go beyond either the pastoral or agricultural stage (although Smith did not seem to consider any society as doomed to remain in the initial hunting stage). Smith's stadial theory thus offered a different perspective than the idea of inverse relations between natural conditions and cultural progress. We might also mention in passing that though stadial theory presupposed a Eurocentric chauvinism vis-à-vis non-European civilizations, not least in the colonies, it was not racist, since the reason for the lack of progress some societies evinced was dependent on the natural environment, not on inborn racial characteristics.[5] In any event, the essentially historiographical origins of stadial theory were transformed in the late eighteenth century into one of the basic elements of nascent modern political-economic discourse. Stadial theory was therefore one of the main sources for the belief in materially-based progress which was to underlie the development of modern economic theory.

Steuart, Hume and other contemporaries

While Smith's version of stadial theory was the most typical, other political economists developed similar outlooks. Here we can return to James Steuart, this time in relation to his more Enlightenment-type ideas on progress and population, rather than his mercantilist notions. While not utilizing a thorough stadial theory, Steuart did outline a conjectural-history discussion which, intentionally or not, was reminiscent of Rousseau's recognition of the possible pitfalls of progress, without, however, deducing from this Rousseau's pessimistic conclusions. In a distinctly non-religious tone, Steuart began from a supposed prelapsarian state in which human beings lived without any needs or any necessity for labor, but also without any change except the acquirement of knowledge. "Banished from Paradise, man began to plow the ground, consequently to change her surface: he built houses, made bridges, traced roads, and by degrees has come, in different ages, to please and gratify his inclinations." This whole process was fueled by the human attempt to fulfil desires. New desires, however, repeatedly surfaced, and therefore there was no visible end to this process, and "man daily becomes more laborious." When human beings lived in total simplicity, they owned land only to the extent that they cultivated it to acquire subsistence. Yet the moment someone required the service of another, he needed an equivalent available for barter. "This equivalent must be something moveable, some fruit of the earth, pure or modified, superfluous, not necessary, not the earth itself, because this is the foundation of his subsistence; and he can never alienate what is essential to his being, in order to procure a superfluity." Therefore, the moment a society made the transition from simple existence to a state where a surplus was produced and trade came into being, this led to the emergence of dependence among human beings, subordination, and the loss of individual independence which a life of simplicity afforded. An economy of this sort might suit those reverting back to a primitive state of innocence or brutality, a state of total spirituality or, conversely, of gratifying animal desires. Human beings existed in an intermediate middle state in between a totally physical and a totally spiritual existence. They needed various things, and required the co-operation of others to acquire them. Steuart termed such things "political-necessary." This situation was of course compatible with society and government, in which case "all simplicity of manners is only relative." Therefore each generation positively considered previous generations as having evinced noble simplicity of manners. Indeed, perhaps one day the manners of the eighteenth century would be considered "the noble simplicity of the ancients." Therefore, since simplicity of manners was relative, so also superfluity might be approved, though only to the extent that it benefited the poor more than it corrupted the rich.[6] Steuart's conjectural history, though devoid of stadial theorizing, was perfectly compatible with the Enlightenment endorsement of cultivating natural resources for the purpose of cultural progress. In a social state the dependence on cultivated land could not be relinquished. This was the consequence of humanity's physical and social constitution. There was no avoiding this dependence on nature.

Steuart differentiated between the "physical-necessary," the catering to basic human needs, and the "political-necessary," those needs beyond these basic ones, which were determined and influenced by social rank, and therefore differed among different people.[7] This came into play throughout his analysis, as did the mercantilist emphasis on the duties of the statesman, the embodiment of the state whose policy Steuart attempted to steer in the desired direction leading to the state's prosperity.[8] This outlook was also influenced by a social elitism which was shared among many Enlightenment literati. The Enlightenment outlook rarely led to support for full democracy. The interests of the masses could be advanced, but not to the extent of full equality, particularly not in guiding political and economic policy. Steuart specifically opposed the idea of natural equality or a social contract.[9] This underlay his observation, somewhat reminiscent of stadial theory, that in a society of hunters subsistence was not something which supported trade, since everyone were supported by what they themselves grew and manufactured. Even in a more advanced society many still lived on their own produce. Only when a class of industrial laborers emerged, did the need arise for them to purchase basic subsistence. The price of these products was determined by the amount of people working in industry and their level of employment. This price could not rise beyond the point where they could not afford purchasing food, a situation which could occur in a country where there was little industry and where many were supported by charity.[10] Steuart consistently presupposed that advanced civilization was preferable to less sophisticated social and economic existence. In this respect he was a typical Enlightenment propagator of the idea of cultural progress.

He also consistently expressed the traditional support for a large population as a sign of progress, though recognizing that "The Number of people, *well employed*, makes the prosperity of a state." The unemployed were a load on the state. Abusive procreation led to hunger and wretchedness. Yet low population levels were a sign of political sickness. Ultimately, a gradual increase of population was better than a rapid one, which would halt at a certain point of distress. It was therefore one of the statesman's tasks to ensure both population and employment.[11] While far from Malthusian apprehensions, Steuart claimed that it was necessary that newlywed couples would be able to feed their children, and would not become a burden to their communities. Such cases occurred of course mainly among the lower classes. Steuart differentiated between the augmentation of a population of those who were able to earn a living, which he termed "multiplication," and the rising population of those whose parents could not properly support them, which he termed "procreation."[12] The connection between population and subsistence also meant that population was connected with the cultivation of natural resources, most significantly agriculture. It was the statesman's responsibility to regulate the multiplication of the population so that it would be commensurate to the fertility of the country's soil. The moment the country was thoroughly cultivated and peopled in proportion to its produce, it was necessary to check the growth of population to avoid either misery and depopulation, or else improper use of national wealth to support the inhabitants.[13] Another example of population policy was the observation that when a nation was in danger of losing its foreign trade, the statesman needed first to see to it that it did not lose the wealth it had already acquired. This might be accomplished either by reducing the population, by establishing colonies, or else by encouraging emigration, till a just level of national subsistence was achieved.[14]

The issue of agricultural production, with and without a connection to the issue of population, received consistent attention from Steuart from several points of view, not least the superiority of advanced civilization, and the emphasis of agriculture as the underpinning for progress in manufactures. Both the growth of population and people's strength of constitution were proportional to the amount of available food. "Were the earth therefore uncultivated, the number of mankind would not exceed the proportion of the spontaneous fruits which she offers for their immediate use, or for that of the animals which might be the proper nourishment of man." Yet when human beings cultivated the land, subject to its relative fertility, this enabled population to grow. This also led to inequality, since those more capable and diligent who chose to cultivate the land more than others, became leaders. Agriculture was the basis for the production of food and preservation of population, and the chief requisite for the state's prosperity.[15] Expressing the common observation regarding the inverse proportion between supportive natural environment and levels of progress, Steuart claimed that in more fertile countries the inhabitants would tend to be lazy, and population would decrease, while in less fertile lands they would tend to be more industrious and their labor would lead to a growth of population, as well as general material and social progress. Thus in countries where labor was required for cultivating the earth there would ultimately also be more workers in other professions, and consequently greater urbanization.[16] It was important to maintain a just proportion between those employed in different occupations, mainly agriculture, otherwise this led to an abusive situation in which not all the population contributed to society's prosperity. Furthermore, it was better that those laboring in various occupations, again mainly in agriculture, would specialize in their work and become interdependent.[17]

Despite the emphasis of agriculture, Steuart recognized the interdependence of all types of production, a point which, in contrast with the Physiocrats, would be emphasized by Smith and all subsequent classical political economists. In a free nation agriculture would enhance population only as long as agricultural surplus would be exchanged with other products the farmers would require. These products would be produced by others not working in agriculture but in need of agricultural produce as food. It was however imperative to avoid overproduction of unused agricultural surplus, and if this was not exported, it was necessary to see that home consumption would not be too limited, otherwise this would lead to discouragement for the farmers. A lazy population would work less and its numbers diminish, and, in Steuart's opinion, no European nation had yet maximized its possible cultivation of land.[18] In a society living only on its agricultural produce without producing a surplus, the inhabitants lived like cattle which fed only on the spontaneous fruits of the earth. Yet agriculture should provide work only for the number of laborers truly required, and no more. Otherwise this would lead to inefficiency, abuse, and ultimately a diminishing population. Agriculture was the basis of economy, yet other professions were also required. The statesman needed to ascertain that sufficient laborers worked in agriculture so that the land was properly cultivated and yielded a surplus, while also making sure that sufficient numbers labored in other occupations. Conversely, if shortage of food occurred, this was caused because industry had progressed more than agriculture. In this situation food became more expensive, since there were more useful inhabitants competing for its purchase. On the other hand, when the number of non-productive inhabitants grew, the price of food would not rise, and only their misery would become greater. This was the reason one often encountered a situation in which a large number of poor existed despite a very low price of necessaries.[19] Maintaining a sufficient and properly priced amount of grain was a prime duty of the statesman. Evincing his mercantilist viewpoint, Steuart noted that the statesman needed to balance the price of subsistence in years of plenty or scarcity, and to strive for its staying lower at home than in rival trading nations. In this way the population would multiply and the expense of manufactures would be reduced, since the number of laborers increased and the price of labor decreased.[20]

A growing population could be maintained as long as demand increased, but no further. When advancing agriculture required increasing investment, food became scarce and people began competing for it, in which case the industrious had an advantage and could continue and multiply, in a situation which might lead to further agricultural improvements. Like other eighteenth-century political economists, Steuart was writing at a time when agricultural improvements, not least in Scotland, were becoming increasingly more significant.[21] A rising value of subsistence raised the price of labor, in which case some of the demand for labor decreased or removed outside the country. Only a decrease in the price of food could lower the price of labor. In such a situation the statesman needed to avoid raising the quantity of labor, while increasing the amount of subsistence. Yet even this was not to be done to an exaggerated extent by large importations, since this would put a stop to agricultural improvements. Only a proper use of public money by the statesman would solve such a dilemma. In any case, the price of industry would necessarily rise with a growing population. This might lead to increased agricultural production, but conversely also, without the statesman's cautious interference, damage manufactures and demand, as well as open the door to foreign consumption. Moreover, what impeded the progress of industry might conversely encourage agriculture. The statesman's role in such situations was to keep the balance between growing agricultural production and growing manufactures, which might even occasionally require importing food for a limited period, although it was important to be wary that such food importation did not damage local agriculture.[22]

In these and other typically meticulous and often repetitious discussions Steuart constantly attempted to address any possible economic contingency. In itself this thoroughness would become part and parcel of subsequent economic analysis, although Steuart's prolixity often made it difficult to comprehend a clear vision. Yet it was clear that he recognized that the growth of agriculture and population could not continue indefinitely. Any chance to maintain growth required a careful balance between the various economic forces, a task which only the statesman could accomplish. Steuart however maintained a cautious optimism about the ability to sustain progress. A country could never become fully peopled, since it was always possible to import food from other countries. A need of imports could also arise when farmers were unable to produce sufficient food for a growing population. In the agricultural infancy of society the spontaneous produce provided by nature led to the multiplication of population. Since then the situation had reversed, and in more advanced civilization population had become what he termed the efficient cause of agriculture. This meant that when poor people consumed food, they had nothing to give in return, and therefore distributed it among themselves and declined to wretchedness. When those, however, who had an equivalent to give in exchange for food asked for it, farmers had an incentive to produce beyond the spontaneous natural yield, or else beyond what they had previously produced.[23] Throughout, Steuart remained consistent about the connection between a proper utilization of natural-resource cultivation, primarily in the form of agriculture, and rising population and prosperity. In this, at least, his vision was not that different from Adam Smith's.

If Steuart combined typical eighteenth-century views with an insistence on outmoded mercantilist notions, other contemporaries developed their insistence on utilization of nature while discarding mercantilism. While not yet classical political economists in the full sense of the term, they already pointed the way to some of the crucial innovations of Adam Smith and his classical followers. One particularly important example of these innovative Enlightenment figures was of course Smith's friend David Hume, philosopher, historian, political commentator and, not least, political economist. Hume's most famous contribution to economic analysis was the idea of the specie-flow mechanism, the anti-mercantilist and anti-bullionist assertion that when a country hoarded gold and silver this inevitably led to inflation (a modern term in itself not used by Hume), and consequently to a reaction which led to the specie flowing out of the country in the direction, and to the benefit, of seemingly poorer countries. Hume's mechanism thus proposed an early notion of economic equilibrium to which international trade predisposed all countries; the amount of money in a country always tended toward approximately the same level – too much, and a condition of decline ensued, too little, and with the proper trading policy, a condition of growth and increasing progress could be initiated.[24] This outlook no doubt influenced Smith's later assertion that a state of progress was preferable to a stationary, not to mention a declining, state. What mattered more than the momentary seeming wealth of a country was whether it was in the process of acquiring more wealth or not. The modern notion of economic growth was in large measure the outcome of these eighteenth-century perceptions.[25]

Hume did not share the common assertion that climate influenced culture, at least not in the emphatic manner outlined by Montesquieu.[26] Nevertheless, despite his doubts on this point, Hume accepted the common theory that a harsh physical environment spurred cultural improvement. In states which had a mild climate and rich soil, farmers lacked the incentive to improve their forms of labor, and governments did not encourage it. But in countries such as England (in contrast with France, Italy or Spain), where the soil was coarse, there was a greater need for more developed methods of cultivation. Therefore, it was specifically in such countries, with less inviting natural surroundings, that one found greater cultural advancement and less poverty. For similar reasons, in a milder climate there was less need of clothing and housing, yet this in turn removed "in part, that necessity, which is the great spur to industry and invention."[27]

Hume was the least affected by stadial theory among the Scottish Enlightenment literati, yet he too acknowledged basic differentiations between various stages of cultural development. He claimed that the moment people quit the savage state of hunting and fishing, they necessarily fell into one of two classes – either husbandmen or manufacturers, although at first most belonged to the former.[28] His conception of growth was intimately connected with his views on population, most notably outlined in his lengthy essay "Of the Populousness of Ancient Nations," in which he asserted that modern nations were more populous than ancient ones.[29] In this bold intervention in a late stage of the *querelle des anciens et des modernes*, Hume regarded modern European civilization as superior not just in population, but also in art and industry, to all earlier civilizations, specifically those of antiquity. Throughout, the argument presupposed that population was essentially a hallmark of cultural progress and prosperity.[30] Hume regarded "art, knowledge, civility, and the best police" as the most appropriate criteria for estimating the size of population in both the ancient and modern eras.[31] A large population was the result of good natural conditions, mainly climate and soil, yet even more so of the virtue of a proper government. This was one of the main reasons for the superiority of the moderns over the ancients.[32] Modern Europe was also more populous than in antiquity because in antiquity many tracts of land were left uncultivated, while in modern Europe most areas were cultivated.[33] Hume thus recognized a direct link between cultivation of natural resources, promoted by proper government, and the resultant growth of population. He evidently regarded the promotion of cultivation of land as one of the duties of government. While he did not emphasize, in the emphatic manner propounded by the famous contemporary naturalist the Comte de Buffon, the ability of human beings to cultivate nature to the point of changing and ameliorating the natural environment itself, Hume did evince some recognition of this possibility. He noted that in antiquity Europe had been much colder than in modern times. This resulted from the fact that by the eighteenth century much more land was cultivated and forests cut down. As a result there was much less shade, and more penetration of warm sunlight, a process which was gradually occurring also in the American colonies, which became warmer in tandem with the cutting down of forests.[34] With more control of nature came more progress, and with more progress more population.

Hume's work on population was the outcome of an amicable exchange with his friend Robert Wallace.[35] According to the latter it was ancient nations which had been more populous, not modern ones. Depopulation might occur as the result of natural causes such as natural disasters. These, however, were prone to the skill and industry of human beings, their laws and institutions. What influenced population more detrimentally were, on the other hand, moral causes such as wars, corruption, sloth and luxuries.[36] Wallace, like Hume, regarded population in itself as a sign of progress. Dangers to population resulted more from human social corruption than from any limit to the ability to cultivate nature. The problem was exacerbated when such corruption impacted cultivation of natural resources. Countries with a natural habitat more amenable to cultivation were capable of sustaining a larger population. Wallace, however, was sensitive to the need for proper cultural abilities to take advantage of such natural surroundings. Relying on stadial notions, he claimed that without agriculture, arts and commerce, it was impossible to cultivate the land and produce subsistence for a growing population at the level achieved by advanced civilizations.[37]

Wallace's political-economic views were rather conservative, not least in not acknowledging any unintended beneficial consequences of the pursuit of luxuries. A nation which cultivated all of its land might sustain the growth of population only with manufactures. Yet in other circumstances manufactures and trade might encourage luxury, and divert labor from agriculture and the production of food, thus damaging the growth of population. A moderate level of elegance and refinement was natural and necessary for human beings and had a civilizing effect, but beyond this it became corrupting. This outlook was connected with a traditional moral support of agriculture. Among the moral causes of the paucity of population in modern as opposed to ancient times, Wallace noted the ancient respect for the occupation of agriculture, with its concomitant cultivation of land, a respect which was lacking in modern times.[38]

Already in his early work on population Wallace exhibited the originality which has rightfully earned him a place in the history of population theories. He noted that it was possible to imagine a situation whereby, at least hypothetically, all the earth would be peopled and cultivated to the full, and the production of additional subsistence would become impossible. This applied to separate nations as much as to the earth *in toto*.[39] Wallace's approach to the issue of population was thus more circumspect than that of most of his optimistic contemporaries. Assuming that all the world would be peopled and cultivated to the full, many would be in danger of perishing in times of famine or bad crops. Yet this, in Wallace's estimate, was only a distant danger not really to be feared. In fact, he perceived a still very large room for cultivating land and peopling countries throughout the world. Scotland in particular was capable of being better cultivated and peopled, if only more attention were given to encouraging a spirited occupation in agriculture. This did not need to come at the expense of occupation, though not excessive, in manufactures. Both types of labor were mutually supportive, and together would make "the lands fertile, the country populous, and society flourish." In the Scottish Highlands the barbarian inhabitants would become civilized if they learned how to labor properly. Since sufficient land amenable to cultivation was lacking there, it was best they did so in fisheries. Wallace thus regarded other types of cultivating natural resources, not only land, as leading to civilization.[40]

This prescient recognition of the limits to population and to natural resources, which has led some scholars to consider Wallace a precursor to Malthus, were developed several years later in more sophisticated fashion in his book *Various Prospects of Mankind, Nature, and Providence*.[41] There he noted how despite nature's riches capable of providing human necessaries, and despite human reason and genius, nature in fact had a capacity to provide much more for these ends. "What vastly greater stores would the earth be able to produce if duly cultivated!" It was possible to enhance progress and population, both the numbers of humanity and their quality of life. "The earth has never been cultivated to the full extent of what it was able to bear… No country has ever been fully cultivated."[42] Greater progress and utilization of natural resources required however more adequate cultural and political conditions. "The earth can never be fully peopled or cultivated in the best manner, and every spot be made to exert its utmost strength, till it becomes the abode of peace, security, and plenty."[43]

To make his point more adamantly Wallace then proceeded to describe in great detail a utopian society devoid of private property, only to ultimately criticize this as an unrealistic aspiration. He began by considering how the abolition of private property would lead to enhanced progress, not least in the cultivation of natural resources. Such a society might purportedly rise either through a revolutionary process, or by a more benign historical process.[44] Nevertheless, after taking great pains to convince his readers of the possibility of establishing such a society, Wallace proceeded to claim that it was the finite limit to physical nature which made it impossible. Assuming a perfect, propertyless society, its conditions would enable a limitless propagation of human beings. Faced with overpopulation, this would inevitably result in violence, and ultimately in the dissolution of that very same, seemingly perfect, political order which had initiated this process to begin with. Philosophizing on the implications of this dialectical process, Wallace raised the possibility that perhaps Providence had created human beings as depraved creatures so that their vices would prevent this situation from ever occurring. On the other hand, he asserted that Providence could not have enabled a situation in which a perfect government would lead to such a disaster. Therefore, he claimed that Utopian societies like the one he had himself painstakingly depicted, were in fact prevented naturally by the moral imperfectability of human beings, as well as by the limited capacity of nature to provide them with room and sustenance.[45] In this respect, if in less sophisticated manner, Wallace preceded Malthus's later apprehensions regarding overpopulation, in a manner quite prescient for a mid-eighteenth-century philosopher. It should also be noted that Wallace, even while engaged in his ultimately fictive depiction of a propertyless Utopia, at no point acquiesced with Rousseau's criticism of advanced civilization, from which he openly distanced himself.[46] On the contrary, Wallace raised the possibility of canceling private property as a means to enhance, not limit, human material and cultural progress. While he then proceeded to cancel the validity of these means, his adherence to this end remained evident.

Wallace's attitude toward nature should be considered in the context of his Enlightened religious view of progress, coupled with his somewhat (though not openly avowed) optimistic Leibnizian theodicy. He claimed that the fact that nature was imperfect and included elements harmful to humanity was divinely ordained to answer the imperfection and depravity of human beings. Had human beings lived in peace and with greater morality, their industry would have been able to overcome all the obstacles offered by nature.[47] However, as already noted, Wallace had earlier dialectically reasoned that the perfection of such a society was ultimately the cause of its own dissolution. Human imperfection was therefore inevitable, the result of divinely ordained wisdom meant to prevent the even greater ills of over-population. The death of human beings, as well as of all living creatures, made room for the following generations of creatures. These included even the most minute animals, which seemed aimed at filling the smallest spaces of physical nature.[48] Wallace thus attempted to balance two opposing forces – on the one hand the tendency of nature, seemingly following the principle of *natura horror vacui*, to fill itself with as much living populations as possible; and on the other the divinely ordained imperfections of nature and human beings, the former in terms of its finality, the latter in terms of their depravity, which ultimately made this imperfect world the best of all possible worlds. This was not yet Malthus's stark propagation of a mathematical law which underlined over-population and its ensuing ills, yet it was, for its time, an unusual departure from the more common and self-confident Enlightenment belief in progress. Wallace presupposed that the maximal utilization of natural resources was a positive end. The problem was in making it as unhindered as possible.

Another contemporary with whom Hume had a friendly intellectual disagreement was Josiah Tucker. The latter, though in favor of free trade, still retained some vestiges of mercantilism. According to his more thorough optimism, all countries could progress equally. Yet he disagreed with the conclusion arising from Hume's specie-flow mechanism, which implied that poor countries could progress at the expense of rich ones. Tucker claimed that rich countries had the advantage particularly in manufactures. They could work raw materials from the poorer countries or colonies, where the manufacturing technology was less advanced. Raw materials were cheaper in poor countries, and complicated manufacturing cheaper in rich ones. This of course was an old mercantilist argument. Yet Tucker also exhibited more novel Enlightenment notions of free trade, in regard to which he was closer to Hume. His special type of conservatism combined free trade on the one hand, and submission to civil authority on the other. Among the duties of the latter was the support of planting of timber. This required a long-term perspective better suited to government rather than to private self-interest. This pointed to Tucker's realization of the significance of natural-resource cultivation, seconded also by a support for a large population suitably employed.[49] He wrote expressly that "Nature has been very bountiful, in bestowing on us [Great Britain] such excellent fisheries… These great advantages are always in our power to cultivate and improve; and it is our fault, and our reproach, that we do not."[50] Among the reasons he gave for his well-known proposition for naturalizing protestant foreigners was the fact that Great Britain was thinly populated in comparison with its potential, "and many hundred thousands acres of good land… lie either entirely waste, or are not sufficiently cultivated, for want of hands, and persons to consume the product." He suggested parceling out land to foreigners choosing a country life, while others would work in manufactures.[51]

Another famous contemporary who favored a large population was Benjamin Franklin.[52] Already as a young man he considered that an abundant population was a positive factor in the development of a nation, raising the value of land.[53] Later in life he retained this belief, as well as the perception that population was limited to the amount of subsistence, though without the pessimistic overtones Malthus would emphasize regarding this point. Yet Franklin was well aware of the connection between the economic well-being of the populace and the tendency to marry and propagate. The abundance of land in America was particularly encouraging in this respect, supporting demand for manufactures, as were its abundant waterways which facilitated commerce. America's "immense forests… many navigable Rivers and Lakes, and its plentiful fisheries," were considered as a resource which could enhance cultural progress. Writing on the eve of the revolution, Franklin still maintained that this would benefit the British empire in general.[54]

Utilizing stadial terminology, Franklin noted that America, still peopled mainly by hunters, had ample uncultivated land, whereas Europe was already practically fully peopled, with many among the populace employed in agriculture and manufactures. This made the appropriation of land, followed by economic advancement, and consequently the inducement to marry and propagate, much easier in America. Franklin therefore perceived a limit to the utilization of land

and the growth of population, but regarded emigration, specifically from Britain to America, as the solution to retaining the empire's continued growth to a very far-off limit, signaled by the full utilization of American land. No Malthusian pessimism was implied in this outlook, despite the perceived connection between the limits of land and sustenance, and those of population. Human causes such as bad government or war might reduce population, but on the other hand a growing population relied more on the industriousness of human beings and the use they made of nature, rather than on the "greater fecundity of Nature" in itself.[55]

4 The Physiocrats and the bread riots

In the early part of the second half of the eighteenth century a prominent group of philosophers coupled an Enlightenment belief in progress with an unprecedentedly systematic discussion of political economy. These were the French Physiocrats, the supporters of the "rule of nature," embodied in a thorough preference of agriculture at the expense of all other types of manufacturing and production. A full overview of their ideas, most importantly as developed by François Quesnay, is out of place here. Yet we should note their claim that only agriculture, due to its motivation of the productive powers of nature, created a surplus which circulated throughout the economy and ultimately stimulated sterile (non-surplus-creating) manufactures and commerce. The idea of economic circulation was probably indebted to Quesnay's medical occupation, and expressed in the famous *tableau économique.*[1] The idea of the pre-eminence of agriculture also required a proper government policy, advocating free trade mainly in agricultural production, and expressed in the famous motto *laissez faire*, which for Quesnay and his associates did not mean free trade in the modern sense, but rather a type of enlightened legal despotism.[2] As is well known, Adam Smith was openly influenced by the Physiocrats, while enhancing the concept of free trade, and not retaining their singular emphasis of agriculture.[3] In terms of the economic recognition of the need to cultivate natural resources, the Physiocratic emphasis of agriculture was quite significant. They evinced the traditional praise of agriculture as morally superior to other types of labor, yet at the same time they added to this a new, distinctly economic argument for this superiority.[4] They also gave a new dimension to the emphasis on a large population, which according to them was a positive thing only if the inhabitants were properly employed in agricultural labor. Furthermore, Quesnay and his disciples recognized that the means of subsistence posed a limit to the growth of population, and, more importantly, they also recognized that the people's quality of life was as important as their absolute numbers.[5] In general, they saw the road to prosperity as based on a proper policy aimed at enhancing the utilization of nature. It was only nature which was truly productive and created wealth through agriculture, and therefore human policy needed to interfere with this productivity, with nature's course, as little as possible.[6]

The emphasis on the importance of agriculture, and the merits of a free trade in grain, were topics regarding which the Physiocrats were influenced by previous political economists. Among these, of particular importance was Pierre le Pesant, sieur de Boisguilbert (or Boisguillebert). Writing around the turn of the eighteenth century, Boisguilbert attempted, less successfully than the Physiocrats later, to have his ideas implemented by the government as direct policy measures. Yet his economic ideas were in many ways innovative and ahead of the times, requiring another half century before they were reformulated in somewhat different form by Quesnay and his followers.[7] Rather expectedly for an early modern political economist, as should be clear by now, Boisguilbert claimed that the fertility of land in itself was not the only thing of importance, and only a proper economic and commercial policy could utilize it to lead to national wealth. Improper taxation, not least the *taille*, had a negative impact on agricultural production and agricultural improvements, diminished the number of sheep, and damaged the general condition of farmers. Improper and unequal taxation ultimately influenced the economy in general and all social classes.[8] This formed the background to Boisguilbert's policy recommendations, but more importantly for our purposes, to his consideration of agricultural production and distribution in general.

Boisguilbert emphasized the foundational significance of agriculture to all economic activity. All types of production and trade, and all sectors of society, were interdependent, and this highlighted the need for the government to protect agricultural production and avoid excessive pricing of necessary products. In comparison with other products grain over time did not retain its price, and therefore the condition of French farmers gradually declined, leading to significant damage to the country in general. It was necessary to maintain a moderate and proper price of grain, not too high and not too low. Boisguilbert made a point of noting that those who wished to lower its price so as to help the poor in fact achieved the opposite effect, hurting the farmers and the incentive to produce an agricultural surplus. Since the prosperity of the farmers was the basis for all other economic activity, this impacted the economy in general.[9] Lowering the price of grain was the result of over-abundance, and in the long run was worse than famine. An excessively low price was in fact just as damaging as an excessively high price, and lowering it eventually, in years of shortage, led to a reactionary violent price rise. What Boisguilbert recommended was striving for a state of equilibrium in terms of a natural price of grain. Yet most people naturally and erroneously viewed it as in their interest to have low grain prices so they would have cheap food, while the proprietors of land, equally erroneously, strived for high prices. The competition between these two was further complicated by the changing circumstances between years of natural plenty and years of shortage. During the latter, public panic exacerbated the situation. It was only a price equilibrium which could evade these two ruinous extremes. The attempts of the government to intervene in the grain market in times of crisis also only served to exacerbate the situation. In fact, in such times the importation of foreign grain was capable of having a stabilizing effect, not because of the augmentation of the quantity of grain in itself, so much as for the recovery of equilibrium between the two price extremes.[10]

Therefore, unsurprising from our modern perspective but much more surprising and unpalatable for most of his contemporaries, one of Boisguilbert's main policy recommendations resulting from these observations, was for diminishing governmental interference in the agricultural market, mainly in the form of improper taxation. Imposts on the importation and exportation of grains ultimately led to famine. One of their chief negative effects was that surplus grain accumulated in years of plenty, and was not stored and kept properly for the inevitable subsequent years of drought and shortage. Furthermore, in contrast with unsubstantiated popular fears, the exportation of grain did not have a negative impact either on the quantity or the price of the harvests. Both the import and the export of grain in fact had no real practical influence on subsistence, but only on the balance of prices.[11] Like the Physiocrats later, Boisguilbert, despite his advocacy for free trade, was not opposed to government intervention, particularly in times of crisis.[12] Free trade in the eighteenth century meant governmentally sanctioned and controlled free trade for particular times and aimed at particular economic sectors, which in France most significantly meant agriculture.

In an almost pre-Ricardian fashion (though without Ricardo's later original inferences from this observation), Boisguilbert was cognizant of how differences in the fertility of land influenced its modes of cultivation. He emphasized that it was less fertile land which could lead to prosperity, since farmers who cultivated it properly tended to invest labor in it, not least manure, the importance of which Boisguilbert particularly emphasized. Therefore the inclination to avoid cultivating less fertile lands was nationally harmful.[13] Nature, which in Boisguilbert's view was tantamount to Providence, supplied human beings with the nourishment they required. As long as the government did not improperly interfere, the raising of grain crops would proceed on its proper natural course. Otherwise, such interference would only lead to misery. Leaving people to behave naturally according to their own self-interests could avoid such problems. Boisguilbert's advocacy for a free trade in grain (free in the relative pre-Smithian sense), was meant to augment agricultural production and thus the general well-being of the French economy, society, and nation. Ultimately, this was based on the common notion of maximizing the cultivation of natural resources as a precondition for general prosperity, and Boisguilbert expressly noted that it was in the interest of all nations to cultivate as much land as possible.[14]

It is easy to see how these ideas preceded subsequent Physiocracy. One of the most prominent of the Physiocrats was Victor de Riqueti, Marquis de Mirabeau, father of the famous revolutionary. The elder Mirabeau acquired fame as the author of a well-known work, *L'ami des hommes, ou Traité de la population*, extolling population and agriculture, which was published just before he came under the influence of Quesnay.[15] In this work Mirabeau already firmly believed in population as the measure of a nation's prosperity, and in the direct connection between the level of subsistence and population. Consequently, the measure of subsistence was also the measure of population ("La mesure de la Subsistance est celle de la Population").[16] Agriculture was the most important of the arts, since it was the source of subsistence, and therefore not only were the other arts dependent on it, but so was the increase of population. Mirabeau therefore emphatically praised farmers and peasants, and advocated for their being similarly appreciated by society at large. Support of agriculture was of prime significance for a nation, not least France.[17] Mirabeau already evinced the Physiocratic preference for agriculture before meeting Quesnay. Slightly later he became acquainted with Quesnay and influenced by him, and in the following years they collaborated in elaborating the Physiocratic position. It was Quesnay, however, who was the more dominant of the two. Under his influence Mirabeau reversed his earlier opinion, claiming not that growing population led to prosperity, but rather that it was prosperity through investment in agriculture, which led to growing population.[18]

Quesnay's political-economic philosophy was based on a conception of progress which included a four-stages analysis of the conjectural-history type which Smith and other Scottish Enlightenment philosophers had developed slightly earlier (although the French had arrived at it independently, not least under the influence of Montesquieu, whose rudimentary stadial observations in *De l'esprit des lois* were known throughout Europe). This framework enabled Quesnay to emphasize the connection between labor and the mastery of nature.[19] In an essay jointly composed with Mirabeau, they claimed that the first three stages of the four-stage process were more states than stages, developing simultaneously and appearing combined in the same societies. In this social reality the settled agricultural form of life was superior. This Physiocratic combination of three states occasionally led to a commercial society which was both secondary and artificial. A commercial society was based on freedom and was therefore republican in nature, yet in such societies there was too much competition, which made them weak, transitory and subject to change. In their own sphere they were strong, yet they could not become empires.[20]

In his own works Quesnay repeatedly addressed the significance of agriculture and the fact that only agricultural labor produced a surplus produce, while manufactures and other types of labor remained sterile.[21] It was important not only to augment the size of a country's population, but also its general wealth, so there would be a proper proportion between its population and wealth, thus avoiding poverty.[22] Progress depended on proper, agricultural, cultivation of natural resources. The savages of Louisiana used to enjoy many natural goods such as water, trees, game and fruit. Yet these did not constitute wealth since they did not have market value. However, the moment the savages began trading with the Europeans, some of their goods acquired such market value and became wealth.[23] For Quesnay nature itself had no significant value for an advanced civilization outside of economic value. The more a nation had both a larger population and a wide and fertile territory, the more its wealth would grow. "It is cultivation, stimulated by men's needs, which is the most fertile source of wealth and the most important mainstay of population."[24] Land had no value other than as such a basis for human progress. This entailed the need for proper governmental policy in favor of agriculture. In a particularly emphatic passage Quesnay emphasized the need for this policy. Farmers would be poor without support, and agriculture was the basis for the prosperity of society in general. "The land, lacking manure and all but uncultivated, can only leave all of them [people in society other than peasants] to languish in poverty."[25]

Given all this, one would not expect to find the Physiocrats starring in a history of modern nature conservation. This, however, is precisely the claim made by Richard Grove in an important study of changing early modern attitudes toward nature, locating the origins of modern environmentalist concerns and management in the early modern colonial setting. Grove has noted the amalgamation of Rousseauian ideas, Robinsonnades, primitivism, and Utopian and Edenic notions of pristine nature regarding tropical islands, which together influenced the rise of early romantic notions about nature. However, as he clearly recognizes, such notions were couched within a rising eighteenth-century recognition that in reality nature was increasingly impacted by human manipulation, a recognition that led to growing attempts to manage natural resources responsibly.[26] Of particular importance in this process, according to Grove, were precisely the ideas of Physiocracy. The Physiocrats applied science to agriculture, forest management, and generally to rural economy. This facilitated the emergence of a conservation policy which was also relevant to broader economic and social objectives.[27]

Grove's thesis requires attention, particularly since our discussion is primarily concerned with outlining how economic considerations increasingly treated nature primarily as a resource meant for human utilization. This outlook would seem to collide with modern notions of sustainability and conservation. Yet as should already be clear, conserving nature for ecological and aesthetic reasons in the modern sense is not equivalent to managing resources for sustainable long-term use. A clearer differentiation between the two is perhaps somewhat lacking in Grove's otherwise perspicacious analysis. This is evident in his discussion of one of the main protagonists of his study, Pierre Poivre, whose adventurous life included, among other things, going as a missionary to China, and undertaking the tasks of French ambassador to Cochinchina (modern southern Vietnam), and intendant of the islands of Mauritius and Bourbon (modern Réunion), where, particularly in Mauritius, he advanced his project of collecting and planting various oriental plants and spices. It was particularly his work in Mauritius which has attracted Grove's notice.[28] Taking a look at Poivre's own ideas can therefore serve to examine the Physiocrats' consideration of nature, since he clearly belonged to their school of thought.

Agriculture, claimed Poivre, was "the universal art of mankind." In his travels he noted that the state of agriculture was a sign of the general state of the various countries he visited.

> If the markets abound in provisions, if the fields are well cultivated, and covered with rich crops, then in general you may conclude that the country is well peopled, that the inhabitants are civilized and happy, that their manners are polished, and their government agreeable to the principles of reason. – You may then say to yourself, I am amongst *Men*. When, on the contrary, I have arrived amongst a people, whom it was necessary to search for amidst forests, whose neglected lands were overgrown with brambles; when I have traversed large tracts of uncultivated desarts, and then at last stumbled on a grubb'd-up wretchedly cultivated field; when arrived at length at some

> canton, I have observed nothing in the public market but a few sorry roots; I no longer hesitated to determine the inhabitants to be wretched savages, or groaning under the most oppressive slavery.

The state of agriculture he observed throughout his extensive travels invariably served as a test for the level of cultural progress, and always confirmed "that a country poorly cultivated is always inhabited by men barbarous or oppressed, and that population there can never be considerable."[29] This confirmed Poivre's Physiocratic perspective, which, like that of Quesnay and Mirabeau, rested on a firm anthropocentric basis. The earth, according to Poivre, was divinely assigned for the use and cultivation of human beings, but this could happen only under a political system which assured liberty and property, and thus enabled good agriculture. Under such conditions prosperity, based on the cultivation of nature, was veritably assured.[30]

The best example of a country where proper agricultural cultivation led to general prosperity was China. In the eighteenth century, at a time when China was used as an example either of prosperity or else of stagnation, the Physiocrats by and large regarded it as a positive example meant for European edification.[31] Poivre, in contrast with most other Physiocrats, was able to do so from first-hand observations. He noted in approval how the Chinese did not lose an inch of ground, and endeavored to cultivate even the most seemingly inaccessible mountain regions, as well as reclaiming parts of the sea in a manner even more impressive than the projects of the Dutch.[32] Among his encomiums to Chinese agricultural efficiency, he noted that they avoided the luxury of chariots, which in Europe required feeding large numbers of horses, at the expense of raising more grain to feed large numbers of hungry human beings. The Chinese, on the contrary, "wish rather to maintain men than horses."[33] It would perhaps not stretch the imagination too much to assume that Poivre would have approved of modern claims that a vegetable-based diet, at the expense of animal products, is a better ecological option for feeding the growing global population. In any event, he described China as the most populous and agriculturally best-cultivated country in the world. This state of affairs was buttressed by an enlightened government in which the emperor considered himself the father of the nation, ensuring equality, freedom, and the advancement of agriculture rather than superfluous luxuries.[34] Poivre thus exemplified the main tenets of Physiocracy – the moral and economic emphasis on agriculture, population, the preference of "enlightened absolutism" (in itself not a Physiocratic term), and the adulation of China as a model for Europe in all these respects. This approach was in accordance with modern notions of sustainable development, as also in accordance with Grove's thesis. It was put into practice in Poivre's agricultural and botanical projects in Mauritius. Nevertheless, claiming Physiocracy as a precursor of modern environmentalism seems like an overstatement.

It would be easy to dismiss Physiocracy as an essentially historiographical topic, a short-lived economic theory which was quickly supplanted by the more correct and influential ideas of classical political economy. This, however, would be overlooking the tremendous immediate influence which the Physiocrats had on the social and economic policies of their time, most significantly regarding the production of corn (the eighteenth- and nineteenth-century term for grain in general). In France, particularly from the 1760s to the eve of the revolution, the issue of food production, most significantly bread, stood at the center of many social and political upheavals, not least the *guerre des farines* (flour war) in the mid-1770s during Anne-Robert-Jacques Turgot's ministry as Controller-General in charge of France's economic policies, with his unsuccessful attempt to institute free trade in grain.[35] Turgot was significant both because to a large (though not indiscriminate) extent he adhered to basic Physiocratic notions and attempted to implement them in practice, but also because he was one of the most original Enlightenment philosophers of historical progress, more sophisticated, indeed, than any of the main Physiocrats. His consideration of natural resources, and specifically agriculture, therefore had both theoretical and political significance.[36] Furthermore, Turgot contributed significantly to rising classical political-economic notions, not least in greater support of free trade than mainstream Physiocrats, and in a sophisticated conception of material growth.[37]

Turgot's outline of historical progress included a consideration of the four-stages theory more sophisticated than any French precursor.[38] Nature, according to Turgot, was unchanging, ruled by repeating life cycles. Yet human beings, by their rational abilities, were capable of breaking this circular regularity by transmitting knowledge from generation to generation. Human history, and different nations at different times, evinced changing fortunes, yet from an overall perspective this history was one of slow but continual progress.[39] Turgot did not accept the assertion that climate was solely responsible for the different levels of progress among various nations. He regarded moral causes as preceding physical causes.[40] All nations began from a similar state of barbarism, yet due to their dissimilar natural settings and uneven abilities in developing various talents, they developed at different rates and to different limits, a fact which was evinced by the varying levels of progress which existed in different places. In North America, for example, the lack of animals amenable to domestication had prevented the development of a pastoral economy. It was, according to Turgot, primarily the ability to acquire safe and abundant subsistence which differentiated between the various stages of progress.[41] He consistently utilized stadial observations to depict how the cultivation of nature served as the basis for the development of human culture.[42]

Turgot went into great detail, from a clearly Physiocratic perspective, in depicting how different social classes developed, beginning from the agricultural stage of progress, in a process where cultural advancement was intertwined with the progressive utilization of natural resources. At first the cultivators and the proprietors of land were the same people. As society progressed, however, a growing lack of fertile land, as well as inequality both in fertility of land and in human capabilities, led to social inequality. When possessed with agricultural surplus, owners of land could afford to stop cultivating it themselves and pay others to do so, while artisans adopted completely different types of labor. As a result, inequality emerged between different proprietors, as well as between them and agricultural laborers who depended on them. The owners of land were left with time which they could devote to state functions such as administration or the conduct of war. In essence, this meant there existed three classes – the cultivators who were the productive class; the artisans who were the stipendiary class; and the landowners (as well as the capitalists) who were the disposable class. In contrast with the proprietors, the other two classes gained their livelihood solely from their wages. In contrast with the artisans, however, the farmer's labor produced not only wages but also further revenue which was paid to the artisans. The proprietors were also completely dependent on the farmers and their labor. Only the farmers were a truly productive class, while the others were sterile. The farmer depended on the proprietor due to civil conventions, while the proprietor depended on the farmer due to the permanent physical situation of nature, since land produced nothing without labor. Therefore, according to Turgot, the primacy of agricultural production as the basis for all social-economic existence was the result of the unchanging attributes of nature itself. He therefore consistently viewed the cultivation of nature as the prerequisite act which both enabled and sustained the existence and development of human civilization.[43]

Had all individuals possessed exactly the amount of land requisite for their livelihood, surplus would not have been produced and commerce would not have developed. Yet such a situation was unrealistic, since the cultivation of land had begun before its division, and the first farmers had probably already cultivated the land as much as possible and created a surplus. Furthermore, the difference between various tracts of land meant that no land could yield every type of produce. Consequently a basic need existed for people to purchase commodities from each other. In addition, most agricultural products needed to be processed before they became food, raiment or other products, and farmers could not do all these tasks. This led to the exchange of products for labor, to everyone's advantage. Ultimately, however, the husbandman was the one whose products remained pre-eminent in terms of developing and preserving trade. Only he could in principle live without the products of other laborers, and consequently his surplus was the basis for their existence. "Nature never bargains with him [the husbandman] in order to oblige him to content himself with what is absolutely necessary. What she grants is proportionate neither to his needs nor to a contractual evaluation of the price of his working day. It is the physical result of the fertility of the soil, and of the correctness, much more than of the difficulty, of the means he has employed to render it fruitful." In this way husbandmen created the surplus which improved their condition and propelled the economic existence of society.[44]

The mastery of nature was evident in specific scientific and technological advances throughout history. While depicting the emergence of Europe from the darkness of the Middle Ages, and the renewed progress in the sciences and arts, Turgot noted that "The arts are nothing but the utilization of nature, and the practice of the arts is a succession of physical experiments which progressively unveil nature." The invention of the compass, for example, turned the seas from a natural element separating nations, to one linking them, while the discovery of new nations made all the world known to the Europeans.[45] At the agricultural stage of progress population grew and a greater need for positive knowledge emerged, which consequently led to enhanced progress in the arts.[46] As already noted, Turgot emphasized the significance of agricultural surplus. He also noted how it led to the development of division of labor, as well as manufactures, commerce and urban culture. Farmers were the productive class in society, while artisans were a stipendiary class. Yet he was less in line with Physiocratic doctrine when he noted that agriculture also enabled the city to rule the country, as well as negative things such as inequality, subjection of women and slavery. For Turgot progress was inevitably connected both with an essentially dynamic social existence as well as with cultural imperfection.[47]

During his short ministry as Controller-General in the mid-1770s, Turgot was given the unique opportunity of implementing in practice the theoretical implications of the Physiocratic emphasis of agriculture, by attempting to deregulate the commerce in grain. This ended in quick and dismal failure. Bad harvests, which repeatedly precipitated social unrest in eighteenth-century France, no doubt played a part. The fact that Turgot's policy was not a comprehensive one of free trade, and that it encountered continual institutional resistance, no doubt played an additional role. In any event, the result was not only social and political unrest, but also a heated intellectual debate involving not just Turgot himself, but several other major figures of the Enlightenment – in support of Turgot the eminent scientist and philosopher Condorcet, and in opposition the Italian Ferdinando Galiani, as well as Turgot's successor as minister of finance, Jacques Necker. Throughout the ensuing debate the issue of the importance of cultivating natural resources, specifically grain, was paramount, both among the Physiocrats and among their critics.[48]

Both Condorcet's position in this debate and that of Turgot were outlined in the former's biography of the latter. Condorcet approvingly described Turgot's policies while advocating his own similar ones. His discussion of Turgot was no less an exposition of his own political and economic philosophy. He advocated Turgot's support of free trade, both internal and international, due in large measure to the influence of the Physiocrat Vincent de Gournay. Turgot supported free trade in corn, which encouraged methods of extending and improving land cultivation, and also lowered taxes and duties.[49] As minister of finances Turgot had encouraged agriculture through regulating the exemption of payment of tythes. The problem with these had been that they were exacted more from the labor of the husbandmen than the shares of the landowners, or in other words, they pertained to the gross rather than the net agricultural product. Turgot therefore made tythes unprofitable. This not only encouraged agriculture but also helped the poor farmers and alleviated their unjust treatment. Condorcet repeatedly emphasized this aspect of Turgot's policies. The only fair tax was a direct one upon the net produce of land. Another praiseworthy policy was the suppression of ecclesiastics of both sexes, which turned large tracts of land into the state's hands. Proper use of this land would create considerable wealth by invigorating agriculture, and by augmenting the number of landowners who would help pay the national debt.[50] Turgot had also initiated a successful support for the inhabitants of Guyenne during a severe cattle plague, though he limited government intervention only to specific necessary cases such as this.[51] Another aspect of Turgot's policies which encouraged the cultivation of natural resources was the construction of waterworks. This improved internal navigation and thus encouraged industry and agriculture, even though Turgot had not been able to support it as much as he intended. Condorcet, indeed, had been one of the advisors for Turgot's canal-building projects.[52]

Condorcet enthusiastically described Turgot's social and political philosophy which emphasized the indefinite and ever-increasing perfectibility of the human race, both at the individual and the collective levels. In modern terms, this outlook also combined both negative and positive liberty, both liberalism and a form of personal accountability in the classical republican mold. Human progress would pertain both to the material-economic level as well as the social and moral one. While eighteenth-century France was the epitome of existing progress in Turgot's and Condorcet's vision, this progress could be extended in the future, not necessarily in France. "This progress, always advancing from age to age, has no bounds, at least no definite bounds, ascertainable by the actual state of knowledge." Part of this intertwined material and moral knowledge included progress in the sciences and arts, as well as their application in agriculture. The ensuing progress would benefit all classes of society and all nations.[53] The support of increasing cultivation of nature was thus part of a general philosophical outlook. Here Condorcet was propagating his own philosophy rather than simply narrating Turgot's. This optimistic Enlightenment vision of the future of the human race would later of course be described in detail in his *Sketch for a Historical Picture of the Progress of the Human Mind*, with its idiosyncratic stadial depiction of human progress, culminating in the future tenth stage of universal progress through science and enlightenment.[54]

As a political economist Condorcet was initially influenced by the Physiocrats, although later he became critical of their emphasis on government authority. He was a transitional figure between the eighteenth and nineteenth centuries, between the Enlightenment and liberalism.[55] His economic opinions were expressed not least in his direct intervention in the corn-trade debate, the *Reflections on the Commerce in Grain*. Condorcet there recognized the connection between the amount of agriculturally produced subsistence, and the rise of population, wages and prosperity. There was an almost mercantilist tone to his logic when he claimed that a nation needed to remain independent of other nations when it came to the production of food. The significance of agriculture overran free commerce even for such a staunch supporter of the latter such as Condorcet.[56] Nevertheless, free trade was usually necessary, not least in the grain trade. This augmented population by improving the quality of life. The rise in population was the result, not the cause, of improved living standards.[57] Grain, after all, was the prime produce sustaining subsistence. Condorcet preceded the later, more sophisticated observations of Malthus and Ricardo, regarding the connection between minimal necessary subsistence and the level of wages.[58]

The Physiocratic emphasis of agriculture was not absent from Condorcet's analysis. He claimed that human beings had a predisposition to rely on nature rather than on other human beings. This explained the attraction to agricultural labor, yet only so long as the freedom of trade in foodstuffs was maintained. He evinced the traditional classical view of agriculture as a noble occupation compared with manufactures. Agriculture in this light was more ethical than the corrupting pursuit of luxury. This meant that liberty in the production and trade in grain would lead to both quantitative and qualitative improvement of the population.[59] His support for free trade notwithstanding, Condorcet still lacked understanding of the law of unintended consequences which underlay the view of free trade developed by Smith and other classical political economists. Like the Physiocrats in general he recognized no beneficial consequences from the free trade and consumption of luxuries.

When it came to agriculture and the commerce in grain, however, commercial prohibitions would result in diminished agricultural production. This pertained not just to domestic trade but to international as well, a point on which Condorcet went beyond common Physiocratic prescriptions. When the commerce in grain was free, and conducted reciprocally between nations, this in fact meant that it covered more extensive ground, thus literally augmenting agricultural production. In this way changing seasons, or the varying conditions from year to year, were less ruinous, and production became more consistent, prompt and proportional. "Thus, this reciprocal exportation is favorable for humanity in general" ("Ainsi, cette exportation réciproque est favorable à l'humanité en général").[60] Condorcet's support of freedom in grain trade thus fit into his general philosophy, which regarded liberty as one of the central preconditions for the progress of the human race in its entirety. This progress was also accompanied by increasing mastery of nature through the aid not just of advanced science, but also the basic cultivation of land, and the increasingly efficient production of food.

So far we have considered Condorcet mainly as a propagator of the increasing emphasis on cultivation of natural resources in growing political-economic discourse. Yet he was also much more modern in his realization of environmental degradation and its accompanying social consequences. One of the exceptional instances in which Condorcet accepted government intervention was to prevent environmental damage due to socially unjust uses of land or water resulting in air pollution, floods and so forth.[61] In this respect he might serve as a better example than Poivre to substantiate Richard Grove's thesis, although, again, Condorcet was not exactly a Physiocrat in the full sense. He was an example of the fact that in the eighteenth century there was a growing awareness not just of the need for proper policy in maintaining the supply of natural resources, primarily regarding forestry, but also increasing recognition of actual environmental damage, and the need for regulating pollution.[62]

Condorcet claimed that it should be lawfully possible to prevent an owner of land from cultivating it in a manner which corrupted the air, causing maladies in the neighboring habitations. Similarly, in marshy areas it should be possible, without the consent of the landlords (though while compensating them), to enact works which would rehabilitate the salubriousness of the air, which otherwise would shorten the life expectancy of the local inhabitants.[63] Similarly, in his biography of Turgot he depicted the latter as almost modern in his recognition of environmental damage and the need for proper policies to ameliorate it. Turgot had acted to drain the marshes in various regions of France, which were a source of diseases and a danger to public health. Their draining, in Condorcet's view, would result in the creation of fertile land, and therefore encourage population and the accumulation of wealth, not to mention the further cultivation of neighboring lands. Yet these marshes were not necessarily natural phenomena. "These evils are not so much the work of nature as of the avidity of men. The obstructions made to the course of waters by the proprietors of rivers and ponds, &c. are the first cause of these inundations; and it is from a mistaken interest in order to add a little to their present revenue, that they consign the lands themselves to sterility, and thousands of their fellow creatures to calamity and death." The only way to combat this danger was to purchase these dangerous lands and drain them. The subsequent local agriculture, fisheries, and enhanced employment, would end up paying for this purchase.[64] Condorcet was thus a prime supporter of maximizing the use of natural resources, but in a responsible manner quite uncommon among Enlightenment political economists.

The supporters of free grain trade, despite their prominence, did not prove the stronger side in eighteenth-century France. One of their prime opponents was of course Turgot's ministerial successor, Jacques Necker, whose own political-economic analysis was as sophisticated as that of Turgot and Condorcet. Necker was not an extremist, and his views were characterized by a moderation aimed at promoting the common good rather than proselytization. Necker agreed with the Physiocratic emphasis on the importance of population, though he regarded the urge to propagate as natural and not amenable to government control, claiming it would probably halt due to natural checks even before food ran out. He was more of a pessimist regarding the social future than a contemporary such as Condorcet.[65] On the grain trade his position, both on the theoretical level, and in his reversal of Turgot's policies, was opposite to that of the Physiocrats.[66] Yet he too shared the assumption that maximizing the utilization of natural resources was a prime goal of social policy.

In his work on the grain trade Necker asserted that had all plots of land been equally divided among proprietors, they would all have cultivated them to the best of their abilities, using the surplus for trading for other necessaries. It was, however, the actual unequal division of land which led the proprietors of large estates to neglect cultivating the full extent of their lands if they could not exchange the resultant surplus for other commodities, thus hindering the progress of agriculture.[67] Free exportation of agricultural products was therefore helpful particularly to countries, such as the North American colonies, which were dependent on such exports to provide a market for their agricultural surpluses, and which were still not developed in their manufacturing industries. France, however, was in a different position, being the most favored country in Europe in terms of its natural surroundings and its historical development. Both its small and large-scale proprietors had ample domestic markets for their produce, and for receiving all the commodities they required, which were also enriched by the rare items from the French colonies. The foreign items imported into France catered to false and unnecessary demand. French agriculture thrived and did not require any exports to continue doing so.[68] Domestic trade of agricultural products was also beneficial because it saved transport expenses, and because of the limited life of agricultural products. It was also the best means of encouraging not just agriculture, but also the French arts and manufactures.[69] Internal freedom in commerce in grain was problematic because it enabled the merchants, the agents of this trade, freedom to augment their profits. While at times grain merchants furthered the public interest, their interest in maximizing their profits often led them to act in opposition to the community's best interest.[70] Necker also opposed the Physiocratic viewpoint when he asserted a positive role for manufacturing production. He objected to the claim that manufactures opposed the interests of agriculture. Both types of industry were interdependent. The only way to stimulate landowners to cultivate their lands and produce a surplus without recourse to trading for manufactured commodities, was to ensure the sustained equal distribution of land, yet that was impossible, thus substantiating the need for government regulation of the economy.[71]

Necker's political-economic views were further elaborated in his later work on the financial administration of France.[72] He there claimed that the wealth of a country was the result of its agricultural cultivation and production of surplus, which in its turn stimulated manufactures. Agricultural and technological improvements made agricultural labor more efficient, thus enhancing profits and stimulating division of labor. Yet those who enjoyed these benefits were not the laborers, but rather the landowners and other wealthy inhabitants, who had more to expend on luxuries. Necker therefore objected to the claim that luxuries stimulated the creation of arts and manufactures, whereas the situation was in fact vice versa.[73] On this point, critical of luxuries, he was closer to the Physiocrats and Condorcet. Nevertheless, Necker's realism and moderation prevented him from adopting an all-out critical view of luxuries. Since luxuries could not be eliminated, it was better to foster those which afforded more opportunities for employment rather than more wasteful luxuries, among which Necker, evincing his instrumental view of nature, included "parks, or barren gardens."[74] He was careful, however, not to disclaim against luxury in general, since France benefited from the commerce in luxury items. Moreover, scientific inventions may have created inequalities and negatively influenced the simplicity of manners, but on the other hand they had also led to progress. Political intervention in the form of sumptuary laws was therefore ill-advised. "If political rigour was to be extended too far, we might in vain be continually anxious about a number of results inseparable from the constant agitation of society, and we should perhaps be brought to regret the invention of the plough, which by accelerating rural industry, yields a greater share of the produce of the earth to the land-proprietors."[75] Necker was therefore aware of the principal of unintended consequences underlining the idea of free trade, and noted it specifically in relation to agricultural improvements.

When it came to the cultivation of natural resources, supported by proper government policy, and to ensuing prosperity and population, Necker allowed himself a more optimistic tone. He claimed that the population of France was greater than at any earlier time. This was due in large measure to advances in agriculture, manufactures and commerce. Among other causes which had contributed to the growth of France's population he mentioned that "the former great extent of forests is no longer the same; marshes and fens have been drained; the sea has retired in several places, and immense waste lands have been rendered productive." Furthermore, "we may likewise observe, that the opening of several canals, and of new highways throughout the kingdom," have "given a great facility to the commerce of corn."[76] On this issue of furthering cultivation of natural resources, and specifically the construction of canals, Necker, Turgot and Condorect were likeminded. Necker's support for the cultivation of nature was also evident when he discussed how government should encourage, and when necessary even finance, the clearing of wastelands. "[T]his branch of expence is very rational: the money does not go out of the kingdom; and the earth generates more numerous inhabitants in proportion to its new produce. No kind of wealth can be more assured, nor more precious: the fertile plough-share, and not the sword procures it; and it is watered with the dew of heaven, and not with the blood of men."[77] Throughout, his view of nature remained firmly instrumental and anthropocentric.

The most vociferous anti-Physiocratic voice in the debate on the grain trade was the Italian Ferdinando Galiani. In contrast with Necker, the tone of his famous *Dialogues sur le commerce des blés*, corrected and prepared for the press by Diderot, was immoderate and consistently witty. He criticized the Physiocrats, but was rather skeptical on many political-economic issues, and while brilliant analytically was not always clear on precise policies to be taken. His work was therefore more of an enunciation of Enlightenment principles than a clear economic treatise.[78]

According to Galiani the policy regarding trade in grain depended on the size of a country. In a small country it was both necessary, and possible, to have in place a permanent governmental price policy. This ensured that the inhabitants would always have access to bread at a fixed price even in years of scarcity, when the country was likely to be closed within its own borders. This policy, however, was impractical both in large countries and large cities.[79] The only countries which could rely solely on agriculture for extended periods of time were those which had vast territories, such as the Roman or Turkish empires, or a land such as America.[80] Unfertile countries which nevertheless had access to the sea and to trade, like Holland, acquired their bread through commerce with other countries. They were thus immune to the influence of the climate, yet on the other hand influenced by war when this affected trade. They were also able to keep bread affordable at a fixed price, even if a high one. Bread therefore remained accessible at all times, unless affected by war.[81] Galiani accepted that climate and geographical conditions influenced human development, yet at the same time recognized the ability of human beings to adapt themselves to natural conditions and thus turn disadvantages into ultimate advantages. Mastering nature enabled cultural development. However, he did not support the claim that agriculture was always the basis for prosperity, and that it required the greatest possible freedom in trade. In countries which were not naturally agricultural, he noted, this principle was invalid. Moreover, in years of scarcity in grain it was commercial nations which prospered.[82] Galiani regarded reliance on agriculture as akin to gambling. In the event of a bad season, the unstable life of a nation relying only on agriculture led the inhabitants into debt, servility such as in feudal times, despotism and superstition. On the other hand, a nation which developed manufactures would in the long run also support agriculture by augmenting demand. In his opinion political liberty was impossible without manufactures.[83]

Relying not exclusively on agriculture did not, however, mean any abatement in the need to maximize the utilization of natural resources, particularly the agricultural cultivation of land. If anything quite the contrary. Galiani may have disagreed with the Physiocrats on the sterility of manufactures, or on the proper grain trading policy, but not on the ultimate aim of enhancing prosperity by augmenting production, not least in agriculture. He supported the maximization of the use of land, claiming that "Any uncultivated land was a stain on the administration, and should cause it to blush."[84] Yet this did not mean that surplus on cultivated lands necessarily meant a high yield of grain. Galiani constantly reiterated that the policy of trade in grain needed to be adjusted to the contingencies of place, time, seasonal conditions, the situation of the state and years of plenty and scarcity. A proper grain policy could improve the general condition of France. Yet when one considered each area of France on its own, it was necessary to implement local contingent solutions rather than general edicts. While addressing this point Galiani also alluded to the human ability to ameliorate the natural environment, writing about the treatment of local evils that "It is necessary to pay particular attention to this issue and to search its causes. If it is a question of insufficient population, it is necessary to found a colony there; if the air is unhealthy, one should drain the waters there; if the soil is bad, it is necessary to search which plants or trees one is able to cultivate there and then to plant them."[85]

For Galiani it was not simply a matter of augmenting the cultivation of nature. Even if France might possess enough surplus grain to enable exporting it, this was not a cause for joy. On the contrary, this meant that France did not yet have a large enough population capable of consuming this surplus grain, and ultimately it was population which constituted the only real wealth of a country. Due to the limits to natural resources, there was also a limit to how much the land could be cultivated and food produced. Once this limit was reached it was impossible to have any surplus food left for export. On the other hand, there was no such limit when it came to the cultivation of manufactures, which could therefore enable the growth of population beyond the level of local food production, by using the money resulting from manufactures to purchase food from other countries. This point, realized at approximately the same time by others such as James Steuart, was to become a common argument for the ability of manufactures to enhance available food and promote population and prosperity. Agriculture supplied food, but only manufactures, according to Galiani, supplied riches. "Thus the art of government should create its masterpiece, for the masterpiece of this art is to force nature and oblige it to provide a miracle such as that of having on a limited land more people than its abilities and means should know how to nourish."[86] Internal commerce in grain was nevertheless more important than its export in achieving national prosperity. Since export, however, was more profitable and easier to implement, government needed to encourage internal trade. The latter, claimed Galiani in a somewhat mercantilist tone, also kept profits inside France, away from foreigners.[87] Importation of grain endangered the state and its agriculture, in contrast with the Physiocrats' view, because it was cheaper than the local grain. A proper duties policy could prevent this damage while still maintaining imports.[88] Furthermore, the support and defense of sailors, and sea trade in general, was particularly important. Countries like England, and other trading nations, which followed this policy, enabled both their manufactures and their agriculture to prosper.[89] The transport of grain by sea required large vessels, and therefore, as a consequence, state support. It also provided work for the lower and uneducated social classes, which otherwise might resort to unlawful and violent behavior.[90]

Despite all his misgivings about the need for adjusting the trade in grain to local circumstances, Galiani was nevertheless in favor of freedom in the grain trade, at least in certain circumstances, for several reasons. These included for example the fact that changes in the size of population took a long time, because the storage of grain was fraught with difficulties. Furthermore, legislation still had to be suited to the real situation of a country and its manufactures. No less important was the fact that freedom was a basic human right important in itself. Therefore, legislative measures were meant mainly to regulate the export of grain in efficient a manner as possible.[91] Thus Galiani was not in fact completely against seeing agriculture as the basis for national prosperity. Yet in contrast with the Physiocrats, he recognized both the limits to free grain trade, and the importance of manufactures.

Galiani, like his Physiocratic rivals, viewed nature primarily as a resource meant to further human progress. He claimed that nature kept all things in equilibrium. Yet due to their minuteness and immediate needs, human beings could not rely on nature to take care of them, whether this applied to grain or to other needs. They therefore needed to control nature so they would be able to provide for themselves.

> We are too small; time, space, movement are nothing compared with her [nature]; yet we are unable to wait. We do not therefore make an alliance with nature, which would be too disproportionate. Our task here below is to combat her. Look around you. See the cultivated fields, the foreign plants introduced to our climates, the ships, the carriages, the tame animals, the buildings, the streets, the ports, the dikes, the roads. Here are the battlements in which we fight; all the pleasures of life and almost our very existence are the prize of victory. With our small art and the spirit which God has given us, we battle nature and often achieve victory over her and master her by employing her forces against herself. A singular combat and one which by this renders man the image of his creator.[92]

These words clearly demonstrated the indebtedness of the Enlightenment to the Baconian view of nature. This emphasis on the human utilization of nature was to bridge the Scientific and the Industrial Revolutions. In the interim, burgeoning political economy provided an increasingly sophisticated analytical and ideological underpinning for the growing emphasis on this utilization, in the process internalizing and transforming Enlightenment historiographical observations on the material and cultural progress of humanity. This general philosophical worldview was shared by both the Physiocrats and their critics, and at approximately the same time received even more sophisticated treatment at the hands of a new generation of political economists who took economic debate into new directions.

The eighteenth-century debates on the grain trade, particularly in France, highlighted a point which should be kept in mind throughout our discussion. In our own age, in which, at least in developed countries, subsistence security is taken for granted, what we perceive as economic activity tends to be focused on monetary and fiscal policies, and on financial transactions. Yet in any other social context, where food is scarce, the economy of subsistence tends to supplant any other economic considerations. This was most often the case even in the West up to the nineteenth century if not later (think of the Dust Bowl and of Steinbeck's *caritas romana*). In other words, humanity's relationship with nature, in the form of utilizing natural resources above all to provide for food, is, both from a historical and an economic perspective, the most foundational human activity. Given modern global, demographic and environmental realities, it is not impossible that even developed countries will once again find themselves coping with this fact. Hunger tends to override all other economic considerations. Human beings are still first and foremost animals.

5 From Adam Smith to classical political economy

Adam Smith and the Enlightenment idea of progress

The developments discussed in the previous chapters were to evolve into what came to be known as classical political economy, originating most significantly in the work of Adam Smith, yet owing many of its early insights to other eighteenth-century intellectuals ranging from Hume to Turgot. Two prominent Italian Enlightenment philosophers, not concerned specifically with the grain trade like Galiani, played a role in this process. These were Cesare Beccaria and Pietro Verri. Beccaria justifiably became famous for the influential penal reforms outlined in his renowned *On Crimes and Punishments*, yet he was also interested in political economy. In discussing economic issues he elaborated a version of the four-stages theory, emphasizing the discovery of the use of metals as the development which had enabled the use of money, thus playing a role in the development of commerce.[1]

Much more significant as a figure in the history of economic thought, specifically the emergence of classical political economy, with its unprecedented analytic rigor, was Verri.[2] Building on common Enlightenment notions such as stadial theory, Verri developed a detailed economic outlook which gave new force to the need for making the utilization of natural resources more efficient. He was well aware of the connection between natural circumstances and cultural progress, outlining his version of the common assertion that a difficult climate and natural obstacles provided a spur for industry and cultural progress.[3] He also noted that as a society advanced, its needs increased. To satisfy new wants it produced more, including agricultural produce, so that the ensuing surplus could be used to trade with other countries and thus satisfy these new needs. Savage nations required less than civilized ones, and therefore did not produce surplus and did not engage in commerce. In Europe the price of progress had been paid by earlier generations, and now this served as the basis for European advancement. Wretchedness preceded civilization, a process which had already been undergone by the European nations.[4]

Verri regarded the size of population as a measure of production and prosperity. A small population accompanied diminishing production and consumption, and was thus an indication of cultural decline. It was therefore advisable to aim at augmenting the size of population. The smaller a state's population, the easier and quicker it became to influence it either positively or negatively. It was also preferable for population not to be spread out over a large territory. On the other hand, there was a risk that population concentrated in one place would not be able to raise enough food for its own maintenance. A middle situation between these two extremes was therefore preferable. Nevertheless, he clearly favored the concentration of population in large cities. This resulted in social fermentation, which in its turn encouraged innovation and creativity.[5] Conquests and colonies might harm a state which had not yet sufficiently established itself in its own territory. In such new territories population would only become scattered over large areas, and even in the mother country land would not always be cultivated. Furthermore, over time colonies tended to lose their affection for the mother country. On the other hand, for countries whose main strength was maritime, colonies might prove a spur for industry and trade, and the immediate depopulation they would create would be short-term, and would eventually be compensated by the economic activity which they encouraged.[6]

The connection between population and a proper cultivation of the land was clearly articulated by Verri. To animate large and sparsely populated countries it was necessary to concentrate the inhabitants in regions with sufficient land for providing them with nourishment. It was, however, also advisable that they would be insulated from other countries by deserts, with which only maritime connections would be kept. Such a situation would stimulate economic growth, as well as increased production enabling exportation, all this leading eventually to prosperity and the growth of population. Subsequently the initially deserted regions would gradually be populated, till they would come in contact with the neighboring nations, only now from a position of strength, industry and cultivation. The more people were distanced from each other the closer they were to the state of savagery, and the closer they were, the more civilized they became. Therefore governments should encourage transportation, canals and the construction of roads, as well as reduce taxation on transport. Even while constructing roads, however, it was important not to waste excessive tracts of land which might be used for agricultural production, and use them instead for gardens, game forests and other luxury uses which did not encourage consumption and growth.[7]

Despite his significance in advancing a new type of political-economic discourse, with clear classical recognition of the significance of maintaining material growth, Verri lacked the comprehensive approach which made Adam Smith the pivotal figure not only in the emergence of classical political economy, but in the formation of modern economics (Marshall's later term) as a new scientific discipline. Joseph Schumpeter's ambivalent but basically critical view of Smith is unacceptable. Schumpeter regarded Smith as an essentially unoriginal thinker, whose main strength was in coordinating earlier ideas into a coherent whole which catered to the common notions of his time, and which, despite its merits, unjustifiably served as the subsequent foundation for nineteenth-century economic discourse.[8] Yet even if one accepts the unmerited assertion that Smith was unoriginal and only coordinated earlier ideas of more original thinkers, this act of coordination lifted all earlier economic notions to a new plain of systematic methodology, which in and of itself gave political economy a systematic rigor without which it might not have become an independent discipline, or would have become so much more slowly. In doing so Smith not only integrated earlier ideas regarding such things as the labor theory of value or the division of labor, but also more general Enlightenment notions of historical progress, as well as ethical issues related to social and economic development. The latter were, for many years, disregarded by generations of liberal economists who preferred to regard Smith as simply the progenitor of the view of *homo economicus*, motivated primarily by rational maximization of self-interest. Today, of course, this view has been completely discarded after several decades of new scholarship which has established beyond doubt the wide compass of ideas, economic, social, political, ethical and historiographical, which combined in Smith's intellectual project.[9] Of these, a consistent attention to the significance of utilizing natural resources, unprecedented in political-economic debates, was far from the least conspicuous. We will begin with his concepts of progress, and how they related to topics such as population and cultivation of nature. We have already noted the significance of his four-stages theory, which should be kept in mind as an underlying theoretical basis for these observations.

Smith began the *Wealth of Nations* with the observation that the state of a nation was determined by the proportion between the quantity of its produce, specifically the necessaries of life, and the number of inhabitants who consumed it. The abundance or scantiness of produce was determined by two things – the proportion between those employed in useful labor and those not so, but more significantly, the manner and judgment which determined how labor was applied. According to Smith this was more important than the geographical and climatic qualities of a country. The total efficiency of a society's labor was what mattered, not the effort of individuals in themselves. At this point Smith alluded to the stadial perceptions developed later in the book, claiming that it was the efficient use of labor which differentiated the existence of savage nations of hunters and fishermen, from the much better condition of civilized and thriving nations.[10]

The four-stages theory underlined many observations in Smith's works. One particularly detailed example was the depiction of the development of military defense. Pastoral nations, claimed Smith like many of his contemporaries, excelled particularly in martial capabilities. On the one hand, they were able to easily move from place to place, loot large quantities of food, and thus maintain large armies, and on the other, while agricultural nations also spent considerable time in outdoor physical activities, shepherds had less need to spend time working, and more time for military pursuits. In more advanced societies, artificers and manufacturers had almost no leisure for martial exercises. At the same time, the military art was developed in advanced cultures to the point of becoming a profession of the few supported by the many, while wars became more long-term affairs. Therefore rich nations, precisely due to their prosperity, invited attacks, while less among their population were capable of fighting. They consequently required defense provided by government-supported professional standing armies superior to ordinary militias. This was the only way advanced nations could combat less advanced but more martially-spirited nations.[11] The interaction with nature had a specific role in this historical development. A husbandman could on occasion afford to go to war, since "Without the intervention of his labour, nature does herself the greater part of the work which remains to be done." A laborer in other types of manufacture could not, however, afford to go to war since "Nature does nothing for him, he does all for himself." Therefore in advanced manufacturing nations the public needed to maintain those who left their work to go and fight.[12]

The cultural development of jurisprudence was also depicted within a stadial framework by Smith. At the hunting stage private property hardly existed and therefore regular administration of justice was less important. As society progressed, the accumulation of private property made administrative justice more necessary. Those with little property supported the lawful defense of those with more property, since in this way their own property was also defended. Those with any property were protected from those with no property at all. The inequality of possessions in which a small minority held large amounts of property required the support of civil government, which in its turn facilitated the accumulation of wealth. These developments were interdependent in Smith's outlook, which implied that with greater material wealth, accompanied by greater utilization of resources and unequally shared property, also came greater progress in government and jurisprudence. The greatest inequality in possession of property occurred in the pastoral stage, which therefore exhibited the most numerous cases of authority of those with material fortune. This social prominence was further enforced by prerogatives of birth. When however a society was sufficiently advanced, jurisprudence was best separated from other governmental powers, both due to a need for greater professionalism and division of labor, and to ensure justice.[13]

The stadial outlook thus provided Smith with a framework for understanding the development of military capabilities, jurisprudence and other aspects of civilization.[14] One point which comes up, and on which too Smith was a representative of other intellectuals of his time, was the realization that progress came at a price. In the historical transition to greater affluence and progress, advanced societies lost something of the independent spirit and military valor of their predecessors. Smith's contemporary Adam Ferguson, in his *An Essay on the History of Civil Society*, famously emphasized this loss in an early romantic vein, which also animated the vogue for the Ossianic poems. Smith, however, belonged to the mainstream who accepted this loss as a necessary but worthwhile price to pay for enabling Scotland, following the union with England in 1707, to attain the final commercial stage of progress. Nevertheless, despite Smith's traditional advocacy for such things as a large population, there is a sense at times of a more modern and cautionary tone regarding the limits to progress, which could not go on indefinitely, particularly when one also took into consideration the need for maintaining not just the size of population, but its quality of life as well.[15] Social and economic progress in Europe in the seventeenth and eighteenth centuries confronted intellectuals with this problem. Some scholars, most notably J. G. A. Pocock, have perceived an interaction in this period between the more commonly recognized

Lockean liberalism, and a classical republican tradition of political thought which emphasized the virtues of the individual acting within the social environment. Smith, according to Pocock, was one of those who evinced recognition of this problem, and worried over the price at which commercial progress came.[16] A detailed consideration of this topic is beyond the scope of the present discussion. Yet, given particularly Smith's stoic proclivities, it seems reasonable that some combination of liberal and republican leanings was at play in his unresolved attempt to arrive at a coherent social, economic and political philosophy.

One topic in which Smith's preference for earlier stages of progress was apparent, was his praise of the agricultural mode of life. This, of course, was in line with the traditional classical praise of agriculture which had been so apparent among the Physiocrats. While Smith did not agree with the Physiocrats regarding the singular producing qualities of agriculture, he still maintained a general preference for the mode of existence based on cultivating the land. Agricultural capital was more dependable than commercial capital and therefore more compatible with long-term growth and progress. Agriculture and manufactures were interdependent according to Smith. Therefore he advocated a golden mean between the virtues of urban and rural life.[17] A claim which he consistently repeated, and which emphasized the superiority of agricultural life to hunting or shepherding, was that in rude ages butcher's meat had been more available than bread and consequently also cheaper. In more advanced and agricultural ages, however, the situation was reversed, and meat became more expensive than bread. Agricultural improvements which made the use of land for feeding cattle more efficient would, in Smith's opinion, lower the price of meat relative to bread, a situation which in London had perhaps already occurred.[18] This observation would later reappear in the work of Smith's disciple John Millar.[19] Smith considered vegetable foodstuffs more essential than meat to feeding the population, and consequently as more pertinent for assessing progress.[20] Significantly, however, the reason for this had nothing to do with ethical vegetarianism or with ecological arguments such as those made in our own time for preferring vegetable food to meat as a source for feeding the masses. For Smith this was an issue of changing prices of different foodstuffs at different stages of historical progress. In rude ages land provided less food and relatively more materials for clothing and lodging, while in advanced ages this situation was reversed. In rude ages there was also an abundance of forests and cheap timber, but with progress these became scarce and expensive.[21] The relative cultural progress of a society determined the price of various cultivated natural resources.

More significant than the wealth of a nation at any given moment, however, was whether it was in a state of growth, in a stationary state, or in a state of decay. The various states were measured by the situation of the wage of labor, whether it was rising, constant or diminishing. Even a stationary condition, such as that of China, might lead many to misery. The situation in some of the English settlements such as Bengal evinced decay and demonstrated, according to Smith, how improper was the suppressive policy of the mercantile companies there, compared with the much better policy implemented in North America, where the protection of the British constitution was in force.[22] Growth meant a dynamic state of progression, not a state of maximum wealth. "The progressive state is in reality the chearful [*sic*] and the hearty state to all the different orders of the society. The stationary is dull; the declining, melancholy."[23] A country which cultivated its natural resources to the maximum, and which was also fully populated, reached the stationary state, and consequently both its wages and profits of stock would be low. Yet, according to Smith, no country had yet attained such a level of opulence. Furthermore, in a country which had acquired its full complement of riches, the level of interest would be so low as to enable only very few people to live on the interest of their money, and consequently almost everyone would need to be employed in some kind of trade. Static wealth, in other words, was detrimental to a nation's well-being.[24]

Smith connected these observations to the level of utilization of natural resources, specifically in the colonial setting, which afforded a suitable context for discussing early levels of progress. In non-European settings one could better assess the problems of pre-commercial societies, and the connection between progress and cultivation of nature in general. "In a fertile country [Bengal] which had before been much depopulated, where subsistence, consequently, should not be very difficult, and where, notwithstanding, three or four hundred thousand people die of hunger in one year, we may be assured that the funds destined for the maintenance of the labouring poor are fast decaying."[25] In new colonies stock produced higher interest and more profit, since it was invested in the most fertile and still uncultivated lands, often well-situated near beaches or navigable rivers. As a colony and its population grew, the profits of stock diminished and interest was lowered. While discussing the state of the British colonies in America and the West Indies, Smith noted how "When the most fertile and best situated lands have been all occupied, less profit can be made by the cultivation of what is inferior both in soil and situation, and less interest can be afforded for the stock which is so employed... As riches, improvement, and population have increased, interest has declined."[26] To a certain extent Smith's observations on interest here preceded Ricardo's subsequent theory of rent. According to Smith, as less fertile land was gradually and necessarily cultivated, interest was determined at a lower rate.

In antiquity colonies were established due to over-population or a lack of land. The situation with modern European colonies was different. Columbus had attempted to emphasize the importance of the lands he had discovered, yet, according to Smith, "in what constitutes the real riches of every country, the animal and vegetable production of the soil," there was nothing there to exhibit. Therefore, Columbus emphasized the New World's deposits of gold, and it was this which became the main stimulus for possessing the newly-discovered continent.[27] For Smith real natural wealth was first and foremost agricultural in nature, particularly in newly-established colonies. Progress was rapid particularly in new colonies with ample uncultivated land, and in which there were agricultural and industrial knowledge, and a regular government among the European settlers not evident among the savage indigenous population. The large regions of uncultivated land encouraged the growth of the population and the accumulation of wealth based on its cultivation. A similar situation had occurred in ancient Greece, though not in ancient Rome, which established new colonies mainly in conquered regions which were already fully populated. The New World colonies thus followed the Greek pattern.[28]

The Europeans had failed to establish thriving colonies in Africa or the East Indies as they had succeeded in America, because in the latter the local inhabitants were still in the hunting stage of historical development, and were therefore more easily subdued compared with the inhabitants of Africa and India, who had already attained the pastoral stage. Shepherding societies were more populous and advanced in cultivating land, and thus more powerful than the American savages, though not including the Mexicans and Peruvians.[29] Smith claimed that the stories on the wealth and progress of pre-colonial Mexico and Peru were exaggerated. In fact the old kingdoms there had attained only limited progress, a small population, and only a limited level of achievement in the arts and the cultivation of resources. The state of the Spanish colonies, due to their government, was less improved than the British ones in terms of agriculture, improvement and population, yet their rate of progress was still faster than all the European states. "In a fertile soil and happy climate, the great abundance and cheapness of land, a circumstance common to all new colonies, is, it seems, so great an advantage as to compensate many defects in civil government."[30] While the Spanish colonies in America were less developed than the British ones, they too encouraged progress and population, and the Spanish Creoles proved superior to the ancient Indian civilizations. The Spanish brought domesticated animals, agricultural arts and implements such as ploughs, the use of iron, as well as trade beyond the local traditional mere barter. "But the populousness of every country must be in proportion to the degree of its improvement and cultivation." Therefore, despite the cruel devastation of the natives they initially induced, the Spanish ultimately enhanced population and prosperity in their colonies.[31] Again, it was the rate of progress more than absolute wealth which was significant. A country with more uncultivated land was better-off than one better governed but lacking such land, but only, of course, up to a point. Ill government could still offset this advantage.

Of all the colonies in America, those which progressed to the greatest extent were the English ones in North America, thanks both to the extent of good local land, and to the freedom the local settlers had to run their affairs. These were the two crucial things necessary for the progress of new colonies. The land in North America was in fact less fertile than in the south, yet the English government was more supportive of land cultivation. An example was the law which imposed on every landowner to cultivate and improve his land, or otherwise to lose his title to it. Primogeniture too was less in force in America compared to England, thus facilitating a more proper distribution of lands.[32] English law also encouraged progress in the colonies by enabling, at times inadvertently, relatively free trade in grain, fish and other commodities. Free trade in timber in particular made clearing grounds profitable, a fact which Smith regarded as a crucial condition for cultivating and improving lands.[33] Nevertheless, the English allowed free colonial trade mainly in rude produce. The more high-level manufacturing procedures were required for working rude products, the more they reserved these for themselves, a mercantilist policy which was essentially unjust in its treatment of the colonies in Smith's estimation. The damage to the North American colonies from this policy would become evident particularly as they advanced culturally, and was therefore still not as serious as it would become when they attained a higher level of progress.[34]

An important sign of progress was population. Among the many ills of the mercantile system which Smith enumerated in detail, was the discouragement it caused to the improvement of land and the growth of population, which were the direct result if its narrow conception of profit.[35] "The most decisive mark of the prosperity of any country is the increase of the number of its inhabitants."[36] The growth of population was always commensurate with the means of subsistence. The poor tended to multiply much more than the rich, yet child mortality among them was higher, and poverty was unfavorable to raising children, mainly due to difficulty providing sufficient food. The more demand for labor, and wages with it, grew or lessened, the more, or less, were poor laborers able to multiply. "It is in this manner that the demand for men, like that for any other commodity, necessarily regulates the production of men."[37] Smith was therefore already thinking in the direction which would subsequently be developed in more detail and somber tone by Ricardo, and particularly by Malthus.

Smith's outlook was still more optimistic in the Enlightenment mold. In most cases, he claimed, a ban on exporting foreign corn and cattle meant limiting the population and industry of a nation to the level that the rude produce of its soil could maintain.[38] Smith regarded free trade as enabling overcoming local natural limitations to population, or in other words, as a way to enhance the efficiency of the utilization of natural resources. The ancient Chinese or Egyptians were examples of great nations surrounded by barbarians, and which therefore acquired riches by cultivating their own lands and by relying on internal, not external, trade. This, however, was ill-advised for modern European nations.[39] Smith, perhaps influenced on this point by Galiani, was sensitive to the fact that local circumstances, both natural and cultural, were relevant to the proper social and economic policy best suited to enhance progress. Staple foods such as potatoes and rice, which had enriched the European diet, were a case in point, since their cultivation was not identical to that of traditional grains. Potatoes, like rice, were able to feed more people per yield for land, than wheat and other sorts of grain. The only difficulty with potatoes concerned their storage and the danger of rotting. Smith, however, claimed that if ever they would become a common food, they would produce more surplus, rent would rise, and population would increase.[40]

With Smith earlier notions of progress, population and cultivation of natural resources attained an unprecedented level of detail and sophistication. As in other fields of economic analysis, he not only gathered together previous ideas, but gave them added weight and systematic rigor which was to seriously influence subsequent political-economic discourse.

Ricardo and Malthus on progress and population

In the early nineteenth century practically any educated European interested in political economy became thoroughly familiar with and influenced by Smith's ideas. These became the fountainhead of the great vogue for the "dismal science," to quote Carlyle's pejorative phrase. Particularly in Britain, where its progress was intertwined with the most emphatic novelties of industrialization, the science of political economy often relied on Smith, elaborating his ideas and at times criticizing them. Even innovations were often recognized as such because Smith had not addressed them. The two most famous early figures of what came to be known as classical political economy, relying on Smith and going beyond him, were David Ricardo and Thomas Robert Malthus, two political economists who greatly influenced the rise of modern economics, yet despite their close friendship held very different opinions on key methodological and economic issues.

It has become customary to differentiate between Ricardo's more deductive approach to political economy, and Malthus's more inductive and empirical approach. This, however, was a matter of relative emphasis, and Ricardo was not impervious to the contingencies of time and place.[41] While historical and geographical circumstances were more significant for Malthus, as they had been for Smith, they were not totally ignored by Ricardo, specifically as they related to cultivating natural resources. In the Preface to his famous *On the Principles of Political Economy and Taxation*, at the very beginning of the work, Ricardo wrote:

> The produce of the earth – all that is derived from its surface by the united application of labour, machines, and capital, is divided among three classes of the community; namely, the proprietor of the land, the owner of the stock or capital necessary for its cultivation, and the labourers by whose industry it is cultivated.
>
> But in different stages of society, the proportions of the whole produce of the earth which will be allotted to each of these classes, under the names of rent, profit, and wages, will be essentially different; depending mainly on the actual fertility of the soil, on the accumulation of capital and population, and on the skill, ingenuity, and instruments employed in agriculture.
>
> To determine the laws which regulate this distribution, is the principle problem in Political Economy.[42]

Ricardo, who famously made criticism of the rent paid to proprietors of land one of the key elements of his economic analysis, here began his discussion of political economy with the division of the population into three social-economic groups – the proprietors of land, the capitalist merchants and manufacturers and the laborers. Two further points are important from our perspective. First, the whole organization of the social-economic structure was based on the natural fertility of land, on the cultivation of the "produce of the earth," and the division of the ensuing profits. In other words, the cultivation of nature was the basis for all economic development. Second, in the "different stages of society," the social relations which determined the distribution of these profits changed. The legacy of the Enlightenment was evident in both respects – regarding the emphasis on the cultivation of nature, and the stadial analysis of historical development – and both points were consistently evident in Ricardo's discussions.

Ricardo claimed that the exchangeable value of commodities produced was proportional to the labor invested in their production, not only the immediate production, but also the effort put into the tools, the implements or the machines required for their production. Ricardo here relied on the four stages theory (and in so doing unsurprisingly mentioned Adam Smith), and claimed that this observation was valid throughout all the historical stages of economic development. In the final stage, when commerce and the arts flourished, the exchangeable value included all the labor which had been invested in producing commodities, taking into consideration the requisite division of labor. This was evident already in the first stage, that of hunters, and in the difference between, for example, the hunters of deer and beaver. The value of their respective commodities was a compound not only of the time and labor invested in their attainment, but also of the time and labor invested in acquiring the hunters' necessary capital, their weapons. The difference in value between these two hunted animals resulted from differences in this context, and in the time and difficulty involved in hunting them, the varying work necessary for producing the various required weapons, and their durability. Even at such an early stage of social development, Ricardo implied, there was already the possibility of division of labor, for example, between the manufacturers of the weapons and the actual hunters. The value of the animals, as products, could vary in accordance with the changing needs of society, conditions of plenty or scarcity.[43]

Like his eighteenth-century predecessors, Ricardo's perception of stages of historical development was intertwined with a value-laden judgment of the worth of various cultures and societies, implying an essential Eurocentrism. The natural price of labor, according to Ricardo, was culturally dependent, and varied in different countries with different accepted needs. What sufficed for the inhabitants of one country, for example wages which only enabled the purchase of potatoes, would be considered as insufficient wages for an English laborer. This also pertained to the comparison between what, in the past, sufficed in England itself, but became in time insufficient. What was common among early nineteenth-century English country inhabitants would have been considered luxuries in the past. This perception was combined with Ricardo's consideration of cultural progress, ultimately based on a firm agricultural utilization of land. In the various stages of the progress of society, the use of capital, and the means of employment of labor, depended on the productive powers of labor, and the latter were greatest when there was an abundance of fertile land. In new settlements (here Ricardo evidently meant mainly European colonies), when the knowledge and arts of more advanced countries were introduced, capital tended to rise more than population. Therefore, without the arrival of external labor, the price of labor would rise. Yet the more population increased, and less fertile land was cultivated, the more the increase of capital tended to diminish.[44]

In barbaric countries where there was an abundance of fertile land accompanied by general scarcity, ameliorating the social situation required a better government. This led to an increase of capital and the cultivation of the abundant fertile land, combined with a growing population and general social-economic improvement. In more advanced countries, however, no improvement or industrial effort would be beneficial without a diminished population.[45] Ricardo's position on population was therefore more sophisticated than that of the eighteenth century, but also less grim than Malthus's. Population might ebb and flow in tandem with economic prosperity, both constantly interacting, as rising and diminishing wages determined the inclination of the laboring class to grow. Ricardo recommended that the laboring class develop a taste for comforts and enjoyments, since this was the best security against a superabundant population. Clearly influenced by Malthus, he opposed the Poor Laws, and advocated letting wages be determined by the fair contest of the market.[46] It should however be remembered that while both Ricardo and Malthus aimed at ameliorating the lot of the poor, Ricardo was much more of a democrat, some would say even with socialist leanings evident in his criticism of landowners. He considered the laboring classes capable of understanding their own interests. If allowed to participate in elections, their decisions, in terms of economics, would benefit the nation as a whole. Democracy in his view was what would enable political economy to operate unfettered, and lead to social amelioration for the laboring class and all society.[47]

Ricardo's attention to the unstable mechanism determining the size of population was connected with the overall relationship between human beings and their natural environment, principally the use of land. His famous theory of rent viewed the rise of rent as related to the different levels of fertility of land, the least fertile always determining the rent for more fertile lands. This, for Ricardo, was also the reason that rent was an unjustified payment to the landlords, who contributed nothing which justified it. Rent was an unjust payment for something which nature offered of itself. A rising rent meant that human beings received less of nature's gifts.[48] In all times and places, claimed Ricardo, profits depended on the amount of labor requisite to supply the laborers' necessaries, but this varied from country to country according to the fertility of the land. Therefore, in a large country with unfertile land, even a small accumulation of capital could lead to diminished profits and a rise in rent, while in a small but fertile country the opposite would happen, particularly when the free importation of food was allowed, and when it was possible to accumulate a large stock of capital without a significant loss of profits or a large rise in rent. In this context Ricardo referred to "the laws of nature, which have limited the productive powers of the land."[49] In this way he described how nature was the basis of human economic activity, but also at the same time set clear limits to this activity and to human progress in general. Since nature was not uniform, particularly regarding the varying fertility of land, the human social and economic mechanisms based on agriculturally producing subsistence were likewise varied, and wages, prosperity and population, constantly rose and fell. In contrast with his Enlightenment predecessors, Ricardo's optimism was more guarded, and he depicted progress as something attainable yet unstable, precisely because nature did not afford unlimited accumulation of necessary produce. In a quite tangible sense, one could say of nature, from this perspective, that "you can't do with it and you can't do without it," or, more precisely, "you can only do with it (as much as it permits), but you can never do without it." Ultimately, however, and notwithstanding its instability, progress was still possible and desirable. "It must be remembered too that the retrograde condition is always an unnatural state of society. Man from youth grows to manhood, then decays, and dies; but this is not the progress of nations. When arrived to a state of the greatest vigour, their further advance may indeed be arrested, but their natural tendency is to continue for ages, to sustain undiminished their wealth, and their population."[50]

This implied a somewhat different, guardedly more optimistic, conception of the stationary state, and its connection with the cultivation of natural resources, than Smith's or Malthus's. According to Ricardo the stationary state was not determined biologically according to the minimum requirements of life. Rather, it was a product of culture and society, reflecting what the poor aspired to. Its meaning was an end to accumulation and economic growth, and it was possible to postpone it by improvements in trade and production. As a result of scarcity of natural resources, economic growth would eventually come to a halt. Like Malthus, Ricardo perceived a connection between population growth and a limit to economic growth. Ricardo however disagreed with Malthus regarding the claim that in countries with abundant fertile land economic growth would not be ensured. For Ricardo this was true only if people were indolent, and if there was insufficient accumulation of capital. For Malthus, as we will see, this was connected to a more pessimistic outlook on the ability to sustain growth and progress.[51] Ricardo, together with Say, famously disagreed with Malthus's view that a general glut was possible. This meant that according to Ricardo and Say the natural limits to production and economic growth were so far-off as to be practically inconsequential, specifically in a well-governed and advanced society. Ricardo therefore claimed that his explanations were about England and advanced countries, where glut could not occur.

Occasionally, improvements in agriculture and manufactures (such as technological improvements in machinery), might cause a temporary diminution in the value of the existing fixed capital belonging to the farmers and manufacturers (such as old machines). Nevertheless, according to Ricardo, one should not attempt to prevent this from happening, or to prevent the importation of corn based on the claim that it would lower the value of the farmers' capital invested in land. Any such preventive measures were opposed to the natural development of economic progress, which contributed to general abundance, and consequently to general happiness. Any deterioration of improvement or progress in such cases was only temporary, and the general direction of change remained positive. In that sense it was clear "that the end of all commerce is to increase production, and that by increasing production, though you may occasion partial loss, you increase the general happiness."[52]

Despite their overall agreement on various issues such as the mechanisms of changing rents or wages, the positions of Ricardo and his friend Malthus differed on major issues. They might agree on the way economic processes occurred, but not on the interpretation of these processes. For example, Malthus agreed with Ricardo that rent depended on varying levels of land fertility. Yet in contrast with Ricardo he regarded rent as contributing to economic development. He was therefore much more supportive of landowners.[53] It was this general difference in worldview which became apparent even to contemporaries. In our own time, Malthus's pessimism regarding the limits to population in particular, and progress based on cultivating natural resources in general, has come to seem particularly prescient and has drawn increasing attention to his doctrines. In the process, the old one-dimensional view of Malthus as an insensitive snob oblivious to the plight of the lower classes has justifiably received less attention. The opposite tendency, however, is also unsubstantiated. Malthus has come to be considered, justifiably, as relevant to the notion of limited natural resources. Yet some have gone a bit too far in viewing him through the lens of modern environmentalism.[54] Malthusian doctrines have proliferated in recent times.[55] Malthus, as we will see, was in fact quite in favor of maximizing the utilization of natural resources. It has even been claimed that Malthus was more optimistic than Smith and Ricardo in allowing that prudent social behavior might enable rising wages and quality of life.[56] For contemporaries, and most subsequent commentators, it was however his pessimism, in stark contrast with Smith and the Enlightenment vision of unfettered human progress, specifically in relation to the limits of natural resources, which was most striking and influential.[57] It is true that the young Malthus was writing at a time, around the turn of the nineteenth century, when notions of over-population and extinction among animals and humans, as well as of the finiteness of natural resources, were beginning to become evident.[58] Yet he gave his own distinct integrating approach, and in this manner was as original and influential as Smith, and like the latter did not deserve the depreciating remarks of Schumpeter.[59] However one interprets his views, it is difficult to deny both his contemporaneous originality and influence, and the modern relevance of his views regarding the limits of natural resources, although our own perspective on these limits is radically different from his.[60] Even if one does not accept his theory of population, it seems difficult, in the early twenty-first century, to deny that growing global population is putting increasing pressure on the planet's natural resources. We are to a considerable extent living in a Malthusian reality, if not exactly as Malthus defined it.

It should be noted that Malthus's famous argument regarding the geometrical ratio growth of population compared with the arithmetical ratio growth of the means of subsistence, a priori assumed that the means of subsistence were raised at optimal efficiency. In other words, in the very best of conditions, with a maximal utilization of natural resources, the gap between a growing population and the sources of food was inevitably widening in an exponential ratio. Anything less than a full cultivation of nature was not even considered.[61] All checks to population, claimed Malthus in another well-known part of his thesis, were either preventive or positive, and were resolved into three types – moral restraint, vice and misery. The preventive check, mainly moral restraint, was less influential than the positive ones. From our perspective, it is the latter, the positive check of misery, which is pertinent. This included all those uncontrollable disasters which occurred when the growth of population and lack of preventive social measures, combined to create a growing gap between population and its means of subsistence. These ranged from war, to diseases, and most disastrously, to famine.[62] But in any event, the law of nature, following an inexorable mathematical logic, meant that the cultivation of nature could never keep up with a growing population. Even under the best conditions, there was not enough food for everyone.[63] Malthus's vision was much less optimistic than the Enlightenment's, and even Ricardo's. It was nature itself which set a limit to human progress. The human cultivation of nature remained a *sine qua non*, but in contrast with his eighteenth-century predecessors, Malthus claimed that it would never suffice for unlimited progress. Nature had to be utilized as efficiently as possible, but would forever remain to a large extent resistant to human mastery.

One significant caveat should, however, be remembered in assessing his seeming pessimism. This is the religious component in his thought, which was much more pronounced than in the more secular outlook of Smith or Ricardo. Malthus's views on population were influenced by his rather heterodox theological outlook, which was part of a current of Christian political economy which was more significant in the early nineteenth century than is at times remembered. Malthus regarded the full cultivation and peopling of the earth as divinely ordained and therefore as a viable goal, and the pressure of population as a stimulus to the development of the human mind. Furthermore, he considered the existence of evil as a divinely ordained spur to exertion and betterment.[64] This type of dialectical logic was not dissimilar to Smith's reliance on the law of unintended consequences, in itself of course famously influenced by Bernard de Mandeville's idea of "private vices, public benefits." From a different perspective, the idea of a severe climate as a spur to progress also shared this dialectical approach, and not surprisingly, as we will see, was shared by Malthus. It is therefore clear that he shared the Enlightenment penchant for dialectical reasoning. This should be kept in mind in assessing his seeming pessimism regarding the limits to progress. He regarded these limits as less imminent than they seem in our own time.

Malthus did not oppose the idea of a large population as a measure of the strength of a country, so long as the size of the population accorded with its means of subsistence. Population in itself was not the problem. The problem was the vice and misery which over-population caused.[65] In itself, a growing population, if it imposed on the means of subsistence, did not increase a country's wealth.[66] In other words, this alluded to Malthus's well-known opposition to Say and Ricardo regarding the impossibility of glut. Say's famous law claimed, as it is often summarized, that "production creates its own demand." In other words, barring outstanding circumstances, increased production could almost indefinitely stimulate economic growth, and the possibility of glut was remote. In contrast with Say, however, Malthus thought that it was demand which preceded production.[67] This was a much more cautious approach to growth. This was a major point of contention in early nineteenth-century political-economic debate, with Say and Ricardo on one side, and Malthus on the other.[68] In his *Letters to Mr. Malthus*

Say reiterated in detail his views on the impossibility of gluts, specifically in an advanced commercial civilization, noting that "It is the power of producing which makes the difference between a country and a desert; and a country is so much the more advanced, so much the more populous, and so much the better provisioned, as it increases in productions."[69] We will come to Say's position shortly, but it is clear that Malthus did not share this optimism, neither regarding the impossibility of gluts and the stimulating influence of production, nor regarding the consequent prosperity and populousness which ensued. Malthus therefore regarded carful policies to mitigate the influence of overproduction, and specifically those related to preventive checks to population, as a necessity.

Much more than for Ricardo, geographical, ethnic, and historical evidence provided, according to Malthus, key insights into the issue of population, and political economy in general. In modern Europe, he claimed, compared to earlier eras or to uncivilized nations, the preventive check to population, particularly moral restraint, was more in force than the positive check.[70] Among barbaric nations population exceeded the limit which could survive in periods of scarcity. Barbarians lacked reason and foresight, which were destroyed by despotism and ignorance. Foresight and security were necessary for industry, and without them barbarians strove to produce only what was necessary for bare existence. Only among those who were not wretchedly poor could one find the hope of bettering their condition, and the fear of want rather than want itself, which was the best stimulus to industry.[71] Malthus did not, however, deny the possibility that less advanced societies could progress. He retained, despite his seeming pessimism, the basic Enlightenment assumption regarding the possibility of historical progress, claiming that societies became more active the more they attained progress. A transition occurred "as the society proceeds from the indolence of the savage to the activity of the civilized state." With more progress came more labor, and consequently more activity, as well as more personal exertion among the laboring classes. "The personal exertions of the South American Indian, the Hindoo, the Polish boor, and the Irish agricultural labourer, may be very different indeed 500 years hence."[72] This also implied that like many of his Enlightenment predecessors, Malthus evinced a Eurocentric cultural chauvinism, yet not a racial outlook.[73] He was amply aware that human nature prevented people from always producing and consuming to the greatest extent they were capable of. This happened due both to their natural indolence, and to the common desire for saving and improving their long-term condition.[74] His assessment of human motivations was therefore sensitive to the varied circumstances of both private and collective behavior, and this left room for affecting positive changes in the social condition. To read Malthus simply as a prophet of doom would be missing the conception he seems to have had that positive changes, given the right social policy, were possible, even if difficult, and could delay the dire consequences of positive checks very far into the future. In this light the limits to natural resources were more a theoretical than an imminent danger.

Malthus's lengthy discussions of various cultures were in large part meant to illustrate the various possibilities that differing geographical and historical circumstances enabled for progress, or the lack thereof. One of the main differences between rude and civilized ages, he claimed, was that in the latter there was greater incentive to attain luxuries beyond bare necessities. Due to the human propensity for indolence, it was the need for necessaries which ultimately stimulated the production of luxuries. One might have expected that precisely in early stages of progress only the few would be occupied in producing food, which would be supplied easily by fertile land, while most would be occupied in producing luxuries. In reality, however, the opposite happened, and in rude societies most people were occupied in agricultural labor. It was in England, despite its lacking particularly fertile land, that the labor of the few was enough to produce sufficient food, while many were occupied in the production of luxuries. This was a measure of English society's progress. What was important, in Malthus's view, was not a country's natural qualities, but rather the nation's physical and moral characteristics, which determined to what extent its natural resources would be cultivated and utilized.[75] This was evident, for example, in the Spanish American colonies, where the dismal political situation usually did not provide sufficient stimulus for labor, which would shake the local population out of their natural indolence. The situation in these colonies included an unequal feudal distribution of lands, as well as lack of international markets for their produce, not to mention insufficient manufacturing production. In this situation there was no stimulus for either enhancing production or enlarging population. Malthus at this point gave his version of the famous assertion that precisely in countries with the best climate and natural surroundings there was a lack of stimulus for cultural ingenuity and progress, whereas this incentive occurred precisely in seemingly less climatically advantageous countries. This was the reason that famines often occurred precisely in fertile countries.[76] Ireland was an example of this. Its fertile soil, lacking proper political and cultural conditions, did not lead to the increase of wealth. Attaining these necessary cultural habits was, in any event, a gradual process in Malthus's opinion.[77]

Malthus was heavily influenced by stadial theory, and this was evident mainly in his discussion of uncivilized peoples. When he described the harsh life of the savage American Indians, and their difficulties in obtaining food, he claimed that the Mexican and Peruvian empires had begun thriving, and their populations expanded, the moment they forsook a nomadic for a sedentary and agricultural mode of life. This was reminiscent of the eighteenth-century stadial emphasis on the crucial transition between a nomadic and sedentary life. There was no clear explanation why most American Indians had not taken this crucial step, and failed to adopt an agricultural existence which would have eased their search for subsistence. Malthus seemed to think that this may have been due to a harsh geographical environment, or to a cultural deficiency, although at no point did he accept a racial explanation.

> [F]rom some cause or other, they [the American Indians] have not adopted in any great degree these more plentiful modes of procuring subsistence [pastoralism, and particularly agriculture], and therefore have not increased so as to become populous. If hunger alone could have prompted the savage tribes of America to such a change in their habits, I do not conceive that

> there would have been a single nation of hunters and fishers remaining; but it is evident that some fortunate train of circumstances, in addition to this stimulus, is necessary for the purpose; and it is undoubtedly probable that these arts of obtaining food will be first invented and improved in those spots which are best suited to them, and where the natural fertility of the situation, by allowing a greater number of people to subsist together, would give the fairest chance to the inventive powers of the human mind.[78]

Here Malthus did not accept the inverse relation between a harsh natural environment and progress. It seems he reserved this for more advanced stages of progress. Like Smith, he regarded a minimally sufficient natural environment as a sine qua non of cultural progress. The ability for contact with the European conquerors to enhance progress was also regrettably untenable. The influence of the Europeans on the American natives was not only unhelpful in terms of obtaining food and enlarging population, but if anything was negative. For example, the natives devoted growing attention to such things as obtaining furs to exchange for destructive liquors, damaging the local wildlife, or working in mines instead of in agriculture. "The attention to agriculture [in America] has every where slackened, rather than increased, as might at first have been expected, from European connexion."[79]

Malthus claimed that discussing the lives of savages in island environments offered an opportunity for understanding the connection between population and subsistence in larger geographical areas. The production of food in the world was not yet completely efficient, and could be enhanced. "There is probably no island yet known, the produce of which could not be further increased. This is all that can be said of the whole world. Both are peopled up to their actual produce. And the whole earth is in this respect like an island."[80] In other words, although production of food still left much to be required, ultimately the finite size of the earth meant that nature put a limit to the growth of population. This reference to the world as an island is of course significant. As already noted, Richard Grove has claimed that island environments were a spur to Physiocratic theorizing about managing natural resources. As we will see, Malthus was significantly influenced by the Physiocrats. Yet he still did not regard the environmental significance of the finiteness of the planet's resources as anything beyond a theoretical possibility, or at least remote enough to remain such.

The four-stages theory was evident when Malthus claimed that the human race in general was prompted to multiply and spread over different geographical areas, varying in their natural accessibility to inhabitation. Shepherds had an advantage over hunters due to their ability to move from place to place. They were also more combative and tended to fight for their sources of livelihood in a manner which agricultural or commercial peoples found difficult to handle. Pastoral societies therefore found it easier to multiply compared to hunters, although "a country in pasture cannot possibly support so many inhabitants as a country in tillage." The populations of pastoral tribes grew, and consequently went in search of new pastures.[81] Again relying on stadial theory, as well as on Edward Gibbon, Malthus continued and described the principle of population as the main historical force which propelled the barbaric invasions from Northern Europe which had led to the demise of the Roman Empire. When the barbarians had finished populating the European continent, they began roaming and looting by sea (an allusion to the Vikings). Only the invention of gunpowder finally enabled the civilized European nations to withstand the incursions of the pastoral barbarians. Furthermore, the main forces which limited the populations of the barbarians in accordance with their scanty means of subsistence were war and famine. The lengthy story of the fall of Rome, due to these large-scale emigrations, "may be traced to the simple cause of the superiority of the power of population to the means of subsistence."[82] Malthus was thinking here like a modern environmental historian. He noted that it was a common error to confound superfluity of inhabitants with a great actual population. It was the ratio between population and food which mattered, not the bare numbers of people. The Germanic tribes were not populous in actual numbers, but rather overly populous in relation to their sources of subsistence. Malthus implied that this was due to a cultural approach which prevented maximizing their utilization of natural resources. "The pastoral manners of the people, and their habits of war and enterprize, prevented them from clearing and cultivating their lands, and then these very forests, by restraining the sources of subsistence within very narrow bounds, contributed to a superfluity of numbers; that is, to a population beyond what the scanty supplies of the country could support."[83]

In similar fashion Malthus described the pastoral life of nations in Asia and Arabia both in past eras and in modern times, claiming they were even more barbarous than the Germanic tribes. In evoking a stadial outlook on cultural progress, he consistently implied that one of the main attributes of barbarism was an inefficient and insufficient utilization of natural resources. There was a limit to the amount of population which a country could support, but barbarians never challenged this limit. The transition from barbarism to civilization was difficult, and Malthus wrote "of the powerful force of habit among nations of shepherds, and the consequent difficulty of the transition from the pastoral to the agricultural state." The problem was not with the physical environment, since Asia was mostly fertile, but was rather a cultural incapacity to utilize natural resources. "The principal defect of this extensive country [the Russian steppes, generally representing much of the middle regions of Asia] is a want of water; but it is said that the parts which are supplied with this necessary article would be sufficient for the support of four times the number of its present inhabitants, if it were properly cultivated." The constant state of war among the Asian pastoral peoples also impeded a proper cultivation of natural resources. "The evils seem mutually to produce each other. A scarcity of subsistence might at first perhaps give occasion to the habits of war, and the habits of war in return powerfully contribute to narrow the means of subsistence."[84] What mattered more than the natural environment was what human beings did with it. There was a reciprocal interaction between environment and culture, yet if the former was more important than the latter at the earliest stage of development, subsequently, even at the hunting stage, and definitely afterwards, Malthus seemed to regard cultural behavior as even more significant than the environment in itself.

Other regions received similar analysis. In Africa as well, noted Malthus, the natural environment was mostly fertile, but the insecurity resulting from constant war and plunder was the main reason for insufficient cultivation of nature. There were no possibilities for a proper use of surplus produce, and therefore the blacks cultivated only the minimal amount of land necessary for survival. Security of property was also lacking, and consequently also industry, and even when population grew, it was sold into slavery or was victimized by war and misery. As with all regions, the African population reached the levels of its means of subsistence, but under the checks of war, pestilential diseases and promiscuous intercourse.[85] Malthus also noted that in less civilized nations the oscillation between large and small populations, and consequently between states of want and plenty, was usually between extremes.[86]

In Siberia the situation was similar to that of the American Indians, only with less influence of war and more of famine. The demand for labor was small, and therefore laborers made do with providing for their families, while conditions for saving and long-term investment in cultivating land were lacking. This prevented accumulation beyond the individual level, which would require not only unoccupied fertile land and a surplus of population to settle it, but also habits of industry and accumulation, and a stable government which would secure property. Siberia also lacked manufactures, and the means to distribute agricultural produce and augment the demand for this produce, things which existed in Europe and America. The efforts and investment of capital made by Peter the Great and the Empress Catherine had ameliorated conditions in Siberia, although Malthus claimed it would take a long time before the Siberian farmers would reach the level of ability of English laborers. "If in the best cultivated and most populous countries of Europe the present divisions of land and farms had taken place, and had not been followed by the introduction of commerce and manufactures, population would long since have come to a stand from the total want of motive to further cultivation, and the consequent want of demand for labour; and it is obvious that the excessive fertility of the country now under consideration [Siberia] would rather aggravate than diminish the difficulty."[87] In other words, the situation would worsen because there would be a greater number of unemployed, who would be unable to take advantage of the land for accumulation beyond their families' needs. This led to insufficient means of subsistence which limited the amount of population. Malthus's clear implication here, alluding to the four-stages theory, was that only in the fourth stage of commerce and industry could a serious utilization of natural resources emerge, although even then, of course, there were limits to how much population could grow. A similar outlook underlined the review of other cultures. In Persia and Turkey bad governments and excessive taxation damaged agriculture and consequently the production of food, and ultimately population.[88] In India and Tibet the small population was due to social and religious customs, and the caste system.[89]

In China, on the other hand, there was a large population, the result of a fertile land, veneration and promotion of agriculture and encouragement of marriage. Nevertheless, most of the Chinese inhabitants, despite their diligence, remained poor and wretched, and poverty, together with constant famines, led to checks to the population (in Japan a similar situation existed, though wars rather than famines constituted the main checks to population). "The population which has arisen naturally from the fertility of the soil (in China), and the encouragements to agriculture, may be considered as genuine and desirable; but all that has been added by the encouragements to marriage has not only been an addition of so much pure misery in itself, but has completely interrupted the happiness which the rest might have enjoyed."[90] In other words, the encouragement of agriculture in a fertile country was in and of itself a positive thing. Yet when other factors supporting a large population, which were not directly connected to the physical relations between human beings and their natural environment (such as encouragement of marriage), disrupted the natural balance between the amount of population and the fertility of the land by leading to over-population, this led to poverty and to the death of multitudes. China indeed belonged in general to the fourth and highest stage of progress which encompassed productive agriculture within commercialism, yet even within this level of civilization there were further sub-levels of progress, and the Chinese remained inferior to the Europeans, because the gap between their growing population and their means of subsistence was greater and more damaging.[91]

Moving from a survey of non-European societies to a consideration of ancient European civilizations, Malthus noted that the ancient Greeks were aware of the national need to encourage the growth of population, but also to keep it at a level commensurate with their means of subsistence.[92] In ancient Rome, compared with Greece, war was a greater factor limiting population.[93] After finishing his survey of ancient civilizations, Malthus proceeded to discuss the modern nations of Europe. In Norway, he claimed, there still existed to a large extent a pastoral economy, with a considerable reliance on cattle, but also with enhanced agricultural improvements and consequently a growing population.[94] His early voyage to Scandinavia seems to have made a deep impression. In a rare instance of poeticism, he expressed sensitivity to the beauty of nature, enthusiastically praising the picturesque and romantic landscapes he had encountered in Norway.[95] This, however, was untypical for Malthus, at least in his official publications, in which he usually discussed nature simply as a resource supporting human existence. In his travel diaries, on the other hand, he more often evinced his delight in the beauty of landscapes.[96] It was, however, in the *Essay on the Principle of Population*, that he claimed, in a rare instance of "environmental-sustainability" thinking, that the Norwegians and Swedes occasionally cleared forests in a hurried manner without considering what the true value of the land would subsequently be. Consequently, at times, for one good crop of rye, they spoiled large quantities of growing timber, as the land itself occasionally even became useless. Malthus here allowed himself a supposition, which seemed to him improbable, yet nevertheless worth mentioning. This was the possibility that such Scandinavian regions which in his time were covered with forests, had, a thousand years earlier, produced corn and been better populated than in modern times. "Wars, plagues, or that greater depopulator than either, a tyrannical government, might have suddenly destroyed or expelled the greatest part of the inhabitants, and a neglect of the land for twenty or thirty years in Norway or Sweden would produce a very strange difference in the face of the country. But this is merely an idea which I could not help mentioning, but which the reader already knows has not had weight enough with me to make me suppose the fact in any degree probable."[97] What exactly were the reasons that all this was not probable remained unclear, although Malthus probably meant the various social factors leading to depopulation which constantly interested him. In any event, however, he evidently thought it worth mentioning that these regions might have been populated in the past. In an almost modern environmental-history approach, Malthus here evinced consciousness of the *longue durée* changing relations between human beings and their natural environment, and of the connection of these relations with cultural developments, all of which was further connected with changes in the cultivation of nature. The implication was that nature was amenable to human cultivation, but also, conversely, that this cultivation (or lack thereof) in its turn affected nature. Malthus's discussion of this topic was brief, but quite remarkable for the early nineteenth century.

He also discussed Scandinavia more in line with his common stadial approach to other regions and civilizations. Writing of mountainous areas in Switzerland and Norway, he noted that in pastoral regions the growth of population was slow, unless manufactures were introduced. When manufactures were however introduced, this also led to damaging health, morals and happiness. Furthermore, pasturage produced food for more people than it was able to employ, and therefore predisposed people to emigration. All this was based on the relationship between nature and the humans who cultivated it. "The limits to the population of a country strictly pastoral, are strikingly obvious. There are no grounds less susceptible of improvement than mountainous pastures. They must necessarily be left chiefly to nature; and when they have been adequately stocked with cattle, little more can be done."[98]

Moving to the most advanced and prominent European nations, Malthus noted that the French population had not diminished during the revolution despite all the ensuing devastation, because in contrast with the damage to manufactures, not only was agriculture not damaged, but actually increased. It continued the means of subsistence unimpaired. Traditionally, the number of small farmers and proprietors in France was large, and encouraged population. During the revolution the distribution of the lands of aristocrats and clergy increased even further the number of landed proprietors.[99] Finally addressing England and its rising population in the early nineteenth century, he claimed that when the natural resources of a state were properly distributed, both regarding agriculture and manufactures, so as to encourage the demand for labor, then the population kept pace with this advantageous situation.[100]

A maximal utilization of land, according to Malthus, was impossible because, assuming private property was retained, not everyone could adequately live on agricultural produce. Therefore it was important to combine agriculture and commerce, despite the greater importance of the former.[101] Here again he made his own idiosyncratic use of stadial terminology, both enforcing the traditional perception of the superiority of European commercial civilization, together with his emphasis on the overarching importance of an agricultural basis to civilization. In commercial nations which supplied some of their food from home agricultural production, and some by importation (not relying exclusively on either), uncertainty occurred in the inevitable cases of years of scarcity, or when the price of corn rose proportionately to the price of wages during overpopulation. This uncertainty was particularly evident in countries with a large territory, when the commercial part of the population grew beyond the surplus produce of its cultivators. The ensuing dearth would impact not only the poor, but all classes of the population. The moment it would not be possible to supply sustenance both by production and by importation, the country would reach the utmost limit to the population it could maintain. This limit to the population of commercial states was achieved when a balance was reached between the funds for the maintenance of labor, and the amount of population. Beyond this limit, the poor could not afford to earn enough to purchase the food at rising prices. Thus, according to Malthus, even at the final stage of the four stages scheme of progress, unlimited progress was impossible in terms of the ability to utilize natural resources. The cultivation of natural resources did not happen in a vacuum. In the best of conditions, it developed within the confines and limitations of a market economy. Progress in the seemingly disparate fields of agriculture, manufactures and commerce, in fact had to be intertwined.[102]

Before 1817, Malthus regarded agriculture as more important than commerce. He claimed that the condition of the poor, and the rise in population, would be better in a country which would invest in agriculture more than in commerce. Stadial progress was possible only so long as agriculture remained the sufficiently productive basis of the more advanced stages of development. He initially supported the Physiocratic position rather than that of Adam Smith, in regard to the precedence of agriculture over manufactures as the measure of a nation's wealth. It was actually the Physiocratic system, according to his early view, with its emphasis on an agricultural basis for economic development, which ultimately enabled the thriving of manufactures and commerce. It was the agricultural surplus of England which explained its thriving manufactures. Nevertheless, not every agricultural improvement which added wealth necessarily supported population. This detrimental development happened, for example, when such an improvement decreased the need for agricultural labor, without at the same time increasing the amount of agricultural produce. Moreover, an over-reliance on manufactures might entail precariously relying on agricultural imports. Malthus, however, also recognized the possibility that if manufactures became efficient enough, in accordance with the division of labor which Adam Smith had mentioned, then they might add to the nation's wealth, though not as much as agriculture.[103] However, over time he changed his mind regarding the Physiocratic emphasis of agriculture. The 1803 edition of the *Essay on the Principle of Population* included several substantial chapters supportive of the Physiocrats.[104] In 1817 he replaced these chapters with a substantially altered discussion, in which he forsook this position in favor of the combination of the agricultural and commercial systems. He then almost disregarded the Physiocratic position, although he continued to regard agricultural production as the basis for economic development.[105] His early position remains, however, pertinent for our discussion, because even later he still remained convinced to a large extent regarding the importance of agriculture. His position vis-à-vis the Physiocrats was therefore not dissimilar to that of Smith.[106] The measure of the Physiocratic influence can be gained from the following 1803 passage, where he noted that a rise in population which did not work in agriculture was always dependent on agricultural surplus.

> Throughout the whole world, the number of manufacturers, of proprietors, and of persons engaged in the various civil and military professions, must be exactly proportioned to this surplus [agricultural] produce, and cannot in the nature of things increase beyond it. If the earth had been so niggardly of her produce as to oblige all her inhabitants to labour for it, no manufacturers or idle persons could ever have existed. But her first intercourse with man was a voluntary present; not very large indeed, but sufficient as a fund for his subsistence, till by the proper exercise of his faculties he could procure a greater. In proportion as the labour and ingenuity of man, exercised upon the land, have increased this surplus produce, leisure has been given to a greater number of persons to employ themselves in all the inventions which embellish civilized life. And though, in its turn, the desire to profit by these inventions has greatly contributed to stimulate the cultivators to increase their surplus produce; yet the order of precedence is clearly the surplus produce.[107]

Like Enlightenment philosophers before him, and Marxists after him, Malthus regarded a firm material basis as the prerequisite for higher cultural progress. In contrast with most Enlightenment philosophers, and more in tune with the Physiocrats, he emphasized, even after 1817, the agricultural over the manufacturing component of this material basis, as well as its finiteness as a source of subsistence. His position was of course ideologically almost diametrically opposed to that of the Marxists. Yet it is significant to note how a stadial outlook on the historical precedence of material culture was shared by most eighteenth- and nineteenth-century European intellectuals interested in economic development and progress.

Malthus's comparative cultural approach, combined with his stadial outlook, provided a means for making general observations on the measure of progress of various civilizations, taking into consideration the social division of labor between the different types of production. It also provided a key to assessing the required steps which societies could take to improve their situation. Although in a different manner than with Smith, Malthus too made a methodological transition from historical observations to political-economic ones. For example, he claimed that the amount of staple grain (the main source of food) which a family could buy with its wages, was a measure of both the condition of the laborers and the encouragement for the growth of population. Yet, he also noted, one needed to bear in mind that there were two ways of gaining command over the necessaries of life – either by increasing resources, which by definition was something limited and inconstant, or else, preferably, by improving the prudential habits of the laboring classes. The laborers were masters of their fate and could improve their own condition much more effectively than others might do for them.[108]

Malthus's historiographical approach constantly implied the ability of human societies to progress based on a proper cultivation of their natural environment. At the same time, however, he recognized that this progress could not go on indefinitely, even under the best of circumstances. Like Smith, Ricardo and other classical political economists, and in fact most modern economists as well, he was concerned not only with the proper conditions for establishing growth, but also with how to sustain this growth for as long as possible. The looming cloud of stationarity has hung over economic analysis for over two hundred years, and the notion of limited natural resources has remained its basic component. When a stationary state emerges (or what modern economics refers to as a recession), an eventuality which seems inevitable, the question then as now, is how to deal with it, perhaps regain growth, and if not, how to minimize its deleterious influences. For Malthus a stationary state meant scarcity of land and the lessening ability to produce food, eventually leading to a consistent decrease in population growth. When stationarity set in, barring technological innovation, population, rent and wages were constant, and agricultural surplus supported those not working in agriculture. Rent and population rose in tandem, and no agricultural laborer was employed unless he produced more than the value of his wages. However, prudential behavior among the laboring class, part of the preventive checks to population, could ensure a consistent level of adequate wages even when approaching the stationary state. In that state the preventive check was able to transfer a part of the surplus produce from the landowners to the laborers and capitalists.[109] Thus, even regarding the stationary state, Malthus was not necessarily as pessimistic as is sometimes assumed. One might easily accept the common view of Malthus (and to some extent also Ricardo) as a cultural pessimist compared with Enlightenment intellectuals. However, despite his grim predictions of the misery that over-population was in all probability bound to continue and indefinitely inflict on the human race, he still retained no small measure of optimism, at least as far as the future of European civilization was concerned. The reason for this optimism was that progress was not dependent on the absolute number of population (which in the early nineteenth century seemed higher than ever before), but rather on the relative proportion between population and food. For this reason, it was thinly populated nations which paradoxically at times suffered the most from the effects of the principle of population. Therefore, Malthus was cautiously optimistic regarding the future of the human race, and viewed his own era, despite all its inherent problems, as the best in history. The preceding century, so he claimed, had seen the smallest amount of diseases and famines in history.[110] Malthus's outlook did not deny the possibility that despite all the many drawbacks which he consistently addressed, perhaps human civilization was after all on a slow path of progress. Any hindrance to this progress came from a human, not a natural, source.

Say and other contemporaries

In the first half of the nineteenth century political economy came into its own as an independent discipline. More and more educated people came to regard it as a prerequisite for any proper understanding of politics and government. The development of political economy was most discernable in Britain, the main scene of the Industrial Revolution. There was a mutual fertilization between industrialization itself, and the theoretical underpinning which political economy provided for it. The Industrial Revolution put into practice the prescripts of the Scientific Revolution, mediated by the Enlightenment's historiographical conception of material progress. Not surprisingly, this provided a stimulus for consistent attention from political economists to the significance of utilizing natural resources. The traditional primary significance of food production, and thus of agriculture, remained in force. Yet industrialization also made other technological and mechanized types of natural-resource cultivation appear increasingly vital. Smith had already recognized this, but it became increasingly more important in subsequent classical political economy. Also important, for practically all European political economists of the early nineteenth century, was a familiarity with the works not just of Smith, but also of Malthus and Ricardo. References of various sorts, supportive, corrective or critical, to the doctrines of all three, became ubiquitous in the thought of the period.

One of the most prominent of the political economists of the era, whom we have already encountered, was the Frenchman Jean-Baptiste Say, whose *Treatise on Political Economy* was very familiar in Britain, not least to Ricardo and Malthus. Say is most famous in the history of economic thought for his famous law stating that "production creates its own demand," and thus implying the impossibility of gluts, an assertion which was shared in basic form by Ricardo and the mainstream of political economists, but denied by Malthus. Yet Say had many other significant things to say about topics germane to the issues of progress, population and natural resources. He openly acknowledged his indebtedness to Smith, though he often disagreed with the latter's opinions.[111] He was also much more radical politically than Smith, openly espousing republican opinions and playing a modest though not insignificant role in revolutionary France. Say combined republican notions with support of free trade in the spirit of Smith. He viewed free trade as a necessary support for a modern republic. During the *Directoire* Say denied both Britain, which he viewed as a corrupt nation whose ascendancy over France was beginning to decline, as well as the republics of antiquity. Both were inadequate as models for the French republic. A modern republic in his view needed to be founded on technological advance, machinery, commerce and agriculture, all of which should lead to a comfortable existence, though avoiding the excesses of luxury. In contrast with the liberal outlook of unintended consequences propounded by Smith, Say, in typical republican fashion, regarded luxury as a socially damaging vice. By the time of the Consulate he mitigated, though not relinquished, some of his republican views, claiming that economic prosperity might be achieved under any type of political system. Political economy needed to be separated from government, which belonged to a different sphere of activity. Thus free trade would be able to enhance prosperity without clashing with republican government.[112] Say was therefore quite modern in both his methodological acceptance of the various types of production, and in his emphasis on the independence of political economy, although this independence was not regarded to the extent common in our time. For Say, as for all classical political economists, economic considerations were still deeply embedded within a broad cultural discourse.

Say, however, relied on historical discussions much less than Smith. He accepted the viability of commercial society, and therefore felt less need to support it by stadial theory.[113] Nevertheless, stadial perceptions surfaced on occasion in his discussion. For example, he noted how the manner in which capital accumulated in various nations depended on their geographical location and their differing cultural characteristics. In a society at an early stage of progress capital thus consisted mainly of buildings, the implements of husbandry, livestock and the improvement of land; in a manufacturing society it was mainly raw materials and machines; and in a commercial society it was mainly capital accumulated in the form of wrought or unwrought goods, which the merchants bought for the purpose of resale. A civilized society, however, invested in all three forms of capital, which resulted in a huge amount of products which, despite large-scale consumption, were constantly renovated and even increased, as long as the industry of the community produced more than consumption destroyed.[114] In this way Say perceived that an advanced civilization simultaneously incorporated all stages of cultural progress, an outlook consistent with the general stadial viewpoint of the eighteenth century, which regarded the stages of progress as accumulative.

Say recognized the significance of natural-resource cultivation for historical progress. Civilization depended on production, and a nation which would create conditions disadvantageous to producers risked reverting from a civilized, back to a savage state. On the other hand, improving technology devoted to utilizing natural resources enhanced civilization.[115] Say was confident about civilization's future prospects for progress, based on advancing science and technology. Just as the savants of previous generations would have been astonished to see the innovations of nineteenth-century Europe, so the people of the future would look on this seemingly progressive civilization as encumbered by unnecessary weight, as they would live in a world that Say's contemporaries could not yet conceive of.[116]

With or without utilizing stadial notions, Say, like other classical political economists influenced by Enlightenment notions of progress, repeatedly recognized the differences between civilized and uncivilized societies. For example, he claimed that nations of savages or shepherds, which devoted almost no attention to the arts, and particularly not to agriculture, found themselves with relatively abundant free time. Therefore they were able to undertake military enterprises in any place which possessed booty and pasture. The Tartars and the Arabs exemplified this state of affairs, which accounted for the vast regions conquered by their various leaders, as well as by the Moors and Turks.[117] Yet like Smith he recognized the superior military efficiency of modern nations. Wars in the modern era, involving standing armies and the preservation of colonies, had become very expensive, and therefore only rich countries, with proper management of their political economy, would be able in future to undertake them. Their overthrow by barbarian nations, which had occurred in past historical eras, would become impossible. Nations in the future, particularly the inhabitants more than their governments, would recognize the futility of wars, and wars without public assent would become rare, while standing armies would be kept mainly for defensive purposes.[118] Say was optimistic about the future of humanity, and about the ability of bridging the gap between civilized and uncivilized nations. This optimism was based primarily on his belief in the ameliorating quality of economic progress.

Say's views on colonization consequently mirrored these ideas. He did not simply oppose European colonialism on liberal and economic grounds. Despite his opposition to slavery, he advocated colonial settlement so long as this included ameliorating the condition of indigenous populations, who would learn such things as agriculture and other types of knowledge and technologies from the Europeans.[119] While differentiating between various civilizations and their respective levels of progress, and consistently recognizing the superiority of European civilization, Say nonetheless called on the European nations to "renounce the costly rights of colonial dominion," since this was in their interest and, implicitly, of all nations trading with each other. Instead, the Europeans should aim at the independent colonization of tropical regions close to Europe and of parts of Africa. This would enable Europe to enjoy the vast cultivation of colonial products.[120] He supported the trade of food between European nations and colonies with large tracts of uncultivated land, in a process which ultimately led to the development of the colonies, and finally to their independence.[121] In this as in other contexts the efficient use of natural resources played a vital and constructive role.

Like all classical political economists following Malthus, Say duly recognized the significance of the issue of population. He noted that the revenue of a state did not depend on its populousness, but rather on the capital and genius of its inhabitants, as these were conducive to promoting its commerce. The inhabitants benefited from these factors and not *vice versa*.[122] While discussing corn laws, he claimed that the size of population and the amount of food were interdependent. Most people, however, lacked the foresight or the possibility to preserve grain in times of plenty for subsequent years of shortage. Say supported free trade in food items as the best means of preventing famine, yet because of the importance of avoiding food shortages, he did not completely oppose certain judicial intervention in cases where agricultural production was damaged.[123] He also claimed that the many improvements in production and in human knowledge in the preceding century, particularly in the natural sciences, had greatly enhanced the efficiency of production. Yet moral improvements in the political and social spheres had been slower, thus preventing reaping the full benefits from these material advancements. Nevertheless, there was some advance in these moral fields as well, and Say claimed that his era (in Europe of course) witnessed a larger population in better material condition than a century earlier.[124] Evincing his acceptance of the independence of economic developments, Say accepted that there were limits to how much human beings could control economic processes. These followed certain physical laws. Therefore, because of the connection between population and food, a peculiarity of agricultural products was that their average price was not raised by growing scarcity, since population would certainly diminish co-extensively with the diminishing quantity of human aliment, as demand was lowered with supply. This happened irrespective of the relative wealth or the level of cultivation of land in various countries.[125] An unprecedented emphasis on the economic significance of demand was one of the main innovations of Say's analysis.

Say criticized Simonde de Sismondi's moderate socialist suggestion that the proprietors of land and manufactures should provide for their workers' sustenance, but should also be given the power to permit or prevent marriage among the workers, so that certain sustenance would not lead to over-population. According to Say, it was not only unfair to make one set of human beings responsible for the maintenance of another, but also to give them control over other human beings, in contrast with the sanctity of personal action. Moreover, the growth of population beyond the means of subsistence was one of the evils consequent on the imperfection of the human race, and on the constitution of nature. It was not dependent on a society's level of progress, nor on social institutions, and was not susceptible to any complete remedy. While government was responsible for the laboring classes, it needed to avoid encroaching on personal liberty, and thus enacting expedients which were worse than the disease itself.[126] Clearly Say's outlook was much more democratic than either that of Smith or Malthus.

He did however agree with them on the connection between population and subsistence, a veritable *idée fixe* in classical political economy. He noted that human beings, like other animals, were in a situation where nature enabled the perpetuation of the species, yet without taking care of the individual. Existence depended on food. In a developed economy this was equivalent to the activity related with things equal in value to food, and thus exchangeable with it. In this manner, with the help of trade, there were nations where more inhabitants lived than would have been able, subsisting only on the local agricultural produce. Even in rich countries there were those who died of hunger. Yet in the condition of an advanced civilization there was an existential need for other products as well, even immaterial ones, which multiplied with demand. Therefore, the size of population in any country was proportional to the sum of its production of every kind. Furthermore, the more the property in a country was evenly distributed, the larger would its population be. All political economists agreed on this point according to Say. What others had not always realized, however, was, he claimed, that a consistent growth of population was dependent above all on the promotion of production. At this point his famous law came into play. Any other attempt to encourage population, as had occurred in various historical cases, was doomed to fail without productive capacity. Viable productive capacity, however, even in cases of disasters, wars or epidemics, would enable the quick renewed growth of population. According to Say, in a rather utilitarian manner, the condition of humanity was measured by the amount of suffering which occurred, or was prevented, as the result of wars and other disasters, yet the size of population was a different matter dependent specifically on production. Population was negatively influenced to a much greater extent by bad economic and political governmental policy which did not support production. A large population was an indicator of enlarged national production, but not of prosperity, since not all products were necessarily diffused among all the population. Therefore population and prosperity did not necessarily grow together. Some countries were directly dependent on the quantity of food they produced, did not save any surplus, and in time of crisis suffered from famine. Others did produce surplus, although not necessarily agricultural, and then they became dependent on trade for the import of food. Yet the best means of feeding the population was domestic agricultural production. In any event, the size of population depended on the quantity of national production, supported by proper government and manners. Say also claimed, prefiguring Max Weber, that this condition was more apparent in protestant than in catholic countries, since Protestantism was more supportive of the habits of production.[127]

Issues related to historical progress also surfaced in the work of other contemporaneous political economists. John Ramsay McCulloch, for example, was clearly influenced by stadial theory, outlining it with clear indebtedness to Smith, even though McCulloch devoted less attention to discriminating between the agricultural and the commercial stages. He was one of those who emphasized particularly the transition to agriculture as the most decisive step in the progress of civilization.[128] He also, like many contemporaries, accepted Malthus's theory of population, despite the fact that he was critical of the latter on many points, and was influenced much more by Ricardo.[129]

A more original political economist was Robert Torrens. While scholars are disagreed on this point, it seems that he played a not insignificant role in developing the famous notion of comparative advantage often accredited only to Ricardo.[130] Torrens became a controversial figure during the 1830s, despite his advocacy of free trade, when he began introducing the "terms of trade" argument in favor of using tarrifs to protect a country's interests in international trade, particularly when this trade was not reciprocally free. Torrens was not the originator of this idea, which in more moderate form became accepted later. Yet it is a testament to his originality as a thinker, not least regarding the utilization of natural resources. He observed four inter-connected types of industry, without which the cultivation of natural resources would cease. These were, based on their relation to natural resources – appropriative industry, the mere collection of natural materials; manufacturing industry, the adaptation of these materials for human use; agricultural industry, meant to augment natural production by seconding the operations of nature; and commercial industry, the transportation and exchange of the articles of wealth acquired by the three previous types of industry.[131] These four types of industry corresponded roughly to the outlines of the four-stages theory of progress, although Torrens did not follow exactly the Enlightenment form of this theory.

Presenting an idiosyncratic version of conjectural history, he depicted how savage societies began using tools (essentially capital) to help appropriate natural materials. With historical progress this type of industry turned from central to relatively marginal in importance.[132] He continued with a brief conjectural history of how manufactures developed almost immediately afterwards, so as to assist the appropriation and cultivation of natural materials.[133] This emphasized the significant role of manufactures, and the mutually enforcing character of the various types of industry as they related to utilizing nature. Consequently it was no surprise that he criticized the Physiocrats and their claim for the barrenness of manufactures.[134] Slightly later he continued his conjectural history with a depiction of the development of agriculture, including both cultivation of the soil and domestication of animals.[135] His departure from the traditional four-stages scheme was apparent by his effectively uniting the shepherding and agricultural stages, and claiming that they had developed after, not before, manufactures.

The fact that all types of industry were interrelated meant that agriculture had not temporally preceded manufactures. It was in fact the latter which fitted for use those natural materials which agriculture, as well as simple gathering, had provided. Without manufactures historical progress was therefore impossible. It was a signal fault of the Physiocrats that they had not realized this mutually enforcing nature of all branches of human industry.[136] While the idea of the interrelatedness of agriculture and manufactures was not new, it was rarely made so explicit before Torrens. This also applied to the importance of trade, which also enabled the extension of the utilization of nature by the other forms of industry.[137] Reiterating Smith's emphasis on transportation, he noted how improvements in roads and navigation consequently assisted the transportation of materials, and helped augment a nation's industry.[138] Returning to a conjectural depiction of human development, of the type which he dispersed throughout his discussion, Torrens briefly described how international trade had developed from simple barter in savage societies. Mercantile capital, a vital consequence of the most advanced societies, was much larger than the capital of all other types of industry.[139] Therefore, even though Torens's stadial outline was not in line with traditional Enlightenment stadial theory, he too considered commerce as the highest stage of progress, due to the ability, at this stage, to apply more capital for the purpose of production, and consequently to augment wealth. He claimed that as long as the improvements in capital and machinery accumulated, "the effective powers of appropriative industry may go on perpetually increasing until the bounty of nature fails, and forests, fisheries, and mines, begin to be exhausted."[140] Torrens therefore perceived a limit to natural resources, though he did not specify how tangible this limit was. He saw no problem with human development in the direction of this limit, and it concerned him much less than Malthus.

Torrens, relying on a logic similar to Locke's agricultural argument, saw no problem with the control that civilized nations took over lands occupied by savages, who in his view did not cultivate their natural surroundings.[141] On this point he was much less progressive, evincing an English nationalist stance which favored a British colonial and commercial empire of the "Anglo-Saxon race." Consequently he maintained a mercantilist-style advocacy of preserving the hegemony of the mother-country over the colonies. Colonization was also a way to alleviate population pressure in England.[142] Torrens claimed that occasionally a mother nation should manage the commerce with its colonies in its own favor, or that a strong nation should do so in trading with a weaker one. This might also benefit the weaker side in such exchanges, since occasionally it might be to its advantage to sacrifice some portion of wealth so as to enhance the protection the stronger trading partner offered.[143] Torrens's rather conservative views on colonization were in contrast with his originality regarding other topics.

Another significant nineteenth-century political economist, though he is often considered more as a philosopher, was Dugald Stewart. As an early biographer of Smith he was influential in transmitting the ideas of the Scottish Enlightenment to England. He played a crucial role in shaping Smith's figure and influence on the development of economic thought, despite some major disagreements with the latter. While he coined the phrase "conjectural history" in his biography of Smith, he himself used conjectural history to a lesser extent, although he did accept Smith's connection of moral issues to political economy. Stewart emphasized the separateness and priority of economics to government, yet he did so from a conservative position aiming for economic thought to play a gradual, not revolutionary, role, in shaping and promoting society. He was less interested in historical circumstances than Smith. For Smith individual actions were important, for Stewart the natural divinely ordained order, and society in general, were paramount over the individual. There was a religious element in Stewart's teleological view of an unfolding divinely ordained progress, on both the physical and moral levels. Political economy for Stewart was an all-encompassing study of the natural order as a whole, which included jurisprudence.[144] He was also significant as an influence on a major contentious methodological debate within early nineteenth-century political economy, favoring a deductive over an inductive approach to political economy, but wary that this could not afford mathematical certainty. On this point he influenced the group of Oxford philosophers known as the Oriel Noetics, who included Richard Whately. These in their turn influenced Nassau William Senior, the first Professor of Political Economy at Oxford, who himself was also directly influenced by Stewart. The deductive approach of this group was criticized by a rival group of Cambridge intellectuals who included William Whewell and Richard Jones.[145] The latter in general lost this debate, as the more deductive approach originating with Ricardo became in the long run more influential in economic studies. This debate has therefore receded to the confines of esoteric scholarship, but for our purposes was significant, since it was the inductive, more empirical approach, which was more sensitive to historical notions, and was far from beaten in the early nineteenth century. We will shortly come to Whately, Senior and Jones, but first a consideration of some relevant ideas of Stewart himself is in order.

Stewart agreed with Malthus's theory regarding the geometrical growth of population compared with the arithmetical growth of subsistence, even though he was less concerned about the danger of over-population.[146] He also favorably considered other ideas of Malthus, for example regarding criticism of the Poor Laws. Stewart discussed at length other means of assisting the poor and improving their condition, particularly education.[147] This was related to his views on cultural progress. A unique human attribute was the attempt to better one's condition, and a central means of doing so was by acquiring property through exertion. When possible, giving the poor the possibility of doing so, even on a small scale, could help improve their condition. This also differentiated between advanced societies and savages, who only hunted and fished when they were hungry, and slept till they were hungry again. It was the legislator's duty in any civilized society to help the poor get out of such a situation, by making them feel that they might improve their condition by becoming owners of land.[148] Cultivating nature was therefore a social route to progress, based on a Lockean notion of acquiring property through labor.[149]

Evincing the influence of Malthus, Stewart claimed that when the growth of population went unchecked, this risked quickly making the world overstocked with inhabitants. This was particularly evident in fertile yet uninhabited regions. "The truth is, that an abundance of rich land, to be had for little or nothing, is so powerful an encouragement to population as to overcome all obstacles." This rapid multiplication of population "is experienced in every instance in which the numbers of the people fall greatly short of what their means of subsistence might support." In such regions the recovery of population numbers following natural disasters or wars was also rapid.[150] Stewart however emphasized human conduct, not just the natural environment, as influencing population numbers. "[I]t appears that population does not depend solely on the fertility of the soil, and the industry of the inhabitants; but on those circumstances, combined with the *habits and ideas* which are generally prevalent concerning the necessaries and accommodations of life." Here Stewart continued with a stadial depiction of the rising efficiency of obtaining sustenance from nature, beginning with the hunting stage, through pastoralism, to the crucial stage of agriculture. He emphasized that in the latter stage, growing potatoes or rice was more productive than growing wheat.[151]

Stewart disagreed with primitivistic notions of the merits of less civilized societies.[152] He noted that the need to apply art to acquire necessaries from nature was what had turned human beings into improving creatures different from brutes. When one class of wants were answered, new desires arose. This was a unique human attribute, which propelled human beings to development fueled by the need to supply these incessantly rising novel demands. In the rude stage of society people catered to their own individual needs. In more advanced stages, however, division of labor was necessary to meet the varying desires and tastes of the members of society.[153] Nevertheless, influenced by the Physiocrats, Stewart still recognized a particular significance for agricultural production. The growth of population depended on agricultural improvements, and therefore it was incumbent upon government to encourage agriculture, by ensuring that husbandmen would enjoy the fruits of their labor.[154] Great Britain, in terms of its geographical characteristics, could afford an increase in both population and agricultural production, as long as this meant a better utilization of its cultivated lands.[155]

Changes in a country's extent of territory or size of population depended in large measure on political institutions and required proper changes in the latter. In many cases, however, the size of territory and population depended on circumstances extraneous to the country itself, for example the situation of neighboring countries, which might require internal changes to enable a country to stay independent of more powerful rivals.[156] Ultimately, a nation's wealth was determined not by the quantity of its inhabitants, but rather of its industrious inhabitants, as opposed to the poor who existed beyond the accessible quantity of subsistence. It was necessary to avoid encouraging manufactures beyond the point where this ceased supporting agriculture, and instead supported the growth of this type of hungry population. Despite his general agreement with Malthus's views, Stewart claimed that Malthus did not sufficiently rely on the means which nature itself used to balance the respective quantities of population and food. It was best not to impede the growth of population or the nation's prosperity from care for the distant future. It was better to rely on the arrangements of Providence, while encouraging both population and national wealth. It was the government's duty to create sufficient employment rather than put obstacles to population growth, at least as long as this was accompanied by a commensurate production of sustenance.[157] Stewart was therefore a clear example of the Malthusian bent in early nineteenth-century political economy.

Among the Oxford group of Oriel Noetics who were influenced by Stewart's generally deductive approach to political economy, and even took this to greater extremes than Stewart himself, who still accepted some level of empiricism, a particularly significant figure was Richard Whately.[158] Like others of the Oxford group he was supportive of Ricardo's methodology. Yet despite Malthus's more inductive approach, Whately was also influenced by the latter's combination of political economy and natural theology.[159] Whately disagreed with conjectural history in its common form, attempting to insert an element of divine intervention into this type of historical analysis.[160] On this point he was an exception among nineteenth-century political economists, no doubt in large measure due to the religious aspect of his thought. He claimed that no evidence existed of a savage society which had lifted itself up to civilization unassisted. Either savages learned civilization from contact with more civilized societies, or else they had degenerated from their own previously more civilized state.[161]

The only assistance human beings had received was from their creator, when they were "placed in a condition, as keepers of domestic animals, and cultivators of the earth, more favourable to the development of the rational faculties, than, we have every reason to think, they could ever have reached by the mere exercise of their rational power; it is probable they were thenceforth left to themselves in all that relates to the invention and improvement of the arts of life." This was a bit in the direction of deism, although Whately did not go that far and was more of a conservative in his religious approach. Human beings, he nevertheless claimed, had been provided by Providence only with the most basic knowledge which they could not attain on their own. From that moment on they were left to discover any further knowledge by their own efforts, unassisted, no matter how lengthy the process of doing so. For this reason he objected to the idea of a state of nature, which was not only an unrealistic invention, but the idyllic depictions of which had no substantial foundation. The only sense in which it had any validity was in the ignorance of arts. The life of savages as depicted from a primitivistic perspective was remote from any notion of what indeed comprised the natural state of humanity, since it did not include the vital human characteristic of enabling progress and improvement.[162] Whately doubted that human beings could have discovered even basic abilities without the aid of Providence. Even something like the use of fire, if not the discovery of fire itself, would have been beyond the abilities of savages and would have required divine assistance. The unassisted domestication of large animals such as oxen also seemed doubtful.[163] Once the historical process of improvement had begun, however, and barring any obstacles which often might and did occur, there was no seeming limit to how far human beings might progress.[164]

From these assertions Whately made a rather abrupt transition to the political-economic claim that what human societies required in order to progress more significantly was the division of labor, and even more important, security of property.[165] This was moving back into more familiar territory in terms of contemporaneous classical political-economic discourse. He noted that the first steps of human advancement would have been the slowest and most difficult, since wealth in the form of basic capital was necessary to produce more wealth. The examples he noted were, not accidentally, chiefly concerned with the difficulty early societies would have had to gain their subsistence from the natural elements. These included the initial stock of corn necessary for sowing, the tools which were produced by other tools, the ax necessary to fell trees whose handle was itself made from wood, and the iron implements necessary for mining iron. "We hardly know how to estimate the impediments to the few first steps, when stakes and sharp stones were the tools, and the labourer's subsistence consisted in the spontaneous products of the earth, and the flesh of wild animals. But it is plain, that each succeeding step must have been easier, and at the same time more effective." Eventually most of the society would have been free from lack of the necessaries of life, and the progress of civilization could advance more rapidly.[166] Despite his criticism of conjectural history, Whately therefore did not really part with it, and his objections centered only on the very earliest stage of human existence, to which he wanted to inject a divine directing force. In other respects he followed a rather common outline of human progress, based on increasing control of natural resources which eventually enabled the attainment of higher culture.

An even more significant figure as a deductively oriented political economist than Whately was his pupil Nassau William Senior. Even more than Ricardo, Senior, like Dugald Stewart, was receptive to empirical evidence despite his deductivism.[167] He referred to capital as "abstinence," in other words the avoidance of using products in favor of investment for future use. This led to the development of implements and technology. Utilizing stadial terminology, he claimed that in this sense the use of capital changed in different stages of progress. The need for abstinence, or capital, increased from stage to stage. The transition from a hunting to a pastoral stage was an exercise in abstinence, while remaining in the hunting stage required very little abstinence. Transitioning from the pastoral to an agricultural stage required even greater abstinence, and this need increased even more with progress to the manufacturing and commercial stages. An agricultural society might remain stationary, but this became impossible in the commercial stage. A nation in this latter stage of advanced progress which, for any reason, did not continually increase its capital, would decline in its power relative to other commercial and manufacturing nations.[168] Senior saw no reason to question the fact that progress in the use of implements, propelled by capital investment and thus enhancing the efficiency of production, would continue in the future, and enable the better utilization of natural resources, "and it is probable that many other powers of equal efficiency lie still undiscovered among the secrets of nature, or, if known, are still unapplied."[169] It was therefore the investment of capital, the abstinence of present wants in favor of future goals, which propelled progress. For Senior this meant above all diminishing the present use of natural resources, or as he termed them, "natural agents," to enhance this use in the long run.[170] This was an outlook which advocated the long-term maximization of utilizing natural resources. One might view this as a precursor of modern views of sustainable development. In fact, however, Senior did not express concern with the danger of limited availability of natural resources. It was the human side of the equation, not the natural one, which determined how much, and how efficiently, these resources were used. Senior thus maintained a somewhat more optimistic view than Malthus's, despite the latter's influence.

Senior implied a type of comparative advantage among nations, connecting this with the manner in which international commerce enhanced the principle of the division of labor. He credited Torrens with recognizing international trade as "the territorial division of labor," noting that "Nature seems to have intended that mutual dependence should unite all the inhabitants of the earth into one commercial family. For this purpose she has indefinitely diversified her own products in every climate and in almost every extensive district. For this purpose, also, she seems to have varied so extensively the wants and the productive powers of the different races of men. The superiority of modern over ancient wealth depends in a great measure on the greater use we make of these varieties."[171] In other words, the greater the historical progress of international trade at the highest stage of historical development, the greater the ability, as well as the need and will, of human beings to utilize natural resources. The natural environment affected the progressive abilities of nations. "To some Countries nature has refused the means of supporting human life; to others she has refused the means of wealth… But, though she can deny riches, she cannot give them." In other words, the combination of both natural riches and the ability to use them, was required to transform them into "the means of wealth." Therefore, "With all the brute and inanimate sources of affluence profusely scattered before them, the inhabitants of the greater part of Africa, America, and Asia want the moral and intellectual qualities by which the raw materials of wealth are to be worked up." It required both the natural treasures of non-European lands, together with the cultural capabilities of European settlers, to take advantage of these treasures for propelling progress. "They [natural "local advantages"] have enabled the Colonies of highly civilized nations to advance to opulence with a rapidity of which we have no other example." Despite their mismanagement, colonies according to Senior were one of the main means by which civilization had been diffused.[172] This was a clear version of Locke's famous agricultural argument.

Senior was influenced by Malthus's combination of political economy and natural theology, as well as by the latter's basic assertions about the growth rate of population versus that of subsistence. Nevertheless, like others in the 1830s, at a time of rising prosperity, growth and agricultural improvements in Britain, he did not accept the pessimism of Ricardo and Malthus. According to Senior a rise in quality of life and luxury accumulation created preventive checks to over-population. Like others of the younger generation he emphasized the possibility of accumulation, while Ricardo and Malthus, despite their differences, had both underlined diminishing returns.[173] Senior emphasized that there never had been, and never would be, a situation in which all the checks to population noted by Malthus, other than famine, would not come into play. This was so, first, because it implied a higher state of civilization than had ever existed, and which by its very definition would implement all possible preventive checks necessary to avoid positive checks, and second, because all positive checks such as pestilence, war and famine, were interconnected.[174] Were the capital and skill of the most advanced European nations applied in all the habitable world, then world population might be maintained and even grow five-hundred-fold. Yet despite this optimism, Senior did not regard this as a realistic possibility, or at least not "in the course of centuries, or rather of hundreds of centuries."[175]

Senior did not accept that growth of population per se was an encouraging sign of progress and prosperity. "No plan for social improvement can be complete unless it embrace the means both of increasing the production of wealth and of preventing population from making a proportionate advance."[176] Expressing an opposite view from Malthus, Senior claimed that with the progress of civilization food would increase in a greater ratio than population. Nonetheless, he accepted that unmitigated growth of population was undesirable. Yet, again in contrast with Malthus, he claimed that what induced people to limit propagation was the inclination to better their situation, which was just as emphatic as the inclination to marry and propagate.[177] He emphasized the more optimistic implications of Malthus's assertions. The progress of Europe, and the gradual advance in quality of life, proved that subsistence might be relatively enhanced compared with population. It was therefore possible to concede "that there exists in the human race a natural tendency to advance from barbarism to civilization, and that the means of subsistence are proportionably more abundant in a civilized than in a savage state, and [if] neither of these propositions can be denied, it must follow that there is a natural tendency in subsistence to increase in a greater ratio than population." Things such as knowledge, security of property, freedom in exchange and social mobility, encouraged the growth of subsistence and decreased the rate of population growth, while the opposite occurred mainly from misgovernment, in itself usually a sign of deeper-seated cultural and moral evils, such as superstition, ignorance and lack of freedom of exchange.[178]

As we will see later, Senior regarded greater efficiency, whether in agriculture or manufactures, accompanied by progress and growing population, as a desirable goal. It was good to cultivate a larger stretch of land. More important, however, was to do so as efficiently as possible, thus producing the same quantities on a smaller stretch of land, consequently also saving on transportation costs. Efficiency in cultivating natural resources was related to progress and population. "The productiveness of the soil of a Country in proportion to its population being given, or, in other words, the amount of raw produce and the number of people being ascertained, the smaller the extent of the land from which that amount is obtained the better."[179] Senior's outlook was thus an interesting combination of Enlightenment optimism and Malthusian apprehension. The result was a belief that proper cultural progress might enable overcoming Malthus's law of population.

A very different perspective was provided by Richard Jones, one of the chief Cambridge opponents of the Oriel Noetics, who preferred a more inductive, historically contextualized approach to the study of political economy, to the deductive methodology of Senior and the Oxford political economists. His attempt to orient the study of political economy in this direction did not have a wide influence, even though he was the first major British historical economist. This lack of influence was probably due in large part to the criticism of John Stuart Mill, whom Jones himself criticized from his side. Jones and Malthus, on the other hand, were mutually appreciative of each other's work, even though Malthus thought Jones's criticism of Ricardo and the latter's theory of rent a bit too harsh, if basically correct. Ricardo, as we have seen, was not completely devoid of empirical considerations. Malthus favored Jones as his successor at the East India College. Jones was also praised by Marx. He was a more considerable figure in his own time, but quickly receded to the periphery of history. Nevertheless, his historical methodology makes him quite relevant for our discussion, even though Scottish stadial theory, and conjectural history in general, were incompatible with his preference for relying on facts in making generalizations.[180] For Jones a historical approach meant contextualized and documented economic history, not the theoretical anthropology of conjectural history. Consequently, despite his heavy reliance on historical and anthropological data, Jones utilized stadial terminology only loosely.

Jones disagreed adamantly with Ricardo's views, and to a lesser extent with those of Malthus. Ricardo, he claimed, was excessively hypothetical and lacking a historical perspective, both European and non-European, regarding the development of humanity. Generalized inferences had no place in political-economic discussions, which required knowledge of the varying circumstances, physical and cultural, of different nations. Once this was realized, it became clear that a declining rate of profit was not necessarily accompanied by a decreasing power of industry, or that in nations in which there was a high rent this was accompanied by a decline of agriculture, whereas the opposite was in fact the case, and in such nations there was usually a large population living in plenty. Jones noted how with the different grades of human progress one saw the accumulation of wealth of generations, which led to "a commanding and increasing productive power, whether employed in unfolding the resources of the earth, or in fashioning the material world to their [advancing human societies'] purposes."[181]

He agreed with Malthus's mathematical model of the comparative growth of population and subsistence. Nevertheless, he claimed that Malthus had erred regarding various aspects of the checks to population, errors which affected

Malthus's followers and cast a gloom over the whole subject. Agriculture would not, in Jones's opinion, yield diminishing returns and prevent the supply of subsistence to a growing population. Moreover, any attempt to halt the growth of population was opposed to human nature, and led to an improper attitude of the higher classes toward the laboring class.[182] Interestingly, Jones's and Senior's seeming opposite approaches led them to very similar views on the issue of population vis-à-vis Malthus. Jones claimed that a growing population usually accompanied poverty, while the higher classes tended to multiply to a lesser extent, a fact which disproved Malthus's claim that the deceleration of reproduction was achieved either through misery, vice or moral restraint. The poor procreated despite their misery, and in any event a growing population could be accompanied by wealth and plenty.[183] Jones therefore adhered to a revised version of the Enlightenment optimism about population. Misery, in his opinion, might come as a result of physical conditions, among other things as a consequence of growing population, or natural disasters. Yet as far as the social behavior of human beings was concerned, these negative consequences of population might be mitigated, as revealed by the differing circumstances of various societies in varying stages of progress situated throughout the world. Therefore, claimed Jones, no society was doomed to suffer the evil consequences of growing population so long as it implemented a proper social policy. In such a case, a slowing rate of reproduction would be accompanied by increasing prosperity, by virtue rather than vice.[184]

In Jones's view human beings moderated the rate of their procreation as their culture progressed, when they "subject the animal passions of man to the partial control of motives, aims and habits peculiar to him as a rational being."[185] He was less in disagreement with Malthus than with Ricardo, but compared with both, he retained a more noticeable level of optimism regarding the ability of human beings to control their social and historical destiny. "Man," he wrote, "in his attempts to obtain or fashion to his wants, the material object of his desire, differs from the lower animals principally in this, that his intellect enables him to contrive the means of using the results of his past labor to push the efficiency of his actual exertions beyond the limits of his mere animal powers."[186] Fashioning "the material object of his desire" meant of course first and foremost the use of natural resources, whether for the provision of subsistence, or as raw materials for manufactures. Jones thus clearly evinced how the Enlightenment notion of historical progress, based on cultivating nature, had been subsumed within the outlook of liberal political economy.

While the most significant work in political economy in the early nineteenth century was written in Britain, other countries, as the example of Say clearly demonstrates, also bred a growing interest in the burgeoning new discipline. Among these was also Germany, who was to become, by the end of the century, the closest continental rival of Britain in terms of industrialization, and eventually also militarily. In the first half of the century one particularly original German political economist was Johann Heinrich von Thünen.[187] Enlightenment optimism about material growth was evident, not least in Thünen's famous theory of the isolated state, by which he meant a putative city-state, surrounded by rings, in which the respective distance from the central town determined agricultural production. In a different way from that of the British political economists, his approach shared a belief in progress built on utilizing natural resources, not least land. He claimed that as a country grew in wealth and population, more intensive cultivation became profitable, thus leading ultimately to the adoption of new and improved farming systems.[188]

While not presenting a detailed stadial analysis, Thünen was aware of the differentiation between nomadic and sedentary societies. He claimed that in certain conditions nomadic shepherds had advantages over settled agricultural societies, not least their ability to escape extreme weather conditions, easier labor and greater freedom. Nevertheless, the nomadic lifestyle was inefficient in terms of utilization of land compared with agriculture, and therefore as the world's population would rise, and land became more valuable, it would become untenable.[189] Furthermore, he noted how richer countries tended to have more fertile soil which was more intensively farmed, thus offsetting the advantage poorer countries had in lower wages and rent. Together with greater industriousness, this enabled the richer countries to produce enough for exports. Nevertheless, poor countries, in Thünen's estimation, were capable of improving their soil and making it more fertile.[190] Fertility of soil was not a natural given, but was amenable to human amelioration given proper advancing agricultural systems.

Thünen regarded the improvement of land and the extension of its cultivation, as the best employment of capital a nation could make. This had bearing on the issue of taxation, specifically related to land rent. Accurately computing land rent was, according to Thünen, extremely complicated, since it was based on the fertility and location of a farm, yet also had to take into account farming practices. To ensure that these would become permanent, and encourage agricultural improvements by avoiding excessive taxation, and given the difficulty of computing the proper rent for this purpose, land rent had to remain constant over long periods, since otherwise it ran the risk of becoming the most damaging tax in terms of checking a nation's progress.[191]

Thünen's belief in the progress of humanity led him to reject the notion of a tangible stationary state in terms of realizable historical conditions. While his notion of an isolated state was in itself a model of a stationary state, Thünen was well aware that these conditions were not applicable in the real world. Even when one generation determined a goal, its attainment often required more than the human life span. One of humanity's highest tasks was therefore discovering and harnessing nature's powers for its benefit. Yet this was a slow process, as was its social and economic influence. This was exactly the reason that Thünen ultimately employed the stationary notion of an isolated state, otherwise the flux of human development and progress was difficult to analyze with precision. Like other classical economists he conceived the stationary state as an intangible possibility at some asymptotic point in the far future. What was tangible, however, was the movement forward, the progress of humanity toward this distant goal, based on the utilization of nature, and hence requiring the proper supportive policy, which in its turn required proper political-economic analysis.[192] On this general point his outlook was similar to his British peers.

6 John Stuart Mill and the idea of progress

The era of classical political economy reached its apogee with John Stuart Mill. Mill's famous life story, his relations with his father (also a political economist but of lesser note) and his many intellectual projects, lie mostly outside the confines of the present discussion. Yet his general philosophy of cultural progress has many bearings for this purpose, and for understanding his political economy in general, not least his view of natural resources. Separating the wheat from the chaff is not easy in this respect, but in what follows we will have to assume a basic familiarity with issues such as Mill's utilitarianism, or his liberalism. Readers sometimes forget that despite the modern renown of these aspects of his social and political philosophy, in his own era his *Principles of Political Economy* was not just his lengthiest work, constantly re-edited by the author, but also a highly influential one, the most comprehensive on the subject since Smith's *Wealth of Nations*, and mirroring the influence (and often taking issue with), the major contributions of Malthus, Ricardo and other political economists of the first half of the nineteenth century.[1] A consistent interest in social, political and historical phenomena underlay the discussions in the book. Mill became gradually liberated from the stringent deductive method of his father and of Jeremy Bentham, and, specifically in sociological and political discussions, evinced greater sensitivity to the particular circumstances of different nations and societies.[2]

In his essay "Civilization" Mill, clearly influenced by Alexis de Tocqueville, expressed concern about the negative aspects of modern democratic civilization, mainly the rising influence of the masses at the expense of individual merit and exertion. There were, however, ways to combat this tendency, mainly through changes in public education, and in any event Mill in no way denied that overall, modern civilization, with all its mass vulgarization, was nevertheless superior to previous less advanced stages of historical development.[3] He viewed civilization as the opposite of savagery and barbarism. Civilized countries, primarily in Europe, and particularly Great Britain, had attained more than any other countries the characteristics of civilization, which Mill clearly viewed as a positive achievement much preferable to barbarism. While savages and barbarians lived vagrant lives in small and scattered communities, civilized societies lived in large and sedentary communities, and were more prosperous both in material and social life. "In savage life there is no commerce, no manufactures, no agriculture, or next to none: a country rich in the fruits of agriculture, commerce, and manufactures, we call civilized." Mill here centered primarily on the stadial emphasis of the difference between nomadic and sedentary societies. In civilized countries, in contrast with savage ones, there were more social intercourse, justice and security, enabling more progress of wealth and population.[4] The Essay "Civilization" thus outlined Mill's clear preference of advanced civilization over less advanced societies.

This viewpoint was elaborated in much greater detail in *Principles of Political Economy*. In the Preliminary Remarks to the work, and after he had substantiated the importance of the human command of natural resources, Mill outlined a stadial overview of the development of human civilization. The hunting stage was the one with the greatest poverty evident in human existence. The pastoral stage enabled more progress, together with luxury and inequality of possessions. Openly cognizant of Malthus's view, Mill claimed that at this stage, so long as the growth of population was not too rapid so as to overstep the means of subsistence, progress could continue. In such a situation the growth of population was a source of new power to the community. Thanks to the leisure and the surplus of food, in nomadic societies one witnessed the development of manufacturing, for example of metals and cloths, and even the beginnings of speculative science such as astronomy. Yet the moment the growth of population created a demand for food beyond what nature yielded without human labor, this, in "the spontaneous course of events," led to the next stage of historical development, that of agriculture.[5]

Here Mill digressed somewhat from the traditional stadial claim that agriculture was a clear progress compared to pastoralism. This was progress, yet at least initially it was also accompanied with cultural digression. At first, the amount of labor and technology required for agricultural production reduced the time left for leisure. It also enhanced inequality and exploitation, not least by governments which took over control of surplus agricultural produce. In this manner progress often became dependent on the will of wealthy individuals or sovereigns. Agricultural existence was also precarious. When natural resources were abundant progress was possible. Yet the moment they became scarce people turned either to trade or to conquest, in which case there emerged conquerors (who were the owners of land), and conquered (the laborers who worked the land). This had happened for example in Rome, where, however, the inequality with which a small minority became wealthy, together with economic and social misgovernment, had enervated the Romans and led to their demise.[6] Elsewhere Mill claimed that in a rude stage of society the individual might be more able than in a state of progress, although in the latter state social co-operation enabled unprecedented achievements.[7] Again alluding to stadial observations, he also claimed that modern society no longer suffered from the existential threats which required the social relations of the strong protecting the weak. These might have had their positive side in the past, but no longer in the modern stage of progress, in which most of these dangers no longer existed, and past protectors had become present oppressors.[8] All this had a bearing on Mill's view of agriculture, which no longer seemed to him to enjoy the privileged position it had held in classical political economy, even though he too, as we will see, recognized its importance as the prime source of food production. A nation completely engaged in agriculture could not, however, in his opinion, on that basis alone attain a high degree of civilization.[9]

Mill continued his broad historical survey, noting how the inequality of late Roman times was followed by the inequality of the Middle Ages, when the owners of land lived alongside the serfs who cultivated it. The latter strove to buy their freedom with the small amounts of wealth which they succeeded in accumulating. They became artisans and city-dwelling manufacturers, who gradually joined the ranks of the aristocracy. The situation in medieval Europe was, according to Mill, better than in contemporaneous Asia, still in a pastoral and nomadic stage of development. Therefore it was in Europe that the proper conditions developed for the social and economic progress which led from a feudal society, eventually to the commercial and manufacturing state of modern civilized Europe. In modern Europe there existed a historically unprecedented state of material bounty, due to the equally unprecedented utilization of natural resources in a safe and stable manner, mainly evident in the cultivation of land for the production of food. This supported a large population and also the production of articles other than food, from luxuries to public works, the maintenance of armies and fleets, the establishment of colonies and so forth. This situation was again accompanied, however, by inequality, both as regards the relative wealth of various nations, and regarding the internal distribution of wealth between the various social classes in each country. Beyond this inequality and multifariousness common in the civilized world, all the earlier stages of human development continued to exist simultaneously in various places around the globe.[10]

Mill ended the Preliminary Remarks to the *Principles of Political Economy* with the claim that these remarkable differences between different portions of the human race led to the observation that some of them resulted from natural laws which governed the natural physical world. These laws were not subject to the inquiries of political economy. Yet the condition of nations was also the result of other causes, social, psychological and moral, which were the province of political economy, both as regards the production of wealth (which was not conditioned by physical laws, but by human labor applied to natural resources, as Mill had claimed earlier), and even more so as regards the distribution of wealth. The latter, even more than production, resulted from human institutions. For Mill the actions of human beings were ultimately more important than physical nature. Therefore abundant natural resources became an advantage only under proper social conditions.[11] By outlining the stadial development of the human race based on the utilization of natural resources, with its economic and social consequences, he set the stage for the lengthy discussions in the *Principles of Political Economy*. The description of this historical development also took notice of the rise of inequality, evident in various ways and degrees in different social circumstances. According to Mill, the manner in which this inequality existed and developed was the subject of the inquiry of political economy, and of his own book on this topic. Before proceeding further to examine his views on this subject as they relate to the utilization of nature, we should note that despite all his attention to the amelioration of this inequality, Mill, like his Enlightenment predecessors which so influenced his views on stadial progress and other issues, did not share the blanket criticism of material wealth which Rousseau had outlined. Mill's aim was not to eliminate inequality by eliminating the material progress which created it, but rather to ameliorate this inequality while retaining this progress with all its consequent benefits, many of which were due specifically to the growing utilization of natural resources during the Industrial Revolution.

In a later section of *Principles of Political Economy* Mill outlined in detail his preference for the commercial stage of cultural progress. Commerce, mainly international commerce, had not only economic advantages, but even more so intellectual and moral advantages. Mill elaborated on the general cultural advantages of the earlier, more narrowly defined, concept of comparative advantage outlined by Ricardo and Torrens. The contact between different peoples was advantageous. Adventurous merchants were often the first to civilize barbarians. Furthermore, commercial contact between civilized nations was the prime cause leading to progress. The comparison with other nations awakened the desire for bettering one's own culture. International trade taught that the prosperity of one nation did not come at the expense of the prosperity of another nation. On the contrary, the prosperity of nations was mutually enhancing. International commerce also rapidly made war obsolete. "And it may be said without exaggeration that the great extent and rapid increase of international trade, in being the principal guarantee of the peace of the world, is the great permanent security for the uninterrupted progress of the ideas, the institutions, and the character of the human race."[12] Modern commerce also enabled moderation of the fluctuation of prices, as well as the transportation of food from place to place. Thus, circumstances which in the past would have led to famine, in the modern age led at most to dearth. Thanks to commerce, there was also more general sufficiency than in the past.[13]

Mill saw the utilization of natural resources as a prime influence on historically developing inequalities between nations. The relative degree of productiveness of natural resources (as well as of labor and capital as components of production) explained the varying levels of prosperity of different civilizations, as well as the varying situations of a specific civilization in different eras. Natural advantages included differences in climate, fertility of soil, abundance of mineral productions, and perhaps most important, the maritime situation, which Mill, like Smith, regarded as crucial for enabling advanced commercial progress. It was the maritime situation which enabled maritime transportation and could compensate for disadvantages in other natural resources. This was particularly evident in antique civilizations, which still had not developed technologies which could substitute maritime transportation (Mill here evidently alluded to trains).[14] Even an advantage in this area was not enough, however, since a society needed the cultural ability to take advantage of natural resources through long-term strenuous labor. Outlining his version of the traditional theory of an inverse relation between the natural environment and cultural progress, Mill claimed that societies living in comfortable climates were those, in fact, which tended to repose rather than labor, while societies living in colder and less hospitable climates, worked harder in utilizing natural resources and thus achieving progress. This, according to Mill, was what explained how the northern nations of Europe had gradually become more dominant than those in the south of the continent.[15] The accessibility of natural resources was not in itself a guarantee of economic abundance and progress. No less important was the ability and knowledge how to properly take advantage of these resources. This could be accomplished by using technologies and machines, or, just as significant, by better utilizing these resources through different methods of land cultivation, such as the rotation of crops, improved methods of planting or of plowing and draining, and so forth.[16]

Human beings' growing command of natural resources enhanced the efficiency of human exertion, and thus diminished the cost of production. Moreover, the increasing intercourse between various regions of the globe also improved economic circumstances, lowering the cost of production, or at least the cost of commodities. Mill was clearly supportive of the situation in which Europeans arrived in various colonies, and took advantage of local natural resources in a more technologically efficient manner than the indigenous population. The situation of both the colonizers and the colonized was improved in this case. "The ignorance and misgovernment in which many of the regions most favoured by nature are still groveling, afford work, probably, for many generations before those countries will be raised even to the present level of the most civilized parts of Europe." With the help of migration of labor and capital, colonization, the importation of science and industrial technology to the colonies, and generally with the help of free trade, the utilization of untapped natural resources around the world would become possible, for the benefit of both Europeans and local populations.[17] This was an updated version of Locke's influential agricultural argument. Mill evinced a Eurocentric viewpoint akin to many of his Enlightenment predecessors in claiming that contact with the Europeans would benefit indigenous colonial societies. He was thus a prime representative of the liberal penchant for colonial expansion. While not racist, this approach evinced a clear European chauvinism, based on a view of historical progress which emphasized how the Europeans, properly utilizing their natural resources, had been able to advance in higher culture more than other societies, who would ultimately benefit by being conquered by the Europeans.[18]

Another important condition for progress, and specifically for successful cultivation of natural resources, was security, mainly security of property, mostly against governmental despotism. When despotism was prevalent there was no incentive to work, which explained the poverty of many Asiatic nations despite their natural fertility. Similarly, in ancient Rome, the government initially had provided defense against external danger, but eventually became despotic. The people consequently stopped willingly working or fighting, and ended up becoming prey to barbaric yet free invaders.[19] Mill also noted that a tendency not to think of the future, thus not encouraging saving, was occasionally evident even in advanced nations, and among certain populations in Europe. In particular he criticized the lack of long-term planning, prevalent among the lower social orders. The desire of accumulation enabled the accumulation of capital and thus enhanced production. This meant thinking of the long term, not just the short-term attention to immediate desires. Such long-term thinking was however less common not just in less developed cultures such as those of hunters, but also in cultures which reached a stage of decline, such as Rome.[20]

Mill's view of progress also included a consistent interest in the issue if population. He agreed with the basic tenets of Malthus's views on population, although regarding most other issues he sided more with Ricardo.[21] Nevertheless, he was more sympathetic to the circumstances of the lower classes than Malthus. He claimed that enhancing the ownership of land among small proprietors did not encourage over-population. On the contrary, it probably had the opposite effect and encouraged frugality, precaution and prudence, as farmers managed their lives and resources with an eye to the future.[22] While outlining his criticism of Irish cottier tenancy, he noted that "A permanent interest in the soil to those who till it, is almost a guarantee for the most unwearied laboriousness: against over-population, though not infallible, it is the best preservative yet known, and where it failed, any other plan would probably fail much more egregiously; the evil would be beyond the reach of merely economic remedies."[23] In other words Mill saw the ownership of land, and of the produce of agricultural labor, as a stimulus for caution and planning for the future. These led to the self-control which ultimately enabled a more moderate rate of births, and thus to a generally better social and economic existence.

Mill acknowledged Ricardo's influence when he discussed how over-population among the laboring class was influenced by wages, and by the aspiration for bettering their living conditions. What determined the condition of the laborers was neither the absolute amount of accumulation or production, nor the amount of funds destined for distribution among the laborers, but rather the proportion between those funds and the number of those among whom they were shared. The only way to ameliorate the condition of the laborers was to alter this proportion in their favor. The implication, of course, was that over-population would harm them because the share of each individual would be smaller. A population could grow in places where advanced civilization existed alongside wide unoccupied tracts of land, such as Australia, America and in new colonies. Conversely, sometimes an unusual investment in a particular industry occurred in Europe, for example in cotton manufacture, in which case the laborers in this particular industry could multiply without their situation worsening. Yet such cases, according to Mill, were rare and transitory, and in most instances over-population would be halted due to either the positive or preventive checks outlined by Malthus.[24]

Only in unoccupied countries colonized by a civilized people, such as in the United States, was fertile land available for cultivation. In Europe, on the other hand, for centuries agricultural improvements only enabled cultivating land of lesser and lesser quality, while the growing population applied continuous pressure to continue this process. "Agricultural improvement may thus be considered to be not so much a counterforce conflicting with increase of population, as a partial relaxation of the bonds which confine that increase." A principal effect of a growing population was that the economic improvement of a society consisting of laborers, capitalists and landlords, tended to benefit and enrich the latter. Agricultural improvements counteracted this only temporarily, because the growth of population tended to transfer all the ensuing benefits of these improvements solely to the landlords.[25] Mill's analysis aimed at understanding the conditions of production which led to progress in order to create a more just and efficient social reality.

One outcome of this was a Malthusian social theory of population more sensitive to the contingencies of the laboring class than that of Malthus. Mill seems to have struggled with the harsher conclusions of the Malthusian thesis with which he basically agreed. He claimed that production resulted from the combination of labor, capital and natural agents. Increase of labor meant increase in population. Mill's view of population was clearly based on Malthus. Like the latter, he favored encouraging the laboring class to multiply in a lesser and more controlled manner.[26] In addition to supporting Malthus's claim for the need to implement a policy encouraging the lower laboring classes to limit their rate of procreation, Mill emphasized in particular the amelioration of the ideas and habits of the poor.[27] When a nation assisted its poor laborers it also had the right to demand that they not proliferate as long as they were unable to make an adequate living. Otherwise the government needed to impose the necessary self-restraint. In discussing this point he constantly connected this type of self-restraint, and the raising of wages, with the improvement of the living conditions of agricultural laborers, and the encouragement offered them to curb their procreation.[28] Mill used a stadial framework in outlining the need to curb the growth of population.

> So long as mankind remained in a semi-barbarous state, with the indolence and the few wants of a savage, it probably was not desirable that population should be restrained; the pressure of physical want may have been a necessary stimulus, in that stage of the human mind, to the exertion of labour and ingenuity required for accomplishing that greatest of all past changes in human modes of existence, by which industrial life attained predominance over the hunting, the pastoral, and the military or predatory state. Want, in that age of the world, had its uses, as even slavery had; and there may be corners of the earth where those uses are not yet superseded, though they might easily be so were a helping hand held out by more civilized communities. But in Europe the time, if it ever existed, is long past, when a life of privation had the smallest tendency to make men either better workmen or more civilized beings.[29]

It was therefore preferable that the condition of European agricultural laborers would be improved by raising their wages, and this required that their numbers would diminish. In other words, Mill regarded over-population as a problem unique to advanced civilization. In less advanced stages of society a growing number of people was in fact an important requirement for progress. While further discussing the need to add restraint of procreation to the life of an advanced civilization, Mill noted that "Poverty, like most social evils, exists because men follow their brute instincts without due consideration. But society is possible, precisely because man is not necessarily a brute. Civilization in every one of its aspects is a struggle against the animal instincts. Over some even of the strongest of them, it has shown itself capable of acquiring abundant control. It has artificialized large portions of mankind to such an extent, that of many of their most natural inclinations they have scarcely a vestige or a remembrance left." This was a positive historical development, to which control of the growth of population had to be added.[30] For Mill civilization thus meant the overcoming not only of external nature but also of humanity's internal animal nature. The historical process of civilization was accompanied by social and moral progress not only in the material sphere. Economic development and social and moral improvements were all intertwined.

Mill was more optimistic than Malthus regarding the possibility that control of the growth of population was achievable. This depended on changing public norms so that these were accepted among the laboring class. In order that this might happen, however, improvement in education was required. Improving women's civic situation was also necessary. It was they, after all, who shouldered most of the effort associated with the growth of population. In order for all this to happen it was vital to alleviate the poverty of the laboring class for at least one generation, and this in turn again required limiting the size of population so that wages might be raised. This in turn could be achieved either by emigration or colonization, or by distributing common tracts of land among the laborers so that there would be many small proprietors. The fact that improvements in transportation made emigration easier and more common created an opportunity for Great Britain, which Mill advocated taking advantage of.[31] The importation of food, or emigration and colonization, might alleviate or even halt the need for limiting population, if only temporarily.[32] The existence of unoccupied land, whether in Britain or elsewhere, became for Mill a precondition for diminishing the rate of the growth of population. Yet it was clear that this logic had its limit. It implied that unoccupied land, if it was not utilized effectively for this purpose, would eventually become scarce outside of Europe as it was within it. Then British society would face the positive checks to population outlined by Malthus, whose outlook on this topic Mill defended against Malthus's critics.

Great Britain, he claimed, no longer depended on the fertility of its own land, but on the soil of the whole world (particularly the United States), from which food of all kinds was imported. Yet if the British population would continue increasing rapidly, some of its inhabitants would need to emigrate, so they could produce the necessary food to support those remaining behind. It was also necessary to send capital for investment to the colonies, to support the production destined to be sent back to Britain. In an advanced country such as Britain, as improvements in production multiplied, and as more capital emigrated to support the cultivation of natural resources in the colonies, this tended to support the growth of gross produce and the demand for labor in the mother country itself, though only so long as the growth of population was not excessive.[33] In other words, the growth of population, and of a national economy in general, required an outlet which would enable the importation of food on the one hand, and the exportation of capital and of labor on the other. Yet an excessively growing population would overstep such a healthy and balanced economic situation.

As we have seen, Malthus was not as pessimistic as is often claimed. Yet Mill was even more of an optimist, if a cautious one. He was optimistic that the growth of population would never be greater than the increase of production, yet he was cautious in noting that this danger could not be completely disregarded. Although the chance of this happening was remote, in such a case the high and middle classes would experience advancement in their situation, while most of the lower laboring class would grow in numbers without improving their material circumstances.[34] Mill was also cautiously optimistic when he claimed that nations recovered quickly from the devastation resulting from war or natural disasters, as long as their population was not seriously affected. Everything else which was ruined would in any case have perished in some manner in a short time. Yet as long as there were enough people capable of working, and these had sufficient food, they would be able to produce again most of what had seemingly been lost. Any period of privation in such a situation would be relatively short.[35]

Mill's optimism regarding population and natural resources was not unbounded. More in line with Malthus, he cautioned against the dangers of over-population, claiming that the rate of improvement of a civilization in general, and its utilization of natural agencies in particular, might enable either a larger population, or conversely a better quality of life for the existing population. However, eventually, the population would reach a stage where a diminished quality of life would become inevitable, and the production of food would become insufficient. At that point any further growth of population would be halted by death.[36] This brings us to the issue of his view of a stationary state. The situation of increasing wealth, according to Mill, was not indefinite, and humanity tended toward a stationary state postponed only by improvements in production, and the sending of capital to the less cultivated regions of the earth. Relying on Malthus, Mill claimed that even advanced countries needed to curb their growing populations. It was precisely a state of economic advancement which gave the lower classes an unjustified sense that they had sufficient labor, and could therefore afford to procreate. In effect, Mill advocated a state of moderate economic growth, which was the healthiest option. "Indeed, even now, the countries in which the greatest prudence is manifested in the regulating of population, are often those in which capital increases least rapidly."[37] There is a sense that Mill was already evincing what would become the modern attempt to balance economic equilibrium with a sustained but moderate and controlled economic growth. Yet Mill went even further. He claimed that in contrast with many other political economists, he regarded the stationary state as preferable to growth, precisely in advanced countries. The mere increase of production and accumulation was not in itself sufficient, if it only led to the unhampered enrichment of the middle and upper classes, while what was truly necessary was the amelioration of the lower classes' circumstances. Furthermore, not just the increase of production was important, but also, and even more, the improved distribution and large remuneration of labor. "It is only in the backward countries of the world that increased production is still an important object: in those most advanced, what is economically needed is a better distribution, of which one indispensable means is a stricter restraint on population."[38]

Furthermore, there was an even more general reason for moderating the growth of population – even if it could continue growing, what was required was not just to live at the physical level, but also to improve the quality of life. "The density of population necessary to enable mankind to obtain, in the greatest degree, all the advantages both of co-operation and of social intercourse, has, in all the most populous countries, been attained." A stationary state of population and capital did not mean a stationary improvement of humanity. On the contrary, in a state in which population did not increase, "when minds ceased to be engrossed by the art of getting on," then an improvement in quality of life became possible. Industrial improvements would then not just increase wealth while the laborers continued living in drudgery and imprisonment, but would contribute to the more legitimate cause of abridging labor. Mill claimed that till his own era technological innovations had only contributed to enhancing the comforts of the middle class; they had not improved the destiny of humanity in general, as they could and should have. "Only when, in addition to just institutions, the increase of mankind shall be under the deliberate guidance of judicious foresight, can the conquests made from the powers of nature by the intellect and energy of scientific discoveries, become the common property of the species, and the means of improving and elevating the universal lot."[39]

Nevertheless, there was also a tangible sense in which the finiteness of nature posed a limit, even if remote, to the growth of humanity. According to Mill's famous observation, the laws of production, in contrast with the laws of distribution, where akin to the physical laws of nature, and as such could not be averted.[40] Consequently nature posed a clear limit, even if very distant and veritably intangible, to the growth of human population, no matter how much utilization of nature might be enhanced. This limit posed by nature to population was evident not least in agricultural production. Agricultural produce belonged to the group of commodities whose value was determined by the difficulty of attainment, and which could be produced in increasing quantities only at increasing price. These commodities included not just agricultural produce, but in fact "generally all the rude produce of the earth." Mines and fisheries also belonged to this group, and in fact there was a greater chance of their becoming scarce than land. This situation enhanced the need to pay rent, and was further reason, according to Mill, for the need to limit the size of population.[41] Despite their similarity as resources, Mill perceived a difference between agriculture and mining (as well as fisheries to a certain extent), since coal and metals were more limited than agricultural land and more prone to the law of diminishing returns. On the other hand, however, they were also more receptive to technological improvements than agriculture, as well as to the discovery of new deposits. Therefore regarding mining, Mill was as optimistic as Smith had been before him.[42] He claimed that with increasing progress the cost of manufactured articles tended to decrease, while the cost of the products of agriculture and mining tended to rise. This was due to the growth of population, which increased the demand for food and agricultural produce, as well as for exhaustible natural resources such as coal and most metals. Only rarely were general progress and a growth of population accompanied by decreasing prices of agricultural produce. This occurred when improvements in agricultural production were sufficient, a situation which Mill perceived in contemporaneous Great Britain. Conversely, the situation in France exemplified another option to attain the same goal – a prudent control of the growth of population.[43]

Clearly evincing his debt to Ricardo's theory of rent, Mill noted that the price of agricultural food production was dependent either on the productiveness of the least fertile land, or on the least productively employed portion of capital devoted to agriculture. This also determined the wages of agricultural laborers. What encouraged cultivation in this downward course of lessening quality of land, was the pressure of a growing population, while the counter-force which checked this descent was scientific agricultural improvements, which enabled a more efficient production of food. "The costliness of the most costly part of the produce of cultivation, is an exact expression of the state, at any given moment, of the race which population and agricultural skill are always running against each other."[44] This meant that in certain circumstances, a growing population could serve as a spur to economic progress, assuming, of course, that the rate of population growth did not exceed the point at which the poverty of the laboring class became excessive. Nevertheless, as the need to cultivate less and less fertile land raised the cost of rent, any improvement of the laborers' condition due to agricultural innovations had only a temporary influence. Eventually, such improvement would become an inducement for new procreation, unless such agricultural innovations were also accompanied by changes in the laborers' lifestyle.[45]

There were two types of improvements in agricultural production – that which enabled cultivating the same amount of produce on the same size of land at a lesser cost and with less labor; or that which enabled cultivating more produce on the same land yet with less labor. In the latter case, assuming there was no demand for more produce, it was possible to dispense with using the less fertile tracts of cultivated land. Thus, according to Mill, agricultural improvements tended to lower the landlords' profits from rent. He criticized those who had opposed Ricardo's similar claim. Yet Mill claimed that this situation occurred only when such agricultural improvements were sudden, while in reality they were usually slow in appearing, and therefore usually did not lower rent.[46] When agricultural improvements advanced more quickly than the growth of population, the situation of the laborers also improved. Yet in reality this was uncommon. Inventions and discoveries also tended to happen sporadically, while population and capital rose almost perpetually. Thus, agricultural advances only rarely lowered rent or raised profits. "Population almost everywhere treads close on the heels of agricultural improvement, and effaces its effects as fast as they are produced." Such improvement only seldom cheapened food, and only prevented food from growing dearer. It also rarely threw land out of cultivation, and usually simply enabled worse and worse land to be cultivated to answer an increasing demand.[47] This points to a significant aspect of Mill's thought – he regarded increased utilization of natural resources as unbeneficial, and occasionally even damaging, if not accompanied by a comparable improvement in social relations. The fruits of the cultivation of nature needed to enter the political-economic fabric in a controlled, equitable and morally consistent manner. This was the true path to making nature serve humanity.

Assuming this goal was attained, Mill, again, was less pessimistic than Malthus regarding the actual chance that nature would indeed be incapable to support a growing population. While repeating his support for Ricardo's theory of rent, Mill claimed that a situation in which a country would be completely populated, and all the cultivable land occupied, was impossible in practicable terms, except perhaps on a small and secluded island. "But this state of things never can have really existed anywhere, unless possibly in some island cut off from the rest of the world; nor is there any danger whatever that it should exist. It certainly exists in no known region at present… In all countries of any extent there is more cultivable land than is yet cultivated; and while there is any such surplus, it is the same thing, so far as that quality of land is concerned, as if there were an infinite quantity."[48] Like Malthus, the island model represented for Mill an abstract model rather than a tangible reality. While he perceived a clear *social* danger in the existence of a large population of poor, on a broader level he did not think there was a true danger for the over-population of a large country, or indeed of a country of any size not completely secluded from the rest of the world. By implication, indeed, this pertained to the whole earth itself. Land, as well as other natural resources, were, in practical terms, unlimited in quantity. There would always be enough land for producing food, even though in many cases the most fertile land would be insufficient for supporting the existing population, and land of lesser and lesser quality would have to be cultivated. The implication of Mill's approach was clear – in purely practical terms, and disregarding (as he did not) the social question of quality of life, nature was capable, with the proper cultivation, of producing food for a practically unlimited quantity of human population. Any theoretical point at which the physical, not social, limit to population would be met, would be asymptotically reached only at some intangible stage in the future. There was no limit to how much human beings could utilize natural resources, which in practical terms were infinite. Nature was capable of accommodating any amount of population and of cultivation. The only practical limit to such utilization was the amount of effort required for cultivating natural resources, and mainly land, of a lesser and lesser quality. This was a social-economic, not a physical-natural, limit, beyond which the population lived in intolerable poverty. Yet in principal, like his even more optimistic predecessors prior to Malthus, Mill regarded nature as an unlimited resource open to human use. In this way, combining a mitigated version of Malthus's population theory with Ricardo's theory of rent, Mill arrived at a cautiously optimistic assessment of the ability of *properly managed* products derived from natural-resource cultivation, to sustain growth and progress.

He continued elaborating this point when he claimed that the situation in which natural resources were truly limited in quantity, and sold at a scarcity value, was an eventuality which "never is, nor has been, nor can be, a permanent condition of any of the great rent-yielding commodities: unless through their approaching exhaustion, if they are mineral products (coal for example), or through an increase of population, continuing after a further increase of production becomes impossible: a contingency, which the almost inevitable progress of human culture and improvement in the long interval which has first to elapse, forbids us to consider as probable."[49] The cultural progress of humanity was an overriding goal which could not, and should not, be hampered by any consideration of limiting the utilization of nature. In Mill's thought there was no recognition of the dialectical tension between progress and the finiteness of natural resources, which has become in our time a mainstay of environmental thinking. However, as we will see later on, he found other reasons for putting a limit to growth and the use of natural resources.

All of this was embedded in a general philosophy of history. The Enlightenment's influence on Mill's thinking went beyond the adherence to stadial conceptions, and included a more general adherence to a progressive outlook on the steady advance of human civilization, even if Mill's and his generation's viewpoint was more circumspect than their pre-revolutionary eighteenth-century predecessors. Mill viewed the human race as living not in a static state, but rather in one of constant progressive change. He claimed that "the economical condition of mankind" is "liable to change, and indeed (in the more advanced portions of the race, and in all regions to which their influence reaches) as at all times undergoing progressive change." Mill was interested in the laws underlining these changes. He wanted to inquire not only into the equilibrium of the various economic components such as production, distribution and exchange (the "statics" of political economy), but also to add to this an examination of the "dynamics" of political economy. The change which, in his view, indisputably happened in all advanced countries and their spheres of influence, was a progress in wealth, principally in material prosperity. "All the nations which we are accustomed to call civilized, increase gradually in production and in population: and there is no reason to doubt, that not only these nations will for some time continue so to increase, but that most of the other nations of the world, including some not yet founded, will successively enter upon the same career."[50]

Among the reasons for Mill's optimism regarding seemingly unending progress, he noted the increased security of person and property, and the growing co-operation in human society. Yet even before these two points, he emphasized the tendency of the progress of society toward increased command over the powers of nature, which specifically influenced economic production. In this context he wrote of "the perpetual, and so far as human foresight can extend, the unlimited, growth of man's power over nature." Scientific progress, which rapidly advanced in various directions, justified "the belief that our acquaintance with nature is still almost in its infancy." Scientific knowledge remained not only in the theoretical realm, but was increasingly applied practically and technologically for the welfare of the human race. "This increasing physical knowledge is now, too, more rapidly than at any former period, converted, by practical ingenuity, into physical power." A prime example of this was the invention of the electro-magnetic telegraph, which Mill considered as an almost magical application of a scientific theory to a marvelous modern invention. Furthermore, increasing theoretical and intellectual progress in science was also accompanied by progress in manual abilities. This meant that there were more and more manual laborers with the required delicate skill necessary for applying scientific knowledge to practical purposes. Therefore, "it is impossible not to look forward to a vast multiplication and long succession of contrivances for economizing labour and increasing its produce; and to an ever wider diffusion of the use and benefit of those contrivances."[51]

Like Malthus, Ricardo and other classical political economists before him, Mill clearly demonstrated that he was a heir to the Enlightenment, not just in his reliance on stadial theory, but more generally in his belief in social and cultural progress based on material progress. This progress in its turn relied on increasingly efficient utilization of natural resources, the outcome of advancing science and technology, all of this ultimately resting on the social and political progress resulting from education and enlightenment. While the nineteenth-century viewpoint was more circumspect than that of the previous century, nascent modern liberalism was clearly a self-conscious continuation of the Enlightenment. One of the main expressions of this historical continuity was the transmutation of the Enlightenment's philosophy of history into the basic tenets of the burgeoning new discipline of political economy. The analysis of Enlightenment historiography became the basis for the prescriptions of liberal political economy. The great pioneer in this respect was Adam Smith, but this intellectual endeavor was to become a central component of classical political economy, culminating in the comprehensive social-political philosophy of Mill. What remains now is to see how these political-economic prescriptions outlined in detail the manner in which proper policies could enhance the utilization of natural resources, and thus cultural progress in general.

Part III

Managing the use of nature

7 Managing nature in the Enlightenment

The philosophical underpinning of classical political economy was based on the Enlightenment notion of historical progress, fueled by a proper material basis. Yet political economists, qua political economists, were concerned with the specific policies which were aimed at advancing this material basis, specifically in enhancing the use of natural resources which stood at its core. In treating this topic they went into great detail, which from a modern perspective often seems abstruse. Yet despite the lackluster nature of these discussions, without entering at least into their basic claims, no proper understanding of the rise of the modern economic consideration of nature is possible. One might speak here of an "economization" of nature, of the manner in which nature was transformed into an economic commodity, with both good and bad, yet almost always far-reaching, consequences.

Relatively little attention has been devoted to this topic in modern scholarship. Regarding the eighteenth-century sources of classical political economy, Fredrik Jonsson has depicted two rival approaches toward natural resources – one, the classical liberalism of Hume, Smith and their followers, which regarded the natural world as a model of self-regulation for markets, and conversely, the market as the best means for managing the balance of nature; the other, what Jonsson terms "civil cameralism," evident in the view of natural historians, landowners and agricultural improvers, which regarded the natural order as too fragile to be left unregulated, and therefore aimed at careful management of population and conservation of natural resources so as to attain social harmony. Both approaches regarded the state as responsible for appropriate policies regarding natural resource cultivation. The clash between these two approaches led to differing models of colonial development, and also contributed to the social disaster of the Scottish Highlands in the nineteenth century. Jonsson centers on the example of Scotland, noting how in the eighteenth century there were already emerging notions of long-term natural resource management, with increasing awareness of the finitude of natural resources. His dichotomic approach to late Enlightenment attitudes toward nature is intriguing and consummately developed, but at the ideological level tends to gloss over the conceptual anthropocentric similarity of both approaches.[1] Like most historians he tends to look for moments of change and disruption rather than continuity. Ultimately, at the practical level, both the approaches he depicts aimed at essentially the same goal – maximizing the efficiency of the use of nature.

A similar observation can be made regarding Margaret Schabas's important survey of economic attitudes toward nature. Schabas claims that in the eighteenth-century the economy was perceived as part of the natural order and subject to the laws of nature, but that by the mid-nineteenth century the economic outlook had undergone a denaturalization process, and economics was perceived as following the human and social order, and much less subject to the physical natural world. In early classical economics nature posed physical constraints to human progress, and while the conquest of nature was already perceived as a viable goal, human agency was still subordinated to nature. In Mill, which Schabas depicts as a transitional figure in this respect, human beings became almost completely responsible for their destiny, although wealth was still bounded. Subsequently, according to the new, modern outlook, the natural, material world, no longer constrained the material progress of humanity, which seemed to have acquired an unlimited ability for expansion. During the second half of the nineteenth century economists ceased to discuss natural resources, specifically land, and concentrated more on individual human deliberation. In contrast with the eighteenth-century outlook, by the second half of the nineteenth century change was perceived as resulting from independence from nature, and the economy was subject to human control. The modern concept of an economy, according to Schabas, is therefore a post-Enlightenment one.[2] This is in contrast to the position developed here, which sees classical political economy, including Mill, as continuing, mutatis mutandis, the Enlightenment approach to natural resources. In neoclassical economics toward the end of the nineteenth century land may indeed have received relatively less attention than before. Yet other natural resources such as coal, which became more important during the industrial age, received proportionally more attention. Furthermore, as we will see, natural resources other than land were not totally ignored before the nineteenth century. Natural resources in general, in other words, continued to be viewed in basically the same fashion in the transition from classical to neoclassical political economy. Schabas describes the era of classical political economy, specifically Mill, as witnessing an almost paradigmatic shift in economic considerations of nature. Yet while change no doubt occurred, it was more a matter of intensification of the basic anthropocentric consideration of the natural world as a resource meant for human use, underlining economic progress, and ultimately cultural progress in general. The changes in economic thought that did occur in this respect were basically concerned with how to enhance the use of natural resources and make it more efficient. Yet the basic consideration of nature as such a resource was evident before, during and after the era of classical political economy. The history of economic thought has been remarkably consistent in this respect. Practically no counterexamples exist to this predominant phenomenon before modern ecological economics, which, as we will see later, has indicatively been considered irrelevant by most mainstream economists.

Hume and Verri

In the eighteenth century the political-economic approach to natural resources was evident even before Smith's detailed analyses. Hume was a prominent and particularly influential example.[3] "Nature," he claimed, "by giving a diversity of geniuses, climates, and soils, to different nations, has secured their mutual intercourse and commerce, as long as they all remain industrious and civilized."[4] In other words, so long as societies were engaged in production, nature supported their cultural progress. The advance of nations in arts was mutual, aided by trade, and not one at the expense of the other. Commercial nations were most often those which did not possess wide tracts of fertile land, and thus were disadvantaged in terms of their natural conditions. Exceptions to this were Holland, England and France.[5] The only nations which had to worry over the progress of their neighbors were commercial nations such as Holland, which not only did not have extensive lands or native commodities, but also subsisted mainly as brokers for other nations. Yet even these, with proper management, could avoid for a long time a situation in which their brokering capacity ceased to be needed.[6] The existence of various nations side by side and trading with each other, supported the development of arts and sciences. In small nations government was usually on a small scale and thus less likely to deteriorate to tyranny. Commerce thus promoted mutual emulation. Among all the regions of the globe Europe, and especially Greece, was the one most broken by seas, rivers and mountains. Therefore, it was there that one encountered several distinct governments, and where the sciences had emerged.[7]

Hume did not deny the significance of agriculture, but saw it as interconnected with other types of production and economic activity. Discussing the social usefulness of moderate luxury, he claimed that in rude nations the arts were neglected and all efforts were devoted to agriculture, with society being divided into tyrannical vassals and oppressed tenants. Yet when luxury encouraged commerce and industry, the farmers, by a proper cultivation of the land, became rich, and the merchants acquired political authority which in their hands became the basis of liberty. In other words, a nation living only on agriculture was likely to lack political liberty.[8] This was a very different perspective from that of Hume's contemporaries the Physiocrats. Hume claimed that agriculture was the underpinning of the general economic welfare of society. More advanced forms of material affluence depended on agriculture, yet in their turn enforced and improved its practitioners. In certain historical instances, for example ancient Sparta and Rome, improvements in agriculture created a superfluity, which instead of maintaining traders and manufacturers, made them available for military service. Such a policy was however inapplicable in modern nations. In these, when manufactures and the mechanical arts were not developed, agricultural laborers had no incentive to produce beyond a basic level, which resulted in the prevalence of indolence and in a limited cultivation of the land. Eventually this also resulted in limited military abilities. On the other hand, when agricultural labor was improved, the resultant superfluity enabled the development of manufactures and eventually a better military.[9]

Hume did not deny the significance of agriculture as the basic source of subsistence, but it was best supported in conjunction with manufactures and commerce. "Every thing useful to the life of man arises from the ground; but few things arise in that condition which is requisite to render them useful." Therefore, in addition to farmers and landlords, society also needed artisans who would work the natural materials, and, at a more advanced stage of progress, merchants who would connect the inhabitants of different regions who manufactured different commodities and needed to trade with each other.[10] Agriculture was the most important underpinning for the growth of population, yet although it might thrive occasionally without manufactures and commerce, with them it would thrive even more. In such better conditions farmers would have a larger market for their produce.[11] The existence of adjacent manufactures was a reason for farmers to enhance their production so that they would have more to trade with. On the other hand, without manufactures they lacked such an incentive. Only the existence of manufactures prompted the production of surplus, leading to greater progress and fortitude. More manufactures meant that agricultural labor also became more remunerative.[12] Hume regarded a free market, both domestic and international, as the best means to assure economic growth based on enhanced utilization of natural resources.

This was also the perspective of Pietro Verri, who noted how commerce and agriculture were mutually supportive, in a process in which growing wants enhanced agricultural production. Verri's outlook was however less radical than Hume's. He criticized the Physiocrats despite agreeing with them on certain points, claiming that manufacturers were not sterile as they had claimed. The whole process of production, whether natural or man-made, was in fact not an act of creation but rather of the transformation of matter. In this respect both agricultural production and manufactures were identical as forms of production. In addition, it was more difficult to create a surplus in agriculture compared with manufactures, and therefore it was easier for the manufacturers to improve their wealth and standing than it was for farmers.[13]

Verri was concerned with creating the best conditions for enhancing agricultural production. He claimed that when ownership of the land was concentrated in the hands of a small section of the population, and the landowners owned large tracts of land, they would tend not to cultivate and improve the land beyond their personal needs. Their tenants would likewise disregard what happened to the land in the long run; it might become barren, but they would be interested in maximizing agricultural yields in the short term. It was therefore preferable that ownership of land would be distributed among as many owners as possible, and then long-term improvements in agricultural production and the quality of the land would ensue. Furthermore, those laboring on the land were more connected to their country, and were more involved in the preservation of the state, which also made a plurality of landowners preferable.[14] Verri approved of freedom in the grain trade, a position more in line with the Physiocrats and Turgot than with his compatriot Galiani. Lack of such freedom, he claimed, resulted in monopolies and the possible rise of prices, and in Italy it also led to the unjust situation in which poor farmers, despite their hard work, had no hope of improving their situation.[15] Like classical political economists later, he searched for a means to ameliorate both production and social inequity. Among his other suggestions for improving agricultural production, and the prosperity of the state in general, he also claimed that when the rate of interest was lowered, and there was more money in circulation, then in an industrious country this would lead to the improvement of land and agriculture, as well as to embarking on great projects of agriculture and trade such as draining swamplands, diverting rivers and digging canals.[16]

Verri regarded agriculture as the truest form of wealth. He claimed that a basic rule of economics was that equations of addition were always successful, while equations of subtraction were always detrimental. It was therefore necessary always to seek for maximum action leading to maximum effect. This meant always preferring the types of agricultural cultivation which most augmented production, and employed the greatest number of laborers. When landowners, aiming to lower costs, did not choose such a course of action on their own, their interest collided with the interest of the state.[17] Verri then proceeded and displayed an almost modern type of environmental viewpoint in his consideration of which types of agricultural cultivation and use of land were preferable. He claimed straightforwardly that the type of land cultivation which should always be preferred was the one least detrimental to climatic conditions. Experience in various regions of Italy taught that when marshlands were cultivated by irrigation, this could benefit production. Yet when there was large-scale use of irrigation in lowlands in which rivers were dispersed, this tended, due to the evaporation of water, to create many fogs, hailstorms and unhealthy air, which would lead to a diminishing population. It was therefore necessary to consider such things when choosing the types of land cultivation for different regions. Furthermore, the interests of landowners collided with those of the state when they preferred land cultivation, which enhanced short-term production yet ruined the soil in the long-term, and eventually made it barren. Another important rule in managing land cultivation was to prefer raising basic food products independently of other nations, even at the expense of more profitable yet less necessary crops. For example, sugar was to be cultivated only after sufficient grain had been produced. For various reasons of economic efficiency, Verri also advised that tenants should pay landowners with produce rather than money.[18]

Despite all this he insisted that a state should not enforce all these rules of land cultivation, since coercion only created an atmosphere of intimidation and discouragement of industry. On the other hand, a state could encourage preferred types of land cultivation by such things as proper tax and duties policy. Eventually, the main thing was to encourage those types of cultivation which most consistently enhanced production.[19] In the conditions of a free market combined with cautious encouragement by the state, when production was increased other aspects of the economy would settle appropriately by themselves. Increased production, population growth and enhanced cultivation of the land, were to be achieved not by governmental coercion, but rather by encouragement and the removal of obstacles.[20]

Verri differentiated between encouraging production as much as possible, and maximal possible production. In practical terms it was always possible to encourage production. In agriculture, therefore, as long as there remained land which for some reason was uncultivated, production could be developed to a greater extent. "There is no land which man's work cannot render fertile, therefore it cannot be said of any part of Europe, that agriculture has reached its peak there." In order for that to happen, all the common land would need to be cultivated, while the grasslands and pastures would be cultivated only to the extent necessary for raising those animals required for human existence. Verri continued to demonstrate again a type of quasi-environmental perception of sustainable balance in the policy of land cultivation. He claimed that when more animals were raised than were necessary for providing for the inhabitants (animals raised as raw material for manufactures), this eventually diminished the size of population, since the number of people a state could feed, and the number of animals it fed, were mutually exclusive.[21] Nature was capable of providing the resources necessary for practically unlimited growth. The issue was providing the proper human policy to enable such growth. Verri claimed that nature in itself usually provided sufficient sustenance for all humanity. In most cases it was human misconduct which was responsible for hunger.[22] With all his almost modern type of recognition of environmental aspects related to the cultivation of natural resources, Verri's approach, if compared with modern outlooks, was more akin to a sustainable-development attempt to maximize the utilization of nature, than to anything remotely reminiscent of an appreciation of nature in itself. This was a more updated version of the traditional anthropocentric and instrumental consideration of nature throughout the Western tradition. From the eighteenth century, increasing attention was devoted specifically to the economic aspects of adjusting human institutions and policies to maximize the efficiency of utilizing nature. Classical political economy would elaborate this point even further, culminating in Mill's detailed treatment of this topic.

Adam Smith and natural resources

The first political economist to consider the use of natural resources in detail was Adam Smith. Despite his emphasis on free trade, he regarded the management of natural resources as one of those vital areas in which government intervention was necessary.[23] According to Smith the improvement and cultivation of the country was the greatest of public advantages.[24] The interdependence of all sectors of the socioeconomic fabric was a consistent part of his discussion of the necessary conditions for proper cultivation of nature. Agriculture was particularly important, but also manufactures, commerce and consequently also transportation, which made other types of mastery of nature, not least water navigation, also significant. The more a region was remote from cities, claimed Smith, the more expensive it became to transport surplus produce, and consequently the profit of both farmers and landowners was smaller. The importance of improved transportation resulted from the lowered cost of the produce. This ultimately benefited everyone, both the country and the city, the farmers and the landowners. Improvements of transportation "encourage the cultivation of the remote, which must always be the most extensive, circle of the country."[25] Here Smith was preceding what would become the much more elaborate discussion of spatial economics developed the following century in Johann Heinrich von Thünen's famous theory of the isolated state, surrounded by rings in which agricultural production was determined by their respective distance from the central town.[26] Smith's prescience was such that he often alluded to original ideas which subsequent political economists would address with greater precision.

He noted how the hunting savages of North America habitually cast aside surplus pelts, yet it was trade with the Europeans which had accorded mercantile value to animal skins. Building materials such as timber were more difficult to transport, and consequently, when at times a surplus of them accumulated, they had no economic value unless a way was found to transport them to where they were needed.[27] Without proper transportation, production was a priori limited. Water-carriage opened more extensive markets than land-carriage. Industries improved first near sea-shores or navigable rivers before reaching the inland. The existence of water transportation had facilitated economic development throughout history, for example in ancient Egypt, in India, in China and in Holland. Rivers which did not split into canals, such as the Danube or most of the African rivers, did not, however, benefit international commerce. Therefore Siberia and Tartary, in which the sea froze and rivers were too distant from each other, "seem in all ages of the world to have been in the same barbarous and uncivilized state in which we find them at present." Smith noted the projects for water distribution in ancient India and Egypt. These encouraged population and the fertility of land, yet due to religious superstition both nations feared naval expeditions, and consequently did not develop naval trade.[28] Good roads, canals and navigable rivers, were "the greatest of all improvements," since they encouraged cultivation of remote provinces, whose situation thus became more similar to that of towns.[29] Smith also noted how judicious operations of banking provided "a sort of wagon-way through the air," and thus enabled dispensing with many of the highways in a country, which could then be converted into pastures and agricultural fields, thus augmenting production.[30] Improving both transportation and communication therefore enhanced the cultivation of nature.

The progress of improvement influenced the price of three types of produce – first, that which nature provided in only limited quantities, and which human industry was almost incapable of augmenting, such as birds and rare fish, whose price rose with progress and a growing demand; second, those which industry was able to multiply in proportion to demand, mainly common foodstuffs such as grain and cattle, and whose price rose so long as it was profitable to produce them; and third, those in relation to which the efficiency of industry was limited or uncertain, and whose price was unstable and changed according to various geographical, natural and political circumstances, and varying levels of demand and accessibility, such as wool, hides, fish and various minerals and metals.[31] The natural properties of various products, and their natural amenability to human cultivation and manipulation, therefore determined the economic viability of investing in their production. The policy of European nations altered for the worse the proper course of capital investment – first in agriculture, then in manufactures and finally in foreign commerce.[32] Thus, in addition to the natural qualities of products, it was the level of how much they were indispensable (particularly food) which determined the need to invest in their production. This complemented the stadial progression of civilization, which relied, particularly in the first three stages, on advancing types of food production, reaching advanced commerce only in the fourth and last stage of historical progress.

This pointed the way to Smith's emphasis of agriculture, and the influence of the Physiocrats, even if he rejected their claim that only agriculture could produce a surplus.[33] Smith considered agricultural production as the basis for the economic activity which maintained all other laborers, whether employed in productive or unproductive labor. Agricultural labor in itself was always productive, and every product of the land was the effect of productive labor, except the spontaneous productions of the earth.[34] Agriculture yielded different quantities of produce, depending on the fertility of the soil, while in industry the same effort always yielded the same produce.[35] The more agricultural improvements were implemented, the greater the amount of surplus, and the larger the number of laborers who could be occupied in other employments. On the other hand, the demand for food was limited by the capacity of the human stomach, but the demand for other products and for luxuries had no certain limits, and consequently the division of labor could increase the quantity and variety of such products.[36] Therefore, according to Smith, the improved cultivation of land for food production led to general progress, and ultimately also to higher rent, even on land which produced products other than food. Furthermore, anything which improved the fertility of the land for producing food, improved the value of neighboring barren lands, since it provided a market for their produce, and also enhanced the demand for other products such as metals and precious stones. "Food not only constitutes the principal part of the riches of the world, but it is the abundance of food which gives the principal part of their value to many other sorts of riches." Food, primarily obtained by agricultural production, was thus the source of material prosperity in general.[37]

The significance of agriculture would later also surface in the work of most classical political economists. Even someone not considered as a political economist per se, such as Smith's disciple John Millar, recognized this significance, claiming that agricultural improvements in Britain had tended historically to improve the condition of farmers, whose capital consequently grew, thus enabling them more independence and longer leases.[38] The question for Smith as for subsequent political economists, was how, and to what extent, should government intervene in managing the economy. Free trade meant minimal intervention, but not complete lack of intervention. According to Smith, when it came to the cultivation of natural resources, this intervention indeed had to be minimal. "Had human institutions… never disturbed the natural course of things, the progressive wealth and increase of the towns would, in every political society, be consequential, and in proportion to the improvement and cultivation of the territory or country."[39]

Agriculture, according to Smith, was more efficient than manufactures. In the latter all of the productive labor was human, while in agriculture human effort put in motion the labor of nature, hence the unequaled value of agriculture, which rather than increase the fertility of nature, guided it in the most profitable direction. "Planting and tillage frequently regulate more than they animate the active fertility of nature; and after all their labour, a great part of the work always remains to be done by her." The farmer's servants, and even his cattle, became productive laborers. Agricultural profit enabled rent, which grew with the natural or improved fertility of the land. This made the investment of capital in agriculture the most advantageous investment for society.[40] In the early stage of societal development, when land was in common, the laborer was also the owner of all the natural fruits of the earth. The moment, however, that land became private property, the laborer was required to pay rent for those same fruits which his labor produced. The proprietor provided materials and necessary maintenance usually unaffordable to the laborers.[41] Rent was determined by the combination of the situation of society and the fertility of the land. When the agricultural produce was expensive due to high demand, the price of rent was significantly higher, for example in the case of some French vineyards.[42]

Rent was not in fact proportional to what the landowners could afford to demand, or the improvements they made, or often did not make, to the land, but rather only to the farmers' ability to pay. Smith therefore implicitly criticized the system of rent precisely due to its lack of incentive for improving land. However, in almost every situation land would create a surplus produce, and would thus enable rent.[43] Nevertheless, better agricultural production meant higher rent. The more the proprietor of land invested in its improvement and cultivation, the higher the rent he received. The more labor, however, that the cultivation of the land required, the more profit was due to the farmer. Smith did not regard both these propositions as mutually exclusive. On the contrary, he implied that the same land could at the same time be improved by the proprietor, and better cultivated by the farmer.[44] Furthermore, as long as the difference between profit on the interest for lending money, and profit from rent on land, remained relatively small in favor of the former, people would prefer to invest in the latter, since investing in land had a superior security which made a smaller profit, at least up to a point, more attractive. This was also true in relation to investment in trade.[45]

Both country and city supplied markets for each other's products and were mutually interdependent. Yet subsistence was more important than other products, and therefore cultivating land preceded the development of cities, which relied on agricultural surplus as their source of subsistence. Country life, in addition, was also attractive due to its charm and the beauty of the countryside, "and as to cultivate the ground was the original destination of man, so in every stage of his existence he seems to retain a predilection for this primitive employment."[46] Labor in husbandry also required more effort and intelligence than urban manufactures. On the other hand, urban laborers found it easier to unite in corporations, and furthermore, regulations such as duties were preferential to their interests. Therefore, trade between the city and the country, which should have been on an equal basis, tended to favor the city. While country laborers were mentally superior, this meant that in reality there situation was worse than that of urban laborers, and they were consequently unjustly scorned. The situation in England had improved in this respect according to Smith. Nevertheless, he claimed that the situation in Europe, whereby agricultural improvements were the result of the overflowing of stock originally accumulated in towns, was unstable, uncertain and slow, as well as contrary to reason and the order of nature.[47]

Despite the superior qualities of agriculture, manufactures also had their advantages. In manufactures the division of labor was more effective than in agriculture, thus enhancing the amelioration of production to a greater degree. Furthermore, manufacturing nations had a greater ability to export rude agricultural produce in exchange for manufactured commodities, thus enabling more subsistence for their inhabitants compared with agricultural nations. The latter, on the other hand, were forced to export more agricultural produce in exchange for a lesser amount of manufactured produce, thus losing subsistence.[48] In contrast with agricultural produce, manufactures exhibited more clearly the relation between lowered prices and progress. In most types of industrial production, particularly the more advanced and sophisticated, so long as there was no shortage of rude materials, progress was accompanied by cheaper production and prices.[49] For Smith, manufactures were on the one hand less necessary for basic survival and progress, but on the other hand were less restrained by natural circumstances.

In any event agriculture, manufactures and commerce were interconnected. Trade between the country and the city led to mutually enhanced progress. "The greatest and most important branch of the commerce of every nation… is that which is carried on between the inhabitants of the town and those of the country."[50] The mercantilist system preferred city to country labor, manufactures to agriculture, yet in contrast with the intention of its propagators, it often damaged the country it intended to advance, while helping other countries, all due to the nature of international trade, which Smith considered as impossible to halt.[51] On the other hand, in contrast with the Physiocrats, Smith claimed that manufactures were required in the advanced commercial stage of progress. Agriculture and manufactures were mutually enhancing, not exclusive. Agricultural surplus enabled the development of urban manufactures. Towns in their turn created markets for country produce, worked the materials produced by agriculture, and provided stable governance, which was also important to maintain agricultural production. Merchants who became landowners proved to be the best improvers of land, more motivated and better informed than country gentlemen.[52] Regarding the trade between European countries and their colonies, Smith noted that the mother countries found in the colonies markets for their manufactures. At the same time, as producers in the mother country developed, they provided new markets for colonial agriculture. Again in contrast to the Physiocratic perspective, it was counter-productive to prefer agriculture to other employments.[53]

Despite this and other points of criticism, Smith's view of the Physiocrats was generally favorable, in contrast with his detailed condemnation of the mercantilists. In contrast with the latter, the Physiocrats had little influence and were unlikely to cause serious damage. On the other hand, the mercantilists at least advanced manufactures as they intended, while the Physiocrats actually did not encourage agriculture as they desired, since agriculture and manufactures, in contrast with their view, were interdependent. The Physiocratic outlook exaggerated its emphasis on country labor, while the mercantilists, opposed by the Physiocrats, belittled the significance of country as compared with city labor. Smith, though much more supportive of the Physiocratic outlook, therefore emphasized the need for a balanced approach combining both types of labor, and enhancing trade between city and country. What he found more appealing in the Physiocratic doctrine was not its singular eulogy of agriculture, but rather its emphasis on economic liberty.[54] In contrast with Quesnay, however, Smith claimed that economic prosperity was possible even without perfect liberty and justice.[55]

The question of the relative merits of agriculture and manufactures offered a unique perspective on the issue of comparable progress in different nations. Poor countries were capable of achieving agricultural development rivaling that of rich countries. Not so, however, in the field of manufactures. This, because the division of labor more effectively influenced manufactures than agriculture, which meant that rich countries progressed more in the former than the latter.[56] In opulent countries the extent of the market enabled people to live by employment in one trade, but this was not possible in poor countries. Therefore, in countries thinly populated and with insufficiently cultivated land, many people, including farmers and cottagers, engaged in subsistence farming, laboring in various occupations, and were only hired on a seasonal basis to engage in extensive agricultural labor.[57] The merits of agriculture notwithstanding, Smith's stadial outlook meant that without manufactures and commerce no nation could maximize its natural-resource utilization and reach the highest level of civilization. In contrast with the mercantilist position, Smith claimed that a country's wealth was not measured by the amount of gold and silver it possessed, which was determined by arbitrary factors such as the accessibility of mines, but rather by the situation of agriculture and manufactures which resulted from proper government. These were the true measures of progress.[58]

History taught as much. The ruin following the fall of Rome, and the subsequent system of inheriting land according to primogeniture or entails, still evident in some places in Smith's time, had an adverse effect on the cultivation of land both due to lack of incentive for proprietors, as well as lack of motivation for the poor laborers who worked the land under the feudal system. Slavery, or working land as tenants, likewise did not provide an incentive for laborers to improve the land beyond their own needs.[59] The existence, since the Middle Ages, of extensive tracts of land as entails in the hands of proprietors, did not constitute an incentive for ameliorating these lands. This was better achieved when lands were divided into small farms. The proprietors of such small estates proved the most intelligent, industrious and successful improvers of land.[60] Smith claimed that land constituted a stable source of public revenue for countries which had passed the pastoral stage of development. It was better, however, that land would be cultivated by the people as private proprietors rather than by the rulers. Otherwise, this would lead to lower income both in rent and in food consumption, and thus also to diminished population. "[I]n all the great monarchies of Europe there are still many large tracts of land which belong to the crown. They are generally forest; and sometimes forest where, after travelling several miles, you will scarce find a single tree; a mere waste and loss of country in respect both of produce and population." It was possible to mend this loss through the cultivation of land by private owners. This would eventually also enhance the crown's income due to cultivation of those lands the king himself did not cultivate. Smith therefore supported private ownership of land.[61]

Another central topic for Smith was elucidating the best policy for sustaining production, whether in agriculture or other types of labor. This raised considerable social issues. The masters, according to Smith, had more legal power to combine so as to prevent the rise of wages, compared to the lesser ability of the laborers, whom the law prevented from combining to raise wages. Laborers occasionally attempted to achieve this by using what Smith considered shocking violence, though their chances of success were unrealistic. Wages, however, had to be at a level enabling the laborers and their families a minimal existence. The moment there was a shortage of laborers in a certain occupation, wages necessarily rose.[62] Smith already outlined the basic tenets of Ricardo's and Malthus's later theories of wages. He did not appear very sensitive to the plight of poor laborers at this point of his discussion. However, elsewhere he noted that the interests of the wage-earning laborers on the one hand, and the landowners reliant on rent on the other, were both in accordance with the general interest of society. Society also depended on a proper investment of stock, which was necessary for progress, and in itself depended on those investors of capital who lived on profit, mainly merchants and large-scale manufacturers. It was precisely these, however, who often acted in opposition to the general interest of society, and often deceived and oppressed the public.[63] Smith recognized that the strict social division between merchants, manufacturers and farmers, raised social tensions, but also became more flexible in a free economy. The welfare of the laborers was a question both of social justice and of economic efficiency. For example, the more the landowners took upon themselves its cultivation, the more they saved expenses otherwise going to the farmers.[64] In this situation rent was less necessary or advantageous. Furthermore, both landowners and farmers were ill-disposed to a spirit of monopoly, and tended to share knowledge regarding agricultural improvements.[65]

Given the interdependence of agriculture, manufactures and commerce, and the fundamental, if not singular, importance of agricultural production, the question of sustaining this production, as well as promoting agricultural improvements, was one of consistent importance for Smith. The state of agriculture in England, for example, was superior to other countries in large part due to the legal protection of the yeomanry.[66] Another example was the rapid progress of the British colonies in America, which resulted mainly from the fact that almost all the capital there was invested in agriculture rather than manufactures. Smith claimed that if the Americans would cease importing manufactured products from Europe, and divert capital to local industrial production, this would in fact retard their nation's progress.[67] For Smith, one of the best and most profitable long-term uses of fixed capital was in improving land. Yet no such improvement was beneficial without the investment of circulating capital to maintain workers. Other resources such as mines and fisheries required similar investment, yet due to its fundamental importance, the produce of land had more significance in supporting economic activity in general.[68] Improvements in agriculture, though also in manufactures and trade, led to rising wages, as well as lowered prices of foodstuffs and other products. The ensuing improvement in the quality of life of the working class was both just and beneficial for the nation in general.[69]

Smith claimed that it was the cheap price of cattle, poultry and various game, in relation to corn, which demonstrated how much land remained uncultivated, and the limit of a country's civilization and population as it was in the infancy of its progress. Vegetable agricultural products were more important than meat for feeding a population, and were thus more significant as a measure of progress. In other words, the more agricultural products were cheap and accessible due to improved cultivation of land, the more civilized a society was. "The land constitutes by far the greatest, the most important, and the most durable part of the wealth of every extensive country."[70] A nation's wealth, when based on agriculture rather than trade, was also more durable and resistant to military devastation. "The capital… that is acquired to any country by commerce and manufactures, is all a very precarious and uncertain possession, till some part of it has been secured and realized in the cultivation and improvement of its lands."[71] Another aspect of the superiority of agriculture to manufactures, was that importing the latter could damage home industrial production, while importing rude produce of the soil, a costly undertaking in itself, was incapable of seriously impeding local agricultural production.[72]

A country's lands could be completely cultivated and improved, only if the price of the produce raised on them was high enough to cover the expense of these improvements, including rent and farming expenses. The price of the product had to be raised before improvements could be implemented. "Gain is the end of all improvement." No true improvements were accompanied by loss. "If the compleat [*sic*] improvement and cultivation of the country be, as it most certainly is, the greatest of all publick advantages, this rise in the price of all those different sorts of rude produce, instead of being considered as a publick calamity, ought to be regarded as the necessary forerunner and attendant of the greatest of all publick advantages."[73] Smith, as usual critical of the mercantilist outlook, claimed that European policy preferred investment in urban trades to that in agriculture. Therefore there remained many tracts of land in Europe which had still not been cultivated or sufficiently improved, and European agriculture could absorb a much greater capital investment.[74]

Tax policy also needed to be attuned to supporting agriculture. Smith discussed in detail various types of land taxes, emphasizing the need for taxation to encourage land cultivation and improvement, as well as the prosperity of agricultural laborers, the landowners, and the income of the sovereign. It was important that the proprietors of land cultivate some of their lands themselves, since compared with tenants, they had more possibilities to conduct experiments in improving the cultivation of land.[75] A proper tax policy needed to take this into consideration, and avoid excessive or damaging taxation. In countries where there was a personal taille, for example, farmers had no interest to cultivate their land to the best of their ability. On the contrary, they had an incentive to counterfeit poverty. "The publick, the farmer, the landlord, all suffer more or less by this degraded cultivation." This type of tax tended "to discourage cultivation and consequently to dry up the principal source of the wealth of every great country."[76]

A further question of policy which Smith considered in detail in relation to enhancing agricultural production, was the issue of bounties on exportation. Like the Physiocrats, Turgot and Condorcet, he supported free commerce in corn. Governmental intervention in the corn trade was admissible in his view only in dire cases of scarcity and suffering, and usually was inefficient in preventing hunger.[77] Smith opposed bounties on the corn trade, which in his estimation raised the price of grain within the exporting country itself. The price of grain also regulated the price of all other products, and thus raised the price of all home-made commodities.[78] The ability of poor laborers to raise their children was consequently diminished, lowering the size of population, or else it diminished the ability of employers to employ large numbers of laborers, thus restraining the country's industry. Therefore in the long run bounties damaged rather than enhanced the home market of grain as well as the consumption of corn. They also degraded the real value of silver, and were therefore detrimental to the economy in general. The only ones to profit from bounties were the corn merchants. Regarding those working in other occupations, this seemed to raise their wages, while in fact the real, as opposed to the nominal, value of money actually declined.[79] Furthermore, a bounty on the exportation of corn raised its price in years of plenty, but on the other hand hindered the plenty of one year from compensating for the scarcity of another, since it was exported rather than stored. As opposed to corn, however, bounties on other types of manufactures could be beneficial and encourage production. Yet nature had established an essential difference between corn and all other sorts of goods. "The nature of things has stamped upon corn a real value which cannot be altered by merely altering its money price." No bounty could raise the price of corn beyond its true value, and no free trade could lower it below this real value. Corn was the commodity which regulated the real value of all other commodities. Thus, in contrast with other commodities, a bounty on corn exportation was unable to encourage its production.[80] Smith implied that agricultural production could not be encouraged beyond the maximum level enabled by nature, while this could be achieved in manufactures. A natural product such as corn (which meant all types of grain), therefore had both advantages and disadvantages vis-à-vis manufactured commodities. Proper management of the corn trade could prevent famine even in the most unfavorable seasons such as droughts or excessive rain.[81]

In contrast with the trade in corn, Smith was more supportive of bounties to its production, which he thought might encourage production, at least under certain conditions. Yet precisely these types of bounties were those less favored by the mercantilist system.[82] In anything related to the commerce in corn, and in agricultural produce in general, free trade was a veritable panacea. Laws which forced farmers to become corn merchants, for example, prevented them from investing all their capital in agricultural production, and consequently impeded the cultivation of the land. Smith favored the freedom and encouragement of corn trade, both internal and foreign, as the best way to encourage agricultural production, lead to prosperity and prevent dearth and famine both on a national and an international level.[83]

Other types of natural-resource cultivation were, however, a different matter. Because they were often risky economic ventures, they belonged to those essential endeavors, such as education or national defense, which were unattractive for private investors, and required the support of the state. As already noted, public works which facilitated transportation and commerce, mainly roads, bridges, canals and harbors, required improvement supported by public investment. This investment grew with the progress of society, due to a greater volume of transported products. In oppressive societies the rich would occasionally construct such projects for their own benefit, inadvertently helping society in general. In a commercial and free society, however, there would be a correlation between the level of trade and the extent of transportation works. Roads, canals and bridges were obviously erected in locations which were amenable to cultivation in the first place, and close to commercial routes, and not in deserts or near remote rivers. In other words, Smith observed a correlation between natural conditions and the possibility of progress, expressed in the utilization of natural resources.[84]

The utilization of natural resources, mainly in agriculture, but also in other areas such as improvements of transportation routes, was therefore a significant theme in Smith's economic analysis. It touched on central issues of his economic outlook more often noted in modern scholarship – division of labor, the relations between various modes of production, the influence (and critique) of the Physiocrats, rent, tax and bounty policies, and social equity, not to mention his general outlook on history and progress. This amalgam of ideas had been addressed in earlier political-economic discourse, but never in such detailed and organic fashion. Subsequently, for close to a century, no self-respecting political economist could afford to disregard how the use of natural resources played its part in the general socioeconomic fabric of society. Even after the rise of neoclassical economics, when a more detail-oriented, technical and mathematical outlook began to overtake economic analysis, this topic could never again be ignored.

One last point regarding Smith's attitude toward nature needs to be mentioned. In modern environmental discourse, particularly among ecocritics, he is often considered as a chief culprit responsible for the rise of the harmful economic outlook which emphasizes growth, irrespective of environmental consequences.[85] Yet, as should be clear by now, his detailed considerations of nature and natural resources were more sophisticated than a simple advocacy for manipulation and growth, and can offer important insights into the development of the modern view of nature.

8 Ricardo and Malthus on the utilization of nature

Ricardo disagreed with Smith's position that land would always permit the demand for rent, even when it was unfertile. According to Ricardo, there always existed the least fertile land which did not enable the demand for rent. Smith, he claimed, was inconsistent on this point, since he had accepted that insufficiently fertile mines did not afford rent. According to Ricardo this pertained both to agricultural land and to mines.[1] However, Ricardo nonetheless recognized that though there was a natural and ordinary connection between rent and the fertility of land, it was nonetheless not a necessary connection.[2] Rent, after all, was a socially determined mechanism. It was not preordained or necessary in Ricardo's opinion, and therefore could be annulled, or at the very least criticized. His theory of rent, which claimed that rent was the result of the cultivation of increasingly less fertile land, was intimately connected with his ideas on the maximization of efficiency in utilizing natural resources, particularly in agriculture. It also related to his criticism of the landowners, who received rent without contributing anything concrete to society's prosperity.[3] He disagreed with the claim that land had an advantage over all other sources of useful produce, due to the surplus it yielded in the form of rent. The reason he disagreed with this view was because when land was most abundant, it did not yield any rent, but did so only when its relative quality was diminished. Assuming air, water and other natural elements would have had various qualities and been limited in quantity, they too would have yielded rent. "With every worse quality employed, the value of the commodities in the manufacture of which they were used, would rise, because equal quantities of labour would be less productive. Man would do more by the sweat of his brow, and nature perform less; and the land would be no longer pre-eminent for its limited powers."[4] This was an early version of the principle of diminishing returns, which played a prominent role in the outlooks of Ricardo, Malthus and their respective followers.

Ricardo claimed that neither Smith nor Malthus had proven that agriculture was pre-eminent in the scale of productiveness.[5] This did not, however, prevent him from giving it due consideration, not least in his criticism of the rent system. As far as consideration of the human cultivation of nature was concerned, Ricardo's outlook seems somewhat paradoxical. In essence he claimed that the healthiest and most productive relations between human beings and their natural environment were evident when no excessive pressure existed, in terms of the resources required to sustain the existing population. In this initial situation (clearly a theoretical abstraction of complete and static economic equilibrium), nature easily yielded all required produce without any particular effort on the part of humanity. What prompted the need for more excessive utilization of natural resources were the rising needs of a growing population, but this was also accompanied with unjustified social inequalities in the form of rent. This, in and of itself, contributed nothing toward a more efficient utilization of nature, and perhaps even impeded it. But in any event Ricardo at no point of this analysis departed from the traditional emphasis on the need to cultivate natural resources for human need. On the contrary, his whole position was based on this widely accepted outlook.

Regarding the relative merits of agriculture and manufactures Ricardo went further than Smith, objecting to the latter's claim that agriculture was the most advantageous way in which society could use its capital, thanks to the work that nature itself contributed to agriculture. In contrast with Smith, Ricardo wrote:

> Does nature nothing [*sic*] for man in manufactures? Are the powers of wind and water, which move our machinery, and assist navigation, nothing? The pressure of the atmosphere and the elasticity of steam, which enable us to work the most stupendous engines – are they not the gifts of nature? to say nothing of the effects of the matter of heat in softening and melting metals, of the decomposition of the atmosphere in the process of dyeing and fermentation. There is not a manufacture which can be mentioned, in which nature does not give her assistance to man, and give it too, generously and gratuitously.[6]

Ricardo's criticism of Smith here in fact did not lessen the latter's claim for the importance of nature for human progress. On the contrary, it strengthened and broadened it. This was probably due to the great industrial advances which happened in the several decades between the writing of their respective works. Ricardo's outlook incorporated Smith's eulogy of the role nature played in agriculture, within the much broader outlook resulting from the dramatic increase in the utilization of natural resources during the Industrial Revolution. Greater reliance on machines made clear that nature could be increasingly harnessed not just in agricultural production.[7]

Again referring to Smith, this time more approvingly, Ricardo claimed that nature limited the amount of capital it was possible to profitably invest in agriculture, due to the naturally limited ability to eat more than a certain quantity. However, no such limitation existed regarding the use of manufactured commodities.[8] In contrast with land, there was no limit to the extent most other natural resources could be utilized by human beings.[9] Ricardo discussed the possibility of utilizing, with the aid of machines, natural agents such as air, sun and atmospheric pressure, so as to reduce the need for manual labor. Such natural agents added to the value in use of produce, but not to its exchangeable value, since the latter diminished the moment less human labor was required for production. Less need for labor lowered prices.[10] However, this did not dispense with the need for adequate wages for all types of labor. "Why," asked Ricardo, "should profits and wages, in agriculture, at any period of society, be greater than in any other employment?"[11]

Nevertheless, even Ricardo admitted that there was a constitutive significance to agriculture as the primary source of subsistence. In contrast with agriculture, manufactures tended to be more vulnerable to changes in the tastes and caprice of purchasers, to the transference of capital from one employment to another, as well as to new taxes. Agricultural produce, on the other hand, was absolutely necessary and could not be dispensed with. "The demands for the produce of agriculture are uniform, they are not under the influence of fashion, prejudice, or caprice. To sustain life, food is necessary, and the demand for food must continue in all ages, and in all countries."[12] Elsewhere, Ricardo similarly noted – "I estimate as the source from which we derive all we possess the power which the earth has of yielding a surplus produce. In proportion to this power we enjoy leisure for study and the obtaining of that knowledge which gives dignity to life. Without it we could neither possess arts or manufactures, and our whole time would be devoted to the procuring food to support a miserable existence."[13] This was reminiscent of stadial progress, of the idea that without agricultural production and the material progress it afforded, higher cultural progress would be impossible. Against this background the concept of rent, as a hindrance to proper agricultural production, became of constitutive significance in Ricardo's political economy.

Ricardo's theory of rent drew strong reaction in the early nineteenth century, both supportive and critical. A prominent example, partially agreeing with Ricardo, was Nassau Senior, who accepted the assertion that with historical progress increasingly less fertile land would come into cultivation. Senior, however, voicing an argument which was relatively common at the time, claimed that Ricardo had erred in causally linking enhanced cultivation with rising rent, since rent existed even when all the cultivated land was of equal fertility. He was, however, more in line with Ricardo's approach in regarding rent as a hindrance to progress and the enhancement of agricultural production.[14] According to Ricardo rent was a symptom, but not a cause, of a nation's wealth. A rising rent resulted from a rise in the nation's wealth, and from the growing difficulty to supply food to an increasing population. Rent rose when there was a lesser amount of fertile land. National wealth rose when there was a larger quantity of disposable fertile land which was more easily cultivated, hence producing less rent.[15] Rent was paid to landlords "for the use of the original and indestructible powers of the soil," not for the interest and profit of capital which included the use of things such as houses, fences, drainage and manure. In this context Ricardo perceived a common error, evinced in his opinion even by Smith, to confuse rent with profit, and to consider profit as if it were rent. In fact rent was an unjustified payment solely for the use of the land itself as a natural resource.[16]

Rent was also destructive because it provided no stimulus to agricultural improvements. When a rise in both population and national wealth occurred, and was also accompanied by agricultural improvements which diminished the need to cultivate less fertile lands, this led to a diminished rent. From this perspective there were two types of agricultural improvements – those which increased the productive powers of the land, such as rotating crops and manure; and those which, through improvements in machinery, enabled creating produce with less labor, for example improvements in agricultural implements such as ploughs, or greater veterinary knowledge. The first type of improvements always lessened rent, the second only under certain conditions.[17] Landowners had in interest in augmenting the fertility of their lands and in advancing agricultural improvements. In the short term, according to Ricardo, this might harm their interests, and also in the long term, had the principle of population, as depicted by Malthus, not been in force. At first agricultural improvements harmed the proprietors of land and worked to the advantage of consumers, yet with the growth of population, the advantages related to these improvements were transposed to the proprietors.[18] Ricardo, however, claimed that it was only in such cases that a clear opposition emerged between the interests of the landlords and those of the state. He objected to Malthus's claim that he, Ricardo, regarded the landlords as enemies of the state, whereas in fact he considered them exactly in the fashion he did all other social classes.[19]

The mechanism which determined rent was evident mainly, but not exclusively, regarding agricultural cultivation of nature. The mining of metals also exhibited a similar phenomenon, with rent rising the more it became necessary to work mines of a lesser quality. "The metals, like other things, are obtained by labour. Nature, indeed, produces them; but it is the labour of man which extracts them from the bowels of the earth, and prepares them for our service."[20] Rent, therefore, was viewed consistently by Ricardo as an obstruction to the efficient and socially useful utilization of natural resources. It interfered with the simple rise in increasing forms of cultivating nature. It thus distorted the relations between the investment of labor, and the consequent rising value of natural resources which had been adapted for human use. Criticizing Malthus's view of rent, and noting a remark by Say in contrast with Malthus's position, Ricardo wrote ironically: "Can any one doubt that if a person could appropriate to himself the wind and the sun, he would be able to command a rent for the uses to be derived from them?"[21]

Ricardo disagreed with Malthus's claim that improvements in agriculture, which would diminish the need for labor, would lead to rising rent. This might happen, but only, according to Ricardo, when the rising amounts of agricultural produce more cheaply produced due to such improvements, and to the cultivation of fertile land, would also be accompanied with a commensurate growth of population. Otherwise, the greater amounts of food would not be required, and consequently rent would be lowered rather than raised, since the price of produce would diminish, and capital would be withdrawn from the land.[22] He also claimed that the more fertile the last land taken into cultivation, the better it was for the people, since their labor was worth more. It was also better for the capitalists, since wages would ultimately be cheaper and profits higher. Ricardo clearly implied, however, that the losers in this situation would be the landlords, who would lose rent. While the fertility of the land was beyond their control, it was nonetheless obvious that increasingly less fertile land was put into cultivation. Had all land been fertile, they of course would not have received rent at all.[23] Nevertheless, Ricardo claimed that with the improvement of the country, despite rents not rising, the landlords' condition could also improve relative to that of the capitalists. Only in the short term were improvements in the productivity of land inimical to the interests of the landlords. In the long run they too profited from this.[24] He therefore clearly supported agricultural improvements. In terms of raising profits they were the same thing as an increase in the land's fertility.[25]

In opposition to Ricardo, Malthus asserted that rent was part of the price of many products, mainly agricultural products. Agricultural improvements raised the rent on more fertile lands, and it was therefore rent which raised the price of agricultural products, even when the price of labor remained the same.[26] Ricardo devoted considerable attention to refuting Malthus's views on rent.[27] On his part he claimed, in opposition to Malthus, that rent was not a necessary constituent of price. In the event of agricultural improvements it was possible that land previously uncultivated would be cultivated. Yet, contrary to what Malthus claimed, this eventuality would not occur with the same price of produce and labor and the same rate of profit, but rather with a lower price of produce and labor and with higher profits. The fact that rent was not a constituent of price did not require proving that all cultivated lands (and consequently all agricultural products such as wool, timber and so forth) paid rent, as Malthus attempted to prove.[28]

While his depiction of how rent rose and fell was similar to Ricardo's, Malthus regarded rent as a constructive element of economic development. Rising rent in fact indicated increased efficiency in the cultivation of land. Conversely, any attempt to reduce the price of products in order to lower the price of rent, ultimately caused a diminution in the amount of land being cultivated, and thus also diminished population and adversely affected the economy.[29] Ricardo, on his side, disagreed with Malthus's view that declining rent was always accompanied by poverty and socioeconomic decline. He noted that other, more positive developments, might cause lowered rent, such as free importation of corn, agricultural improvements, or adoption of cheaper food which would throw land out of cultivation.[30]

The exchange on rent between the two friends went, however, into even greater detail, indicating just how vital they considered this issue. This significance might easily be lost on modern readers. In contrast with Ricardo, Malthus claimed that the rent mechanism would have operated even had all tracts of land been equally fertile. In reality, of course, such differences in fertility nonetheless existed.[31] In fact, according to Malthus, a more efficient investment of capital, for example in the form of agricultural improvements, or in the laborers' exertion, could prevent diminished profits connected with the cultivation of less and less fertile lands. Agricultural profits did affect profits of other types, yet this was not an incontrovertible influence, and capital investment could at times influence profits more than the relative fertility of land.[32] Ricardo, according to Malthus, had insufficiently noticed the effect agricultural improvements had on the profits of stock. Therefore Ricardo was in error when he claimed that accumulation of capital in an extensive country with infertile land would lead to lowered profits and rising rent, while in a small but fertile country, capital accumulation would lead to higher profits without rising rent. In fact, claimed Malthus, the opposite would happen, thanks to the agricultural improvements which the extensive country could maintain for hundreds of years, which was impossible in a small country.[33] What mattered was not a country's prima facie fertility, but rather the long-term potential it offered for continuing and ever-increasing human cultivation. It was not nature in itself that mattered, but rather its amenability to human mastery. "[T]he bounty of nature furnishes but few of the necessaries, conveniences and amusements of life to man without the aid of his own exertions."[34] Malthus praised Ricardo personally, as well as in his capacity as the owner of land, yet claimed that Ricardo himself, who profited from rent, underrated its national significance. On the other hand he, Malthus, who did not profit from rent, recognized this significance. This was, in his opinion, proof of the sincerity and lack of bias in the economic analyses developed by both Ricardo and himself.[35]

The two friends also disagreed on the burning contemporary issue of the Corn Laws. While Malthus struggled with this issue, Ricardo firmly supported the free importation of corn, claiming that the Corn Laws assisted the landowners by raising the price of grain and encouraging the cultivation of less fertile land, thus raising rent on land. Importing corn from countries which had more fertile land than the least fertile land of the importing country, meant that the latter could divert labor to other things besides the production of food.[36]

On the issues of labor, wages and population, Ricardo and Malthus were less divided. Ricardo claimed that the natural price of labor depended on the price of food and other necessaries which supported the laborer and his family. As society progressed the price of labor tended to rise, yet agricultural improvements and commercial development might lower the price of labor for some time.The price of most commodities, though not of labor and raw produce, tended to diminish with the rise in wealth and population. When the market price of labor rose above its natural price the condition of the laboring class improved. However, when this eventually led to a rise in wages and consequently to a rising population, the growing number of laborers, above the existing demand for labor, caused wages to be lowered again to their natural level, and even lower, and then the condition of the laboring class worsened, occasionally even to the point of poverty. Only when their privations reduced their numbers, or the demand for labor rose, did the price of labor also rise, and their situation again improved. Like Malthus, and probably under his influence, Ricardo no longer adhered to the earlier optimistic Enlightenment belief that a growing population was always a good sign of progress. And yet Ricardo, more than Malthus, still retained more of this optimism, claiming that in an improving society, a situation of general amelioration and high wages could be retained for an indefinite period.[37]

There were many similarities between the claims of Ricardo and Malthus, which made their disagreements all the more striking. The idea of the oscillating condition of laborers was with minor differences shared by both. This perceived mechanism claimed that wages and then numbers of laborers would rise, leading to decreased demand for their labor, poverty, lesser population, but then consequently a renewed growing demand for labor, rising population, and so forth. Malthus combined an observation on agricultural labor into this process.

He claimed that when a population was growing, the resultant surplus of laborers, whose condition was worsening, would find themselves working in cultivating the land, and their situation would ultimately improve. Yet this would again eventually lead to a growing population, and to a repeated oscillation between retrograde and progressive conditions of society. Malthus claimed that this oscillation had not been previously understood, because most commentators had concentrated on the higher classes, and there was much less information regarding the history of the lower classes.[38]

Malthus's population theory put particular emphasis on the significance of subsistence production, hence on agriculture. This put human beings in large measure at the mercy of nature. Something as basic as the changing seasons had a significant influence on the availability and the price of corn.[39] The limit to the ability of a geographical region to supply its inhabitants with food was defined by the scarcest season. "The profusion of nourishment which is poured forth in the seasons of plenty cannot all be consumed by the scanty numbers that were able to subsist through the season of scarcity. When human industry and foresight are directed in the best manner, the population that the soil can support is regulated by the average produce throughout the year; but among animals, and in the uncivilized states of man, it will be much below this average."[40] In other words, with greater progress came greater ability to overcome, if not completely, the natural limitations to food production. The most devastating positive check to population was lack of food, but even the damage this caused was not incontrovertible, given the right measures. States could recover, their subsistence resume its increase, and their population resume its growth, so long as the inhabitants' industry remained intact. In the long term, despite his emphasis on the negative influence of famine, Malthus regarded bad governance as equally devastating. A government which did not encourage agriculture had a more negative impact than the plague. "The traces of the most destructive famines in China, Indostan, Egypt, and other countries, are by all accounts very soon obliterated; and the most tremendous convulsions of nature, such as volcanic eruptions and earthquakes, if they do not happen so frequently as to drive away the inhabitants, or destroy their spirit of industry, have been found to produce but a trifling effect on the average population of any state."[41] The human ability to combat the forces of nature was such, that it could overcome all but the worst natural disasters. Any failure to cultivate nature to the utmost extent possible was therefore a failure of will, a sign of cultural and political debility, and therefore inexcusable. This message – that it was human response to natural disasters that mattered more than these disasters themselves – had been a central claim of the Enlightenment ever since the 1755 Lisbon earthquake and Voltaire's famous poem following the event.

Malthus consistently regarded agriculture as the most basic requisite for the existence of an abundant population, writing that "[N]o greater evil can easily happen to a country than the loss of agricultural stock and capital."[42] Country life was healthier and happier than city life, and country employments less damaging to health than those of manufactures.[43] Malthus was emphatically influenced by the Physiocrats, even if this influence diminished over time, particularly following the 1817 edition of the *Essay on the Principle of Population*. By then, he viewed their definition of wealth as too narrow, yet continued to accept their assumption of the superior productiveness of agriculture to other types of labor.[44] His position was similar to that of the Physiocrats in viewing land as unique, due to its capacity to produce a surplus, which then enabled the growth of population and consequently also a rise in production of, and demand for, other types of products.[45] The influence of the Physiocrats was also evident when Malthus claimed that a country's wealth was dependent first and foremost on the combination of the fertility of its land, with the level of efficiency of the cultivation of that land. Investing capital in agriculture was favorable to investing it in commerce or manufactures, which were less stable. "The fertility of the land, either natural or acquired, may be said to be the only source of permanently high returns for capital."[46] Before 1817, when he was still heavily influenced by the Physiocratic preference for agriculture, he even worried that a situation was beginning to emerge in England where the commercial system predominated. This put all the English economy, including its manufactures, in danger. This also demonstrated how it was best for a nation to produce an agricultural surplus with which it could trade with other countries, rather than be dependent on agricultural imports. A country which voluntarily stopped producing an agricultural surplus beyond the consumption of its population, in fact undermined its own prosperity. England in this respect shared the unjustified preference of modern European countries for trade over agriculture.[47] Malthus ultimately retained the Physiocrats' predilection for agriculture, but forsook their view of its singularity. Quoting Smith, he noted the importance of combining agriculture with commerce.[48] For Malthus agriculture was significant primarily as the most important source of food production, hence also for maintaining a large population.

Malthus praised James Steuart for recognizing the connection between agricultural production and populousness.[49] The main force influencing the size of the population remained its compatibility with the amount of food which it was possible to produce. "[P]opulation… will always be in proportion to the food which the earth is made to produce. And no cause, physical or moral, unless it operate in an excessive and unusual manner, can have any considerable and permanent effect on the population, except in as far as it influences the production and distribution of the means of subsistence."[50] Improvements in the means of subsistence almost always led to a rising population, yet this was not all that mattered. The compatibility between the amount of food (acquired or produced) and the amount of population, was a veritable incontrovertible law of nature. The populousness of countries therefore followed the amount of food they possessed. The happiness of their inhabitants, on the other hand, was in accordance with the amount of food which a day's work could purchase, or the liberality with which food was distributed. What really mattered for the general happiness was not the absolute quantity of food, but rather how it was proportionately distributed. "The proportion is generally the most favourable in new colonies, where the knowledge and industry of an old state operate on the fertile unappropriated land of a new one."[51] This also emphasized the significance of the natural environment and the extent of its cultivation. Writing of the quickly growing population in America following the arrival of the Europeans (mainly the Spaniards), despite their bad governance, Malthus noted that "Plenty of rich land, to be had for little or nothing, is so powerful a cause of population as generally to overcome all obstacles." Similarly, population also increased under the bad colonial governance of the Dutch and French exclusive companies of merchants. A fortiori this happened in the North American colonies, where liberty and equality were more prevalent.[52]

All this raised the question of the proper policies necessary for enhancing agricultural production under the proper social conditions. The government's role in regard to agriculture was even more important than in regard to commerce or manufactures.[53] For example, one of the main reasons Malthus opposed the Poor Laws, was that they increased population without increasing the amount of food necessary to support it.[54] Regarding the need to combine agriculture and commerce, he claimed that "[T]he question whether a balance between the agricultural and commercial classes of society, which would not take place naturally, ought, under certain circumstances, to be maintained artificially [for example by restrictions upon the importation of foreign grain], must appear to be the most important [Malthus later altered this to 'a most important'] practical question in the whole of political economy."[55] No government, however, could force its inhabitants and industry to "produce the greatest quantity of human sustenance that the earth could bear." That would necessitate the violation of private property, "from which everything that is valuable to man has hitherto arisen." It would necessitate devoting all the nation's industry to growing potatoes at the expense of other food such as animal produce. This was practically impossible, and could not prevent the eventual emergence of want, only with less available resources than ever.[56] Malthus therefore perceived a limit to how much nature might be cultivated, without leading to either over-population or to economic and cultural decline. Cultivating natural resources was to be encouraged, but only within the limits of proper cultural, social, and political progress. His chauvinistic attitude toward the lower classes underlined this observation, but it should be noted that one of the main aspects of his outlook was the view that any attempt to controvert the proper policy was bound to fail. Even the best of governments could not obviate the limit to population and to progress, which the means of subsistence posed. This was a law of nature, and a bad government only made the inevitable depopulation happen quicker and with more devastating force. The acquisition of food, whether, preferably, through domestic production, but also by means of importation, was therefore a signal role of government.

All this raises the question of Malthus's support for the Corn Laws, in contrast with the position of Ricardo. Scholars are divided as to whether he eventually reneged on this support, but it is clear that at least for a significant time he did support these laws.[57] Malthus supported government intervention through Corn Laws, as well as bounties on the exportation of corn, both of which had been neglected since the seventeenth century, and in his opinion, contrary to that of Ricardo, needed to be renewed. These would maintain the situation of surplus agricultural production in England.[58] In contrast with Ricardo, who claimed that he unnecessarily let moral issues influence his opinion on this issue, Malthus made an exception to his general advocacy of free trade, in the case of a need for a measure of protection for domestic agriculture. While Ricardo opposed the Corn Laws, Malthus emphasized the negative impact that adopting free trade in corn would have on the agriculture of a nation, if it was not reciprocated by similar free trade policy in the countries with which it traded. It would also reduce the rent on land and thus hurt the landowners, whose interests he regarded as intimately connected with those of the nation. This view was criticized by most contemporaries, and after 1815 Malthus's position on this point became more moderate, accepting at least some arguments for free trade in corn.[59] It should therefore be considered in conjunction with his early support for Physiocracy, yet like the latter, it is not at all certain that he ever really completely reneged on this point. The significance of agricultural production of food was simply too important for his general socio-economic outlook.

Malthus favored limiting the importation of foreign corn, as long as this led to increased capital investment in long-term agricultural improvements. "Permanent improvements in agriculture are like the acquisition of additional land."[60] He discussed in detail the pros and cons of taxing the importation of grain. In certain conditions this might be advantageous. Ideally, a system of completely free international trade was the best option. Yet the competing interests of different countries made such a situation practically impossible. Therefore, limits on the importation of corn were requisite under certain conditions, mainly regarding the proper combination and the balance between agriculture and commerce.[61] It was therefore a matter not just of the importation of corn, but of a general proper economic policy. Malthus claimed that neglect of agricultural production, as well as of agricultural importation, explained how empires had declined in history, in favor of weaker nations which eventually replaced them. He accepted the assertion that commerce and manufactures, as well as luxury, were culturally important. However, when luxury became excessively important, it damaged the funds necessary for agriculture, and turned from an encouragement, to an impediment, to agriculture. In ancient times wars may have been the main reason for the fall of empires, but in fact they usually only finished what an excess of luxury, and a neglect of agriculture, had begun.[62] Ancient Rome was an example of such decline, since its population began declining the moment it began importing all its corn, and lay all Italy into pasture.[63] While corn importation, therefore, was not to be prohibited, it should never come at the expense of the main source of subsistence – proper domestic agricultural production. This entailed various policy measures which Malthus considered in detail.

He noted the importance of proper division of land, which was necessary to enable the accumulation of wealth and the growth of population. Even without advanced trade, this could enable economic development, as the example of the United States proved. In contrast, the situation in some parts of Europe still remained in a feudal stage as far as the unequal distribution of land and the lack of small-scale proprietors were concerned. Owners of large tracts of land did not provide sufficient demand for production, which could lead their countries to adequately utilize their natural resources. On the other hand, owners of small tracts of land were also incapable of providing such demand. As things stood, it was therefore impossible that the limit to enlarging population relative to cultivating land would be reached quickly enough. In the division of land, Malthus aimed therefore at proportionality, which could enhance agricultural production and thus also population.[64] It was possible, nevertheless, to leave large tracts of land in an uncultivated condition, without this indicating a bad government, particularly in large countries. The truly significant thing was to maintain a surplus of agricultural produce. It was therefore possible to imagine a situation in which it was preferable to invest in bettering the cultivation of land already in a state of cultivation, rather than investing the substantial sums necessary for beginning cultivation in previously uncultivated land. It was never possible to cultivate all a country's land, and it was also never possible to activate preventive checks to population in a completely sufficient manner. All that was practically attainable was attempting to maintain the best possible ratio between food and its production on the one hand, and the size of the population on the other.[65]

Malthus claimed that in order for land to be properly cultivated, it needed to be someone's property. In fact, for society it did not matter whether the owner of land was also the one laboring on it. For the laborer himself it was clearly also preferable to own the land. Yet in essence, this did not affect the contribution of the cultivation of the land for society in general.[66] Malthus perceived a correlation between the interests of individuals and those of the nation in general, at least as long as the economy functioned properly, and individuals such as landlords did not put short-term profit interests ahead of long-term ones. Proper investment in land cultivation was precisely a case of worthy long-term investment.[67] The landowners, in any event, needed to provide their tenants with sufficient capital to enable proper cultivation of the land. Furthermore, in the event of rising prices, the proprietors should wait and not raise rents immediately, so that the farmers could accumulate capital and improve the land.[68] Malthus's approach meant that proprietors had to put aside their short-term interests in the form of rent, in favor of the long-term interests related to the improvement of land cultivation, and the prosperity of the nation in general.

He was more in line with Smith's approach than with that of Ricardo when he noted the affinity between the interests of landlords and those of the nation in general. In contrast with Ricardo, he regarded rising rent as a positive development which resulted from agricultural improvements. Only in the case of superabundant fertile land could one imagine no need for rent, yet Malthus regarded this as an unrealistic possibility. Like Smith, he was more sensitive to contingencies than Ricardo. In reality, population grew as much as possible, while land was cultivated with the increasing success connected with gradual agricultural improvements. In this situation rent would always rise together with agricultural improvements.[69] It should be noted, however, that Ricardo on his part claimed that in fact the landlords' interest was in variance with agricultural improvements only in the short term. In the long term, with the rising population which would accompany the increased facility of food production, the landlords' condition would also improve, as a result of the increased productive power of the land to yield food.[70]

In Malthus's view, hearkening back to Robert Wallace, the fact that land, in contrast with air and water, was limited in its capacity for sustaining the population's need for sustenance, was a divinely ordained reality which prevented the unlimited growth of population, with all the consequent ills which inevitably occurred. Therefore, in contrast with Ricardo's position, it was important to maintain a surplus of agricultural produce, which enabled rent and thus posed a realistic limit, in the form of limited food, to the growth of population and the economy. This was in fact the proper limit to a nation's prosperity.[71] Ricardo was unwilling to accept Malthus's claim that the inability to produce unlimited amounts of food was providentially ordained to prevent over-population. For Ricardo this was not a moral issue but rather a factual one – the need to investigate whether the ability to produce food was indeed limited or not, at least in the context of political economy. Ricardo claimed that Malthus had misunderstood his position on the limits to land fertility. Their main point of disagreement, at least in Ricardo's view, centered on the fact that rent resulted from decreasing fertility. Ricardo implied that Malthus had created a seeming disagreement which in fact did not exist. He, Ricardo, did not complain either against Providence or against the wanting liberality of nature, and therefore he and Malthus were not in disagreement on this point as the latter contended.[72] Ricardo also claimed that Malthus had been mistaken in ascribing to him the claim that profits depended on the fertility of the land last cultivated. In fact, claimed Ricardo, what he meant was that profits were in proportion to wages, to the productiveness of labor on the land last cultivated.[73] What mattered, in other words, was not the relative fertility of the land in itself, but rather the changing amount of labor that was consequently required in order to produce food on variably fertile lands. As elsewhere, for Ricardo it was not nature in itself that mattered, but rather what human beings derived from it by cultivating it. On this both he and Malthus agreed, but the latter remained more pessimistic about the extent to which such cultivation could be maintained.

Malthus's position was that the human control of nature had a clear limit – the ratio between the amount of population and the means of subsistence. It was this perspective which underlay his claim that attempts to find cures for diseases were in vain, since nature created other diseases at times even more deadly. The depletion of excessive population was simply unavoidable, since "Nature will not, nor cannot, be defeated in her purposes." The removal of particular causes of mortality did not affect population beyond what the means of subsistence allowed, and the laws of nature permitted. Nevertheless, Malthus remained optimistic that the extinction of a mortal disease such as smallpox might still lead to social improvement, for example by influencing more circumspection in marriage and births. Yet it was neither advisable nor effectively possible to implement restraint in such matters. Things should be left to run their course, while leaving people with freedom of choice, even if, as seemed to be the case, correct choices in such matters were not yet being taken. Free choice, particularly among the poor, would occur only when they would be educated to understand that they were responsible for their own condition, their own over-population, and their own poverty.[74] Here Malthus demonstrated both his social chauvinism on the one hand, as well as the emphasis on the importance of education of the masses on the other, both of which he shared with his Enlightenment predecessors.

At times Malthus seemed to justify his bad reputation for social insensitivity, and at other times quite the contrary. One example of his relatively more sensitive opinions was his claim that it was better to augment the size of the population not by enlarging the proportion of births, but rather by diminishing the proportion of those dying under the age of puberty. For this reason he supported vaccinations.[75] Yet his general approach to the poor was, at the very least, paternalistic. He unstintingly voiced his demand that the nation should not support the poor, who should support themselves and their families on their own, or otherwise take responsibility for their actions and starve. He claimed that his position on this matter was not motivated by insensitivity to the suffering of the masses, but on the contrary, that supporting them in the short term only increased their suffering in the long term.[76] This point remains of course a point of contention in modern debates between right and left socioeconomic positions.

Where governments did need to act in support of the poor was therefore not by Poor Laws, but by investing in education for all classes of the population.[77] Education, as well as civil and political liberty, were key to improving the condition of the poor and slowing the growth of population.[78] Another point on which he seemed sensitive to the condition of the socially disadvantaged, was his worry for the mental welfare of laborers. On this issue he may have been influenced by both Smith on the one hand, and early socialists on the other, but in any event he supported affording laborers time for leisure.[79] He was also in favor of public works, supplying work for the poor when this became necessary.[80] Nevertheless, Malthus claimed that no matter the effort devoted through charity or other forms of investment, no plan could enable the laboring class of society to marry and raise families in an old and fully peopled country, with the same safety they might have in a new country.[81] Once again, he regarded the means of subsistence as an incontrovertible limit defining the amount of food which the cultivation of land would enable, and consequently the number of inhabitants it could support. In a new land, where cultivation of natural resources, primarily land, had only just begun, there was still much room left for further development. But it was a clear implication of Malthus's position, reiterated throughout the *Essay on the Principle of Population*, that even in such a new country, the relative freedom to grow was only temporary, and would narrow the more it would become cultivated and populated. From a strictly economic, physical point of view, nature set a limit to how much it could be cultivated for human benefit.

We need to keep in mind that Malthus viewed the state of true over-population as a distant, almost theoretical possibility, so long as human beings made the best social arrangements and put into effect preventive checks to population. The fact that there were poverty and misery due to over-population was the result of improper policies which could be ameliorated. Therefore, in the real world of his times, Malthus thought that as long as preventive checks to population were better implemented, the actual utilization of land and other natural resources could still be considerably enhanced, in themselves enabling a larger population. Therefore, he claimed that the attempt of landlords to accumulate their capital so as to save for the future, meant that they did not cultivate their lands to the maximal limit supporting the largest population. "The very definition of fertile land is, land that will support a much greater number of persons than are necessary to cultivate it." Yet a landlord who would utilize all his surplus produce to employ laborers in cultivating his land would become impoverished. Malthus aimed at a moderate mean in this respect, balancing the short-term needs of the landlords, with the overall prosperity of the nation. The impoverishment of landlords was justified only to augment population, yet human beings in fact were motivated by other desires, such as pleasure and the acquisition of luxury products. Proprietors of land aimed to preserve their command of wealth for the future, and once this became impossible they ceased to hire new agricultural laborers. This created a process whereby population was eventually reduced, till a new balance of produce and consumption was reached. Without governmental intervention such as agrarian laws, the landlords would lack the incentive to invest their money in a manner which stimulated industry and commerce. Without such government intervention, relying on the landlords doing the right thing risked impoverishing the state.[82] In this way, although their conception of the role that landlords, and rent, played in social-economic relations was almost opposite, both Malthus and Ricardo reached the conclusion that the state could not leave the proprietors of land to do as they wished, since this would almost surely be contrary to the greater good. Furthermore, these observations demonstrated Malthus's observation that human behavior prevented the maximization of utilizing and cultivating land. It was not nature itself, but rather defective human conduct, which limited the maximal cultivation of land, at a point much lower than when the maximal amount of population might be reached.

Continuing to hammer in this point, Malthus claimed that Ricardo was right when he regarded increasing difficulty in obtaining food for laborers as a cause of diminishing profits, but had erred in not perceiving other reasons for this process. In Malthus's opinion such a situation could occur long before the maximal cultivation of land had been attained. This could happen when there was insufficient demand for labor, a situation in which encouraging births would be harmful. This, in Malthus's view, happened even if there was still land available for cultivation. Once again, in the real world the social limits to population were reached long before the maximization of population, available based on nature's limits, was attained.[83] From a different perspective, he noted that "A fertile soil gives at once the greatest natural capability of wealth that a country can possibly possess." Occasionally one encountered small and unfertile countries which had attained wealth disproportional to their natural condition thanks to foreign commerce, yet "no instance has occurred, in modern times, of a large and very fertile country having made full use of its natural resources." Fertile land without commerce could not in itself ensure the accumulation of wealth.[84] The potential for growth was larger in more extensive and fertile countries. Yet discrepancies in social and political circumstances meant that small countries could at times surpass large ones, despite having a scantier natural potential for prosperity. For Malthus what mattered was not nature, but what human beings did with it. It was impossible to utilize natural resources indefinitely, and it was difficult to define the exact limit to the amount of food which could be produced by cultivating the land. On the other hand, the negative effects of over-population were much clearer and more tangible.

> The power of the earth to produce subsistence is certainly not unlimited, but it is strictly speaking indefinite; that is, its limits are not defined, and the time will probably never arrive when we shall be able to say, that no farther labour or ingenuity of man could make further additions to it. But the power of obtaining an additional quantity of food from the earth by proper management, and in a certain time, has the most remote relation imaginable to the power of keeping pace with an unrestricted increase of population.[85]

That is to say, there was no limit to how much human beings could cultivate and utilize nature. Yet there was a limit to how much they could do so while maintaining a proper ratio between this utilization (in terms of the amount of food it produced), and the growth of population. Malthus posed no limit to the level of cultivation of nature. On the contrary, he unambiguously encouraged it. Yet he did claim that humanity would never reach a state in which what obstructed its progress would be an insufficient utilization of nature. Long before that, human beings would reach a point where the healthy ratio between the size of the population and the means of subsistence would be violated. Realistically speaking, no amount of cultivation of natural resources would ever be enough in this respect, no matter how much it was advisable to try and augment it. From our own twenty-first-century environmental perspective, a Malthusian viewpoint would lead to the prediction that were a global environmental catastrophe to occur, this would happen while many areas of wild nature would still remain in relatively pristine condition.

Both Malthus and Ricardo therefore agreed on the basic assumption that use of natural resources was a policy goal which could be pursued irrespective of any physical natural limitations, which they did not consider as imminent. They differed on how to adjust social policies given this use, and in their respective optimism or pessimism regarding the ability to sustain socioeconomic growth based on this seemingly unlimited potential for natural-resource utilization. Both their views had a profound effect on classical political-economic thought. It is Malthus's pessimism, however, which seems more relevant from our modern vantage point. Till Malthus's time there was a common belief in European thought in the uncontested human control of nature. Beginning with Malthus, however, there began creeping in a gradual process of rational recognition of nature's ability to harm human beings if they did not conduct themselves wisely in their use of natural resources. This outlook has of course moved much beyond Malthus's own views, let alone their providential religious underpinning. The old idea of religious propitiation to assuage divine wrath in the face of natural calamities no longer seemed convincing even to Malthus and most of his contemporaries, raised as they were on a rationalistic Enlightenment outlook. This pertained even to the Christian political economists like Malthus himself. Their religiosity was combined with a modern and scientific type of social analysis. As the scientific and industrial view of nature gained increasing hold, the omnipotent quality of nature became increasingly evident, and has remained consistently so in modern civilization. "Managing natural resources" has thus become increasingly necessary, particularly in the face of the growing world population. This was the truly revolutionary implication of Malthus's population principle, which in our times seems more realistic than ever.

9 Jean-Baptiste Say and other contemporaries

The influence of Smith, Ricardo and Malthus, both appreciative and censorious, was evident in the work of practically all nineteenth-century political economists. One could simply not write on this topic without sharing in the common familiarity with their respective works. Yet others were able to make significant original contributions of their own, not least on the subject of the use of natural resources. Jean-Baptiste Say's writings were particularly prominent. Say claimed that Adam Smith had exaggerated the importance of labor as the sole source of value and wealth. In fact, value was the result of labor and industry, combined with the operation of natural agents and capital. Therefore Smith, according to Say, had not given sufficient attention to the utilization of the powers of nature, nor to its connection with machinery and the production of wealth. "Nature," he claimed, "executes an essential part of the production of values; and her agency is in most cases paid for, and forms a portion of the value of the product… the portion of value contributed by nature is not the product of human labour."[1] The Physiocrats also merited criticism. The actual production of wealth was not the creation of matter, but rather of utility, accomplished by three types of industry – agriculture, manufactures and commerce – while capital also contributed to this production. Most products were actually created by a combination of all three, a point which afforded Say the opportunity of criticizing both the Physiocratic emphasis on agriculture, and the mercantilist emphasis on commerce.[2]

Say outlined his own version of the common perception of reciprocal interconnections between town and country, emphasizing their mutual support of agriculture, production and trade, and how they supplied markets one for the other.[3] Yet even he recognized the importance of agricultural production, though he seems to have been ambivalent about the singularity of this importance. The most consistently utilized products were articles of food, "and no occupations are so regular as those which minister to human sustenance." Therefore, agricultural occupations yielded the most certain profit.[4] In antiquity agriculture was considered an honorable occupation, with the result that there was an influx of labor and capital to agriculture, more than to manufactures or trade. Consequently, the ancients' agricultural skill was equal, and in some respects perhaps even superior, to that of the moderns. Only agricultural products were truly essential for the multiplication of humanity, and since in antiquity agriculture was advanced compared with mechanical manufacture, there were many who found themselves unemployed. The ruling class, seeking to find them employment, were forced to engage them in warfare, since they lacked land, capital or other work, and refused to labor in subordinate employments usually reserved for slaves. These patron-client relations resulted in continual civil disorder and discord. Rich nations were consistently attacked by poorer and more warlike nations. Rome fell due to such circumstances, and this barbaric situation continued in the Middle Ages, in the relations between the aristocratic landowners and their vassals. Despite the general declension of arts, medieval cultivation of land remained advanced. In modern times, on the other hand, there was more emphasis on manufactures and commerce, and most of the population made a living from industry independent of large proprietors. Even the poorest individual, thanks to some accumulation of capital, was his own master, and nations in general became self-sufficient. Wars were not concerned any more with destroying the sources of wealth, but rather with the control of colonial assets or commercial monopoly. Wars were mainly conducted between civilized nations, and Say hoped that the principles of political economy would teach that all wars were harmful, and that domestic production was the best path to progress.[5] As far as modern civilization was concerned, he did not regard agriculture in itself as the prime source of wealth, as it had been in earlier eras. A particular aspect of historical progress was the modern ability to advance beyond the reliance on agricultural production. This was based on a wider use of natural resources, not just on land.

Agriculture, according to Say, was in itself only the bare collection of natural products. When, beyond this, there was also a fashioning of these natural products, this became manufacturing industry, and when objects, otherwise inaccessible, were put within reach, this became commerce. Industry, in all its manifestations, thus manufactured products and made them accessible, even if they were not completely necessary for survival. It was such seemingly superfluous products, beyond bare existence, which differentiated between a savage and a civilized existence. "Nature, left entirely to itself, would provide a very scanty subsistence to a small number of human beings. Fertile but desert tracts have been found inadequate to the bare nourishment of a few wretches, cast upon them by the chances of shipwreck: while the presence of industry often exhibits the spectacle of a dense population, plentifully supplied upon the most ungrateful soil."[6]

Say went into some detail in defining the precise processes through which natural resources were labored upon and turned into consumable products. Utility itself was a natural quality which human beings, through labor, extracted from nature. "No human being has the faculty of originally creating matter with utility. In fact, industry is nothing more or less than the human employment of natural agents."[7] Human beings did not create anything new in nature. What they did was "to change the combinations of things," thus giving them economic value as consumable products. Say quoted Bacon on the need to obey nature so as to command it, referring to how bettering technological use of natural resources was the foundation of human industry.[8] At times the differentiation between the three types of industry was indistinct, as in fishing or mining, which combined agriculture and commerce, or the production of wine, which combined agriculture and manufacture. Industry could thus be infinitely subdivided, or conversely, generalized to the point of viewing it as one action. In any event, it was "the employment of natural substances and agents in the adaptation of products to human consumption."[9] Although scientific discoveries contributed to production, ultimately its increase was due to the productive power of natural agents. It was irrelevant how the means of employing those natural agents were first conceived. Nature itself retained an irreplaceable constitutive role in production.[10] The attainment of a product consisted of three stages – first, its scientific study; second, the application of this knowledge for useful purposes by landowners, manufacturers and merchants; and third, the actual labor supervised by those responsible for the first two stages. Industry, according to Say, was therefore always divided into theory, application and execution. All three were almost always performed by different people. Nations would progress as much as they excelled in all three stages, otherwise they became dependent on other nations.[11]

Occasionally, in viewing the production of wealth, it was difficult to differentiate between the action of natural agents, and that of capital invested in such things as machines, buildings or the improvement of land. For example, a flock of sheep was produced by a combination of the activity of nature in the animals themselves, the labor of the proprietors and shepherds, as well as the capital invested in their feeding and habitation. "Thus nature is commonly the fellow-labourer of man and his instruments; a fellowship advantageous to him in proportion as he succeeds in dispensing with his own personal agency, and that of his capital, and in throwing upon nature a large part of the burthen of production."[12] Among the advantages Say perceived in the introduction of machines to the process of production, was that "by its means man makes a conquest of nature and compels the powers of nature and the properties of natural agents to work for his use and advantage."[13]

Different natural agents offered different productive services to human beings. Water, for example, provided motion for machines, fish and means of transportation, while wind turned mills. Yet they did so equally for all people, while the land, limited in quantity, was subject to ownership, which made it worthwhile for the investment of capital and industry. In civilized nations even those who did not own land gained from this. Savages, in places where land was unappropriated, were often in need of food, but even the poor in Europe, where all the land was appropriated, as long as they were healthy and willing to work, had at least a minimum of shelter, clothing and food.[14] It was in the interest of the landowners, as well as of the agricultural laborers and tenants, that the laborers would be able to enjoy the improvements which they made to the soil. The productive power of the soil was valuable only so long as its products were objects of demand beyond subsistence level. It was then that profit made the payment of rent possible, something which did not occur with elements such as water or air. In this way the appropriation of land become profitable for the individual only with rising demand for agricultural products. Say, like Malthus, and in contrast with Ricardo, viewed rent as an indicator of progress and civilization. The only thing, however, which could truly augment the productive agency of land in circulation was the actual amelioration of the soil, either by cultivating new land or by enlarging the productive power of old land.[15]

Like others before him, Say noted that there was such a thing as natural wealth constituted by the gratuitous agency of natural objects. Among these were air, water and solar light, which were the spontaneous offering of nature, though since there was no exertion involved in obtaining them, they had no exchangeable value.[16] Objects of utility which, on the other hand, could be obtained only with some modification by human agency involved with some difficulty, became subject to exchange of property, or in other words, depended on social institutions, and constituted social wealth. In Say's opinion it was only this latter type of social wealth which could form the subject of scientific research.[17] Were the cost of production of all products to become null, then all products, similarly to water and air, would not be required to be either produced or purchased, everything would be free, everyone would be rich, and the acme of wealth would be attained. In this case political economy would no longer be a science, and it would be unnecessary to learn how to acquire wealth, since it would be ready-made for all.[18] This, however, was of course only a hypothetical possibility.

Like other classical political economists Say was acutely aware of the need to define the proper governmental policies which would enhance the use of natural resources, whether in agricultural production, in manufactures or in trade. For example, he generally opposed excessive taxation, particularly when accompanied by excessive spending and improper government policy, which did not use public expenditure for the benefit of the population. Yet he recognized one advantage in such a situation, in that the effort to pay such excessive taxes operated to stimulate the perfection of the art of production, by forcing human beings to turn natural agents to better account. Therefore, the moment taxation would be limited to its desirable level, the advantages attained in this way would become evident. On the other hand, if this did not occur and improper governance continued, then perhaps the depressed working classes might even prefer a savage yet free existence to despotism which took from them the fruits of their labor without any recompense.[19] This in effect was Say's cautionary approach to avoiding the road to socialism.

He also advocated for government support of science and academies, particularly of theoretical science, and most of all of activities which were not pursued by individuals. Scientific advances which enabled greater control and utilization of nature were essential for progress, and despite his general support of free markets, this was one of the areas where Say preferred governmental intervention.[20] Increased efficiency in the control of nature could, for example, help reduce the price of products by reducing their cost of production, thus benefiting all classes in society.

> But whence is derived this accession of enjoyment, this larger supply of wealth, that nobody pays for? From the increased command acquired by human intelligence over the productive powers and agents presented gratuitously by nature. A power has been rendered available for human purposes,

> that had before been not known, or not directed to any human object; as in the instance of wind, water, and steam-engines: or one before known and available is directed with superior skill and effect, as in the case of every improvement in mechanism, whereby human or animal power is assisted or expanded.

Say then continued and noted how "The discovery of a new mineral, animal, or vegetable, possessed of the properties of utility in a novel form, or in a greater degree of abundance or perfection, is an acquisition of the same kind. The productive means of mankind were amplified, and a larger product rendered procurable by an equal degree of human exertion."[21]

Agriculture, however, posed the greatest difficulties to human mastery. While discussing which branches of production yielded the greatest recompense to productive agency, and in which it was best to invest capital, Say observed that "the land may stubbornly resist that kind of cultivation, whose products are in the greatest demand."[22] There was a limit to the utilization of nature, especially when it came to the agricultural production of food. "[A]lthough the same surface of soil may be rendered more productive, it can not be so to an indefinite degree."[23] Furthermore, occasionally, whether due to the distance of land from markets, to unfavorable seasons, wars or taxation, the cultivation of land yielded no profit and it was thrown out of cultivation, or else the proprietors worked the land themselves for personal subsistence, while earning profits elsewhere from capital or personal industry.[24] Nature placed numerous obstacles to injurious interference of government in agricultural production, such as the vast number of people involved, and the small value of produce in relation to its volume. Nevertheless, governmental involvement in agriculture, in contrast with manufactures and commerce, was usually beneficial, for example by granting encouragements or by helping research and the diffusion of knowledge.[25] It was advisable to raise the suitable crops for each tract of land, and to otherwise purchase them from places where they were produced with advantage, thus reducing expenses. "It is the very acme of skill, to turn the powers of nature to best account, and the height of madness to contend against them; which is in fact wasting part of our strength in destroying those powers she designed for our aid." Similarly, in manufactures it was advisable to import raw materials, when these were superior to local materials and more compatible with national industry, although this in itself seemed at first like an act limiting the bounty of nature. "Whenever human efforts succeed in attaching to these gifts of nature a value, that is to say, a degree of utility, whether by their import, or by any modification we may subject them to, a useful act is performed, and an item added to national wealth."[26] The human control of nature was therefore not unlimited, yet with the proper conduct and accommodation to contingencies, its efficiency could be maximized.

In addition to enhancing agricultural production Say recognized the positive role government could have in other areas crucial to production, such as the construction of roads, which enabled easier and cheaper transport of produce. He supported enhancing the construction of canals in France, which would help sustain a republic by supporting communication and the unification of manners.[27]

Say's view of the need to utilize natural resources was comprehensive. "Were it possible," he wrote, "to transplant from the mountain to the plain the beautiful forests, that flourish and rot neglected upon the inaccessible sides of the Alps and Pyrenees, the value of these forests would be an entirely new creation of value to mankind, a clear gain of revenue both to the landholder and the consumer also."[28] In contrast with contemporaneous romantics, Say perceived no real value in nature "in itself," and very little in the beauty of nature. The main positive aspect of untouched nature was its potential, when eventually touched, of becoming a source of economic material gain for all classes of society.

This did not mean, however, that Say was not capable of demonstrating a more nuanced and modern approach to the use of nature. While discussing the benefits of government intervention in agriculture, for example, he mentioned such things as punishing those engaged in "the destroying of caterpillars and other noxious insects." In other words, he recognized the importance of these insects for what today would be termed ecological balance, though specifically from the perspective of sustainable development. Thus, the regulations regarding the felling of trees in France, which were indispensable for preserving their growth, were in some respects at least discouraging for the growing of trees, a "branch of cultivation, which, though particularly adapted to certain soils and sites, and conducive to the attraction of atmospheric moisture, yet seems to be daily on the decline."[29] Here again Say recognized the limited control humans had of nature, which could nevertheless be maximized with the proper economic policy. When he did note the beauties of nature, these were beauties resulting from the human improvement of nature, not from pristine wilderness.

> Capital employed under intelligent direction, may make barren rocks to bear increase. The Cevennes, the Pyrenees, and the Pays de Vaud, present on every side the view of mountains, once the scene of unvaried sterility, now covered with verdure and enriched by cultivation. Parts of these rocks have been blasted with gunpowder, and the shivered fragments employed in the construction of terraces one above another, supporting a thin stratum of earth carried thither by human labour. In this manner is the barren surface of the rock transformed into shelving platforms, richly furnished with verdure, and teeming with produce and population… capital cannot be more beneficially employed, than in strengthening and aiding the productive powers of nature.[30]

Nature could be beautiful, but it was precisely human activity, the blast of gunpowder, which endowed it with beauty.

Say's views, particularly regarding his departure from Smith through accentuating the role that nature played in creating value in all forms of production, influenced another contemporary French political economist, Frédéric Bastiat, known for his wit, staunch support of free trade and critique of socialism.[31] Bastiat developed his own idiosyncratic approach. He claimed that nature provided materials and forces which when used by human beings gratuitously, had utility, but in effect no value. "We do not buy Nature's goods; we gather them in, and if, to gather them in, an effort of some sort has to be made, it is in this *effort*, not in the gift of Nature, that the value consists." This was more in line with Locke than either Smith or Say. In fact, claimed Bastiat, the greater the satisfaction derived from natural objects without labor, the less value these had, or in other words, use and value were in inverse proportions. The more use could be derived from objects without the onerous requirement of labor, the greater their utility, but the lesser their economic value. Utility, wealth and value were not synonymous, contrary to the claims of many other political economists, according to Bastiat. At this point he referred to the authority of Say. Furthermore, he claimed that all this meant that the materiality of nature was gratuitous, and therefore lacked value, whereas it was human actions which created value. Human beings could not create matter, but they could render services to each other, and these constituted value. Smith's mistake on this point had led to the socialist doctrine, which regarded all those working in occupations which did not deal directly with matter, such as merchants and businessmen, as unproductive parasites (the Physiocrats of course merited Bastiat's criticism here more than Smith). This, for Bastiat the champion of free trade, was obviously an error. Furthermore, value was the result of the exchange of quantifiable services in society. This fortified Bastiat's disdain for what he regarded as the eighteenth-century infatuation with the state of nature in Rousseau's sense, in which no exchange was relevant.[32]

This led him to a defense of private property, and specifically of landed property. If value consisted not in the utility of free natural materials, but in the services rendered by human beings to each other, this meant that human labor was in fact what was ultimately exchanged, not the natural materials it worked upon. Those who confused utility with value, however, attributed value to the free gifts of nature, and thus erroneously undermined the right to property, most conspicuously regarding landed property. The criticism of rent on land might be partially justified, or at least comprehended, by the notion of landlords who did not work, and inherited land occupied by conquest and not under normal conditions. Yet under such normal conditions it was unjustified, just as was the criticism of interest on capital, which was also paid for the seeming use of free natural materials and forces. Once one realized that the forces of nature were not what created value, all the criticisms of landed property appeared erroneous.[33]

Bastiat proceeded on this score to criticize the theories of rent of the Physiocrats, Smith, Ricardo, Senior, Malthus, J. S. Mill and other political economists, most of whom he in other respects admired, not to mention the socialists and the communists, of whom he was much more critical. They had all, in his opinion, made the same error stemming from the confusion of utility and value, of the free gifts of nature and the laboriously rendered services created and exchanged by human beings. Even Say, according to Bastiat, had not recognized this sufficiently. Rent was not paid in return for the free gifts of nature, but for the efforts of the landowners in improving the instruments that made cheaper the production of wheat, wool, fruit and other products. The landowners did not charge rent for the land itself, but for the improvements to it made possible by their investments and efforts, which were for the benefit of all society, including those who did not own land. So long as liberty and justice were maintained, the ownership of land was justified. Rent was therefore part of the principal of reciprocal services which constituted political economy, and indeed human social interaction in general. Even assuming the remote possibility of a fully peopled and cultivated earth, this situation would probably only spur the landowners to curb their own procreation, and maximize their production of food. The contingencies of such a situation were, however, inconceivable for all the sciences, not just political economy.[34] Bastiat was therefore a much stauncher defender of the landowners than Malthus. While he agreed with Malthus's population theory, he regarded Malthus as over-pessimistic.[35]

For Bastiat it was precisely the addition of human labor to the free gifts of nature which made social existence possible, and optimism about human progress the obvious conclusion. This was an elaborate version of the Lockean theory of value. The mere utility of natural resources had no social or economic value as long as they were freely available for all. It was what human beings added to nature, not nature in itself, which constituted the foundation of social and political-economic development. "Show me," he retorted, "in any part of the world whatsoever, a piece of land that has not directly or indirectly been the object of man's activity, and I will show you a piece of land totally lacking in value."[36]

In Britain, reactions to Smith, Ricardo and Malthus were more pervasive and elaborate. John Ramsay McCulloch repeated the essentially Lockean theory of value, noting that "Nature spontaneously furnishes the matter of which commodities are made; but until labour has been applied to appropriate matter, or to adapt it to our use, it is destitute of value, and is not, and never has been, considered as forming wealth."[37] He emphasized nature's unlimited bounty, and the human ability to control it in manufactures as much as in agriculture.[38] Agriculture was the most vital form of production, since the utilization of the land was the most central aspect of labor for the provision of food, as well as other necessary items. Yet manufactures and trade were also important. McCulloch claimed that both the Physiocrats and Smith had erred in regarding agriculture as the most efficient type of labor because of the work that nature itself contributed in the process, which was unavailable in manufactures. He went so far as to claim that the passage in the *Wealth of Nations* where Smith outlined this view was "perhaps the most objectionable passage" in the whole work.[39] In fact, nature contributed just as much to manufactures, machinery, navigation and other endeavors, as it did to agriculture. If anything, due to soil exhaustion, nature contributed even more to manufactures, since once a technological invention was made, its reproduction maintained its efficiency indefinitely.[40]

A more detailed consideration of natural resources was outlined by the independently-minded Robert Torrens. Torrens claimed that no matter how fertile the land might be, and how bountiful nature, it had no meaning for human beings before they made use of nature with the aid of labor, and of capital in the form of tools. "The productions of nature possess no utility for man until he has rendered them his own. The ungathered fruits of the earth, and the beasts of the chase roaming at large in the forest, constitute no portion of wealth.

The circumstance of nature's having abundantly bestowed the materials for supplying our wants would have been of no consequence whatever, unless we had possessed the skill to apply our labour to the appropriation of her gifts."[41] Torrens repeated the well-known differentiation between uncultivated natural elements on which no labor was bestowed, and which were consequently not part of capital, and cultivated elements which consequently became capital, hence a particular species of wealth.[42] Human beings were incapable of creating anything, only of modifying the materials provided by nature through the use of labor. "With the economist, riches are always more or less an artificial requisition, requiring for their formation that some portion of human exertion should second the agency of nature."[43]

Like Say and Nassau Senior he often used the term "natural agents" in referring to the natural elements. He noted that the term "land" referred to those natural agents which were primary instruments of production, and did not mean just the land itself, which he termed "soil" (though this was the most prominent element), but rather all the natural elements from which wealth was derived. Torrens thus made explicit what had long been clear in political-economic discourse – that the reference to "land" was synonymous with natural resources in general.

> When we contemplate the world which we inhabit, we not only observe order and regularity in the succession of events, but discover a system of adaptation and harmony, and see one part of nature corresponding with, and answering to, another. The earth supplies, spontaneously, productions calculated to supply the wants and gratify the desires of the sensitive beings which dwell upon her surface. The surrounding atmosphere, the depths of the waters, the bowels of the earth, and, above all, the exterior soil, abound with materials adapted to our use. Hence, the air, the waters, and the earth, and even the physical laws which determine their combinations, may be considered as the primary instruments in the formation of wealth.[44]

Torrens claimed that production was based on three factors – land, labor and capital. He differentiated between production itself, which was the formation of wealth, and industry, which was "the means employed in order to effect such formation." Use of capital in particular was unique to the human race. Any use of implements, tools, was in effect use of capital. Such use had begun at the savage stage of social development, and had reached much higher forms with historical progress, till by Torrens's own time "[I]mprovements are perpetually taking place in all kinds of implements and machinery, until, in the application of wind, water, and steam, in our mechanical operations, we press the powers of nature into our service, and, in the literal sense of the terms, 'arm us with the force of all the elements.'"[45] Torrens based his discussion on the differentiation between four types of industry – appropriation of natural materials, adaptation of these materials, the agricultural augmentation of natural production and the commercial transportation and exchange of these materials. He thus viewed the various types of industry as advancing forms of utilizing natural resources.[46]

Torrens was influenced, though only up to a point, by Ricardo's theory of rent.[47] He claimed there were diminishing returns not only regarding the same amount of labor on less, as compared with more, fertile land, but also regarding the application of more labor and capital on the most fertile land in itself. Only when this application of additional capital yielded less on fertile land than on less fertile land, was there a motive to cultivate the soil of the next degree of fertility. Once the cultivation of even the least fertile soil became disadvantageous, then the limits to cultivation had been reached. Since all types of industry – appropriation, manufactures, agriculture and trade – were mutually dependent, this limit to cultivation would apply not only to agriculture, but to all manufactures dependent on agricultural production. Therefore, all agricultural improvements were in effect also manufacturing improvements, and vice versa; they both pushed ahead the limit at which agricultural production became disadvantageous. In addition, Torrens noted that agricultural improvements did not cause unemployment, since by providing additional raw materials for manufactures, they enabled more employment in that branch of industry.[48]

Torrens developed a singular view of the significance of commerce. Without mercantile industry all other types of industry would cease to exist, division of labor would also disappear, and cultivation of nature would come to a halt.[49] Home trade, much more than foreign trade, formed the main part of a country's commerce, and without it all production would cease. "Abolish the home trade, and the home divisions of employment will cease; and the efforts of man, uncombined and unconcurring, will no longer be able to subdue the earth."[50] International trade, however, like home or colonial trade, also initiated prosperity through what Torrens termed "foreign or international division of employment." This recalls the scholarly debate regarding the development of the concept of comparative advantage by Torrens and Ricardo. In Torrens's version there existed a mechanical division of labor, roughly equivalent to Smith's famous concept of division of labor, as well as a territorial division of labor, resulting from international trade. Both contributed to prosperity. International trade helped both new countries which had abundant fertile land but a small population and little capital and "mechanical" division of labor, as well as old countries in which the opposite conditions prevailed – little land, but abundant population, capital and mechanical abilities. Therefore commerce between old and new countries was mutually beneficial. Torrens thus viewed commerce in general as the summit of human progress, enabling societies of all types, and in all stages of development, to maximize their production and utilization of resources.[51] Only in the case where a nation approached the limit of its agricultural production but still imported luxuries, might international trade be self-damaging. Yet Torrens considered this as a far off possibility which would probably not occur for centuries to come. He also objected to Malthus's view that growing population would make trade between old and new countries disadvantageous. This too was a danger which seemed to him centuries away.[52]

Torrens's view of comparative advantage had, however, a further aspect which made it particularly original. This was his recognition of natural and geographical factors as part and parcel of a nation's commercial advantages.[53] Commerce in general, and international commerce in particular, propelled the division of labor. In this way it became possible to take advantage of the different natural advantages amenable to cultivation which different regions possessed.[54] Torrens's connection between geographical territory and the division of labor was a further original departure from Ricardo's view of comparative advantage, as Nassau Senior would later note.[55] Torrens emphasized how the different geographical qualities of different countries, or of colonies in relation to their mother country, enabled cultivating different natural resources. He called this "a mutually beneficial territorial division of employment."[56] This notion, of an international "territorial division of labor" between countries, to which we might add a concept of "territorial comparative advantage" (not spelled out by Torrens himself), was his most original contribution to the idea of utilizing natural resources to enhance progress.

A different consideration of natural resources was outlined by Dugald Stewart, who claimed that both geography and cultural customs influenced the economic situation of a country. Britain's situation was good thanks to proper utilization of its agricultural riches and its system of inland navigation, on which Stewart continued and wrote "of the prodigies which the industry and spirit of the people, improving on their natural advantages, have already effected, under the protecting influence of civil liberty; connecting the different parts of our islands by an extended system of inland navigation, which (considering the mountainous surface of the country) may be justly regarded as one of the proudest monuments of human power."[57] The need for a proper political order and cultural basis to sustain economic prosperity and progress, was central to Stewart's outlook. The transition from an agrarian-based economy to an industrial one, with which all classical political economists had to come to terms, was one of his central economic preoccupations. He claimed that in his time, in contrast with a century earlier, the attachment to landed property was greatly diminished in favor of trade and luxury, as the rank of individuals was determined mainly by their expenses. City dissipation was preferred to country frugality. Land, like other property, was measured according to the revenue it afforded. Land still retained advantages over all other types of property, though not as much as in the past. This situation was in stark contrast to that in the infancy of English trade in feudal times.[58]

The interdependence between agriculture, manufactures and commerce was a key element of a modern economic order. Nature supplied rude materials, most of which required cultivation or manipulation before they could serve human needs. Therefore, in addition to cultivators of the land, artisans appeared who traded with their farmer neighbors already in the infancy of society. As society developed and the number of new commodities increased, this trade was done from greater distances with the aid of the new class of merchants. The resulting trade also in turn encouraged the production of agricultural surplus.[59] Commerce of course required proper transportation, which also enhanced the circulation of knowledge and the transmission of advanced political ideas.[60] Like Smith, Stewart emphasized maritime trade in particular. In modern times maritime trade had a positive cultural influence, in large part due to improvements in navigation. In antiquity, by comparison, reliance on land carriage had not been the result solely of less knowledge of maritime navigation, but rather of the proximity of the three known continents, and the broad terrestrial structure of Asia and Africa. It was water-based trade, both within continents and between them, which had led to the clear superiority of the modern age over antiquity in terms of prosperity, and the improvement of the human condition in general. The discovery of the passage to India through the Cape of Good Hope, and even more so the discovery of the New World, were the watershed points in this respect. They did so by enhancing the mutual connection between nations, "and by encouraging the art of man to contend with the dangers of the ocean, throwing a new light on those beneficent arrangements which Providence has made for the improvement of the human race."[61]

Nevertheless, Stewart found it difficult to forgo the traditional emphasis on the preeminence of agricultural production. He discussed in detail the interdependence of agriculture and manufactures. Manufactures created a stimulus for agricultural development, which he regarded as the basis for a state's greatness much more than the size of its population. A one-sided preference for either agriculture or manufactures was wrong. This was the reason he criticized the extreme position of the Physiocrats. On the other hand, however, he claimed that agriculture had indeed been neglected by modern Europeans, a fact which governments needed to amend.[62] Stewart did agree with the Physiocrats and Turgot in considering agricultural laborers as pre-eminent among the social classes. Smith's criticism of Quesnay and the Physiocrats was excessive in his opinion. Nevertheless, it was necessary that advancing agriculture would be accompanied by increasing trade and division of labor, so that farmers could cultivate their lands more efficiently, and all of society enjoy the fruits of their labor.[63] Stewart dealt at some length with his preference for the Physiocratic position regarding agriculture as the basis for national wealth, over Smith's criticism of it. On other points, however, he was more in agreement with Smith, criticizing the Physiocrats for their support of monarchy. He also preferred Smith's sensitivity to the contingencies of reality to Quesnay's generalizations.[64]

The benefits of division of labor were least significant for agricultural labor. This emphasized the significance of machines as enhancing both better working conditions and advancing prosperity. Yet without agriculture and the provision of subsistence, society could not benefit from the division of labor in other types of production.[65] Stewart repeatedly noted the pre-eminence of agriculture over all other types of industry in Britain.[66] This logically entailed enhancing the cultivation of land. "The wastes and commons of the kingdom [Great Britain]… afford ample resources for a much greater population than we possess… Every exertion for their improvement may be ranked among the wisest national measures."[67] Among such measures Stewart recommended portioning out small rather than large tracts of land, which would encourage land cultivation and the growth of population.[68] Nevertheless, he claimed that the situation of modern Europe was quite different from that of antiquity in this respect. In the early stages of Roman history small farms were well-cultivated yet self-dependent. The result was insufficient development of trade and manufactures, which gave modern Europe a clear advantage over antiquity. Development of trade and manufactures was also impeded by the fact that the ancient Romans held non-agricultural and non-military occupations in contempt. In modern Europe, on the other hand, farmers did not just grow food for self-consumption, but also produced a surplus meant to acquire manufactured goods through trade. Stewart also claimed that an equal distribution of lands was incompatible with the natural order. In modern Europe, however, the danger was not the existence of excessively small tracts, but rather the opposite, the accumulation of large tracts in too few hands.[69]

Stewart discussed the progress England had made throughout the eighteenth century in terms of its growing population and advancing agriculture, supported by interconnected advancements in trade and manufactures. Other positive developments in the preceding century had included enclosure of lands, and the construction of roads, bridges, harbors and particularly canals which enabled inland trade vital to England's prosperity. Yet the growth of population during this period had not been combined with sufficient increase of agricultural production necessary to maintain more inhabitants. Therefore, the growth of population had not been accompanied by a comparable increase of the general happiness of the nation. Stewart claimed that Adam Smith had not sufficiently realized this fact when he had discussed national wealth.[70]

Openly influenced by Smith, however, Stewart supported complete freedom of inland trade in corn in Britain, since in most cases in which a country enjoyed large-scale production of grain, free inland commerce and frugal use of grain would usually enable overcoming years of scarcity.[71] Stewart did not oppose the importation of grain when necessary. Prohibiting such imports risked enhancing the misery of the poor while assisting the rich. Such a step, meant to raise the price of grain, "is nearly the same as prohibiting the improvement of land, and consequent multiplication of the means of subsistence, in order to serve the owners of those lands that cannot be farther improved, or converting the half of the kingdom into a forest, in order to serve the proprietors of the other half."[72] Prohibiting grain importation, in other words, was not only socially unjust, but also impeded efficient utilization of the country's natural resources. Had grain importation to Britain been allowed, in America more land would have been cultivated to answer British demand. Despite plentiful available land, the Americans would not cultivate more than required to answer their own home demand and that common in Europe.[73]

Other aspects of the utilization of natural resources, and the proper political and economic measures of enhancing it, also interested Stewart. He discussed, for example, the long-term advantages of growing timber.[74] His underlying assumption, like most early discussions of forestry, was akin to the modern sustainability approach. The best use of land was for agriculture, the raising of cattle and growing timber. Stewart considered land solely as an economic resource which required proper political support. One of the disadvantages of a despotic government was that even in countries with abundant natural resources their cultivation was neglected. In despotically governed countries, "Agriculture is neglected, and the earth is left in a state of nature."[75] Legislative measures might amend the imperfections in the political-economic system and thus bring it "nearer and nearer to the order of nature." What Stewart meant by "the order of nature," however, was in fact an anthropocentric conception of an economically and socially efficient system, built upon interdependent classes of society, and enhancing a nation's prosperity by maximizing the utilization of its natural resources. "It is only in such a state of society as that in which we live, in which commerce, agriculture, and manufactures act and react upon each other, that the human character and genius can be completely developed."[76]

Stewart's intellectual outlook straddled two centuries. While he wrote and attained most of his influence in the nineteenth century, he still persisted in an optimism about cultural progress which rested on the foundations of Smith and the Enlightenment view of progress. Among the many advantages of commercial civilization which led to Stewart's optimism was its capability of enabling the overcoming of natural obstacles, which nations on their own were not always capable of accomplishing. "In the present state of the *commercial* world, we no longer dread the miseries of famine, because we find that where nature withholds her bounty from one quarter, she lavishes it on another." Stewart hoped that a similar remedy would emerge to other ills with which humanity had battled for ages.[77]

As noted earlier, Stewart had a considerable influence on the more deductively oriented political economists of the early nineteenth century, not least on Nassau Senior. Expectedly, Senior also demonstrated a consistent interest in enhancing the use of natural resources, coupled with an optimistic vision of how this use could lead to progress. Commenting on the climatic influence on culture, he claimed that this influence on commodities necessary for life remained relatively constant over time, while that on luxuries changed with progress.[78] In other words, the relationship between human beings and their natural environment changed with time. The ability to control this relationship was less evident regarding basic forms of cultivation such as agriculture, and more evident regarding advanced manufactures. For Senior, the true limit to human progress was nature per se, not the ability to utilize what was produced from it. "The only check by which we can predict that the progress of our manufactures will in time be retarded, is the increasing difficulty of importing materials and food. If the importation of raw produce could keep pace with the power of working it up, there would be no limit to the increase of wealth and population."[79]

Senior gave his own version of Smith's differentiation between value in use and value in exchange. According to Senior, both utility and limitation in supply were constituents of value. Nothing in its existing state was limited in supply. It was purposive use which gave value to natural things. Thus the water in a river was freely open to everyone's use, but was limited for those intending to use it to turn mills, thus entailing the need for payment. The more obstacles existed for procuring a product, for example gold, the greater the exertion involved and consequently the value. Furthermore, the propensity to be transferable also constituted an ingredient of value.[80] For Senior being amenable to human use and appropriation was what made natural resources economically valuable. This of course evinced a clear influence of Locke's labor theory of value. Senior, however, claimed that the limit to supply, not only the labor involved, constituted an efficient cause of value, writing that "If all the commodities used by man were supplied by nature without any intervention whatever of human labour, but were supplied in precisely the same quantities as they now are, there is no reason to suppose either that they would cease to be valuable, or would exchange in any other than their present proportions."[81]

Senior, like Say and Torrens, preferred the term "natural agents" to "land," thus emphasizing that this meant not only "land, with its mines, its rivers, its natural forests with their wild inhabitants, and, in short, all its spontaneous productions," but also "the ocean, the atmosphere, light, and heat and even those physical laws, such as gravitation and electricity." Nevertheless, land was the most important of these as a source of profit, as amenable to appropriation, and as leading to the command of other natural agents. This entailed the use of the term "land" in this wider sense.[82] Similarly, he preferred the term "proprietor of a natural agent" to "landlord." Furthermore, even someone who made a useful discovery and let out the privilege of using it, in essence received rent similar to that on land.[83] In contrast with Ricardo, Senior regarded rent as an expression of nature's bounty, and as pure profit. Senior's nature was more generous than Ricardo's. It was practically an agent with intentionality, favoring human prosperity.[84]

Adam Smith, though not a Physiocrat, still claimed that agriculture had an advantage over manufactures due to the labor provided freely by nature. Like others of his generation, who were witnessing the dramatic innovations of the Industrial Revolution, Senior came to doubt Smith's position on this point. While demonstrating an early recognition of the idea of diminishing returns (though without the term itself), Senior claimed that this was the reason that labor in manufactures had an advantage over labor in agriculture. The absolute amount of manufactured product, no matter how efficient the industrial effort involved, seemed at first sight limited by the amount of produce provided by the cultivation of nature. Yet this seeming advantage of agriculture over manufactures was only theoretical. It was clear that the cultivation of land was incapable of being improved indefinitely, otherwise there would have been no need to cultivate lands of lesser and lesser fertility. This was an inherent quality of the soil which limited the efficiency of its use beyond a certain point. This limiting quality did not exist in manufactures, which, in the conditions of the real world, were capable of becoming increasingly more efficient, much more so than agriculture. This did not mean that Senior was not in favor of enhancing the utilization of natural resources as much as possible. On the contrary. The road to this, however, was as much, if not more, through manufactures as through agriculture.[85]

Nature, in any event, was usually amenable to cultivation. In England and Wales there were few lands, even those which seemed uninviting at first sight, which it was truly impossible to bring under cultivation, given the proper effort.

> If the utmost use were made of lime, and marl, and the other mineral manures; if by a perfect system of drainage and irrigation water were nowhere allowed to be excessive or deficient; if all our wastes were protected by enclosures and planting; if all the land in tillage, instead of being scratched by the plough, were deeply and repeatedly trenched by manual labour; if minute care were

> employed in the selecting and planting of every seed or root, and watchfulness sufficient to prevent the appearance of a weed; if all live stock, instead of being pastured, had their food cut and brought to them; in short, if the whole Country were subjected to the labour which a rich citizen lavishes on his patch of suburban garden; if it were possible that all this should be effected, the agricultural produce of the Country might be raised to ten times, or indeed to much more than ten times, its present amount.[86]

Prima facie, there seemed no limit to enhancing the use of nature. Yet in the conditions of the real world, the true ability to augment the efficiency of land use in England was perhaps to quadruple it, and even that was doubtful, let alone to decuple it. Manufactures, on the other hand, had a much greater potential for progress in the real world. "The advantage possessed by land in repaying increased labour, though employed on the same materials, with a constantly increasing produce, is overbalanced by the diminishing proportion which the increase of the produce generally bears to the increase of the labour. And the disadvantage of manufactures in requiring for every increase of produce an equal increase of materials, is overbalanced by the constantly increasing facility with which the increased quantity of materials is worked up."[87] For this reason each additional quantity of produce obtained in agriculture was at a greater proportionate cost, while any similar addition in manufactures came at a lesser proportionate price.[88] Senior positively considered the enhancement of utilizing land and other natural resources. What was even easier to implement, however, was enhancing the efficiency of using the raw materials provided by nature. In contrast with Smith, let alone the Physiocrats, Senior did not regard agriculture as a field in which labor was more efficient thanks to the characteristics of nature.[89] On the contrary, nature itself put a limit to the manner in which it could be utilized, even though it was advisable to try and approach this limit as close as possible. Manufactures, on the other hand, were almost limitless in terms of ingenuity, and of increasing efficiency in using the materials which direct cultivation of nature, primarily agriculture, provided. Either way, whether directly (through agriculture), or indirectly (through manufactures), Senior approved of augmenting the utilization of natural resources to the utmost possible limit.[90] He agreed with the goal of Smith and other Enlightenment predecessors, but differed from them regarding the means to achieve this goal.

Combining his views on the utilization of natural resources, on commerce and on cultural progress, Senior, in the closing sentence of *An Outline of the Science of Political Economy*, noted that "[T]he general progress of improvement tends more and more to equalize the advantages possessed by Different countries in government and habits, and even in salubrity of climate."[91] This was an echo of the earlier Enlightenment view in the style of the Comte de Buffon, which emphasized not only the influence of climate on human beings, but also the reciprocal, often ameliorative, influence of human activity on the climate and the natural environment in general. Senior therefore manifested, in a clearer manner than most other classical political economists, the transmutation of Enlightenment notions of historical progress into the prescriptions of classical political economy. This outlook was based in large part on the crucial and constantly augmenting role that utilization of natural resources played in the cultural, social, economic and political progress of humanity. This optimism was in stark contrast to Ricardo's vision, let alone that of Malthus.

Malthus had a much greater influence on the Christian political economist Thomas Chalmers. Malthus's combination of political economy and natural theology, as well as his criticism of Ricardo, were shared by Chalmers, who also supported Malthus's population principle, and the need to combat it with moral restraint. He also advocated agriculture in a neo-Physiocratic fashion. His main aim as a political economist was to provide a political-economic foundation for the significance of church establishments. His abstract thinking and dogmatism, however, prevented him from having a long-term influence as a political economist, despite his great renown as a preacher.[92]

Basing his approach on Malthus, Chalmers outlined a view of human material progress based on the relation between the production of food and the size of population. The more efficient the labor engaged in production of food, a factor dependent on progress and division of labor, the greater the amount of population which could work to supply necessaries beyond food. If possible, a "disposable" population would even be able to produce luxuries. This latter population was not however really disposable in Chalmers's view. In fact, the more the so-called disposable population could afford to work in producing luxuries, the higher the level of progress of a nation, so long as this did not come at the expense of food and other necessaries. What made this possible was precisely the ability of the agricultural laborers to produce a surplus. This was up to a point a neo-Physiocratic analysis, although Chalmers did not claim that manufactures were strictly sterile.[93] The relative progress which each nation attained determined how efficient its agricultural labor was, and therefore how many inhabitants would be free to cater to other needs. Yet "the generosity of nature" assured that almost always, some amount of agricultural surplus would be produced. Agricultural labor could become indefinitely more efficient, "from the gradual amelioration of the soil, the improvements in the art of farm-management, and the application of machinery, which abridges the work of man, and renders the implements of husbandry more effective."[94]

Chalmers claimed that the manufacture of luxuries could be transferred from one commodity to another, whether because of changing tastes and demand in society, or due to extraneous circumstances, not least of which was the possible exhaustion of natural resources. For example, the exhaustion of particular mined metals might bring an end to the production of dependent articles. This would be only a temporary loss to the laborers, since the surplus food to maintain them would remain, and they would find different occupations, catering to different luxury items which would take the place of the now unavailable ones. The real loss would be to the consumers who would be deprived of an item they had formerly desired. This problem, however, became much more emphatic when the resource in question was required for producing not luxuries but necessaries. Chalmers gave as an example the exhaustion of coal. This was an example how, by the first decade of the nineteenth century, coal was considered of vital importance, although it seems that Chalmers did not consider such a shortage as imminently possible.[95] He did seem aware, however, of the basic problem that the limited supply of natural resources posed to a society, another sign of the significant influence of Malthus.

Beyond food, necessaries were often defined by the natural and climatic conditions in which human beings lived. "If the temperature of our climate was so mild and uniform, as to save us the necessity of houses, the occupation of a mason would be utterly unknown." The surplus agricultural produce expended on houses might then have been spent on other items. Yet this of course was not the case. "It is a pity that the elements of nature should be so unkindly, and that, to defend himself against them, man must surrender so much of that wealth which secures him the blessings and the advantages of existence." In the same manner, if the nature of human beings themselves had been better, the necessity of providing for armies would have been redundant.[96] The issue of military expense was significant for Chalmers, particularly during the war with Napoleon. While not raising ethically based criticism of luxury, he noted that the emphasis placed on manufactures was misplaced. The manufacturers were the servants of the customers, or in other words of society at large, which through its instrument, the government, might transfer its demand from one product to another, with no lasting negative damage to the interests of the manufacturers. Chalmers therefore emphasized the possibility of transferring, not least through taxation, public funds to military expenditure. This came at no loss to the economy, so long as the diminished manufactures were those produced by the "disposable" population, who would find different employment as the servants of the state rather than the market. Openly recognizing Smith's analysis, Chalmers noted that in an advanced society such as Britain, the division of labor had reached the level where agricultural workers, and even those producing other necessaries, worked at their occupation year-round, and could not find time to labor in military occupations, which themselves became specialized. The production of agriculture and necessaries therefore had to be exempt from wartime taxation. On the surplus of these items depended the ability of the country to consume luxuries in peacetime, and support the military in wartime. In this fashion Chalmers demonstrated how efficient use of natural resources enabled the surplus necessary for expenditure on such things as high culture on the one hand, or military defense on the other.[97]

The pressing need to support military expenditure during the Napoleonic wars was also the starting-point for a quite outstanding simile which Chalmers outlined:

> Let us suppose, that a gentleman's estate is situated upon the sea coast, and that, from its level situation, it may come in time to be exposed to the influx of the waters. It is conceivable that a permanent elevation may take place on the surface of the ocean, and that, unless the necessary precautions are resorted to by the owner, it may in time make such an encroachment upon the land, as to annihilate his whole property. Two expedients may be proposed for saving the estate. The first is, to reduce the sea to its former level: The second is to throw

> an embankment along the beach and defend his territory from its encroachments. The first expedient is visionary and impracticable. The second is more likely of success. He cannot destroy the cause; but this is no reason why he should not try to defend himself from the effects of it. He cannot reduce the elevation of the water; but this is no reason why he should not try to prevent the elevation from spreading over upon him, and to save himself from that ruin which inevitably awaits him, if he looks on, an unconcerned spectator, without defence and without preparation.[98]

This was a natural simile for the danger which could also come from human sources, which in this case meant Napoleon. Yet such human dangers were usually more short-term than natural ones, which might be intransigent. Combating the latter was possible for the landowner only so long as it was economically viable, entailing less expenses than the income of rent on the endangered land. Like his mention of the exhaustibility of resources, it seems that in this case too Chalmers was mentioning a possible natural danger which did not seem imminent, but which served his allegorical argument. From our modern perspective it is, however, rather striking that he detailed such a possibility, which in times of global warming has become a distinct danger for many coastline areas. Chalmers of course would have known of reclamation projects such as those famously undertaken by the Dutch since medieval times. A "permanent elevation… on the surface of the ocean," however, was a less imaginable idea in the nineteenth century. In any event, Chalmers accepted the need, and the possibility, of combating natural forces so long as it was physically and economically viable to do so.

Another interesting figure was the inductively inclined Richard Jones, who as already noted relied heavily on historical evidence in his political-economic analysis. He disagreed sharply with Ricardo's views, and to a certain extent also with Malthus's, presenting a more optimistic vision of the possibility of progress based on utilization of natural resources. Jones claimed that throughout all stages of social progress the interests of the landlords, and their growing profits, were attuned to those of society in general. Furthermore, a lowered rate of profit was usually accompanied by an increasing productive power, and the ability to accumulate more fresh resources. Contrary to the claims of other political economists, a situation of lowered profits was therefore not a sign of decline but rather of prosperity. Likewise, a growing population was not a hindrance to the happiness of all the classes of society.[99] Jones was optimistic, claiming that with a proper social policy the interests of all classes concurred. There was no reason to fear that anything, "either in the physical constitution of man, or in that of the earth which he inhabits," would impede a country's progress.[100]

Jones devoted considerable attention to the issue of rent, and specifically to a sustained critique of Ricardo's theory of rent.[101] First and foremost, Jones claimed that rent would be charged even were all the land of identical quality. Ricardo's theory, he claimed, was the source of the erroneous view that there was an opposition between the interests of the proprietors of land and those of the rest of the community. Ricardo's theory was correct only regarding farmers' rents (by which he meant those cases when the owners of the land were capitalists, and rent was in fact the surplus profit realized on the land). Yet such rents were barely one percent of all rents, and appeared mainly in England and the Netherlands. Most rents were straightforward peasants' rents.[102] In any event, the cultivation of less fertile land did not raise the rent on more fertile land, though it did put a limit to the rise of rent, since the price of raw produce would never rise beyond the price of procuring it from the least fertile land. This limit to rent ensured a continued protection of the consumers' interests without hurting those of the landowners.[103]

Jones went into great detail in refuting the Ricardian outlook on all types of both peasant and farmer rents, using a classification which would be adopted by John Stuart Mill, despite the latter's criticism of Jones.[104] The first type of peasant rent was the system of serf labor, or rents on land, which was not only unjust, but also failed to motivate an efficient cultivation of the land. However, even in the east-European countries this type of rent was gradually disappearing, with the result that these countries were beginning to acquire a station proportional to their natural resources.[105] The situation of metayer tenants was better than that of serfs. Their subjugation was less oppressive, and all the care of land cultivation was in their hands, and therefore more efficient than with serfs. It was in the landlords' interest that the metayers would cultivate the land properly and pay rent. Therefore, even when the metayers' condition was bad, not least as a result of depressive taxation, the landlords took care of them. Nevertheless, the discrepancy of interests between the landlords and the metayer tenants became apparent in the lack of proper investment in agricultural improvements.[106]

Jones then addressed ryot rents, those rents paid to the sovereign, which in modern times were common mainly in Asia, not least in Persia. In the latter, as a result of scarcity of water, those who erected waterworks and brought water to previously dry localities received from the sovereign hereditary rights to the land which had turned fertile, while of course paying a rent to the sovereign.[107] This, however, was practically the only positive thing Jones had to say about the depressive Persian ryot rent system. In themselves ryot rents were not incompatible with prosperity, being in essence a type of land tax. Yet in Asia they were connected with political corruption, and thus hindered any possible prosperity and progress which could have been achieved with better government.[108] On the other hand, among the disadvantages of cottier rents (rents, according to Jones's definition, paid in money rather than produce), was the fact that they created no checks to population, thus enabling the peasants to procreate till they reached a state of penury. With other rents, the interests of the landlords or sovereigns created such checks by halting the division of the soil. In the cottier system the division of the land would cease only when the peasants were already in a state of wretchedness, as the occurrences in Ireland had demonstrated.[109]

Jones admitted that all types of peasant rents prevented the full development of the productive powers of the earth, because the landlords tended to detach themselves from a true interest in cultivation, while the peasants, due to their poverty, were unable to invest capital or apply science to advance agricultural improvements. Only capitalists could do so, yet they were absent from the task of cultivating land.[110] The real problem for Jones was not, in contrast with Ricardo's outlook, with rent in itself, but rather with the fact that the less inhabitants, whether agricultural or non-agricultural, were concerned with agriculture, the less a nation was able to progress both in agriculture and in other fields. Coming closer to Ricardo's viewpoint than in most other passages of his discussion, Jones claimed that even an increase in the wealth of the peasants would not in itself improve their condition, or that of society in general, so long as the other classes were unwilling to sacrifice something for the sake of such progress.[111] When rent of any type rose as a result of pressure on the tenants, this became detrimental to production and prosperity. Yet when rent rose as a result of prosperity and improved cultivation, it created an indefinite power of increase which favored the peasants, the landlords and all society.[112] Jones perceived no tangible limit to enhancing the cultivation of land under the proper social and political circumstances.

Having finished his discussion of peasant rents, he next addressed the less common farmer rents, by which he meant rent on lands owned by capitalists. Ricardo, he claimed, had erred regarding these also, since the investment of capital in agriculture came with progress, enhancing both production and consequently rent, which was not the result of the cultivation of increasingly less fertile lands. Ricardo and his followers were indeed correct in claiming that there were diminishing returns on agricultural labor. Yet the influence of this fact was less decisive in Jones's opinion compared with the influence of increasingly efficient agricultural labor. Rent was dependent on the amount of produce, not the relative fertility of the land. Ricardo, so he claimed, had also erred in regarding agricultural improvements as detrimental to the interests of the landlords.[113] Jones's repeated criticism of Ricardo was expressed in particularly emphatic tone when he objected to the "repulsive doctrine" regarding the opposition of the interests of the proprietors of land to those of the other classes of the community. The interests of all classes were intertwined. The profits of one class might come at the expense of another class, but they might also rise as the result of enhanced production, in which case they could continue rising securely, thus benefiting society in general.[114]

Like other classical political economists, Jones addressed the relative merits of agriculture and manufactures. Investment of capital in machinery and implements, he claimed, was equivalent to the investment of auxiliary capital in labor, making it more efficient, compared with the investment of capital simply in enlarging the quantity and power of labor.[115] Auxiliary capital invested in agricultural production also diminished the amount of agricultural laborers in the population compared with the non-agricultural laborers. This, as the situation of England demonstrated, was a sign of progress.[116] Agricultural production did not enjoy superiority in every respect. Social, political and moral progress were expressed in a nation's advance in manufactures, but not in agriculture. Agriculture, on the other hand, might remain at the same level of efficiency, while in other fields, including manufactures, there was a general cultural decline.[117] This implied both a strength and a weakness of agriculture – strength in its self-sufficiency, and weakness in its relative irrelevance to higher forms of cultural progress. Yet this also pointed to Jones's repeated emphasis on the inter-dependency of all sectors of the economy, a point on which he was more in tune with other classical political economists.

Agriculture, however, enjoyed a privileged place in his political-economic analysis. While criticizing Ricardo's notion of diminishing returns on agricultural labor, Jones accepted that there was an indefinite point where this indeed became valid, though he regarded this point as less close and tangible than Ricardo did. "Surely it is neither impossible nor improbable, that the earth under an improving system of husbandry, may disclose powers of rewarding as bountifully the skilful and efficient industry bestowed upon her, as she did the languid and ignorant operations of a less laborious cultivation."[118] Ricardo had also erred in claiming that agricultural improvements would move land out of cultivation and lower rent, because he had abstractly hypothesized in assuming this would happen overnight. In fact, according to Jones, agricultural improvements were implemented gradually over time, and were accompanied with growing population and increasing demand. According to Jones's outlook all society, including the landlords, were instrumental in advancing agricultural improvements. Therefore a rising rent was not the mere transference of wealth, as Ricardo had claimed, but was rather part and parcel of the creation of wealth, equivalent to the enlargement of the territory itself.[119]

Agricultural improvements brought into cultivation land which had previously been regarded barren, a process which was accompanied with prosperity, growing population as well as rising rent.[120] Writing of ryot rents, but in fact addressing all types of rent, Jones noted that "While an increase of produce rents [which rose in tandem with the amount of produce] has its source in greater crops, it may go on till the skill of man and the fertility of the earth have reached their maximum, that is, indefinitely."[121] Improved agricultural production therefore enabled general socioeconomic progress. England served as an example how agricultural improvements enabled the growth of the non-agricultural population, thus changing the national character, customs and politics of any nation which would undergo a similar process of making agriculture more efficient. It was probable that England's progress would continue and even be enhanced, hand in hand with the rising efficiency of land cultivation, including bringing yet unproductive land into cultivation.[122] England's agricultural improvements, apparent in few other places, afforded incomparable cultural progress. "Were the whole of the earth's surface cultivated with like efficiency, how different would be the aggregate of the commercial means, political institutions, the intellect and civilization of the inhabitants of our planet!"[123]

Jones, like the other nineteenth-century classical political economists who followed in the wake of Ricardo and Malthus, felt compelled to grapple with the main tenets of the theories of these two formative figures, all the while cognizant of Smith's foundational analysis. Major topics such as Smith's division of labor, Ricardo's theory of rent, Malthus's population theory as well as the debate on general gluts which included Say's important contribution, all received consistent attention in the first half of the nineteenth century. In most cases, as we have seen, this involved a consideration of the use of natural resources. Some political economists presented a more optimistic vision, others less so. Yet they all shared the common anthropocentric assumption that nature was first and foremost a resource meant for human use, and even the most pessimistic of them, including Malthus himself, considered the notion of a finite limit to natural resources as a remote and far from imminent possibility. If such a limit seemed acute, this was the result of improper social and economic policies, and could therefore be amended. Enhancing the efficiency of utilizing natural resources was therefore considered both a precondition, and a result, of cultural progress in general.

10 John Stuart Mill's attitude toward nature

With all due respect to other classical political economists beyond Smith, Ricardo and Malthus, the next, and last, giant of this tradition was John Stuart Mill, whose *Principles of Political Economy* was the most comprehensive work in the field since Smith's *Wealth of Nations*, and also the most intellectually diversified. This pertained, not least, to the issue of nature. As noted above, Margaret Schabas regards Mill as a pivotal figure in the denaturalization process from the classical political-economic view in which nature posed distinct limits to human development, to the modern view in which human beings were perceived as more independent of, and consequently more in command of, nature. Schabas claims that Mill considered nature as something which humanity needed to confront and control, not something with which to conform. Mill influenced the turn in modern economic thought in the direction of dealing with the human and the artificial, which was separate and superior from the physical and the natural. In this respect she regards Mill as largely responsible for the process of denaturalization in economic thought. While, she claims, contemporaneous naturalists, mainly Darwin, inserted humanity into nature, economists, following Mill, removed humanity from nature.[1] However, as should have become clear by this point of our discussion, the "denaturalization" which appeared in the history of economic thought was in fact a persistent manifestation of the anthropocentric cosmology which had been evident in human culture for millennia. What was novel at different stages of this process was the intensification of this outlook, and its increasingly reflexive character, and not any new emergence in the modern era. In the main, the history of human attitudes toward nature has been consistent and linear. Eighteenth-century stadial theory was a particularly significant stage in this history, since it demonstrated how Enlightenment intellectuals consciously and deliberately viewed the command of the natural environment as a sine qua non of historical progress. It was this outlook, as we saw, which was transmuted into the new science of political economy, becoming a key prescriptive element in the modern economic outlook on the natural environment qua natural resources. In contrast with Schabas's interpretation, therefore, classical political economists, including and culminating in Mill, should be considered as continuators of the Enlightenment view of nature. What was novel to Mill's outlook, as we will see, was recognition of the problematical aspects of the new modern control of nature, alongside advocacy for it.

Nature, in quite a forthright manner, played a leading role in Mill's political economy. He indicatively began the Preliminary Remarks to the *Principles of Political Economy* with the statement that "In every department of human affairs, Practice long precedes Science: systematic enquiry into the modes of action of the powers of nature, is the tardy product of a long course of efforts to use those powers for practical ends."[2] Many pages later, he ended the lengthy text of the book with the observation that "It is the proper end of government to reduce this wretched waste [efforts devoted to neutralizing injurious conduct] to the smallest possible amount, by taking such measures as shall cause the energies now spent by mankind in injuring one another, or in protecting themselves against injury, to be turned to the legitimate employment of the human faculties, that of compelling the powers of nature to be more and more subservient to physical and moral good."[3] The emphasis on the vital importance of the human use of nature thus framed the whole text of *Principles of Political Economy*, and was constantly discussed either implicitly or explicitly throughout it. We have already addressed some facets of Mill's views on this topic, mainly those associated with his consideration of progress and over-population. Yet there were other vital aspects of his views on nature. It is easy to overlook the significance of the opening remark quoted above. Mill of course was discussing the rise of the science of political economy in the modern age. Yet there is a further significance to this statement. It is an essentially historical claim, stating that forms of utilization of nature precede their systematization and transformation into an ordered scientific praxis. In other words, as the *Principles of Political Economy* would proceed to demonstrate at great length, science – whether this was what today we would term natural or exact science, but also the social sciences such as economics – was in fact a late, a posteriori chapter in the historical development of the human race, preceded by long centuries of material and social progress. Of prime importance, in this respect, was the human utilization of natural resources. This underlying logic influenced Mill's various discussions of topics such as stadial social progress or over-population. As the closing sentence of the work quoted above demonstrates, the utilization of nature was also intimately intertwined with Mill's more famously known views on the moral condition and progress of society.

Mill claimed that "everything… which serves any human purpose, and which nature does not afford gratuitously, is wealth." This was evidently a late reformulation of Locke's labor theory of value. Not all aspects of nature were considered as wealth, only those which required human labor to transform them into valuable items. Following earlier political economists, Mill noted that air, for example, was not wealth, since it was naturally and abundantly available. Assuming, however, a scarcity of air for some reason, then whoever would be able to supply it would make it into wealth, since then it would gain exchangeable value, due to the fact that labor was necessary for producing or acquiring it. In other words, the human utilization of natural resources formed the basis for the production of valuable and exchangeable products, and thus for all human material progress from its very historical beginnings.[4] There were two requisites of production – labor, and appropriate natural objects. Nature spontaneously provided certain products, for example fruits, although even then gathering them required effort. Anything beyond that, however, required specific effort at cultivation. Occasionally the resulting product appeared completely different and unassociated with its original natural source, for example the relation between the fleece of sheep and manufactured cloth. In addition, nature supplied things such as wind and water which served as substitutes for labor.[5]

The differentiation between nature and labor was not a simple matter. In essence, human beings only gave motion to various natural objects, and the laws of nature then did all the remaining work. This was evident from such things as cloth production, through the planting of seeds, to the production of steam-propelled machines. "This one operation, of putting things into fit places for being acted upon by their own internal forces, and by those residing in other natural objects, is all that man does, or can do, with matter… But this [motion and resistance to motion] is enough to have given all the command which mankind have acquired over natural forces immeasurably more powerful than themselves; a command which, great as it is already, is without doubt destined to become indefinitely greater."[6] It was impossible to assess the relative importance of nature in relation to labor, as these two elements played their respective roles in producing various products. This was the origin of the Physiocrats' error, as well as that of Adam Smith, in thinking that nature assisted human beings in agricultural more than in manufacturing labor. Nature provided not only materials but also powers, and in this respect contributed equally to all human activity, to manufactures as much as to agriculture.[7] According to Mill, it was the fact of the lesser quantity of agricultural land in comparison with natural elements such as air, heat or electricity necessary for manufactures, which resulted in the payment of rent on land. Rent was not paid for a greater service rendered by nature, but simply because of the lesser quantity of land.[8] Different natural elements varied in quantity from place to place and at different times. Land might be fertile and abundant in one country and scarce in another, as water might vary in abundance in various regions.[9] The moment a scarcity of a particular natural resource occurred as a result of increased demand for its use, it acquired exchangeable value and became the subject of economic interactions. According to Mill's outlook, this was the crucial point at which natural elements became natural resources in the full economic sense.[10]

Agriculture, the actual work upon the soil, was according to Mill unique and different from any other type of labor, or from any other stage of production which resulted from agricultural labor.[11] Almost anything which was produced perished more or less quickly. Even most buildings and bridges did not survive long, particularly if they were intended for industrial purposes. Almost all types of capital thus had a limited survival period. However, "The land subsists, and the land is almost the only thing that subsists."[12] Therefore, when it came to fixed capital, land was superior. The most useful utilization of fixed capital was that which was invested in the improvement of natural resources. "The most permanent of all kinds of fixed capital is that employed in giving increased productiveness to a natural agent, such as land." This might include things such as the draining of marshes or permanent manuring. Such types of labor required some level of repeated investment for maintenance, yet enhanced the value of the land itself, and as such were a good investment which eventually yielded a surplus. In contrast with improvements invested in machines, improvements in land remained effective forever. The capital invested in such labor was consumed, "But it was consumed productively, and has left a permanent result in the improved productiveness of an appropriated natural agent, the land."[13] In other words, an investment in natural resources, principally in land, was the best and most remunerative investment. This approach underlay Mill's, and in fact the whole tradition of eighteenth- and early nineteenth-century political-economic thought's, emphasis on the importance of agriculture. It was the cultivation of land which was not only the sine qua non of human existence in its capacity of supplying sustenance, but also, under properly managed economic and social conditions, was both the most remunerative economic investment, as well as the firm basis for all other economic production and activity. Put succinctly, the labor invested in manipulating natural elements, thus turning them into natural resources, was the ineluctable and permanent basis for all human economic and social development. As Mill had learned from his Enlightenment predecessors, this was the starting point for the progressive history of humanity.

Capital was a component of production in addition to labor and natural agents. The latter implied land, although Mill included in this not only what was grown on land, but also the products of mines and fisheries, which were subject to generally similar economic rules.[14] In order for a country's agriculture to be truly productive, there was need for an outlet for agricultural production. This outlet became a stimulus for farmers to produce more than was necessary for basic consumption. Such a stimulus was provided mainly by the proximity of cities to agricultural regions, or by the exportation of agricultural produce outside of the country, both which created a demand for such produce.[15] The true limit to production was the amount of land. Assuming otherwise was "not only an error, but the most serious one, to be found in the whole field of political economy." Humanity was still far from reaching the stage when land would be unavailable. Nevertheless, the fact that there still remained many uncultivated tracts of land did not mean that it was possible to continue and cultivate the land unabated, without this having a negative impact on production.[16] Like other post-Malthusian political economists, Mill had to consider the idea of finite resources.

Following Ricardo and Malthus, Mill recognized that the law of production from the soil was a law of diminishing returns, proportional to the increased application of labor and capital. In order for the proportional increase of agricultural produce to be maintained, it was necessary to invest a similarly proportioned amount of labor. Mill noted that "This general law of agricultural industry is the most important proposition in political economy." This fact resulted from the uneven quality and fertility of land, as well as from the varying proximity or distance of land from markets. The more amount of land was cultivated, the more the need to cultivate less qualitative land became evident, land which consequently demanded more labor, while giving lesser returns and profits.[17] What weakened the effect of the law of diminishing returns in relation to the cultivation of land was the progress of civilization, and in particular the progress and growing efficiency of agricultural knowledge, agricultural tools, methods of land cultivation and so forth. The law of diminishing returns also affected manufactures, yet there, technological innovations had an even more dramatic effect in enhancing the efficiency of labor and production. Improvements in manufactures, however, also occasionally influenced agriculture, which utilized manufactured tools. Agriculture became more efficient also as a result of progress in transportation, and of general cultural progress evident in government, ethics, society and education.[18] The command of natural resources was both the basis for human historical development, and also the domain in which progress in other cultural fields became most clearly evident, in mutually enhancing fashion. "[A]ll natural agents which are limited in quantity, are not only limited in their ultimate productive power, but, long before that power is stretched to the utmost, they yield to any additional demands on progressively harder terms. This law may however be suspended, or temporarily controlled, by whatever adds to the general power of mankind over nature; and especially by any extension of their knowledge, and their consequent command, of the properties and powers of natural agents."[19] Nature posed a physical-quantitative limit to the growth and progress of humanity, yet humanity, with the aid of progress in all fields of culture, from economics, through technology, and on to ethics and government, could make the utilization of natural resources more efficient, and thus maximize it.

Mill, alluding to, though not exactly following, Ricardo's theory of rent, noted that in an early stage of social development people labored on the land most easily cultivated, only later turning to cultivating the most fertile land (the varying fertility of land not necessarily implying how commensurably easy or difficult it might be to cultivate).[20] When a landlord improved the fertility of his land, he became entitled to the same higher rent which he would have received if the same level of fertility had been natural to the land.[21] Mill went into great detail as he outlined and supported Ricardo's theory of rent. There always existed cultivated land which was the least fertile, or less advantageously situated in the vicinity of markets, and which consequently did not require payment of rent, although it determined the level of rent paid for land which was more fertile or better situated than it was.[22] In itself, according to Mill, and clearly echoing Locke, a natural resource was not something which could be held as private property. The moment, however, that labor was invested in the cultivation of the land, it became private property. Improvement of it was what conveyed the right to property of land.[23]

Ricardo's criticism of landowners evoked a socialist perspective. Mill, at a time when socialism had made a much greater impression, famously struggled much more to reconcile certain socialist ideas with his general advocacy for free markets.[24] The appropriation of land as property, he claimed, was different from the appropriation of manufactured products. Property in movables, so long as it was harmless, was to remain unlimited. Ownership of land, on the other hand, had to be restricted much more strenuously the moment it damaged the common good. The rights of landlords in this respect were less important compared to the community's interest. In case these two interests collided, society in general should not leave it to the landlords to decide how the land was to be used. Land, in contrast with movables, was limited in quantity, and therefore when one individual had more of it, others, unjustly, had less. When it came to land, no such thing as "sacredness of property" existed. "No man made the land. It is the original inheritance of the whole species. Its appropriation is wholly a question of general expediency. When private property in land is not expedient, it is unjust." Even when the owners of land cultivated it, this did not permit them to abuse this right contrary to the common good, a fortiori when they desired to limit accessibility to the land not for purposes of cultivation, but only for their own private enjoyment.

> When land is not intended to be cultivated, no good reason can in general be given for its being private property at all; and if any one is permitted to call it his, he ought to know that he holds it by the sufferance of the community, and on an implied condition that his ownership, since it cannot possibly do them any good, at least shall not deprive them of any, which could have derived from the land if it had been unappropriated… The species at large still retains, of its original claim to the soil of the planet which it inhabits, as much as is compatible with the purposes for which it has parted with the remainder.[25]

The constitutive significance which Mill perceived regarding the role which cultivation of land played in the development of society, was mirrored by the fact that when he addressed social and economic injustice and inequality, he perceived the ownership of land as a pivotal issue through which the amelioration of society could be achieved. Mill as both political economist and as social reformer thus equally emphasized the cultivation of nature, with all its accompanying social phenomena, as the constitutive basis for cultural progress.

On this, as on many other issues, Mill made a considerable impact on contemporaneous political-economic discussions. A prominent example was the Irish political economist John Elliott Cairnes.[26] Writing of the difficult situation of Ireland, and basing his reasoning on Ricardo's theory of rent, Cairnes claimed that *laissez-faire* principles were not always paramount. At times governmental intervention was required, particularly regarding land, which economically was a different object of wealth than other types of property. Farmers were not capitalists, and did not have the true freedom to choose to labor in other occupations. They were therefore at the mercy of the landowners, who could charge exorbitant rent and leave them only with bare subsistence. Therefore, the free market did not work properly or justly in the case of landed property. Cairnes, basing his argument on Mill, claimed that in contrast with moveable property, land, which no human being had made, existed in limited quantity and was the inheritance of all humanity, and therefore should not be the object of personal property. The labor invested in land did not change this situation, since neither labor to raise immediate crops, nor the construction of, for example, buildings or railroads in the vicinity of agricultural land, constituted an improvement in the land itself. The latter occurred only when the land, by labor, became more qualitative as cultivable land, when permanent improvements were made to the soil itself. However, those who enjoyed this improvement in the quality of land were not those who had invested the required labor, but rather the proprietors. Therefore the singularity of land as an object of property pertained both to land in the state of nature, and in many cases to cultivated land as well.[27]

As for Mill, he supported peasant proprietorship of land, but only so long as the tracts of land owned by the farmers were not too small, and thus inadequate for providing sufficient food for them and their families.[28] Mill had greater confidence than Malthus in the laboring class's ability to act in a way conducive to their well-being. He claimed that enhancing the ownership of land among small proprietors did not encourage over-population. On the contrary, it probably had the opposite effect, encouraging prudence, as farmers managed their lives and resources with an eye to the future. This was one of the main reasons that, according to Mill, the system of ownership of small tracts of land by the agricultural laborers was best, and clearly superior to the traditional English system of large farms cultivated by hired labor.[29] He devoted considerable attention to the need for enlarging the number of small farms in England. Among his arguments supporting the assertion that small farms were no less productive than large ones, he noted that the skill and knowledge of farmers in small farms were not inferior, and in fact were occasionally superior, to those of farmers of large farms. Farmers in small farms perhaps had less opportunities to conduct experiments or implement agricultural novelties, yet their traditional expertise and ardor of industry were greater.[30] Alongside peasant proprietorship, however, it was important to preserve a certain amount of large farms owned by large capital and by well-educated people, who could support the long-term investment required for scientific improvements to agriculture.[31]

Mill's consideration of rent was influenced by this general outlook. Despite his criticism of Richard Jones, he adopted the latter's classification of rents.[32] Outlining his criticism of the Irish system of cottier tenancy, Mill wrote:

> The land of Ireland, the land of every country, belongs to the people of that country. The individuals called landowners have no right in morality and justice, to anything but the rent, or compensation for its saleable value. With regard to the land itself, the paramount consideration is, by what mode of appropriation and of cultivation it can be made most useful to the collective body of its inhabitants… There is no necessity for depriving the landlords of one farthing of the pecuniary value of their legal rights; but justice requires that the actual cultivators should be enabled to become in Ireland what they will become in America – proprietors of the soil which they cultivate.[33]

Mill consistently followed Locke's approach to the connection between cultivation and ownership of land. Yet he also extended this approach to a consideration of social justice, in a fashion which would have been impossible in the social and intellectual climate of the late seventeenth century, and even during the eighteenth century. He was the first major figure in the history of political-economic thought to come to grips with the intransigent problem of accommodating certain socialist principles within an overall free-market capitalistic system. This pertained to the use of natural resources as much as to any other socioeconomic issue. Then as now, no clear solution to this pressing problem yet emerged.[34]

Mill claimed that proprietorship of land was preferable for laborers over living as agricultural laborers for hire. It could also lead to a more prudential check to population. Yet this was preferable specifically in an underdeveloped economy. At a later and more advanced stage of progress, the association and co-operation among people were to be preferred to their division into small familial and paternalistic units. Evincing his moderate socialist ideas, Mill noted that this, however, would become possible only if the association between the capitalists and the laborers would be one of partnership. It should not be based on exploiting the laborers, but rather on enabling them the proper progress resulting from their labor. Furthermore, it was also possible for the laborers to form associations among themselves.[35] Mill discussed many examples of such associations. He did, however, criticize those socialists opposed to competition, which was necessary for progress, and the prevention of idleness and monopolies.[36]

It is clear that like earlier classical political economists, Mill considered the cultivation of natural resources, primarily though not solely the land, as a foundation of human progress, and an underlying factor of social interactions. His view of this important issue gave due consideration to new developments, manifested in the repeated revisions of the *Principles of Political Economy* between 1848 and 1871, and evident not least in its consideration of socialism, a development which was unanticipated by Smith, and only a fledgling phenomenon during the prime of Ricardo and Malthus. In Mill's case, however, there was a further layer of meaning to the concept of nature than most other classical political economists, who did not demonstrate the wide philosophical interests which he habitually did. The only comparable figure in this group of intellectuals was Adam Smith, yet the latter, in contrast with Mill, found writing a difficult task, and did not produce the wide-ranging oeuvre that Mill was able to put forth. Smith did not develop any systematic consideration of the concept of nature. Mill, in contrast, did just that, most notably in his essay "Nature."[37]

In this essay he claimed that everything artificial or produced was part of nature, and thus in effect natural. Human agency consisted merely in moving things, thus leading to certain effects. It was therefore possible to differentiate between two types of nature – either everything which existed, or else everything which was not influenced by human agency. Mill claimed that this essay was meant to examine appeals to nature as a universal moral standard to which human beings should obey. Intelligent action, however, meant that human beings had the possibility of placing themselves in circumstances which led to the acting or not acting of one or other law of nature, or to one law of nature counteracting another.[38] He also observed that admonitions to follow the dictates of nature were absurd, since all human action would thus be negative, whereas in fact many operations of human beings to master and cultivate natural forces were constructive actions. Openly paraphrasing Bacon, he noted that to commend such actions was

> to acknowledge that the ways of Nature are to be conquered, not obeyed: that her powers are often towards man in the position of enemies, from whom he must wrest, by force and ingenuity, what little he can for his own use,

> and deserves to be applauded when that little is rather more than might be expected from his physical weakness in comparison to those gigantic powers. All praise of Civilization, or Art, or Contrivance, is so much dispraise of Nature; and admission of imperfection, which it is man's business, and merit, to be always endeavouring to correct or mitigate.[39]

Mill then proceeded to criticize traditional religious claims to regard acts of mastering natural resources as either infringements of divine will, or the result of divine beneficence. Furthermore, he objected to any religious injunction putting limits to the level of control of nature, the infringement of which was viewed as impious. This led to the religiously motivated disposition to obey or follow divinely ordained nature. Mill, however, claimed that nature, even if divinely created, was imperfect. It was therefore the duty of human beings, indeed their religious duty, not only to ameliorate themselves, but also to ameliorate the material world, "the order of physical nature" itself.[40]

The human admiration of awe-inspiring natural phenomena was due to their vastness and power, and their ability to overpower human beings. This admiration, however, actually had no moral basis, since these forces were neither good nor bad. Nature imperviously inflicted on human beings, whatever their moral or immoral constitution, tortures and suffering worse than anything they inflicted on each other. Therefore nature could not be considered a guide to moral conduct. Mill, however, claimed that no one, either religious or not, really regarded natural calamities as good in themselves. The attempt to obviate such calamities by commanding natural forces was therefore commonly considered a positive undertaking, and only a lunatic would think otherwise.[41] Mill disagreed with the optimistic Leibnizian view of the world as the best possible world which Providence could create. The world was imperfect and full of human and animal suffering, contrary to the intention of its necessarily imperfect creator. This meant that human beings had a necessity, perhaps even a duty, to combat the ills of the natural world. Indeed, assuming that Providence was just, then by necessity it had "intended Nature as a scheme to be amended, not imitated, by Man." This non-omnipotent being had at least created human beings with the power to ameliorate themselves gradually over generations, thus improving themselves and progressing from savagery to civilization.[42]

Mill continued and criticized claims for the superiority of instinctual "natural" behavior to rational deliberative action. The former was the mark of a primitive human existence, inferior to higher cultured existence. Almost everything good in the natural condition of humanity was potential, to be realized only by the artificial means afforded by cultural progress. Furthermore, some behaviors resulting from natural inclination, such as destructiveness, cruelty, or the inclination to despotism, were patently harmful, and best eradicated.[43] Mill claimed that all human virtues, from simple private ones such as cleanliness, to social virtues such as sympathy, self-command, truthfulness, and justice, were all acquired and cultivated. He opposed this to the Rousseauian notion of primitive virtue. Both the human command of outer physical nature, and that of inner human nature, were equally desirable. "[T]he duty of man is the same in respect to his own nature as in respect to the nature of all other things, namely not to follow but to amend it."[44]

The essay "Nature" afforded Mill the opportunity for outlining his advocacy for the interrelated progress of human material culture based on the cultivation of natural resources, and higher cultural progress based both on material advancement, and on the rising command of human nature itself. Both these forms of cultivation were evidence of a gradually acquired independence from simple superstitious religiosity, and in this respect Mill displayed his debt to the Enlightenment's predominantly deistic outlook. This perspective, as we have seen, was also evident throughout the *Principles of Political Economy*.[45] Nevertheless, Mill there also outlined a very different aspect of the human interaction with nature, one which differentiated him sharply from other classical political economists, who were unstinting in their support for maximization of the human utilization of natural resources. Mill in this respect proved more sophisticated, and more willing to take into consideration contemporaneous romantic views of nature.

We have already discussed in a previous chapter Mill's claim that population had to be limited to a stationary state, so as to enable the improvement of the quality of human life, as this pertained to the social and economic condition of the laboring class. Yet Mill outlined an even more interesting reason for moderating economic growth. Surprisingly, given his constant attention to the need to utilize natural resources, this was an aesthetic and romantic reason.

> A population may be too crowded, though all be amply supplied with food and raiment. It is not good for man to be kept perforce at all times in the presence of his species. A world from which solitude is extirpated, is a very poor ideal. Solitude, in the sense of being often alone, is essential to any depth of meditation or of character; and solitude in the presence of natural beauty and grandeur, is the cradle of thoughts and aspirations which are not only good for the individual, but which society could ill do without. Nor is there much satisfaction in contemplating the world with nothing left to the spontaneous activity of nature; with every rood of land brought into cultivation, which is capable of growing food for human beings; every flowery waste or natural pasture ploughed up, all quadrupeds or birds which are not domesticated for man's use exterminated as his rivals for food, every hedgerow or superfluous tree rooted out, and scarcely a place left where a wild shrub or flower could grow without being eradicated as a weed in the name of improved agriculture. If the earth must lose that great portion of its pleasantness which it owes to things that the unlimited increase of wealth and population would extirpate from it, for the mere purpose of enabling it to support a larger, but not a better or a happier population, I sincerely hope, for the sake of posterity, that they will be content to be stationary, long before necessity compels them to it.[46]

This was Mill's famous and quite original argument in favor of a stationary state. It was premised on the idea that quality of life was as important as quantity, in the sense of the size of population or the amount of wealth.[47] Such sentiments were of course common in the nineteenth century and even earlier, not least in romantic art. Yet in the context of classical political-economic debate they were almost apostasy. Following Malthus, of course, it was no longer possible to disregard the limit to natural resources. Yet no other political economist inferred from this a similar conclusion. Mill, who appreciated natural scenery, had an affection for Wordsworth's poetry and attitude toward nature.[48] Yet it seems that he intentionally outlined these ideas regarding the stationary state in the a priori incongruous context of the *Principles of Political Economy* rather than in one of his other works. He seemed aware that precisely in this seemingly paradoxical context this passage would be most effective. He was evidently correct in assuming as much, since from a modern environmentally conscious perspective, these words have been considered both premonitory and influential.[49] Yet this influence, as Mill seemed already aware, was a limited one in the face of the inexorable, and to his mind generally positive, advance of human material development.[50]

Mill's discussion of this idea was prescient and original in an even deeper sense. We should be wary of the easy temptation of ascribing to him a sentiment akin to modern environmentalism. It should be kept in mind that rising sentimental attitudes toward nature during the Industrial Revolution were often a reaction to the growing distance of urban dwellers from nature. Ever since Norbert Elias, sophisticated modern scholars have been aware that the aesthetic appreciation of nature was the province precisely of those advanced societies which had sufficiently mastered nature. Elias noted how from the Middle Ages onward, with growing control of nature, "as forest and field cease to be the scene of unbridled passions, of the savage pursuit of man and beast, wild joy and wild fear; as they are moulded more and more by intertwining peaceful activities, the production of goods, trade and transport; now, to pacified men a corresponding pacified nature becomes visible, and in a new way. It becomes… to a high degree an object of visual pleasure." Moreover, Elias recognized that this new aesthetic appreciation of nature was primarily the province of urban populations removed from direct and perilous contact with nature.[51] More recently, Keith Thomas has made a similar observation, noting the "growing conflict between the new sensibilities [toward nature circa 1800] and the material foundations of human society… It is one of the contradictions upon which modern civilization may be said to rest. About its ultimate consequences we can only speculate."[52] Other scholars have similarly discussed the rising sensitivity to nature which emerged from the late eighteenth century, and the conflict between this new sensitivity and the wish to control nature.[53] Early signs of this tension in fact became evident specifically in Scotland, the scene of so many of the most significant innovations in eighteenth-century economic thought.[54] Prominent studies of American environmentalism have also observed a comparable development.[55] This dialectical phenomenon unfolded parallel to the rise of classical political-economic considerations of nature. The nineteenth century witnessed, on the one hand, an increasing emphasis on the practice of modern science, and on the other, an aesthetic-artistic romantic valorization of nature.[56] For some romantics the economic sphere was considered something natural, yet opposed to the human, and consequently they viewed naturalistic explanations of human phenomena as practically anathema, an outlook which led specifically to criticism of both Malthus and Darwin.[57] Yet the scientific and the romantic viewpoints were not always mutually exclusive. Denise Phillips has claimed that in the 1830s and 1840s there was an increasing combination of romantic idealization of nature on the one hand, with a more practical, scientific and industrial attitude toward nature on the other. This approach continued earlier German idealism and the combination of art and science in the spirit of Goethe, and underlined the liberal approach to mass education in the fields of both art and science. Only in the second half of the century did there develop a more distinct separation of the scientific and humanistic approaches to nature, although even this separation was not a total one.[58] While Phillips has made these observations mainly in relation to German culture, they might help explain Mill's seemingly ambiguous consideration of nature.

Some modern environmentalists have been tempted to regard Mill's notion of the stationary state as an early example of modern ecological sensitivity or environmental ethics. This is part of a popular recent approach which seeks to reread various canonical figures from various eras through the lens of modern environmentalism. While this might be a valuable exercise in philosophical terms, as a historiographical approach it remains lacking. One might take Mill's remarks as a starting point for an environmental philosophy. Yet it seems doubtful, to say the least, that he intended anything of the sort. His remarks regarding the need for spiritual contemplation of nature in fact addressed both an anthropocentric and an unavoidable use of nature. Perhaps this was more a contemplative than a physical use. Yet Mill did not advocate "leaving nature alone" in the modern environmentalist sense. His approach was one of enjoyment of nature precisely *after* sufficient control of it for enhancing material life had been achieved, and specifically not prior to this stage of material progress. Aesthetic enjoyment of nature was thus a luxury, not a necessity. It was something to aspire to and perhaps attain. It became possible only in the last stages of cultural progress, when all the material problems associated with controlling the size of population, and addressing social evils, had led to a just and prosperous state of all classes of a country's population.

Therefore, Mill's aesthetic musings on nature, contrary to first impressions, were perfectly in tune with his advocacy for utilizing natural resources. As we have seen, he claimed that for any practical purposes nature could never be completely cultivated, although social ills and poverty would probably become prevalent long before any chance of this happening would even become tangible. In addition, either preventive or positive checks to population, in Malthus's sense, would halt any process of over-population long before natural resources in themselves would become scarce. Therefore, whether in an unplanned and tragic contingency, or in a planned and civilized manner, human societies would always be left with uncultivated natural regions, even if only small ones. The aesthetic contemplation of nature was thus a reality, not an unattained ideal, precisely in an advanced civilization heavily reliant on utilizing natural resources. It is therefore quite indicative that Mill made these aesthetic observations precisely within a discussion of material and economic issues. Despite these remarks, he chose to end the *Principles of Political Economy* with his customary admonition for maximizing the use of natural resources, noting that it was the government's task to support "the legitimate employment of the human faculties, that of compelling the powers of nature to be more and more subservient to physical and moral good."[59] Any observed affinity between Mill's, and the modern, sense of environmental crisis, risks projecting a historically foreign outlook onto the nineteenth-century *Weltanschauung*, at a time when the sense that natural resources were truly finite was not immanently evident, not even for Malthus, let alone for Mill.

It is interesting to note that the possibility of putting aside at least some uncultivated natural spaces for public aesthetic enjoyment was occasionally addressed in political-economic discussions long before Mill. Nevertheless, most commentators chose to criticize this option, and even if not, none were, or could be, aware of the need for such conservation, as were the political economists of the industrial age. In the Middle Ages St. Thomas Aquinas had recommended establishing cities in places which were pleasant due to their natural beauty, since moderate enjoyment and pleasure were a human necessity.[60] By the Renaissance, the more common instrumental approach was evident in Giovanni Botero's claim that using land for parks rather than for agriculture was unprofitable and ill-advised, as proven by the complaints of the English people, who due to such practice found themselves short of grain.[61] Among the seventeenth-century mercantilists Thomas Mun was even more adamant, writing:

> [W]ould men haue vs to keepe our woods and goodly trees to looke vpon? they might as well forbid the working of our woolls, & sending forth our cloth to forraine parts; for both are meanes alike to procure the necessarie wares, which this Kingdome wanteth. Doe they not know that trees doe liue and grow; and being great, they haue a time to dye and rot, if oportunity make no better vse of them; and what more noble or profitable vse then goodly ships for Trade and warre? are they not our barns for wealth and plenty, seruing us walles and Bulwarkes for our peace and happinesse? Do not their yearely buildings maintaine many hundred poore people, and greatly increase the number of those Artesmen which are so needfull for this common wealth?[62]

Among eighteenth-century commentators this approach, to various extents, remained predominant. Robert Wallace enthusiastically, and at some length, described the beauties and grandeur of nature. At the same time, however, he also noted the human achievements in harnessing natural resources through knowledge and science.[63] The Physiocrat Pierre Poivre was more unequivocal. While praising Chinese agriculture, he noted approvingly that the Chinese had no use for immense parks, where deer rather than people lived. Even the country houses of the rich were adorned with "useful cultures," in which "every where reigns a happy imitation of that beautiful disorder of nature, from whence art has borrowed all her charms."[64] From a different perspective Jacques Necker reached similar conclusions, claiming that land utilized for parks, decorative gardens and other unproductive purposes, would come at the expense of food production and population.[65] He specifically criticized the consumption of luxuries as a hindrance to the growth of population. Among such luxuries he noted the exaggerated attention and space allotted to the care of military horses or the horses which commodiously transported the wealthy, and "those parks and sumptuous gardens that the ploughshare shall no longer furrow."[66] Similarly, according to Pietro Verri it was important not to waste land which might be used for agriculture, by devoting it instead to gardens, game forests and other luxury uses which did not encourage economic growth.[67]

Among classical political economists, as expected, a similar outlook persisted. Adam Smith noted that "Lands, for the purposes of pleasure and magnificence, parks, gardens, public walks, &c. possessions which are every where considered as causes of expence, not as sources of revenue, seem to be the only lands which, in a great and civilized monarchy, ought to belong to the crown."[68] While this seems a more moderate position, it is clear that for Smith uncultivated lands, even if preserved for human leisure, were less important to society than agriculturally cultivated ones. Aesthetic contemplation or recreational use of land were a luxury for the few, not a necessity for the many. As for any "environmental" consideration of the spiritual worth of nature, this was clearly not part of Smith's purview, either in Mill's sense, let alone a modern one. Later, Jean-Baptiste Say, in an untypical passage, expressed a rare recognition of the positive influence of beautiful natural surroundings. Yet even this was beauty created by human cultivation, not purely natural beauty, as Say noted the advantages of beautiful cultivated public spaces, where people could enjoy healthy exercise, watch pleasant landscapes and breathe clean air.[69] As noted in a previous chapter, Malthus, rather surprisingly, demonstrated sensitivity to the attraction of nature when he ardently praised the beauty of the Norwegian landscape. This, however, was even more untypical for him than for Mill, even though in his travel diaries Malthus often expressed delight in the beauties of landscape.[70] This might suggest that he regarded aesthetic appreciation of nature as outside the realm of economic analysis. Assuming this was the case, he was presaging a problem which would become persistent in modern economic discussions, particularly with the rise of ecologically motivated critiques of economic discussions of the environment. The mainstream in economic discourse, however, has retained Malthus's outlook. Robert Solow, to note one prominent example, while discussing the conservation of nonrenewable natural resources, has claimed that what one generation owes to the future, if at all, might be construed in terms of similar resources, but also, from a different outlook, in terms of the equivalent of these resources in capital or technological knowledge. Yet he also recognizes, though rather abruptly, that "The preservation of natural beauty is a different matter since that is more a question of direct consumption than of instrumental productive capacity."[71]

It is interesting also to take a look at one of the most prominent nineteenth-century critics of Mill's political economy, John Ruskin. Ruskin preferred the ancient Greek concept of *oikonomia*, household management, to the precepts of classical political economy, which he criticized by aiming at the latter's most prominent contemporaneous figure, Mill.[72] One might expect that Ruskin, the great admirer of J. M. W. Turner's romantic landscape paintings, would have sided with the romantic critique of scientific and economic utilizations of nature. Oddly enough, however, in the course of his sustained criticism of the basic tenets of nineteenth-century political economy, Ruskin was almost reactionary in his views on population and the environment. Perhaps this was due to his idiosyncratic mix of an advocacy for a free but fair economy with criticism of socialism, coupled with his critique of the political-economic quantitative, instead of qualitative, assessment of life.

In any event, Ruskin disagreed expressly with Mill's view of the value of natural scenery. He considered the possibility of over-population to the point of leaving no undeveloped nature as impossible. He also claimed that precisely in a putative state of maximal population, mechanization and industrialization, pure air and water would still be necessary to maintain the population, the flora and fauna, and even desert regions would continue to exist alongside habitable areas. Despite, or perhaps due to, his advocacy of landscape painting, Ruskin perceived no value in a nature in which the air was silent. He preferred a world teeming with the life and sounds of humans and animals, a world of feral nature alongside cultivated and domesticated nature.[73] "There is no wealth but life." Not only was the richest nation the one possessing the most "noble and happy" inhabitants, but, according to Ruskin, a greater number of people was also vital to enhancing their quality. Population numbers and human virtue were mutually enhancing. The issue was quality of life more than quantity. "It will, indeed, be long before the world has been all colonized, and its deserts all brought under cultivation. But the radical question is, not how much habitable land is in the world, but how many human beings ought to be maintained on a given space of habitable land." For Ruskin the limit to population growth was not one set by nature itself, which could and ought to be utilized in unlimited fashion, but rather the social and ethical qualities of the population. Ultimately, his outlook on nature was very similar to Mill's.[74]

Mill's view of nature, and even of the stationary state, was therefore a continuation, though an original one, of earlier notions. This predominant political-economic consideration of nature aimed at a situation in which the fruits of both the material and the aesthetic enjoyment originating from the utilization of nature, would become the common lot of humanity. What Mill defined as property was not only what was produced by human beings. The earth itself, the forests, waters and all nature's riches, were the inheritance of the human race, and there was consequently a need for regulations governing the common enjoyment of these riches. Such regulation was among the necessary tasks of government, and an inseparable part of the very idea of a civilized society.[75] Nineteenth-century liberal political economists like Mill still did not face the acute environmental hazards, including over-population, which confront twenty-first-century civilization. Despite growing awareness of the pollution and squalor resulting from unbridled industrialization, they regarded such hazards as at most a distant and far from imminent prospect. For Mill, one of the most acute and prescient observers of this era, writing of the beauty of nature, and noting its melancholy decline in the face of otherwise praiseworthy industrialization, was ultimately a romantically inspired lament of the inevitable. It was a sad yet well-worth price for the progress of the human race. Those modern scholars, such as Norbert Elias and Keith Thomas, who emphasized the ambiguity in modern attitudes toward nature, had been anticipated in the nineteenth century. The intellectual perspicuity of a figure such as Mill was, however, more impressive, since he recognized this problem at the very moment when it was emerging as an integral element of the modern world. He offered no solution, but accepted this as an insurmountable aspect of cultural progress, and in this sense, a century and a half later, no effective solution to this problem has yet emerged.

Many modern environmentalists criticize the economic view of nature as a leading culprit in the tale of humanity's desolation of the earth. This is an attractive approach, displaying a clear separation of bad guys and good guys, and laying out simple steps, some of them no doubt necessary, to reversing this desolation. Often, this "ecocriticism" is coupled with an extreme socialist critique of Western capitalism, and demonstrates other leftist agendas, including specifically criticism of the Enlightenment. This approach is no less simplistic than the "neo-conservative" advocacies of diametrically opposed policies, including unhindered use of natural resources. A more balanced approach, taking its cue from Mill, and avoiding the Scylla and Charybdis of extreme politics, should recognize the complicated difficulty of finding any easy solution to the dilemma between nature and progress. Critics of the Enlightenment often conveniently forget the crucial contribution of industrial, technological and generally scientific utilization of nature, to the creation of the modern world, with its vastly superior advantages in quality of human life compared with earlier eras in the history of humanity. Both sides of the equation are therefore inconvenient truths – on the one hand the environmental ravages of uninhibited industrialization, yet on the other the indispensable dependency of human beings on the continued cultivation of natural resources. The question, at least in realistic political terms, is therefore not one of continuing or discontinuing the large-scale, and rapidly growing, utilization of nature by human action, but rather one of making this inescapable utilization a better, more environmentally sensitive, and ultimately more efficient and long-term option. Making the aesthetic contemplation of nature part of this vision, in Mill's sense, as in that of romantically disposed artists before, during and following him, seems initially a self-evident goal. Yet this is also a luxury of the well-to-do. We should keep this in mind if we admonish less-fortunate societies and individuals who are still, regrettably, unable to wrestle with this dilemma due to their limited material and social circumstances. Perhaps the road to a more environmentally progressive and concomitantly socially and politically just world lies in the direction of greater, but more careful and sophisticated, utilization of nature, rather than in the Rousseauistic dream of suspended-animation progress. As classical political economists recognized, arresting the progress of humanity, with its foundation in utilizing nature, was as futile as it was ill-advised.

Epilogue

From socialism to modernity

The history of political-economic thought demonstrates a consistent emphasis of the need for a proper utilization of natural resources. By the eighteenth century this was viewed as a foundation of material progress without which no higher cultural progress could be achieved. Consequently, classical political economists gave detailed attention both to the role that natural resources played in historical progress, and to the proper economic policies which could maximize the efficiency of the production of wealth resulting from the use of these resources, while also attempting to distribute this ensuing wealth in the most socially just manner. By Mill's time it became clear that industrialized progress came at an environmental price, although this price, though regrettable, was considered worth paying. Nature was first and foremost meant for human use. Even the contemplation of pristine nature was ultimately an anthropocentric activity, preconditioned by the earlier mastery of nature, which made this contemplation possible to begin with.

What remains to be discussed is how this view of nature has remained evident in other types of political-economic discourse, both those which in the nineteenth century opted for a different outlook than the dominant classical one, and subsequently in the more modern context of twentieth-century economics. Like the overview of classical and medieval political economy outlined above, this discussion is necessarily desultory. It does, however, consider sufficient examples to make clear that the history of economic considerations of nature, from antiquity to our own time, is a linear one of consistent and increasing emphasis on the ineluctable necessity of utilizing natural resources.

The most significant nineteenth-century political-economic alternative to the classical school was of course socialism. One has to keep in mind that there was no clear socialist school at any given moment, and socialists of various ilk, often quite at odds with each other, proliferated in the face of the social ills of nascent industrialization. One interesting and relatively moderate example, well-known and oft-criticized by the classical political economists, was the Swiss Simonde de Sismondi.[1] In fact, Sismondi shared with the classical political economists many presuppositions, not least a reliance on Enlightenment ideas about progress, including conjectural history. He described how a man destitute on an island, even though the soil would be fertile and the animals abundant, would remain poor unless he applied his industry to utilizing these resources. Were he, instead of only immediately consuming the available vegetables, to plant them, plough the fields and domesticate the animals, he would become rich. Relieved from the immediate danger of hunger, he could further augment his wealth by producing such things as clothes, furniture and habitation. This, according to Sismondi's short conjectural history, was in fact how the whole human race had developed. By applying labor to natural resources human beings had created wealth, or in other words an excess of products of daily labor over daily needs. The efficient utilization of natural resources was eventually augmented even further by the division of labor. "However great the beneficence of nature, she gives nothing gratuitously to man, though, when addressed by him, she is ready to lend her assistance in multiplying his powers to an indefinite extent."[2]

Sismondi loosely utilized stadial notions when he discussed how, in the transition from a shepherding to an agricultural existence, cultivation of the land was followed at times only for short periods. It was only a stable government, and the security of property in land for those who cultivated it, which were able to ensure a consistent cultivation of land for the long term, to the benefit of all society, including the urban population. This cultivation included such things as irrigation, drainage, the planting of trees and other investments beneficial only to farmers, who knew that their descendants would enjoy these investments. To this Sismondi added the love of working the land in itself as a motivating factor. All this emphasized the importance of the government's ensuring the proprietorship of land to those who worked it. Eventually this would also create the proper conditions for accumulating agricultural knowledge and improvements.[3] He criticized Ricardo's theory of rent, claiming that uncultivated land was not necessarily inferior in quality to land already under cultivation. In fact, in most European countries, as a result of centuries of feudal order, there were many lands belonging to the commons, which due to long periods of lack of cultivation might require initial investment, but in general were not less fertile than some lands already under cultivation.[4] Sismondi was enthusiastic about agriculture. He wanted to prevent the evils of industrialization in afflicting the rural classes, and this underlined his discussion of systems of rent. An essential element of the necessary policy was advocating for the possession of small farms for as many proprietors as possible, in place of small numbers of large estates.[5]

Sismondi's views on natural resources and social-economic progress were evident in his detailed discussion of population.[6] He claimed that so long as the size of population was commensurate with the people's level of income and did not exceed it, then misery could be avoided. In the conditions of the existing social order, the misery of population was the fault of the rich, but those who suffered from it were the working poor. Their wages were not guaranteed, and they could find themselves, through no fault of their own, suddenly deprived of their wages, thus plunging their families into poverty.[7] Sismondi was in disagreement with Malthus's views, although Malthus claimed that Sismondi had not properly understood his claims about population.[8] According to Sismondi, the growth of population would halt long before the limit of food production was reached, whether this happened due to the inability of people to purchase food, or to the inability of labor to produce it. Malthus's theory of population was true only as an abstraction, but not in the actual conditions of the real world. In the latter, the discontinuation of production of subsistence almost always occurred wilfully, the result of decisions made by landowners who saw no advantage in augmenting it. It was human policy, not inability to cultivate the land, which almost always led to widespread famine. Even the influence of natural disasters on food production was only short in duration. In contrast with Malthus's mathematical model, proper policy could encourage food production to the point where it too would grow at a geometrical rate.[9] Sismondi perceived a much greater potential for future cultivation of natural resources than Malthus.

As long as uncultivated lands remained, it was useful to increase the class of cultivators, provided they were amply rewarded. This also applied to industrial laborers, as long as their productions did not exceed consumer demand, and similarly to traders, soldiers, and all types of laborers. A proper social order and governance were always required for this, otherwise land might remain uncultivated to the detriment of society, and population would eventually decline rather than grow. Such growth, though, needed to be continuous and not intermittent, otherwise the workers would be led to hunger and misery. In the long term, population was always proportionate to the demand for labor, which in its turn was an incentive for the proportionate production of subsistence, even if by importation.[10] Sismondi criticized the encouragement to procreation by the religious establishment, as well as by improper government policy. He advocated for a proper policy which would make something like mechanization useful and conducive to the condition of the laborers, rather than leading to unemployment and poverty.[11] He viewed the various factors of the social and economic order as intertwined. Given the proper stable social policy, population, in itself a sign of healthy progress, and cultivation of the land, therefore went hand in hand.

On the one hand Sismondi opposed the existing order, yet on the other he distanced himself from the more extreme socialist programs of his time, which aimed at fundamentally altering the existing state of ownership. In contrast, he aimed at "gentle and indirect legislative measures." Yet he also objected to the contemporaneous British model of a free economy of unfettered competition, which sanctioned individual greed at the expense of the general interest of humanity.[12] His moderate social-democratic viewpoint, as it would be termed today, thus shunned both communism and extreme liberalism. Yet at no point did he depart from the common contemporary advocacy for increased utilization of the natural environment.

Other socialists were of course more extreme, not least Marx and Engels, whose views of natural resources have received significant scholarly attention in recent years. As with Sismondi, anyone seeking a foundation for forthright environmentalism in the original Marxist outlook would face a difficult task.[13] Criticizing the modern manipulation of nature, William Leiss presented an outlook similar to the earlier position of Marx and Engels, highlighting the connection between domination of nature by human beings and domination of human beings by each other. In his words, "If the idea of the *domination* of nature has any meaning at all, it is that by such means – that is, through the possession of superior technological capabilities – some men attempt to dominate and control other men. The notion of a common domination of the human race over external nature is nonsensical."[14] This mirrors quite closely the view of Marx and Engels, who were concerned less with the environment per se, and more with the social injustice resulting from the inequitable distribution of the wealth produced by utilizing natural resources.[15] They considered the maximal use of these resources as a commendable goal in itself. On this point they were quite in line with the classical political economists. It is doubtful if Marx should be considered as belonging to the classical political-economic tradition, as some scholars claim.[16] As regards the consideration of nature, however, this was no doubt the case.

Just how emphatic was this connection with classical political economy, and with the Enlightenment view of progress, can be gleaned from several sections of Friedrich Engels's *Dialectics of Nature*.[17] Engels objected to the idealistic inclination to attribute human progress to ideas and the mind, and to forget the crucial role of the physical side, mainly due to the use of hands, in historical progress.[18] Despite the truth of Hume's observations, there was causality in nature. What proved this was the human ability to use nature, to conduct experiments in which the anticipated results occurred. In this way human activity changed human thought. It was not nature in itself, but rather its alteration at the hands of humans, which constituted the basis of human understanding and the development of human intelligence. Nature acted on human beings, but they in their turn acted on nature, creating new conditions for their existence. In Germany almost nothing remained of "nature" in itself as it had existed when the Germanic tribes emigrated there, and almost all the changes which had happened to its soil, climate, flora, fauna and the people themselves, had been induced by human activity.[19]

In an essay titled "The Part Played by Labour in the Transition from Ape to Man," Engels outlined a conjectural, though not stadial, history of how human beings developed from apes, by standing upright and freeing their hands for labor.[20] The development of the hands led to the development of other organs, and eventually to the social implications of enhanced physical abilities. "The mastery over nature, which begins with the development of the hand, with labour, widened man's horizon at every new advance." This inter-related physical and social development led to the development of the larynx and to language.[21] Reliance on conjectural history was one avenue of the Enlightenment's influence on Engels. Another was his view of population. He rejected Malthus's population theory, claiming it did not take into consideration scientific and technological progress, which also increased, like population, in a geometric rate from generation to generation. Yet Engels agreed with Malthus's claim regarding the need for moral restraint, thus in fact accepting that there was a Malthusian population problem. In his view, however, only communism could enable moral restraint. His position on population was therefore contradictory.[22] He did, however, accept the assumption that a large population, in the proper social conditions, was a positive sign of prosperity.

Everything in nature, according to Engels, was interconnected. Even animals changed nature by their actions, and in their turn were influenced by these changes. He anticipated the insights of modern environmental history when he noted how goats had prevented the regeneration of forests in Greece, or how in St. Helena the goats and pigs brought by navigators almost exterminated the local vegetation, making room for plants subsequently introduced by colonists. Animals, however, did such things unintentionally, while human beings did so deliberately. Human action transfers "useful plants and domestic animals from one country to another and thus changes the flora and fauna of whole continents. More than this. Through artificial breeding, both plants and animals are so changed by the hand of man that they become unrecognizable."[23] Yet despite the intent of human use of nature, unintended consequences ensued. "Let us not, however, flatter ourselves overmuch on account of our human conquests over nature. For each such conquest takes its revenge on us. Each of them, it is true, has in the first place the consequences on which we counted, but in the second and third places it has quite different, unforeseen effects which only too often cancel out the first." Thus, the ancient nations who engaged in deforestation to obtain cultivable land, never anticipated the subsequent devastating consequences this would have centuries later, due to the related removal of reservoirs of moisture. Similarly, in Italy deforestation damaged water sources and the dairy industry, and the spreading use of potatoes, in Engels's estimation, spread scrofula. "Thus at every step we are reminded that we by no means rule over nature like a conqueror over a foreign people, like someone standing outside nature – but that we, with flesh, blood, and brain, belong to nature, and exist in its midst." Human mastery of nature consisted only in the ability to comprehend and utilize its laws.[24]

These insights, prescient though they were, did not mean that Engels forsook the admonition to maximize the use of nature. They were simply a caution to do so warily. Maximizing human mastery and comprehension of nature would ultimately lead to the understanding that human beings were "one with nature," thus diminishing the damaging influence of Christianity. The greater and more difficult challenge, however, was not to understand the natural consequences of human manipulation of nature, but rather to realize its more important social consequences. One example was the importation of potatoes to Europe, which spread famine, and another was the invention of the steam-engine, which enhanced the struggle between the bourgeoisie and the proletariat (though regarding the outcome of the latter Engels was more optimistic). Mastery of the social consequences of the use of nature was feasible in his opinion.[25] The use the social elite made of nature centered on gratifying immediate desires, and was insensitive to the long-term consequences of the destruction of natural resources. Engels implied that use of nature which would accommodate the needs of the proletariat would by definition take into account long-term social needs, and this would constitute a new development in human history.[26] Despite human superiority over nature, only when social production and distribution would be sufficiently realized could humanity emerge beyond the world not just biologically but also socially.[27]

The relative conservatism of Engels, shared also by Marx, in assessing nature primarily as a resource meant for socioeconomic progress, albeit in their own terms, was not shared by all their modern neo-Marxist heirs. The most prominent examples were the members of the Frankfurt School. In their famous *Dialectic of*

Enlightenment Max Horkheimer and Theodor Adorno raised the possibility that modern science might lead to the destruction of nature, including all of its flora, fauna and the human race itself, "and if the earth is then still young enough, the whole thing will have to be started again at a much lower stage."[28] This criticism of the predominant attitude toward nature shared by both the Enlightenment and by classical political economy was essentially criticism of scientific rational manipulation of nature. In the second half of the twentieth century it was to have considerable influence. Although much of this lies outside the realm of economic thought, one famous example merits mention, and that is Carolyn Merchant's ecofeminist critique of the Scientific Revolution's (and by implication the Enlightenment's) view of nature in her *The Death of Nature*, aptly titled following her view that the modern attitude toward nature is a deadening one. She contends that the language used during the Scientific Revolution, specifically by Bacon, to describe the conquest of nature, was similar to paternalistic language used to describe the male domination of women. According to this outlook feminist and environmental problems are intimately linked.[29] While the historiographical aspects of her study are controversial, Merchant's argument is an eloquent example of the extent to which the socialist critique of mainstream economic considerations of nature might go. It preserves the connection between social equity and the management of natural resources that was evident in nineteenth-century socialism, but on both scores goes to greater extremes than its intellectual progenitors.

In the second half of the nineteenth century a major methodological transformation occurred in mainstream economic discourse. The marginalist revolution and the rise of neoclassical economics at the expense of classical political economy shifted the interest from production and the evaluation of wealth, to supply and demand, emphasizing marginal utility. From a wider perspective it was also a stage in the professionalization of economics, emphasizing the rational maximization of utility and the increasing use of mathematics. It was the beginning of economic analysis in the modern sense still taught to students to this day, symbolized, following Alfred Marshall, by the adoption of the term "economics" instead of "political economy." It would be a mistake, however, to disregard the great debt that the neoclassicists had to the classicists. In a way they did to the latter what the latter had done to Adam Smith – they based many of their ideas on their predecessors' work, while constantly supplementing and amending it. All the while they retained the traditional emphasis on the significance of natural resources, updating it for the contingencies of increasingly modern realities.

One of the major neoclassicists who gave ample attention to the issue of natural resources was the Austrian economist Eugen von Böhm-Bawerk. Natural, material goods, according to Böhm-Bawerk, served human beings by providing material services. Natural goods might appear in a form serviceable to human beings either by chance, or by intentional human effort. The former was teleologically accidental and insufficient, not providing nearly enough to satisfy human needs, even if "Thus originate fruitful islands in the courses of streams; thus the grass on natural pastures and prairies; thus berries and trees of the wood; thus deposits of useful minerals." The latter, purposeful means, therefore supplied the majority of human material demands. In doing so human beings did not straightforwardly press nature to their service. The process was much more limited. They simply put objects in motion, since the power resided in the natural objects in themselves, and was only guided by human intervention.[30] In this respect human beings' mastery of nature was quite limited. "Man has a certain power to make natural forces act where, when, and how he will; but this power he possesses only in so far as he can control the matter in which these forces reside." In doing so humans relied on their intellect, which enabled them to utilize natural forces against each other.[31]

The productive process therefore included the natural forces endowed by nature on the one hand, and the more limited powers residing in the human organism on the other. Most natural forces, however, were not part of the natural endowment, but on the contrary, were useless or even harmful to humanity. Human beings had in fact harnessed only a small part of nature's forces. Humanity's "natural endowment" was

> an infinite treasure-house from which the producing man may draw as much as he will and can. As yet it is only the very smallest part of this treasure that has been touched… The resistless rise and fall of the tide, the rush of rivers and waterfalls, the atmospheric movements, the giant forces of electricity, magnetism, and gravitation slumbering in our earth, are powers turned to human account only to a very small extent. Others again, such as the vegetative powers of land, have been utilised to a greater, but still very far from complete extent.

Yet even in agriculture much greater advance seemed possible. It was the combination of nature and labor, and nothing else, which constituted the process of production. "What nature by herself does, and what man does along with her – these form the double source from which all our goods come, and the only source from which they can come."[32]

From an economic point of view, however, not all natural endowments were significant. Those natural elements and powers which were freely and abundantly at hand had no economic significance. It was those which were limited in quantity which gained economic value, and according to Böhm-Bawerk, most of these were connected in one way or other with the land, to which most human labor was devoted.[33] This was strictly in line with earlier classical emphasis on agriculture. Furthermore, Böhm-Bawerk defined capital as to a certain extent a store of useful natural powers (as also of labor), meant for a long-term production process. In this sense capital was a tool of production, although it was not by any means an independent factor in production. Only nature and labor constituted factors of production. Capital was only the medium through which these two exerted themselves in the act of production. Its contribution was in enabling nature and labor to influence production at different stages, extending it for lengthy time periods, a process which had been enhanced by the division of labor. Ultimately economic production remained, in essence, the result of two things – nature on the one hand, and human labor on the other.[34] In this way Böhm-Bawerk elaborated Locke's labor theory of value, with its underlining anthropocentric view of nature as a resource meant for human use. "If today we allow a fruitful field to lie fallow, or a mine or water power to remain unexploited; if, in short, we do not act economically with valuable uses of land, we act as directly against our economic wellbeing as when we throw away labour uneconomically."[35]

Böhm-Bawerk's attitude toward nature was therefore rather conservative, in fact more a continuation of eighteenth-century notions than the more cautionary approach to limited natural resources which emerged following Malthus. This cannot, however, be said about another major neoclassical figure, William Stanley Jevons, who dealt with the issue of finite resources in his early work *The Coal Question*. Consequently, Jevons has even been considered a precursor of environmental and even ecological economics, developing an early notion of intergenerational equity akin to modern weak sustainability.[36] It remains however doubtful, to say the least, that reading such intentions into Jevons's words follows his intent. Jevons's opening motto to this work was a citation of Adam Smith's cautionary note regarding the stationary state.[37] This was the foundation of his consideration of a pressing resource problem – the depletion of coal reserves. Then, and often still today, coal was the main energy resource, fueling the demands of increasing industrialization. It was therefore not just a question of limited resources in general, not even of the production of food. It was a more modern issue than had faced political economists earlier in the century.

Jevons considered the complete physical exhaustion of Britain's coal-mines an impossibility. His idea of exhaustion of coal was an economic one. He worried over the growing difficulty and cost of extracting coal from increasingly deeper mines. Britain's economic supremacy was relative to that of other nations as this related to coal deposits. What was at stake was Britain's ability to remain in a progressive state, hence Jevons's citation of Smith. Despite the country's incomparable utilization of coal, other countries were also advancing in this field. The stationary state had not yet been reached, but it loomed threateningly in the imminent future. Jevons depicted Britain's reliance on coal as essentially a two-edged sword – on the one hand the engine which had fueled its astonishing progress, yet on the other creating a dependence which threatened prosperity and population. The quality of the country's population, and its ability to continue and strive for progress based on scientific and technological advances, were not in question. Only its material resources were limited. Other countries were also capable of enhancing their utilization of natural resources. It was this utilization which had enabled Britain's supremacy, and its future economic role was likely to become even more prominent. Therefore, it was precisely at the point of Britain's supremacy, in Jevons's present, that the opportunity emerged for cultural amelioration which would be both impossible and sorely needed in the bleaker future. Among the necessary steps to be taken was the education of the lower classes and the cessation of child labor. Such steps, beyond their ethical necessity, would lead to more efficient labor in the future, reducing the burdens of future generations.[38]

At the heart of Jevons's approach was the idea of maximizing the efficiency of resource utilization. In discussing the application of various technologies to extract energy from natural sources, he noted how human beings actually utilized only a small part of this available energy.

> [N]ature is to us almost unbounded, but that economy consists in discovering and picking out those almost infinitesimal portions which best serve our purpose… So material nature presents to us the aspect of one continuous waste of force and matter beyond our control. The power we employ in the greatest engine is but an infinitesimal portion withdrawn from the immeasurable expense of natural forces… The rude forces of nature are too great for us, as well as too slight. It is often all we can do to escape injury from them, instead of making them obey us. And while the sun annually showers down upon us about a thousand times as much heat-power as is contained in all the coal we raise annually; yet that thousandth part, being under perfect control, is a sufficient basis of all our economy and progress.[39]

The aim of human technology was to harness energy as motive power, which was controlled as far as possible by human will. In this respect Jevons considered coal the best source of power that nature afforded to human command, specifically in fueling steam-engines. With further scientific progress the reliance on coal was only likely to increase. This emphasized the importance of coal deposits for Britain, since supposing some other source of fuel would be discovered in the future, there was no certainty that Britain would have superior reserves of that putative resource. Should technology emerge to enhance the utilization of electricity, or to collect sunlight, this would destroy Britain's natural-resource basis for supremacy.[40]

Jevons accepted Malthus's population theory, while emphasizing the principle of diminishing returns on the use of resources. "[E]xterior nature presents a certain absolute and inexorable limit." What had once been true of corn was now true of coal – it was the staple produce of the country on which the production of subsistence ultimately depended. Here Jevons sounded a note of optimism, emphasizing how future technological possibilities might enable the efficiency of extracting energy from coal, relative to consumer demand, to advance in a geometrical ratio similar to that of population. "No *à priori* reason here presents itself why each generation should not use its resource of knowledge and material possessions to make as large a proportional advance [in utilizing coal] as did a preceding generation." This was an updated version of the claim for the superiority of manufactures to agriculture. Nevertheless, all this optimism was conditional and temporary, since in contrast with agricultural land, which could continue yielding a produce indefinitely, coal deposits were not unlimited. "For once it would seem as if in fuel, as the source of universal power, we had found an unlimited means of multiplying our command over nature. But alas no! The coal is itself limited in quantity; not absolutely, as regards us, but so that each year we gain our supplies with some increase of difficulty." Decreasing returns on labor, as it applied to gaining utility from coal, were tantamount to a physical limit to this natural resource. Jevons therefore accepted the Malthusian position with two essential updated caveats – he applied a similar model based on coal rather than food as the basis of growth; and he noted that advancing technology pushed the limit of stationarity to a farther and more slowly-approaching future. Ultimately, however, this limit could not be avoided. Therefore, the advisable thing to do was not only to continue enhancing the consumption of coal, but even to scale it back precisely at the present point when it was in abundance, for the benefit of the nation's future.[41]

Jevons, on this point, was practically an environmental (though not an ecological) economist, in the modern sense. He recognized a key problem regarding the use of natural resources – the relation between the available quantity of raw material and the amount of its consumption. In an efficiently functioning economy the ratio between the two could be controlled, at least to a certain extent. It was this which emphasized the importance of proper policies. What Jevons realized was that increasing efficiency of resource utilization did not decrease consumption, but in fact increased it. Scholars have termed this "Jevons's paradox," or the "rebound effect."[42] In fact there is nothing really paradoxical about it. It is an inveterate phenomenon in human behavior, particularly in modern free economies with their consumer culture and practically limitless variety of products, that when a product becomes more accessible or cheaper demand for it in many cases rises. This is the reason that various products are often sold cheaply on sale. This is true of luxuries, but even more of necessaries. This made consumption of the latter, specifically in a situation of advancing technological efficiency, a policy problem, since the limited availability of resources risked being overstepped by the temptation to increase consumption. The obvious, though not easily implemented, solution, was to curb consumption by self-restraint, if need be by rationing. Yet this was not exactly Jevons's prescription.

This problem was enhanced by growing population, yet Jevons remained more optimistic than Malthus. The Malthusian worry regarding overpopulation was unfounded, and relative to its resources Britain was in fact underpopulated, though Jevons did not claim that this would always remain so. The threat of a future stationary state, whether due to a limit to coal production or to other causes, remained tangible.[43] Nevertheless, when it came to practical policies, Jevons, in contrast with modern economists dealing with resource depletion, made no substantial recommendation. He regarded all aspects of culture, including the economic, to be inscrutably interdependent. The unintended consequences of various human inventions and ideas meant that in the past various contributions had furthered unintentional aims, and in the future, no attempt to further a specific cause would indeed attain its proclaimed goal rather than another, no less beneficial. The choice, in fact, was between decelerating Britain's present consumption and prosperity, or else disregarding its future. Both options, and particularly the former, held no promise of success. The choice ultimately was between "brief greatness and longer continued mediocrity." But for Jevons the implication was that there was in fact no choice. Not only was it ill-advised to relinquish Britain's cultural superiority, it was also merely a counter-factual exercise, since the actions of past ages had set it on a path to greatness. Evoking earlier Enlightenment notions,

Jevons seemed convinced that even were Britain eventually to recede into mediocrity, it will already have contributed its own to the overall progress of humanity, to be continued by other nations. This was based on its contributions in all fields of cultural endeavor, but not least in its utilization of natural resources, specifically coal. "In our contributions to the arts… we have unintentionally done a work that will endure for ever. In whatever part of the world fuel exists, whether wood, or peat, or coal, we have rendered it the possible basis of a new civilization. In the ancient mythology, fire was a stolen gift from heaven, but it is our countrymen who have shown the powers of fire, and conferred a second Promethean gift upon the world."[44] Enhancing the utilization of natural resources was a prominent contribution of the British nation to human civilization.

Though less original, the neoclassical approach to natural resources received a particularly detailed treatment at the hands of its last major figure, Alfred Marshall. Like earlier classical political economists, Marshall developed his ideas in a culturally nuanced manner, evincing social and historical concerns.[45] This included an interest in nature, and specifically in biological notions.[46] This outlook, however, was distinctly anthropocentric, and relied heavily on earlier classical considerations of nature.

Marshall demonstrated Locke's influence when he differentiated between the free gifts of nature and those acquired by labor. He did, however, also differentiate between the points of view of individuals and of nations. A resource such as natural oyster beds might be free from the nation's point of view, but since the nation allowed them to become appropriated and vested by individuals, from the latter's point of view they were not free.[47] A free gift of nature such as the Thames had added more to England's wealth than man-made things such as canals or railroads.[48] Marshall broadened the conception of wealth from national boundaries to cosmopolitan wealth, the aggregate of all global manifestations of national wealth.[49] He extended the Lockean labor theory of value from his neoclassical perspective emphasizing utility. "[I]f inventions have increased man's power over nature very much, then the real value of money is better measured for some purposes in labour than in commodities." Human beings could create material things, but only utilities, changing matter to adapt it to the satisfaction of want. "All that he [man] can do in the physical world is either to readjust matter so as to make it more useful, as when he makes a log of wood into a table; or to put it in the way of being made more useful by nature, as when he puts seeds where the forces of nature will make it burst out into life."[50]

Marshall had a clear conception of how historical progress was intertwined with material-economic progress, although he did not always think in the earlier terms of stadial theory. In the uncivilized state human beings were easily satisfied with what nature afforded, but with every step of progress their desires became more varied, and were not satisfied by mere physical wants, instead striving for variety for its own sake. With variety in wants came variety in the means of acquiring them. This explained the discrepancy between more and less civilized societies. "[A]lthough it is man's wants in the earliest stages of his development that give rise to his activities, yet afterwards each new step upwards is to be regarded as the development of new activities giving rise to new wants, rather than of new wants giving rise to new activities."[51] While Marshall did not explicitly detail the implication this had for the human utilization of natural resources, this seemed clear – progress was a self-perpetuating process. The more human culture developed, the greater the variety of wants that surfaced, instigating a comparable growth in the means of satisfying them, or in other words a growing number of means of utilizing nature to satisfy these wants. At some point, evidently already manifest in civilized countries, these ever-varying and developing means of production through manipulating nature, became in a way independent. They no longer catered to specific wants but actually invented new wants by affording new means of creating novel products. Marshall's perspective in fact made room for an unlimited process of increasing the utilization of nature, since the limits to this were set not so much by what nature ostensibly offered, but rather by the human imagination. Utilizing nature was bounded only by the difficulties of finding new ways to master it to cater to ever new, previously unimagined, wants. This was a more modern, and in a way more comprehensive conception, of the limits, or rather the lack thereof, of utilizing nature.

Marshall did not ignore traditional topics such as agricultural production.[52] His contribution to the consideration of natural resources was, however, this more expansive recognition of the increasingly diversified use of nature that modern life enabled. Human development was inexorably dependent on the use of nature. "Knowledge is our most powerful engine of production; it enables us to subdue Nature and force her to satisfy our wants." Nature and human beings were in fact the only two agents of production, and understanding them led to comprehending human development. "But on the other hand man is himself largely formed by his surroundings, in which nature plays a great part: and thus from every point of view man is the centre of the problem of production as well as that of consumption."[53]

Marshall did however realize that human progress required proper social conditions. He noted how from the late eighteenth century there was a growing realization that even if a greater population strengthened the state, it was unjust to do so at the ensuing expense of misery. Acknowledging the contribution of Malthus, he nonetheless did not appear as pessimistic as the latter, observing how social progress had enabled a more balanced growth of population in England. It was dangerous that there was a growing tendency among some of the more able and intelligent segments of the working population to be disinclined to have large families. Given the proper moral and physical bounds which should reign in the obvious dangers of inadequate raising of children, Marshall was cautiously optimistic about the future growth in population, which would enhance both England's, and the whole world's, physical and mental condition.[54] It would not be the want of essentials which would curtail population, but rather that of comforts beyond bare necessaries.[55] Yet there was no tangible danger of that happening. Sustainable progress was slow and gradual, not sudden and over-ambitious.[56] There was no reason to regard a stationary state as imminent. The surplus of production over the necessaries of life was constantly augmenting. "The whole history of man shows that his wants expand with the growth of his wealth and knowledge."[57]

Though the distribution of wealth was not always socially equitable, and though wars and military expenditure posed a constant inhibiting force to progress, Marshall remained optimistic, noting that population, the material means for its maintenance, and the "proportionate increase in the aggregate income of enjoyment of all kinds," advanced in tandem. Moreover, "[t]he accumulated wealth of civilized countries is at present growing faster than the population… as a matter of fact an increase of population is likely to continue to be accompanied by a more than proportionate increase of the material aids to production."[58] Growing ability to utilize natural resources outweighed the growth of population. "[O]ur growing power over nature makes her yield an ever larger surplus above necessaries; and this is not absorbed by an unlimited increase of the population."[59] Marshall's optimism highlights a basic fact regarding the neoclassical view of nature – despite its increasing methodological sophistication compared with classical political economy, neoclassical economics owed more in this respect to eighteenth-century political economy, than to the more cautious approach of the later classicists following Ricardo and Malthus. In the transition to modernity, Malthusian pessimism was a bump on the otherwise confident road emphasizing the increasing human ability to utilize natural resources. The next, and more tangible, bump of this sort, would have to wait for the late twentieth century.

In assessing modern economics our discussion necessarily has to turn from desultory to almost superficial. A detailed consideration of the unprecedented variety of approaches to nature in modern economics is completely beyond the scope of the present discussion, and those looking for a survey of this large topic will have to look elsewhere.[60] Here we will center on two points – first, the persistence of the advocacy for enhancing the use of nature among mainstream economists; and second, the increasing interest in environmental issues both among mainstream economists, and in more heterodox debates.

Probably the most influential modern economist, Marshall's disciple John Maynard Keynes, definitely belonged to the former group, although he did not accord natural resources any systematic attention. However, like Marshall, he grounded his economic perspective within a wide cultural context, which makes it possible to assess his view of this issue. Keynes regarded economics as one of the moral sciences.[61] Human motivation was a mixture of rational mathematical deliberation, together with the probably even more prevalent spontaneous reactions due to the activity of "animal spirits." In particular, decisions to act positively, to undertake action, were based on the innate human propensity for action rather than inaction, often augmented by a spontaneous, if irrational, optimism about the future outcome of such actions. Not all human decisions regarding the future were based on irrational psychology. Yet people should be reminded that such decisions "cannot depend on strict mathematical expectation, since the basis for making such calculations does not exist; and that it is our innate urge to activity which makes the wheels go round, our rational selves choosing between the alternatives as best we are able, calculating where we can, but often falling back for our motive on whim or sentiment or chance."[62] For Keynes, however, this did not by any means lead to relinquishing an inherent optimism about future human development. This has led to environmentally oriented criticism claiming that he erroneously emphasized the short at the expense of the long term, dismissing environmental problems as long-term problems which do not require immediate attention.[63]

In his famous (though latently anti-Semitic) 1930 essay "Economic Possibilities for Our Grandchildren," Keynes claimed that since the sixteenth century there had been an unprecedented advance in the quality of life in developed countries, due to significant increase in two things – accumulation of capital, and scientific and technological innovation. In a hundred years it was perfectly possible that human beings would solve the "economic problem," the struggle for subsistence. This had always been the prime issue for human societies. Once it was solved, however, the difficulty facing humans would be how to deal with leisure and abundance, as they would no longer need to cater to their natural innate impulse to deal with the economic problem. Keynes regarded this emerging psychological problem as a serious social and moral challenge.[64] Despite his prescience, however, he seemed unaware of the possibility, today so apparent, of globalization, which would make generalizations about the developed world as a separate entity almost impractical. While in the sphere of personal life his predictions were perhaps more accurate, when it came to human societies in general these changes have proven more pervasive, not least regarding the problem of over-population. Keynes claimed that quality of life had risen in developed countries even with increase in population, and he estimated that this growth of population in developed countries had a good chance of slowing down in the future. This, in other words, would enhance prosperity and leisure, with their attendant problems.[65] Keynes did not elaborate the implications this had for the human interaction with the natural environment, but it is not difficult to infer this conclusion. He presented an updated and more cautious version of the Enlightenment optimistic view of human progress based on increasing control of natural resources. His vision of the solution to the "economic problem" was an optimistic overcoming of Malthus's pessimism. His concept of "animal spirits" assumed that human beings would continue to operate and enhance their control of the natural environment, even in the face of rational evidence that this might be a precarious road of action. While Keynes himself was therefore far from sensitive to environmental concerns and limitations to socio-economic progress, his theoretical assumptions provide a prognostic framework for explaining why, in the twentieth century, despite growing evidence of the negative impact of human activity on the environment, human beings continue to enhance this activity, and not only due to rising global population.

Moreover, as Keynes noted, the "mathematical" information necessary for making strictly rational choices was usually unavailable. In our own time the debate about global warming is a clear example of how the claim, made in some quarters, for lack of full information, hinders a solution to an acute environmental and socio-economic problem. On the other hand, a case could be made that sufficient information regarding this issue already exists, and human beings, animated by either irrational optimism or lack of will, continue to act in defiance of this information. If so, this might suggest that when it comes to utilizing natural resources, and perhaps in other fields as well, human beings tend to operate in defiance of their long-term interests. This, of course, is not in itself surprising, and does not bode well for those intent on educating the public to these dangers. On the other hand, there is some evidence that at least those living in the developed world, and possessing the abundance and leisure Keynes foresaw, are increasingly prone to listen and respond to environmental cautionary information. The situation, of course, is very different when it comes to the inhabitants of less developed countries, still dealing, at times desperately, with the economic problem, and who are gradually becoming the proportionately larger segment of global population. Yet this is moving a long way from Keynes's original views, which did not evince such environmental interests.

At one point he did address directly the issue of land cultivation. He noted that in the modern world, the influence of fluctuations in harvests on the agricultural cycle was much less significant than in previous eras. One reason was that agricultural output held a much smaller proportion to the overall output than previously. The second, more pertinent to our discussion, was that the development of a world market for most agricultural products led "to an averaging out of the effects of good and bad seasons." Compared with the "old days," when individual countries were more dependent on their own harvests, the conditions of modern international trade meant that harvest fluctuations in the global market were less acute than in individual countries.[66] While Keynes himself did not elaborate this point, this meant that international trade reduced the dependence of human beings, in the production of subsistence, on the vagaries of natural phenomena. This viewpoint was clearly indebted to the classical outlook we considered above.

In the late twentieth century there finally occurred a novel development in the economic consideration of nature, although even this has remained confined mainly to heterodox circles among economists. Political economy since antiquity had almost universally accepted that utilizing the natural environment was a human prerogative, that it was essential for material and cultural existence and progress, and that there were no tangible physical limits to the extent that natural resources could be used, and human civilization expanded. Malthus raised serious concerns about this optimism. Yet even he did not perceive any imminent environmental problem. This overall optimism continued to reign in economic discourse till the modern environmental crisis, increasingly evident in the last generation, has made such disregard seem like oblivious insouciance. However, this does not mean that coming to terms with environmental problems has necessarily led economists to adopt an environmental outlook. Quite the contrary. Among mainstream economists, grappling with this problem has led to a new, cautious yet also reinvigorated, optimism about the prospects for future progress. A similar process, as we have seen, occurred following the nineteenth-century discussion of Malthus's population theory.

In modern economics the dividing line between mainstream economists and their more environmentally inclined peers is most clearly manifest in the different outlooks of environmental versus ecological economics. Mainstream environmental economics is concerned with efficiently managing the use of natural resources, in the attempt to maintain their utilization to the furthest extent possible. While it accepts the possibility of finite resources, it does not see this as a reason to discontinue this utilization. This is evident in the concept of weak sustainability, the idea that a natural resource might be used till exhaustion, so long as sufficient investment in other resources or capital is made, so that future generations will have at their disposal complementary economic resources. An example could be the idea that we might exhaust our natural supply of fossil fuels so long as we develop other types of energy technologies in their stead. The different approach of strong sustainability, on the other hand, claims that some natural resources are incommensurable, and cannot be compensated by other resources or capital. The singular qualities of a landscape devastated by mining, for example, are lost forever, and no compensation for future generations is possible. Endangering the Alaskan countryside for oil drilling is therefore, according to the extreme version of this outlook, unthinkable. This approach has been a mainstay of the new sub-discipline of ecological economics. It should however be noted that among mainstream economists environmental economics and weak sustainability have dominated, while the opposite approach has been confined, at least so far, to a minority among the profession, although it has welcomed contributions by scholars from other disciplines, not least environmental philosophers.[67] We should also note, albeit briefly, that the question of the existence of wilderness has come to the fore in recent environmental debate. Some environmental historians, most notably William Cronon, question whether any real wilderness, removed from humanity, exists at all anymore.[68] If not, this requires a major reassessment of what manifestations of the natural environment, or what is left of it, should be "conserved."

A prominent figure in developing the concept of weak sustainability has been economist Robert Solow. Acknowledging the finiteness of nonrenewable natural resources, Solow nonetheless sees ways of offsetting this by capital investment, which can maintain consumption, and thus also economic growth, from generation to generation. He has proposed the weak-sustainability idea of the substitutability of other resources for depleted nonrenewable natural resources. This is a way, if imperfect, to sustain the level of consumption and living standards into the indefinite future. Solow provides a sober vision of weak sustainability far from disdainful of environmental concerns.[69]

Ecological economists, however, and many environmentalists in general, have felt ill at ease with this predominantly traditional economic view of nature. Since the advent of the modern environmental movement there has been a deep-seated, and expected, suspicion of economics in general. Aldo Leopold, for example, one of the founding fathers of modern environmentalism, became disillusioned with the ability of economists to deal with a true appreciation of nature and provide a way to conserve it.[70] Nevertheless, some heterodox economists became increasingly concerned with the depletion of natural resources. Kenneth Boulding's concept of "spaceship earth," highlighting the realization of the ineluctable finite quality of the earth and its material resources, proved a famous and influential example of this growing realization.[71] Another approach, particularly among ecological economists, has grappled with the economic assessment of environmental values such as clean air or landscapes. It has become increasingly clear that there are serious difficulties when environmental issues become a matter of cultural and communal values.[72] This "messiness" of ecological economics has proven a hindrance to its acceptance among mainstream economics, with its preference for neat mathematical formulations and clear-cut scientific solutions.

Nonetheless, some prominent economists have insisted on approaching environmental issues in a nonconformist manner. Amartya Sen is one of the most influential among them. Sen propounds a more expansive view of sustainable development than the common one developed for example by Solow. He advocates for a concept of sustainability encompassing cultural values and citizenship and going beyond immediate material needs.[73] Sen has objected to the claim that the natural environment should be valued and conserved mainly by separating it from human interference as much as possible. "[T]he value of the environment cannot be just a matter of what there is, but must also consist of the opportunities it offers to people. The impact of the environment on human lives must be among the principal considerations in assessing the value of the environment." He is however optimistic that human impact on the natural world might be positive as well as negative. "[T]he environment is not only a matter of passive preservation, but also one of active pursuit." Human development need not have only destructive consequences, but also many forms of positive involvement. Proper developmental activity, which for Sen means of course a social arrangement based on justice, therefore bodes well both for humans and for nature. "Development is fundamentally an empowering process, and this power can be used to preserve and enrich the environment, and not only to decimate it. We must not, therefore, think of the environment exclusively in terms of conserving pre-existing natural conditions, since the environment can also include the results of human creation." Sen thus continues the modern recognition, already evident in classical political economic thought, that human impact on the environment is inevitable. It is a measure of his optimism that despite the dire lessons of modern environmental degradation, he continues to assert a vision of human impact as the source not just of damage to the environment, but also of the amelioration of that damage.[74]

Nevertheless, Sen remains in the minority among mainstream economists, most of whom consistently maintain a belief in progress based on the use of natural resources, continuing the long tradition of political-economic thought we have surveyed. Robert Fogel, one of the leading proponents of the modern subdiscipline of cliometrics, the application of quantitative economic methodology to the study of economic history, has presented one of the most updated versions of this outlook. Fogel has included in his purview not only advanced industrial economies, but those of the third, developing, world as well. He has outlined a much more global and encompassing economic vision of human progress than that envisioned by his classical-economic predecessors, and even by a later figure such as Keynes. In fact, it now seems that any serious scholar tackling the issues of population and resources cannot regard the idea of limits to these factors as only theoretical or far-off possibilities. Fogel, however, does not see this as a reason for pessimism. On the contrary.

Fogel centers his discussion on the concept of "technophysio evolution," referring to the complicated interaction between progress in the technology of production (including scientific, industrial, biomedical and cultural advances, which have vastly increased human control of the environment), and improvements in human physiology (including such things as body size, longevity, age of onset of chronic diseases and the great increase in population size), particularly since 1700, and most prominently since the beginning of the twentieth century. This connection between technological and physiological improvements is perceived by Fogel as synergistic, as mutually enforcing. In other words, improvements in nutrition and physiology contributed to economic growth and technological progress, and not just the other way around. Technophysio evolution, however, has created a new set of contemporary problems related to the solvency of pension funds, and other socioeconomic and intergenerational difficulties. Yet these have nothing to do with any theoretical finiteness to natural resources, which seems inconsequential in Fogel's outlook.[75] His notion of technophysio evolution rests on the firm belief that "human beings have gained an unprecedented degree of control over their environment – a degree of control so great that it sets them apart not only from all other species, but also from all previous generations of *Homo Sapiens*."[76] This is clearly, for Fogel, a positive historical development, and his aim is to enhance it into the future.

His views on population are a logical emanation from this point of departure. He claims that there have in fact been numerous historical moments in which an equilibrium between the sizes of population and of subsistence was reached (though with different levels of body size and mortality), not, as Malthus had claimed, that there existed one level beyond which the limit to subsistence spelled demographic disaster.[77] In the last half century or so not only has agricultural production kept pace with the dramatic increase in population, but the world's per capita consumption of food has in fact even increased in a sustained manner, although fifteen percent of the global population still suffers chronic malnutrition. Technophysio evolution, according to Fogel, has not only conquered the severe malnutrition of previous eras, but has even created a problem of overnutrition and corpulence as a result of cheaply priced food.[78] In time, technophysio evolution will enable almost all the population to realize their fullest potential for self-fulfillment. Fogel optimistically claims to "believe that the desire to understand ourselves and our environment is one of the fundamental driving forces of humanity, on a par with the most basic material needs."[79] By "understand" he in fact means also to control, and by "environment" he alludes both to the natural and to the social environments. In any event, he regards the utilization of natural resources as a significant factor contributing to the amelioration of human life in the modern age, in which new technologies improve the environment.[80] Obviously, this outlook is diametrically opposed to that of ecological economics and the environmental movement in general. It does however prove the claim we have been discussing throughout these pages – that the history of economic considerations of nature is a linear one of increasing emphasis on the need to maximize the use of natural resources, and thus to advance human civilization to the highest level possible.

It is not my intent here to judge whether this outlook is commendable or not. I suppose proponents of various and even conflicting approaches to economic considerations of nature will find material here to buttress their respective arguments. Personally, I think that as with most things in life, moderation is the best option. Irresponsible unhindered use of natural resources oblivious to environmental and social costs is a bad course of action. So, however, is also any attempt, futile to begin with, to arrest development, and deny the inexorable fact, proven by history in general, and by the history of economic thought in particular, that without the constant cultivation of natural resources, human progress and the amelioration of human life among all populations, is impossible.

Notes

Chapter 1: From antiquity to the Renaissance

1 It is imperative to note at the start that we will be concerned with nature specifically as a physical natural resource meant for human utilization. The term "nature" has of course many other meanings, and studies of cultural attitudes toward nature abound, not least in its political sense related to natural law and other similar concepts. This body of scholarship is not, however, particularly relevant for our present discussion. For more pertinent broad-ranging surveys see Clarence J. Glacken, *Traces on the Rhodian Shore: Nature and Culture in Western Thought from Ancient Times to the End of the Eighteenth Century* (Berkeley: University of California Press, 1967); and Keith Thomas, *Man and the Natural World: Changing Attitudes in England 1500–1800* (Harmondsworth: Penguin Books, 1984). Even these justly famous studies, though, accord economic thought relatively little attention.

2 The *locus classicus* of this approach is Lynn White Jr.'s famous article, "The Historical Roots of our Ecological Crisis," *Science*, 155 (10 March 1967), 1203–7. See also J. Edward de Steiguer, *The Origins of Modern Environmental Thought* (Tucson: University of Arizona Press, 2006), 99–109.

3 See Arthur O. Lovejoy, *The Great Chain of Being: A Study of the History of an Idea* (New York: Harper and Row, 1960).

4 On the combination of these two attitudes see Francis Oakley, "Lovejoy's Unexplored Option," *Journal of the History of Ideas*, 48 (1987), 231–45.

5 See S. Todd Lowry, "The Classical Greek Theory of Natural Resource Economics," *Land Economics*, 41 (1965), 203–8.

6 On this and other aspects of Greek political-economic thought, and specifically Aristotle, see the various approaches in Scott Meikle, *Aristotle's Economic Thought* (Oxford: Clarendon Press, 1995), 180–200; Barry Gordon, *Economic Analysis Before Adam Smith: Hesiod to Lessius* (London and Basingstoke: Macmillan, 1975), 21–69; and Joseph A. Schumpeter, *History of Economic Analysis*, ed. Elizabeth Boody Schumpeter (New York: Oxford University Press, 1954), 57–65.

7 See Dotan Leshem, "Oikonomia Redefined," *Journal of the History of Economic Thought*, 35 (2013), 43–61.

8 Aristotle, *The Politics*, trans. Benjamin Jowett, revised by Jonathan Barnes, ed. Stephen Everson (Cambridge: Cambridge University Press, 1988), 10–11, 15, 18.

9 Ibid., 15–16.

10 Ibid., 86–8, 151, 169.

11 Ibid., 162–4, 171.

12 Ibid., 146–8. See also Gordon, *Economic Analysis Before Adam Smith*, 30.

13 Aristotle, *Politics*, 12–15.

14 See Gordon, *Economic Analysis Before Adam Smith*, 27–39.

15 Aristotle, *Politics*, 31.

16 Ibid., 11.
17 For this, and Xenophon's political economy in general, see Willie Henderson, *John Ruskin's Political Economy* (London and New York: Routledge, 2000), 64–85; Jane Garnett, "Political and Domestic Economy in Victorian Social Thought: Ruskin and Xenophon," in *Economy, Polity, and Society: British Intellectual History 1750–1950*, eds. Stefan Collini, Richard Whatmore, and Brian Young (Cambridge: Cambridge University Press, 2000), 205–23; and also L. N. Christofides, "On Share Contracts and Other Economic Contributions of Xenophon," *Scottish Journal of Political Economy*, 39 (1992), 111–22.
18 See Gordon, *Economic Analysis Before Adam Smith*, 39–41.
19 See Xenophon, "Ways and Means," in *Scripta Minora*, trans. E. C. Marchant (Loeb Classical Library; London: William Heinemann, and Cambridge, MA: Harvard University Press, 1925), 193–231, at 193–5.
20 See Xenophon, "Oeconomicus," in *Memorabilia and Oeconomicus*, trans. E. C. Marchant (Loeb Classical Library; London: William Heinemann, and Cambridge, MA: Harvard University Press, 1923), 363–525, at 391, 393–9.
21 Ibid., 365.
22 Ibid., 401–5 (405 for the quotation), 409–11, 479–521.
23 For general surveys see Joel Kaye, *Economy and Nature in the Fourteenth Century: Money, Market Exchange, and the Emergence of Scientific Thought* (Cambridge: Cambridge University Press, 1998); and Odd Langholm, "The Medieval Schoolmen (1200–1400)," in *Ancient and Medieval Economic Ideas and Concepts of Social Justice*, eds. S. Todd Lowry and Barry Gordon (Leiden: Brill, 1998), 439–501.
24 See Edgar Scully, "La philosophie politique de saint Thomas d'Aquin: économie politique?" *Laval théologique et philosophique*, 38 (1982), 49–59. For Aquinas's economic views in general see Kaye, *Economy and Nature in the Fourteenth Century*, 56–78, 85–6, 95–100; Langholm, "Medieval Schoolmen," 444–5, 447, 450, 452, 455, 462–4, 470–84, 487–8, 491, 495; Gordon, *Economic Analysis Before Adam Smith*, 153–86; and Germano Maifreda, *From* Oikonomia *to Political Economy: Constructing Economic Knowledge from the Renaissance to the Scientific Revolution*, trans. Loretta Valtz Mannucci (Farnham and Burlington: Ashgate, 2012), 47–50.
25 See St. Thomas Aquinas, *Political Writings*, ed. and trans. R. W. Dyson (Cambridge: Cambridge University Press, 2002), 58, 68, 110, 164, 251–3, 256. For Aquinas's consideration of nature in general see Glacken, *Traces on the Rhodian Shore*, 229–36, 273–6.
26 Aquinas, *Political Writings*, 6, 9, 206.
27 See Gordon, *Economic Analysis Before Adam Smith*, 181–6.
28 Aquinas, *Political Writings*, 38–9, 45.
29 Ibid., 49–52.
30 See Gordon, *Economic Analysis Before Adam Smith*, 186.
31 On Scotus's economic ideas see Langholm, "Medieval Schoolmen," 455–6, 458, 471–2, 478, 481–2, 486–8, 493; Kaye, *Economy and Nature in the Fourteenth Century*, 125–7, 140, 184.
32 John Duns Scotus, *Political and Economic Philosophy*, ed. and trans. Allan B. Wolter (St. Bonaventure, NY: Franciscan Institute, 2001), 45.
33 Ibid., 29–31.
34 Ibid., 35, 37–9.
35 See *The De Moneta of Nicholas Oresme and English Mint Documents*, trans. and ed. Charles Johnson (Edinburgh: Thomas Nelson and Sons, 1956), 6. On Oresme see Kaye, *Economy and Nature in the Fourteenth Century*, 29–31, 148–51, 155–6, 160–1, 201–19, 222–5, 235–45; and also Langholm, "Medieval Schoolmen," 490–1, 495–7; Gordon, *Economic Analysis Before Adam Smith*, 188–90.
36 See Kaye, *Economy and Nature in the Fourteenth Century*, passim.
37 See Nicholas Copernicus, *Minor Works*, trans. Edward Rosen, with Erna Hilfstein (Baltimore and London: Johns Hopkins University Press, 1985), 176.

38 Ibid., 191–2.
39 On Botero and his influence on early modern thought see Richard Tuck, *Philosophy and Government 1572–1651* (Cambridge: Cambridge University Press, 1993), 65–119.
40 On these points see Andrew Fitzmaurice, "The Commercial Ideology of Colonization in Jacobean England: Robert Johnson, Giovanni Botero, and the Pursuit of Greatness," *William and Mary Quarterly*, 64 (2007), 791–820.
41 Giovanni Botero, *The Reason of State & The Greatness of Cities*, trans. [respectively] P. J. and D. P. Waley, and Robert Peterson (1606) (London: Routledge and Kegan Paul, 1956), 35.
42 Ibid., 257–8. See 264–9 for further praise of China's natural treasures and their efficient use. This enabled an excess of products which fueled international trade and growing population.
43 Ibid., 135.
44 Ibid., 38–40.
45 See Mauro Boianovsky, "Humboldt and the Economists on Natural Resources, Institutions and Underdevelopment (1752–1859)," *European Journal of the History of Economic Thought*, 20 (2013), 58–88. On Botero in this context see Istvan Hont, *Jealousy of Trade: International Competition and the Nation-State in Historical Perspective* (Cambridge, MA, and London: Harvard University Press, 2005), 431–9 (these pages authored by Hont jointly with Michael Ignatieff).
46 Botero, *Reason of State*, 235–6, 255–7.
47 Ibid., 237–8, 269. See 236–42 for a detailed discussion of rivers, canals and their navigability.
48 Ibid., 102, 172.
49 Ibid., 148–50, 185–6.
50 Ibid., 144–6; see also 227, 231–2, 274–5.
51 Ibid., 233–43, and also 244–73.
52 Ibid., 148–67. See also 246–7, on how colonies enriched and augmented the population of the mother country.
53 Ibid., 150–3, 160.
54 See Joseph A. Schumpeter, *History of Economic Analysis*, 254–5. For Botero's population theory see also Terence Hutchison, *Before Adam Smith: The Emergence of Political Economy, 1662–1776* (Oxford and Cambridge, MA: Basil Blackwell, 1988), 18–19; Charles Emil Stangeland, *Pre-Malthusian Doctrines of Population: A Study in the History of Economic Theory* (New York: AMS Press, 1967), 105–7.
55 Botero, *Reason of State*, 154–7.
56 On this topic see John M. Headley, "Geography and Empire in the Late Renaissance: Botero's Assignment, Western Universalism, and the Civilizing Process," *Renaissance Quarterly*, 53 (2000), 1119–55.
57 Botero, *Reason of State*, 275–9.
58 See John Hales, *A Discourse of the Common Weal of this Realm of England*, ed. Elizabeth Lamond (New York: Burt Franklin, 1971 [1893]). It was probably written around 1548–1549, though published only in 1581. On Hales see E. A. J. Johnson, *Predecessors of Adam Smith: The Growth of British Economic Thought* (New York: Augustus M. Kelley, 1965), 19–37. For Hales as a mercantilist see Eli F. Heckscher, *Mercantilism*, trans. Mendel Shapiro, ed. E. F. Söderlund, 2 vols. (London: George Allen & Unwin, and New York: Macmillan, 1962), 2: 20, 104–5, 109, 175–6n, 211–12, 227, 238, 278–9, 293–4, 260, 313–14.
59 Hales, *Discourse of the Common Weal*, 48–53.
60 Ibid., 54–5.
61 Ibid., 60–5.
62 Ibid., 59, and see also 120–4.
63 Ibid., 92–3.

Chapter 2: Mercantilism and natural resources

1 For a recent introduction see Lars Magnusson, *The Political Economy of Mercantilism* (Abingdon and New York: Routledge, 2015). On the varying assessments of mercantilism in modern scholarship see Philip J. Stern and Carl Wennerlind, "Introduction," in *Mercantilism Reimagined: Political Economy in Early Modern Britain and Its Empire*, eds. Philip J. Stern and Carl Wennerlind (Oxford: Oxford University Press, 2014), 3–22.
2 See Andrea Finkelstein, *Harmony and the Balance: An Intellectual History of Seventeenth-Century English Economic Thought* (Ann Arbor: University of Michigan Press, 2000), 89–97.
3 As far as raw materials, including foodstuffs and even machines, were considered, since they were perceived as factors of production, mercantilist policy was often in essence reversed – and due to their importance their export was forbidden, and import encouraged. This led to internal contradictions in policy. See Heckscher, *Mercantilism*, 2: 146–52.
4 For aspects of the mercantilist consideration of natural resources see Fredrik Albritton Jonsson, "Natural History and Improvement: The Case of Tobacco," in Stern and Wennerlind, *Mercantilism Reimagined*, 117–33; Johnson, *Predecessors of Adam Smith*, 239–43, 265–6, 272–6; and Lars Herlitz, "Art and Nature in Pre-Classical Economics of the Seventeenth and Eighteenth Centuries," in *Nature and Society in Historical Context*, eds. Mikuláš Teich, Roy Porter, and Bo Gustafsson (Cambridge: Cambridge University Press, 1997), 163–75, who also discusses Cantillon and the Physiocrats.
5 See Heckscher, *Mercantilism*, 2: 157–65; Stangeland, *Pre-Malthusian Doctrines of Population*, 118–84; Johnson, *Predecessors of Adam Smith*, 247–56; and Ted McCormick, "Population: Modes of Seventeenth-Century Demographic Thought," in Stern and Wennerlind, *Mercantilism Reimagined*, 25–45.
6 Joyce Oldham Appleby, *Economic Thought and Ideology in Seventeenth-Century England* (Princeton: Princeton University Press, 1978), 84–5.
7 See Heckscher, *Mercantilism*, 2: 308–15; and Andrea Finkelstein, *Harmony and the Balance*, 101–6. Appleby, *Economic Thought and Ideology*, at 84, has noted that in the seventeenth century the extension of market analysis from commodities, to people and land, was a critical stage in the transformation of modern society, in which economic processes rather than more traditional modes of thought directed social relations.
8 See Maifreda, *From* Oikonomia *to Political Economy*, passim; Kaye, *Economy and Nature in the Fourteenth Century*, passim.
9 See Peter Harrison, *The Bible, Protestantism, and the Rise of Natural Science* (Cambridge: Cambridge University Press, 1998).
10 See Francis Bacon, *The New Organon*, eds. and trans. Lisa Jardine and Michael Silverthorne (Cambridge: Cambridge University Press, 2000), 101, 221. Also see Glacken, *Traces on the Rhodian Shore*, 471–97.
11 See Lewes Roberts, "The Treasure of Traffike, or a Discourse of Forraigne Trade" (London, 1641), in *EET*, 49–113, at 60–3. On Roberts see Johnson, *Predecessors of Adam Smith*, 240, 242; Appleby, *Economic Thought and Ideology*, 106–7, 121–2, 160, 216.
12 See Johnson, *Predecessors of Adam Smith*, 242, 253–4; and also Appleby, *Economic Thought and Ideology*, 86–7, 136–7, 207–8.
13 Samuel Fortrey, "England's Interest and Improvement, Consisting in the Increase of the Store, and Trade of this Kingdom" (London, 1673), in *EET*, 211–49, at 217–18.
14 Ibid., 218–19.
15 Ibid., 226–31.
16 On this work see Heckscher, *Mercantilism*, 1: 319–20; 2: 115, 188, 314; Appleby, *Economic Thought and Ideology*, 125, 135–6, 147; Johnson, *Predecessors of Adam Smith*, 249, 251, 254.

17 "Britannia Languens, or a Discourse of Trade" (London, 1680), in *EET*, 275–508, at 291–2. On the importance of a growing population, see also 300, 458.
18 Ibid., 349–52.
19 Ibid., 493.
20 On Mun see Finkelstein, *Harmony and the Balance*, 74–88; Johnson, *Predecessors of Adam Smith*, 73–89; Heckscher, *Mercantilism*, 2: 113, 189–90, 212, 223–4, 232, 242–3, 248–9, 281, 321.
21 See Appleby, *Economic Thought and Ideology*, 37–41, 48–50, 116, 118, 158–61, 203–5.
22 See Mauro Boianovsky, "Humboldt and the Economists on Natural Resources," 87.
23 On Mun's consideration of nature see Johnson, *Predecessors of Adam Smith*, 242.
24 Thomas Mun, "A Discovrse of Trade, From England vnto the East-Indies" (London, 1621), in *EET*, 1–47, at 40–1. On Mun's differentiation between natural and artificial wealth see also Johnson, *Predecessors of Adam Smith*, 79, 88–9, 240–1, 264–5, 302–3; Andrea Finkelstein, *Harmony and the Balance*, 81–4.
25 Mun, "Discovrse of Trade," 46.
26 Thomas Mun, "England's Treasure by Forraign Trade, or the Ballance of our Forraign Trade is the Rule of our Treasure" (London, 1664), in *EET*, 115–209, at 191–204.
27 Ibid., 127–34.
28 See Johnson, *Predecessors of Adam Smith*, 76.
29 Mun, "Discovrse of Trade," 24–6.
30 On Petty see Alessandro Roncaglia, *Petty: The Origins of Political Economy*, trans. Isabella Cherubini (Armonk, NY: M. E. Sharpe, 1985); Tony Aspromourgos, "The Life of William Petty in Relation to His Economics: A Tercentenary Interpretation," *History of Political Economy*, 20 (1988), 337–56; Andrea Finkelstein, *Harmony and the Balance*, 107–29; Heckscher, *Mercantilism*, 1: 52–3, 311; 2: 117, 165, 190, 207, 213, 260, 297–8; Hutchison, *Before Adam Smith*, 27–41; Johnson, *Predecessors of Adam Smith*, 93–113, 241, 243, 248, 252–5, 269–70, 274.
31 See Roncaglia, *Petty*, 19–28; Heckscher, *Mercantilism*, 2: 309–10.
32 See Carl Wennerlind, "Money: Hartlibian Political Economy and the New Culture of Credit," in Stern and Wennerlind, *Mercantilism Reimagined*, 74–93, esp. 77–9.
33 See Ted McCormick, *William Petty and the Ambitions of Political Arithmetic* (Oxford: Oxford University Press, 2009), 179–81, 183–4. Also see James Bonar, *Theories of Population from Raleigh to Arthur Young* (London: Frank Cass, 1966), 82–100.
34 See William Petty, *Several Essays in Political Arithmetick* (London, D. Browne et al., 1755; reprint London: Routledge and Thoemmes Press, and Tokyo: Kinokuniya, 1992), 148.
35 Ibid., 23–32.
36 Andrea Finkelstein, *Harmony and the Balance*, 123–4.
37 See Anthony Brewer, "The Concept of an Agricultural Surplus, from Petty to Smith," *Journal of the History of Economic Thought*, 33 (2011), 487–505.
38 See Petty, *Several Essays*, 100–25 (quotation at 108). Also see Roncaglia, *Petty*, 56.
39 On these aspects of Davenant's thought see Andrea Finkelstein, *Harmony and the Balance*, 219–46. Also see Hont, *Jealousy of Trade*, 57, 59–62; Hutchison, *Before Adam Smith*, 48–53; Heckscher, *Mercantilism*, 2: 115–16, 163, 169, 190, 192, 203, 233–4, 260–1, 282, 322–3.
40 See Andrea Finkelstein, *Harmony and the Balance*, 239–42; Johnson, *Predecessors of Adam Smith*, 242, 248–50, 252–5, 265, 268, 275.
41 See Charles Davenant, "An Essay on the East-India Trade," [1697] in *The Political and Commercial Works of That Celebrated Writer Charles D'Avenant*, collected and revised by Sir Charles Whitworth, 5 vols. (London: R. Horsfield et al., 1771; reprint Farnborough: Gregg Press, 1967), 1: 83–123, at 86, and also 88.
42 Ibid., 104–5, and see also 110–11, and 106–7, on the possibility of developing fishing on England's shores.

43 On Child's economic ideas see Andrea Finkelstein, *Harmony and the Balance*, 130–46; Appleby, *Economic Thought and Ideology*, 88–93, 113–14, 149, 190; Hutchison, *Before Adam Smith*, 58–60; Johnson, *Predecessors of Adam Smith*, 241, 254; Heckscher, *Mercantilism*, 1: 311, 319, 354–5, 374, 414; 2: 29, 117, 124–5, 158–9, 224, 229, 306, 321.
44 See Josiah Child, "A New Discourse of Trade" (London: John Everingham, 1693), reprinted in *Sir Josiah Child, Selected Works 1668–1697* (Farnborough: Gregg Press, 1968), 135–64.
45 Ibid., 13–19, 36–7, 44, 52, 122.
46 Ibid., 29–30.
47 Ibid., 35, 39, 64.
48 Ibid., 209–16, 223–4, 228.
49 Ibid., 211–12.
50 Ibid., 216.
51 Ibid., 164–8.
52 Ibid., 164–79, 207–8.
53 Ibid., 189–93.
54 See Josiah Child, "A Discourse of the Nature, Use and Advantages of Trade" (London: Randal Taylor, 1694), reprinted in *Sir Josiah Child, Selected Works*.
55 Ibid., 1–6 (5 for the quotation), and see also 30, and 10, for fishery as another foundation of trade.
56 Ibid., 7–9.
57 Ibid., 11.
58 Ibid., 26–8, 30.
59 Ibid., 17–18.
60 On Montchrestien see Maifreda, *From* Oikonomia *to Political Economy*, 170–80.
61 See Antoine de Montchrestien, *Traicté de l'œconomie politique*, ed. François Billacois (Geneva: Librairie Droz, 1999), 51–2, 54–5, 66.
62 Ibid., 81–2, 280.
63 Ibid., 75–81 (quotation at 81).
64 On Uztáriz see Robert S. Smith, "Spanish Mercantilism: A Hardy Perennial," *Southern Economic Journal*, 38 (1971), 1–11; and also Stangeland, *Pre-Malthusian Doctrines of Population*, 170–2.
65 See Jerónimo de Uztáriz, *The Theory and Practice of Commerce and Maritime Affairs*, trans. John Kippax (Dublin: George Faulkner, 1752), 26–33 (quotation at 29).
66 Ibid., 99–109 (quotation at 100).
67 Ibid., 216–19.
68 Ibid., 403, 410–11.
69 Ibid., 411–21.
70 Ibid., 416.
71 One explanation which has been offered is that precisely Dutch dominance in international trade raised the concern in other countries, particularly England, which led to the development of mercantilist thought, while in Holland itself commercial success made such theorizing seem less necessary. See Th. van Tijn, "Dutch Economic Thought in the Seventeenth Century," in *Economic Thought in the Netherlands: 1650–1950*, eds. J. van Daal and A. Heertje (Aldershot: Avebury, 1992), 7–28.
72 On de la Court's political-economic views, and his views on interconnected commercial and republican issues, and freedom of trade, see Arthur Weststeijn, *Commercial Republicanism in the Dutch Golden Age: The Political Thought of Johan & Pieter de la Court* (Leiden and Boston: Brill, 2012), 205–83.
73 Pieter de la Court, *The True Interest and Political Maxims, Of the Republic of Holland*, trans. John Campbell (London: J. Nourse, 1746), 17–22.
74 Ibid., 22–5, 30–1, 36–7.
75 Ibid., 25–8, 70–7.
76 Ibid., 29, 65–8, 94–5.

77 Ibid., 13–15, 32–3. For de la Court's views on population see also Philip van Praag, "Un populationniste hollandais: Pieter de la Court (1618–1685)," *Population (French Edition)*, 18 (1963), 349–58; and Stangeland, *Pre-Malthusian Doctrines of Population*, 168–9.

78 De la Court, *True Interest and Political Maxims*, 120–4.

79 Ibid., 130–1.

80 For a pertinent discussion see Craig Muldrew: "Afterword: Mercantilism to Macroeconomics," in Stern and Wennerlind, *Mercantilism Reimagined*, 371–83.

81 On Locke as a mercantilist see Heckscher, *Mercantilism*, 2: 27, 47, 203–4, 239–42, 289; and for a more cautious assessment, Hutchison, *Before Adam Smith*, 60–73.

82 On these points see Appleby, *Economic Thought and Ideology*, 219–41, 270–1.

83 See John Locke, "Understanding" (1677), in *Political Essays*, ed. Mark Goldie (Cambridge: Cambridge University Press, 1997), 260–5.

84 On these points see the remarks (jointly authored by Hont with Michael Ignatieff) in Hont, *Jealousy of Trade*, 431–9.

85 John Locke, *The Works of John Locke, in Nine Volumes*, twelfth edition, vol. 4 (London: C. and J. Rivington et al., 1824), 12–13, 72 (from "Some Considerations of the Lowering of Interest, and Raising the Value of Money"). And see also the remarks at 148, from "Further Considerations Concerning Raising the Value of Money."

86 Ibid., 41 (from "Some Considerations of the Lowering of Interest, and Raising the Value of Money"). And see also Hutchison, *Before Adam Smith*, 68.

87 See Andrea Finkelstein, *Harmony and the Balance*, 166.

88 See *Works of John Locke*, vol. 4, 222–44 ("First Treatise of Government," chapters III–IV).

89 Ibid., 62–3 (from "Some Considerations of the Lowering of Interest, and Raising the Value of Money").

90 For the general discussion of this idea in the early modern era, see Maifreda, *From* Oikonomia *to Political Economy*, 143–82 (166–70 on Locke).

91 See chapter V, "Of Property," in "Second Treatise of Government," in *Works of John Locke*, vol. 4, 352–67.

92 Ibid., 356.

93 Ibid., 362.

94 Ibid., 366.

95 Ibid., 362.

96 On *res nullius* and the agriculturalist argument see Anthony Pagden, *Lords of All the World: Ideologies of Empire in Spain, Britain and France c. 1500-c. 1800* (New Haven and London: Yale University Press, 1995), 73–86. On *vacuum domicilium* see Barbara Arneil, *John Locke and America: The Defence of English Colonialism* (Oxford: Clarendon Press, 1996), 79–80, 109–17, 141–5, and passim for Locke's notions regarding the possession of land through investment of labor. Also see Andrew Fitzmaurice, "The Genealogy of *Terra Nullius*," *Australian Historical Studies*, 38 (2007), 1–15.

97 See Paul Warde, "The Invention of Sustainability," *Modern Intellectual History*, 8 (2011), 153–70; also Mark Stoll, "'Sagacious' Bernard Palissy: Pinchot, Marsh, and the Connecticut Origins of American Conservation," *Environmental History*, 16 (2011), 4–37.

98 See S. Todd Lowry, "The Agricultural Foundation of the Seventeenth-Century English Oeconomy," *History of Political Economy*, 35, Supplement (2003), 74–100.

99 See the remarks in Michael Williams, *Deforesting the Earth: From Prehistory to Global Crisis* (Chicago and London: University of Chicago Press, 2003), 130–6, 145–9, 160–7, 179–209, 222–33, 265–75.

100 See John F. Richards, *The Unending Frontier: An Environmental History of the Early Modern World* (Berkeley: University of California Press, 2005), 11–12, 20, 22, 178–80, 183–7, 190–1, 221–41, 617–22. For an overview of early modern forest management in Japan see Conrad Totman, *The Green Archipelago: Forestry in Pre-Industrial Japan* (Athens: Ohio University Press, 1998), 1–6, 171–90.

101 For Venice see Karl Appuhn, *A Forest on the Sea: Environmental Expertise in Renaissance Venice* (Baltimore: Johns Hopkins University Press, 2009), 1–19, 272–302. On Germany see Paul Warde, *Ecology, Economy and State Formation in Early Modern Germany* (Cambridge: Cambridge University Press, 2006).
102 See Richard H. Grove, *Green Imperialism: Colonial Expansion, Tropical Island Edens and the Origins of Environmentalism, 1600–1860* (Cambridge, 1995), 153–67, 222–37 and passim. For a different perspective see E. C. Spary, "'Peaches Which the Patriarchs Lacked': Natural History, Natural Resources, and the Natural Economy in France," *History of Political Economy*, 35, Supplement (2003), 14–41.
103 See Georges-Louis Leclerc, Comte de Buffon, "Sur la conservation & le rétablissement des forêts," and "Sur la culture & l'exploitation des forêts," in *Histoire naturelle, générale et particulière*, Supplément, vol. 2 (Paris: Imprimerie Royale, 1775), 249–71 and 271–90, respectively.
104 See Fredrik Albritton Jonsson, *Enlightenment's Frontier: The Scottish Highlands and the Origins of Environmentalism* (New Haven and London: Yale University Press, 2013), 147–63. And see also ibid., 73–4, on how eighteenth-century intellectuals were aware, critically or not, of the ability of human activity such as deforestation to influence the climate.
105 See Gregory Allen Barton, *Empire Forestry and the Origins of Environmentalism* (Cambridge: Cambridge University Press, 2002).
106 See Jean-François Melon, *A Political Essay Upon Commerce*, trans. David Bindon (Dublin: Philip Crampton, 1738), 77–88. For Melon and his influence in Naples and Scotland, see John Robertson, *The Case for the Enlightenment: Scotland and Naples 1680–1760* (Cambridge: Cambridge University Press, 2005), 340–76. Also see Hont, *Jealousy of Trade*, 30–4.
107 Melon, *Political Essay Upon Commerce*, 173–99. See also Hutchison, *Before Adam Smith*, 219–20.
108 Melon, *Political Essay Upon Commerce*, 328.
109 For his views on this point see Carol Blum, *Strength in Numbers: Population, Reproduction, and Power in Eighteenth-Century France* (Baltimore and London: Johns Hopkins University Press, 2002), 31, 87–8; Joseph J. Spengler, *French Predecessors of Malthus: A Study in Eighteenth-Century Wage and Population Theory* (New York: Octagon Books, 1965), 48–9, 53–6.
110 Melon, *Political Essay Upon Commerce*, 142, and more generally 55–62.
111 Ibid., 4–5, 145–7, 151–2.
112 Ibid., 60–1.
113 Ibid., 11, 39.
114 Ibid., 76.
115 Ibid., 6.
116 For a general discussion see Hutchison, *Before Adam Smith*, 163–78. For a view of Cantillon as an anti-mercantilist, see Mark Thornton, "Cantillon, Hume, and the Rise of Antimercantilism," *History of Political Economy*, 39 (2007), 453–80. Among Cantillon's prescient observations may have been recognition of the specie-flow mechanism later attributed to Hume, for which see ibid.
117 Richard Cantillon, *Essai sur la Nature du Commerce en Général*, ed. and trans. Henry Higgs (London: Frank Cass, 1959), 3. On land as the basis for all other produce see also 123, 175 and passim.
118 See Anthony Brewer, "Cantillon and the Land Theory of Value," *History of Political Economy*, 20 (1988), 1–14.
119 See Cantillon, *Essai*, 31, 41, 113.
120 Ibid., 97–9.
121 Ibid., 3–7, and also 31–3.
122 Ibid., 9, 13–17, 43, 47, 55–7, 59–65, 93–4.
123 Ibid., 39.

124 See Spengler, *French Predecessors of Malthus*, 113–28; Hutchison, *Before Adam Smith*, 169–70.
125 Cantillon, *Essai*, 65–7.
126 Ibid., 67–9.
127 Ibid., 69–85.
128 Ibid., 185–7, 193–5, 235. And see also 195–9 on how ancient Rome underwent this process.
129 Ibid., 189–91.
130 For general assessments of Steuart see A. S. Skinner, "Sir James Steuart: Author of a System," *Scottish Journal of Political Economy*, 28 (1981), 20–42; Johnson, *Predecessors of Adam Smith*, 209–34; Hutchison, *Before Adam Smith*, 335–51; Ikuo Omori, "The 'Scottish Triangle' in the Shaping of Political Economy: David Hume, Sir James Steuart, and Adam Smith," in *The Rise of Political Economy in the Scottish Enlightenment*, eds. Tatsuya Sakamoto and Hideo Tanaka (London and New York: Routledge, 2003), 103–18.
131 *SPPO*, 1: 360–2.
132 Ibid., 1: 273–5, 296.
133 Ibid., 1: 246, 271, 285.
134 Ibid., 1: 342–3.
135 Ibid., 2: 199; 3: 262n, 362, and for more on land taxes see 3: 232, 335–6, 376–7, 427.
136 Ibid., 3: 270–4, 281, 345–63, 373–4, 428–30.
137 Ibid., 3: 288–90, and for more on the inverse connection between natural conditions and cultural vitality, see 1: 34–5, 47–8.

Chapter 3: Pre-classical Enlightenment developments

1 For Schumpeter's well-known, though unconvincing, claim that most of Smith's political economy was not really original, see Schumpeter, *History of Economic Analysis*, 181–94.
2 Much has been written on this topic. For a general overview see e.g. David Spadafora, *The Idea of Progress in Eighteenth-Century Britain* (New Haven and London: Yale University Press, 1990).
3 See Dugald Stewart, "Account of the Life and Writings of Adam Smith, LL.D.," in Adam Smith, *Essays on Philosophical Subjects*, eds. W. P. D. Wightman and J. C. Bryce (Oxford: Clarendon Press, 1980) 269–351, at 292–6.
4 On conjectural history and stadial theory see Ronald L. Meek, *Social Science and the Ignoble Savage* (Cambridge: Cambridge University Press, 1976); J. G. A. Pocock, *Barbarism and Religion*, vol. 4: *Barbarians, Savages and Empires* (Cambridge: Cambridge University Press, 2005); Silvia Sebastiani, *The Scottish Enlightenment: Race, Gender, and the Limits of Progress*, trans. Jeremy Carden (New York: Palgrave Macmillan, 2013); Nathaniel Wolloch, *History and Nature in the Enlightenment: Praise of the Mastery of Nature in Eighteenth-Century Historical Literature* (Farnham and Burlington: Ashgate, 2011); Hont, *Jealousy of Trade*, 159–84, 364–6; H. M. Höpfl, "From Savage to Scotsman: Conjectural History in the Scottish Enlightenment," *Journal of British Studies*, 17 (1978), 19–40; Christopher J. Berry. *Social Theory of the Scottish Enlightenment* (Edinburgh: Edinburgh University Press, 2001), 61–73, 93–9; Aaron Garrett, "Anthropology: the 'Original' of Human Nature," in *The Cambridge Companion to the Scottish Enlightenment*, ed. Alexander Broadie (Cambridge: Cambridge University Press, 2003), 79–93; Roger L. Emerson, "Conjectural History and Scottish Philosophers," *Historical Papers/Communications Historiques*, 19 (1984), 63–90; and for nineteenth-century influences, Frank Palmeri, "Conjectural History and the Origins of Sociology," *Studies in Eighteenth Century Culture*, 37 (2008), 1–21.

5 See Adam Smith, *Lectures on Jurisprudence*, eds. R. L. Meek, D. D. Raphael, and P. G. Stein (Oxford: Clarendon Press, 1978), 14–16, 223, 244. Also see J. G. A. Pocock, *Barbarism and Religion*, vol. 2: *Narratives of Civil Government* (Cambridge: Cambridge University Press, 1999), 309–29; Christian Marouby, "Adam Smith and the Anthropology of the Enlightenment: The 'Ethnographic' Sources of Economic Progress," in *The Anthropology of the Enlightenment*, eds. Larry Wolff and Marco Cipolloni (Stanford: Stanford University Press, 2007), 85–102; Jennifer Pitts, *A Turn to Empire: The Rise of Imperial Liberalism in Britain and France* (Princeton: Princeton University Press, 2005), 25–58; Jerry Evensky, *Adam Smith's Moral Philosophy: A Historical and Contemporary Perspective on Markets, Law, Ethics, and Culture* (Cambridge: Cambridge University Press, 2005), 10–12, 16–19, 63–6, 115–16, 132–6, 215–16.

6 *SPPO*, 2: 29–31. For Steuart's uncommon stadial notions see Skinner, "Sir James Steuart: Author of a System," 22–5; and for this and other relevant topics, Andrew S. Skinner, "The Shaping of Political Economy in the Enlightenment," *Scottish Journal of Political Economy*, 37 (1990), 145–65, esp. 150–4, 159. For an interpretation which emphasizes Steuart's view of progress as pessimistic, see Anthony Brewer, "The Concept of Growth in Eighteenth-Century Economics," *History of Political Economy*, 27 (1995), 609–38, at 625–9.

7 *SPPO*, 2: 76–7 and passim.

8 For relevant remarks see, e.g., Donald Winch, *Riches and Poverty: An Intellectual History of Political Economy in Britain, 1750–1834* (Cambridge: Cambridge University Press, 1996), 86, 88; Murray Milgate and Shannon C. Stimson, *After Adam Smith: A Century of Transformations in Politics and Political Economy* (Princeton and Oxford: Princeton University Press, 2009), 39–42.

9 *SPPO*, 1: 240–3.

10 Ibid., 1: 395–8.

11 Ibid., 3: 336. See also 1: 59–60, 66, 69, 75, 80; and Jean-Jacques Gislain, "James Steuart: Economy and Population," in *The Economics of James Steuart*, ed. Ramón Tortajada (London and New York: Routledge, 1999), 169–85.

12 *SPPO*, 1: 71–2, 155–6.

13 Ibid., 1: 347–8.

14 Ibid., 1: 339–41.

15 Ibid., 1: 17–25 (quotation at 18), 150–1.

16 Ibid., 1: 34–5, 47–8, and see also 3: 288–90.

17 Ibid., 1: 82–95, 156–7.

18 Ibid., 1: 26–31, 151, 175–6.

19 Ibid., 1: 101–8, 129, 225, 284; 2: 41–2.

20 Ibid., 1: 291–5; 2: 64.

21 See T. C. Smout, "A New Look at the Scottish Improvers," *Scottish Historical Review*, 91 (2012), 125–49; and for a more general overview, Simon Schaffer, "The Earth's Fertility as a Social Fact in Early Modern Britain," in Teich, Porter, and Gustafsson, *Nature and Society in Historical Context*, 124–47.

22 *SPPO*, 1: 225–31, and see also the discussion of foreign trade at 267–9, and the remarks at 1: 101–8; 2: 66–7.

23 Ibid., 1: 114–16, 132.

24 For the specie-flow mechanism see, e.g., Samuel Hollander, *Classical Economics* (Oxford and New York: Basil Blackwell, 1987), 24, 282, 319; and for this and other aspects of his political economy, see also Hont, *Jealousy of Trade*, 267–96, 325–53; Robertson, *The Case for the Enlightenment*, 360–71; Hutchison, *Before Adam Smith*, 199–214; and Tatsuya Sakamoto, "Hume's Political Economy as a System of Manners," in Sakamoto and Tanaka, *The Rise of Political Economy in the Scottish Enlightenment*, 86–102.

25 See Brewer, "The Concept of Growth in Eighteenth-Century Economics"; and also Joel Mokyr, "The Intellectual Origins of Modern Economic Growth," *Journal of Economic History*, 65 (2005), 285–351.

26 See Silvia Sebastiani, *The Scottish Enlightenment: Race, Gender, and the Limits of Progress*, trans. Jeremy Carden (New York: Palgrave Macmillan, 2013), 23–43.
27 David Hume, "Of Commerce," in *Essays, Moral, Political, and Literary*, ed. Eugene F. Miller (Indianapolis: Liberty Classics, 1987), 253–67, at 266–7.
28 Ibid., 256.
29 David Hume, "Of the Populousness of Ancient Nations," in *Essays, Moral, Political, and Literary*, 377–464.
30 For Hume's views on population see Bonar, *Theories of Population*, 163–78.
31 Hume, "Of the Populousness of Ancient Nations," 448.
32 Ibid., 382, 403.
33 Ibid., 445–7.
34 Ibid., 448–52. For Buffon's views see Georges-Louis Leclerc, Comte de Buffon, "Septième et dernière Époque, lorsque la Puissance de l'Homme a secondé celle de la Nature," in *Histoire naturelle, générale et particulière*, Supplément, vol. 5 (Paris: Imprimerie Royale, 1778), 225–54; and also Glacken, *Traces on the Rhodian Shore*, 587–91, 663–81.
35 On Hume's and Wallace's longstanding friendship see Ernest C. Mossner, *The Forgotten Hume (Le Bon David)* (New York: Columbia University Press, 1943), 105–31. Also see Yasuo Amoh, "The Ancient-Modern Controversy in the Scottish Enlightenment," in Sakamoto and Tanaka, *The Rise of Political Economy in the Scottish Enlightenment*, 69–85. For general assessments of Wallace see Robert B. Luehrs, "Population and Utopia in the Thought of Robert Wallace," *Eighteenth-Century Studies*, 20 (1987), 313–35; Jonsson, *Enlightenment's Frontier*, 6–23; Yoshio Nagai, "Robert Wallace and the Irish and Scottish Enlightenment," in Sakamoto and Tanaka, *The Rise of Political Economy in the Scottish Enlightenment*, 55–68.
36 Robert Wallace, *A Dissertation on the Numbers of Mankind in Antient and Modern Times* (Edinburgh: G. Hamilton and J. Balfour, 1753; reprint London: Routledge/Thoemmes Press, and Tokyo: Kinokuniya, 1992), 12–13, 80–4.
37 Ibid., 15–20.
38 Ibid., 21–31, 97–104, 267–70, 302, 328–31.
39 Ibid., 21.
40 Ibid., 148–59.
41 See, e.g., John M. Hartwick, "Robert Wallace and Malthus and the Ratios," *History of Political Economy*, 20 (1988), 357–79. Also see the survey of this book in Caroline Robbins, *The Eighteenth-Century Commonwealthman: Studies in the Transmission, Development, and Circumstance of English Liberal Thought from the Restoration of Charles II Until the War with the Thirteen Colonies* (Indianapolis: Liberty Fund, 2004 [1959]), 197–2005.
42 Robert Wallace, *Various Prospects of Mankind, Nature, and Providence* (London: A. Millar, 1761), 3–10; and for more on nature as meant for human use see also 275, 279.
43 Ibid., 26.
44 Ibid., 27–8, 38–105.
45 Ibid., 109–25.
46 Ibid., 111–12n.
47 Ibid., 276–81, 289–90, 299, 359–60.
48 Ibid., 293–5, 297–8, 336.
49 On the friendly debate between Tucker and Hume see Bernard Semmel, "The Hume-Tucker Debate and Pitt's Trade Proposals," *Economic Journal*, 75 (1965), 759–70; idem, *The Rise of Free Trade Imperialism: Classical Political Economy, the Empire of Free Trade and Imperialism, 1750–1850* (Cambridge: Cambridge University Press, 1970), 14–24; and see also J. G. A. Pocock, "Josiah Tucker on Burke, Locke, and Price: A Study in the Varieties of Eighteenth-Century Conservatism," in *Virtue, Commerce, and History: Essays on Political Thought and History, Chiefly in the Eighteenth Century* (Cambridge: Cambridge University Press, 1985), 157–91; B. W. Young, "Christianity,

Commerce and the Cannon: Josiah Tucker and Richard Woodward on Political Economy," *History of European Ideas*, 22 (1996), 385–400; Hont, *Jealousy of Trade*, 70–1, 283–9, 294–6; Hutchison, *Before Adam Smith*, 209–10, 228–38; George Shelton, *Dean Tucker and Eighteenth-Century Economic and Political Thought* (London and Basingstoke: Macmillan, 1981), 51, 56, 59, 76–8, 93, 96.

50 Josiah Tucker, *An Essay on the Advantages and Disadvantages which Respectively Attend France and Great Britain, with Regard to Trade* (Glasgow: no printer, 1756), 40–1.

51 Ibid., 104–5.

52 See Alfred Owen Aldridge, "Franklin as Demographer," *Journal of Economic History*, 9 (1949), 25–44.

53 Benjamin Franklin, *The Autobiography and Other Writings on Politics, Economics, and Virtue*, ed. Alan Houston (Cambridge: Cambridge University Press, 2004), 144–58 (from "A Modest Enquiry into the Nature and Necessity of a Paper Currency").

54 Ibid., 307–12 (from "On a Proposed Act to Prevent Emigration").

55 Ibid., 215–21 (from "Observations Concerning the Increase of Mankind, Peopling of Countries, &c.").

Chapter 4: The Physiocrats and the bread riots

1 On Quesnay's medical thought and its influence on his economics see Paul P. Christensen, "Fire, Motion, and Productivity: The Proto-Energetics of Nature and Economy in François Quesnay," in *Natural Images in Economic Thought: "Markets Read in Tooth and Claw"*, ed. Philip Mirowski (Cambridge: Cambridge University Press, 1994), 249–88.

2 For the political aspect of Physiocracy see Liana Vardi, *The Physiocrats and the World of the Enlightenment* (Cambridge: Cambridge University Press, 2012).

3 For Smith's criticism of Physiocratic ideas, see Hont, *Jealousy of Trade*, 80–3, 354–88.

4 See Georges Weulersse, *Le mouvement physiocratique en France (de 1756 a 1770)*, 2 vols. (Paris: Félix Alcan, 1910), 1: 243–80; H. Spencer Banzhaf, "Productive Nature and the Net Product: Quesnay's Economies Animal and Political," *History of Political Economy*, 32 (2000), 517–51; and also Paul H. Johnstone, "The Rural Socrates," *Journal of the History of Ideas*, 5 (1944), 151–75.

5 See Weulersse, *Le mouvement physiocratique en France*, 2: 268–95; Stangeland, *Pre-Malthusian Doctrines of Population*, 254–65; Spengler, *French Predecessors of Malthus*, 170–211, esp. 187–9.

6 See Margaret Schabas, *The Natural Origins of Economics* (Chicago and London: University of Chicago Press, 2005), 45–50.

7 On Boisguilbert see Gilbert Faccarello, *The Foundations of* Laissez-faire*: The Economics of Pierre de Boisguilbert*, trans. Carolyn Shread (London and New York: Routledge, 1999); and Hutchison, *Before Adam Smith*, 107–15.

8 See Pierre Le Pesant, sieur de Boisguillebert (or Boisguilbert), "Le detail de la France," in *Économistes financiers du XVIIIe siècle*, ed. Eugène Daire (Geneva: Slatkine Reprints, 1971 [1851]), 163–247, at 163, 179–80, 218–20.

9 Pierre Le Pesant, sieur de Boisguillebert (or Boisguilbert), "Traité de la nature, culture, commerce et intérêt des grains," in Daire, *Économistes financiers du XVIIIe siècle*, 323–71, at 325–33. For Boisguilbert's discussions of the grain trade see also Faccarello, *The Foundations of* Laissez-faire, 75–7, 97–8, 122–30, 138–40.

10 Boisguilbert, "Traité de la nature, culture, commerce et intérêt des grains," 339–42, 345–6, 353–6, 367.

11 Ibid., 352, 356–8. Also see Boisguilbert, "Le detail de la France," 195–6.

12 See Faccarello, *The Foundations of* Laissez-faire, 138–40.

13 Boisguilbert, "Traité de la nature, culture, commerce et intérêt des grains," 350–1, 370.

14 Ibid., 363–4, 366. According to Gilbert Faccarello, for Boisguilbert nature and Providence in the economic realm meant competition. See Faccarello, *The Foundations of* Laissez-faire, 99–100. It should be remembered, however, that the equation of nature with God, and not necessarily in the Spinozistic pantheistic version which was obviously far from Boisguilbert's outlook, was common in the early modern era. It was often part of a traditional theistic cosmology.

15 On this work and Mirabeau in general see Vardi, *Physiocrats and the World of the Enlightenment*, 117–22 and passim; Blum, *Strength in Numbers*, 43–4, 48–9; Spengler, *French Predecessors of Malthus*, 128–36.

16 Victor de Riqueti, Marquis de Mirabeau, *L'ami des hommes, ou Traité de la population*, 2 vols. (Avignon, 1756–1760; reprint Aalen: Scientia Verlag, 1970), 1: Part 1: 11–24; Part 3: 171–3.

17 Ibid., 1: Part 1: 24–34, also 68–85; Part 3: 173, 177–9.

18 See Vardi, *Physiocrats and the World of the Enlightenment*, 113–14; and also Spengler, *French Predecessors of Malthus*, 190–2.

19 See his essay "Natural Right" in Ronald L. Meek, *The Economics of Physiocracy: Essays and Translations* (Cambridge, MA: Harvard University Press, 1963), 43–56.

20 See the extract from "Rural Philosophy" in ibid., 60–4; and see also the passage from "Miscellaneous Extracts" at 65–6. A republican strain had been evident in Mirabeau's pre-Physiocratic views. See Michael Kwass, "Consumption and the World of Ideas: Consumer Revolution and the Moral Economy of the Marquis de Mirabeau," *Eighteenth-Century Studies*, 37 (2004), 187–213.

21 See Meek, *Economics of Physiocracy*, 203–30 (from Quesnay's "Dialogue on the Work of Artisans").

22 Ibid., 259–60 and passim (from "General Maxims for the Economic Government of an Agricultural Kingdom").

23 Ibid., 257.

24 Ibid., 84 (from Quesnay's *Encyclopédie* article "Corn").

25 Ibid., 81–2.

26 See Richard H. Grove, *Green Imperialism: Colonial Expansion, Tropical Island Edens and the Origins of Environmentalism, 1600–1860* (Cambridge: Cambridge University Press, 1995), 222–37 and passim.

27 Ibid., 6, 9–11, 168–9, 189–94, 200–5, 221–2, 262, 334–42, 477–8.

28 See ibid., 168–263and passim. For Poivre's adventurous life and career see Lewis A. Maverick, "Pierre Poivre: Eighteenth Century Explorer of Southeast Asia," *Pacific Historical Review*, 10 (1941), 165–77. Also see P. M. Harman, *The Culture of Nature in Britain 1680–1860* (New Haven and London: Yale University Press, 2009), 64–8.

29 Pierre Poivre, *Travels of a Philosopher: Or, Observations on the Manners and Arts of Various Nations in Africa and Asia*, trans. anon. (Dublin: P. and W. Wilson et al., 1770), 1–5.

30 Ibid., 121–2.

31 See Virgile Pinot, "Les physiocrates et la Chine au XVIIIe siècle," *Revue d'histoire modern et contemporaine*, 8 (1906/1907), 200–14.

32 Poivre, *Travels of a Philosopher*, 151–5, 181.

33 Ibid., 150.

34 Ibid., 137–73. And see also 174–83 for a positive comparison of China with all other regions of the world, including Europe.

35 On Turgot's ministry as Controller-General see Steven L. Kaplan, *Bread, Politics and Political Economy in the Reign of Louis XV*, 2 vols. (The Hague: Martinus Nijhoff, 1976), 2: 405–6, 611–13, 660–76.

36 For Turgot's Physiocratic ideas, but also his disagreements with them, see Jessica Riskin, "The 'Spirit of System' and the Fortunes of Physiocracy," *History of Political Economy*, 35, Supplement (2003), 42–73; and Schabas, *Natural Origins of Economics*, 52–4.

37 See Peter Groenewegen, "Turgot's Place in the History of Economic Thought: A Bicentenary Estimate," *History of Political Economy*, 15 (1983), 585–616; Brewer, "The Concept of Growth in Eighteenth-Century Economics," 629–31; Hutchison, *Before Adam Smith*, 308–21. On the topic of population Turgot was more in line with mainstream Physiocracy. See Spengler, *French Predecessors of Malthus*, 282–90.
38 See *Turgot on Progress, Sociology and Economics*, ed. and trans. Ronald L. Meek (Cambridge: Cambridge University Press, 1973), 5–10, 20.
39 Ibid., 41, 56 (from the important essay "A Philosophical Review of the Successive Advances of the Human Mind," in ibid., 41–59).
40 Ibid., 88–90 (from "On Universal History," in ibid., 61–118).
41 Ibid., 42–4, and also 64–9. And see also 80–3, for the advantages of early hunting and shepherding societies on the one hand, and republics on the other, as pertains to the status of women and the relative lack of despotism.
42 Ibid., 147–8, 151, 180–1 (from "Reflections on the Formation and the Distribution of Wealth," in ibid., 119–82).
43 Ibid., 124–8, and also 153, 176–7 on the capitalists.
44 Ibid., 119–23 (quotation at 123).
45 Ibid., 56–7.
46 Ibid., 93.
47 Ibid., 43, 69–71, 123–4.
48 On the Physiocrats, their debates with their critics, and their political involvement and influence during the ancien régime, see Kaplan, *Bread, Politics and Political Economy*, 1: 113–17, 146–52; 2: 472–81, 590–613. On the eighteenth-century grain trade debate in general see also Hont, *Jealousy of Trade*, 88–99, and 403–19 (the latter pages authored by Hont jointly with Michael Ignatieff).
49 Antoine-Nicolas de Condorcet, *The Life of M. Turgot*, trans. anon. (London: J. Johnson, 1787), 39–42, 61–7, 69–73, 299–301, and passim. At 325–7, Condorcet even outlined an early version of the principle of comparative advantage.
50 Ibid., 132–4, 212–17, 230–1, 302–3, 357, 398–409.
51 Ibid., 166–9.
52 Ibid., 134–6. See also Baker, *Condorcet*, 67–9.
53 Condorcet, *Life of M. Turgot*, 315, 360–6 (quotation at 362).
54 See Antoine-Nicolas de Condorcet, *Sketch for a Historical Picture of the Progress of the Human Mind*, trans. June Barraclough (London: Weidenfeld and Nicolson, 1955).
55 For a discussion of these points see Emma Rothschild, *Economic Sentiments: Adam Smith, Condorcet, and the Enlightenment* (Cambridge, MA, and London: Harvard University Press, 2001), 157–217.
56 Antoine-Nicolas de Condorcet, "Réflexions sur le commerce des blés (1776)," in *Oeuvres de Condorcet*, eds. A. Condorcet O'Connor and M. F. Arago (Paris: Firmin Didot Frères, 1847–1849), 11: 99–252, at 118–19, 136.
57 Ibid., 154.
58 Ibid., 132–4.
59 Ibid., 145, 157–61, 170.
60 Ibid., 217, and also 222. Translations are mine unless otherwise noted.
61 For Condorcet's consistent interest in this topic see Rothschild, *Economic Sentiments*, 172–3.
62 See for example Pierre Claude Reynard, "Public Order and Privilege: Eighteenth-Century French Roots of Environmental Regulation," *Technology and Culture*, 43 (2002), 1–28.
63 Condorcet, "Réflexions sur le commerce des blés (1776)," 165.
64 Condorcet, *Life of M. Turgot*, 232–5 (quotation at 233).
65 See Spengler, *French Predecessors of Malthus*, 323–33.
66 See Robert D. Harris, *Necker: Reform Statesman of the Ancien Régime* (Berkeley: University of California Press, 1979), 53–67; Gilbert Faccarello, "'Nil Repente!': Galiani and Necker on Economic Reforms," *European Journal of the History of Economic Thought*, 1 (1994), 519–50; Kaplan, *Bread, Politics and Political Economy*, 258–9, 403.

67 Jacques Necker, *Sur la législation et le commerce des grains* (Paris: Pissot, 1776), 35–6.
68 Ibid., 36–41.
69 Ibid., 42–4.
70 Ibid., 194–9.
71 Ibid., 44–7.
72 Jacques Necker, *A Treatise on the Administration of the Finances of France*, trans. Thomas Mortimer, 3 vols. (London: Logographic Press, 1785). See 3: 231–5, for a short summary of Necker's position regarding the regulation of commerce in grain.
73 Ibid., 3: 96–9.
74 Ibid., 3: 102.
75 Ibid., 3: 117–19.
76 Ibid., 1: 212–13. But see 3: 104, where Necker mentions that these improvements in communications also advanced the consumption of luxuries, some at least of which were detrimental to the state.
77 Ibid., 3: 236–40.
78 See the discussions in Franco Venturi, *Italy and the Enlightenment: Studies in a Cosmopolitan Century*, trans. Susan Corsi, ed. Stuart Woolf (London: Longman, 1972), 180–97; Kaplan, *Bread, Politics and Political Economy*, 1: 257–8, 266–7, 2: 591–611; Robertson, *The Case for the Enlightenment*, 347–50; Hutchison, *Before Adam Smith*, 255–70, 293–4; Maifreda, *From* Oikonomia *to Political Economy*, 237–41; and Faccarello, "'Nil Repente!': Galiani and Necker on Economic Reforms."
79 Ferdinand Galiani, *Dialogues sur le commerce des blés* ([Paris]: Fayard, 1984), 25–47.
80 Ibid., 142–3.
81 Ibid., 49–67.
82 Ibid., 70.
83 Ibid., 110–16.
84 Ibid., 132: "Toute terre inculte est une tache à l'administration, elle en doit rougir."
85 Ibid., 133: "Il faut porter une attention particuliere à cet objet et en rechercher les causes. Si c'est un défaut de population, il faudra y fonder une colonie; si l'air y est mal sain, il en faudra faire écouler les eaux; si le sol est mauvais, il faut chercher quelques plantes ou quelques arbres qu'on puisse y cultiver et ensuite les y faire planter."
86 Ibid., 137–9 (quotation at 139): "Alors l'art du gouvernement aura fait son chef-d'œuvre, car le chef-d'œuvre de l'art est de forcer la Nature et de l'obliger à un miracle tel que celui d'avoir sur un sol limité plus d'hommes que ses forces et ses moyens n'en sauraient nourrir."
87 Ibid., 230–8.
88 Ibid., 260–8.
89 Ibid., 192–5.
90 Ibid., 196–201.
91 Ibid., 188–90.
92 Ibid., 209–11 (quotation at 210): "Nous sommes trop petits; le temps, l'espace, le mouvement devant elle ne sont rien; mais nous ne pouvons pas attendre. Ne faisons donc point alliance avec la nature, elle serait trop disproportionnée. Notre métier ici bas est de la combattre. Regardez au tour de vous. Voyez les champs cultivés, les plantes étrangeres introduites dans nos climats, les vaisseaux, les voitures, les animaux apprivoisés, les maisons, les rues, les ports, les digues, les chaussées. Voilà les retranchemens dans lesquels nous combattons; tous les agrémens de la vie et presque notre existence même est le prix de la victoire. Avec notre petit art et l'esprit que Dieu nous a donné, nous livrons bataille à la nature et nous parvenons souvent à la vaincre et à la maitriser en employant ses forces contre elle. Combat singulier et qui par là rend l'homme l'image de son créateur." See also Hutchison, *Before Adam Smith*, 267.

Chapter 5: From Adam Smith to classical political economy

1 See Cesare Beccaria, *A Discourse on Public Economy and Commerce*, trans. anon. (n.p., 1769; reprint New York: Burt Franklin, 1970), 20–4. On Beccaria see Venturi, *Italy and the Enlightenment*, 154–64; and also Hutchison, *Before Adam Smith*, 298–302; and Luigino Bruni and Pier Luigi Porta, "*Economia civile* and *pubblica felicità* in the Italian Enlightenment," *History of Political Economy*, 35, Supplement (2003), 361–85, at 372–3.

2 For Verri's influential work as a political economist see Pier Luigi Porta and Roberto Scazzieri, "Pietro Verri's Political Economy: Commercial Society, Civil Society, and the Science of the Legislator," *History of Political Economy*, 34 (2002), 83–110; Venturi, *Italy and the Enlightenment*, 165–79; Bruni and Porta, "*Economia civile* and *pubblica felicità* in the Italian Enlightenment," 364–71; Hutchison, *Before Adam Smith*, 302–6.

3 Pietro Verri, *Reflections on Political Economy*, trans. Barbara McGilvray and Peter D. Groenewegen, ed. Peter D. Groenewegen (Fairfield, NJ: Augustus M. Kelley, 1993), 112.

4 Ibid., 5–6.

5 Ibid., 12–13, 21, 42, 67–71, 112.

6 Ibid., 76–7.

7 Ibid., 77–9.

8 Schumpeter, *History of Economic Analysis*, 181–94.

9 The number of studies emphasizing this viewpoint has been steadily growing in recent years. For a few (and only selective) examples see Rothschild, *Economic Sentiments*; Winch, *Riches and Poverty* (also emphasizing other figures in addition to Smith in this respect, particularly Malthus); Evensky, *Adam Smith's Moral Philosophy* (emphasizes both the moral and the historiographical components of Smith's thought); Charles L. Griswold, Jr., *Adam Smith and the Virtues of Enlightenment* (Cambridge: Cambridge University Press, 1999); James R. Otteson, *Adam Smith's Marketplace of Life* (Cambridge: Cambridge University Press, 2002); Jack Russell Weinstein, *Adam Smith's Pluralism: Rationality, Education, and the Moral Sentiments* (New Haven and London: Yale University Press, 2013).

10 *WN*, 1: 10.

11 Ibid., 2: 689–708.

12 Ibid., 2: 694–5.

13 Ibid., 2: 708–23.

14 On the stadial development of proprietary notions in Smith see the remarks in Evensky, *Adam Smith's Moral Philosophy*, 63–6.

15 For Smith on population see, e.g., Winch, *Riches and Poverty*, 80–9, 233–6. On Smith's recognition of the limit to progress see Evensky, *Adam Smith's Moral Philosophy*, 308–12. For the claim that Smith already recognized a "Malthusian" over-populated limit to progress, see Robert L. Heilbroner, "The Paradox of Progress: Decline and Decay in *The Wealth of Nations*," *Journal of the History of Ideas*, 34 (1973), 243–62.

16 See Pocock, *Virtue, Commerce, and History*, 103–23; and also Heilbroner, "The Paradox of Progress."

17 On Smith and agriculture see, e.g., D. P. O'Brien, *The Classical Economists Revisited* (Princeton and Oxford: Princeton University Press, 2004), 249–53; Evensky, *Adam Smith's Moral Philosophy*, 132–4, 179–80; Winch, *Riches and Poverty*, 83–5; Schabas, *Natural Origins of Economics*, 93–5; Hont, *Jealousy of Trade*, 307–10. For Smith's economic discussions of agriculture in general, see Samuel Hollander, *The Economics of Adam Smith* (London: Heinemann Educational Books, 1973), 95–9, 208–41, 285–93 and passim.

18 *WN*, 1: 164–7, 205–7, 234, 237, 240; 2: 577, 652–3.

19 See John Millar, *The Origin of the Distinction of Ranks and other Writings*, in William C. Lehmann, *John Millar of Glasgow 1735–1801* (Cambridge: Cambridge

University Press, 1960; reprinted New York: Arno Press, 1979), 326–7. For Millar's political-economic ideas see Hont, *Jealousy of Trade*, 311–15.

20 *WN*, 1: 251, 256–9.
21 Ibid., 1: 178–83.
22 Ibid., 1: 87–91.
23 Ibid., 1: 99. On Smith's stationary state see, e.g., Milgate and Stimson, *After Adam Smith*, 191–3; O'Brien, *The Classical Economists Revisited*, 253.
24 *WN*, 1: 111–13.
25 Ibid., 1: 91.
26 Ibid., 1: 109.
27 Ibid., 2: 560–1, 556–8.
28 Ibid., 2: 564–7.
29 Ibid., 2: 634.
30 Ibid., 1: 221–2.
31 Ibid., 2: 568.
32 Ibid., 2: 571–3.
33 Ibid., 2: 577–80, 583–90.
34 Ibid., 2: 581–2.
35 Ibid., 2: 611, 636, 639.
36 Ibid., 1: 87–8.
37 Ibid., 1: 96–9, 162.
38 Ibid., 1: 463.
39 Ibid., 1: 495.
40 Ibid., 1: 176–7, 223.
41 On their differing approaches see Stefan Collini, Donald Winch, and John Burrow, *That Noble Science of Politics: A Study in Nineteenth-Century Intellectual History* (Cambridge: Cambridge University Press, 1983), 63–89; Sergio Cremaschi and Marcelo Dascal, "Malthus and Ricardo: Two Styles for Economic Theory," *Science in Context*, 11 (1998), 229–54; Winch, *Riches and Poverty*, 349–88. On Ricardo as an empiricist see Timothy Davis, *Ricardo's Macroeconomics: Money, Trade Cycles, and Growth* (Cambridge: Cambridge University Press, 2005), 214–16. On Ricardo's basic tenets and influence, although presented as less original than is sometimes claimed, see O'Brien, *The Classical Economists Revisited*, 44–52.
42 *RPPE*, 5.
43 Ibid., 22–5. On hunting and fishing in the same context see also 26–30. Ricardo's discussion of animals centered solely on their role as economic products, with no mention whatsoever of modern ecological concerns or the suffering involved in hunting.
44 Ibid., 96–8.
45 Ibid., 99–100.
46 Ibid., 100–9.
47 See Milgate and Stimson, *After Adam Smith*, 160–85; and William Dixon, "Ricardo: Economic Thought and Social Order," *Journal of the History of Economic Thought*, 30 (2008), 235–53.
48 See Schabas, *Natural Origins of Economics*, 102–5, 113–20; and also the overview in Hollander, *Classical Economics*, 97–100.
49 *RPPE*, 126. See also Stanley Moore, "Ricardo and the State of Nature," *Scottish Journal of Political Economy*, 13 (1966), 317–31.
50 *RPPE*, 265. For Ricardo's guarded optimism and views on progress see also ibid., 265–72, 393–4.
51 On these various points see Milgate and Stimson, *After Adam Smith*, 195–9; Boianovsky, "Humboldt and the Economists on Natural Resources," 72–7; E. Kula, *History of Environmental Economic Thought* (London and New York: Routledge, 1998), 36–40.

52 *RPPE*, 270–1. And see also 386–97, for more on the importance of not avoiding improvements in machinery despite their temporary disadvantage in reducing the need for labor, and lowering prices. Any attempt to avoid such improvements would tend to lead to the exportation of capital and would ultimately increase unemployment.
53 See on this point Patricia James, *Population Malthus: His Life and Times* (London: Routledge & Kegan Paul, 1979), 274–85.
54 See, e.g., David Wells, "Resurrecting the Dismal Parson: Malthus, Ecology, and Political Thought," *Political Studies*, 30 (1982), 1–15. For a more critical assessment see Christian Becker, Malte Faber, Kirsten Hertel, and Reiner Manstetten, "Malthus vs. Wordsworth: Perspectives on Humankind, Nature and Economy. A Contribution to the History and the Foundations of Ecological Economics," *Ecological Economics*, 53 (2005), 299–310. Also see Glacken, *Traces on the Rhodian Shore*, 637–54.
55 On Malthus and modern Malthusian doctrines see Kula, *History of Environmental Economic Thought*, 22–35.
56 See E. A. Wrigley, "The Limits to Growth: Malthus and the Classical Economists," *Population and Development Review*, 14, Supplement (1988), 30–48.
57 See Robert M. Young, *Darwin's Metaphor: Nature's Place in Victorian Culture* (Cambridge: Cambridge University Press, 1985), 23–55, 187–9. On Smith's limited influence on Malthus see Milgate and Stimson, *After Adam Smith*, 121–38.
58 See Jonsson, *Enlightenment's Frontier*, 167–261. Jonsson claims that the concept, though not the actual modern term, of carrying capacity, was already emerging at this time.
59 According to Schumpeter, Malthus's population theory, and apprehension of overpopulation, was not only to a large extent unoriginal, but also erroneous, devoid of significant empirical foundation, and irrelevant to economic analysis. See Schumpeter, *History of Economic Analysis*, 250–8, 578–84.
60 For an important appreciative discussion of Malthus see Winch, *Riches and Poverty*, 221–405.
61 *EPP*, 1: 9–15.
62 On positive checks and the inability of human beings to control natural disasters, see, e.g., Jonsson, *Enlightenment's Frontier*, 139–40, 193–5.
63 *EPP*, 1: 23, 147; 2: 87, 296–7, 303–4 and passim.
64 On the significance of Malthus's religiosity, and on Christian political economy in general, see A. M. C. Waterman, *Revolution, Economics and Religion: Christian Political Economy, 1798–1833* (Cambridge: Cambridge University Press, 1991); and on the points mentioned here ibid., esp. 101–12, 130; and also J. M. Pullen, "Malthus' Theological Ideas and Their Influence on His Principal of Population," *History of Political Economy*, 13 (1981), 39–54.
65 *EPP*, 2: 205–6.
66 T. R. Malthus, *Principles of Political Economy, Variorum Edition*, ed. John Pullen, 2 vols. (Cambridge: Cambridge University Press, 1989), 1: 347–51.
67 See, e.g., ibid., 1: 353–4, 360–6, and also the editorial comments at 2: 433.
68 On Malthus's disagreement with Say's Law see, e.g., Semmel, *The Rise of Free Trade Imperialism*, 48–75.
69 Jean-Baptiste Say, *Letters to Mr. Malthus, On Several Subjects of Political Economy, and on the Cause of the Stagnation of Commerce. To Which is Added a Catechism of Political Economy, or Familiar Conversations on the Manner in which Wealth is Produced, Distributed, and Consumed in Society*, trans. John Richter (London: Sherwood, Neely, and Jones, 1821), 5.
70 *EPP*, 1: 304–5.
71 Ibid., 1: 438–9.
72 Malthus, *Principles of Political Economy*, 1: 314–15.
73 On this aspect of liberal thought see Pitts, *A Turn to Empire*.
74 Malthus, *Principles of Political Economy*, 1: 503.
75 Ibid., 1: 376–81, 472–3.

76 Ibid., 1: 382–93.
77 Ibid., 1: 393–401; 2: 260.
78 *EPP*, 1: 44, and see also 40.
79 Ibid., 1: 45.
80 Ibid., 1:46.
81 Ibid., 1: 60–1.
82 Ibid., 1: 62–73 (quotation at 66).
83 Ibid., 1: 72.
84 Ibid., 1: 74–86 (quotations at 74–5, 79).
85 Ibid., 1: 87–98.
86 Ibid., 1: 147.
87 Ibid., 1: 99–107 (quotation at 102).
88 Ibid., 1: 108–12.
89 Ibid., 1: 113–20.
90 Ibid., 1: 121–33 (quotation at 126).
91 Malthus noted that encouragement of marriage to promote a growing population (rather than from religious reasons), usually evinced ignorance on the part of governments, and in most cases, such as China, did not achieve its objective. It usually also indicated a moral and political depravity in the state, vicious manners and political institutions unfavorable to enhancing population. See ibid., 1: 142–3.
92 Ibid., 1: 135–9.
93 Ibid., 1: 140–7.
94 Ibid., 1: 155–6.
95 Ibid., 1: 159.
96 T. R. Malthus, *The Travel Diaries of Thomas Robert Malthus*, ed. Patricia James (Cambridge: Cambridge University Press, 1966), 45, 65, 68, 70–1, 77, 88, 93, 96, 109–10, 124–8, 133–4, 138, 263–4. On Malthus's early tour of Scandinavia and his delight in landscape see James, *Population Malthus*, 69–76.
97 *EPP*, 1: 163–4.
98 Ibid., 1: 225.
99 Ibid., 1: 233.
100 Ibid., 1: 276.
101 Ibid., 2: 44–5. On the combination of agriculture and commerce, see also 2: 40–8, 62–3.
102 Ibid., 1: 385–6.
103 Ibid., 1: 388–9.
104 See ibid., 1: 380–431.
105 Ibid.
106 For Malthus's view of the Physiocrats see Semmel, *The Rise of Free Trade Imperialism*, 48–75; Schabas, *Natural Origins of Economics*, 105–13; Winch, *Riches and Poverty*, 266–7, 272.
107 *EPP*, 1: 393.
108 Malthus, *Principles of Political Economy*, 1: 289–91, 305–6. And see also 2: 247–50, for a general discussion on how to assess and compare the wealth of various nations.
109 On Malthus's stationary state see Waterman, *Revolution, Economics and Religion*, 51–7; Hollander, *Classical Economics*, 202–5; Milgate and Stimson, *After Adam Smith*, 193–5.
110 See *EPP*, 2: 202–3, and regarding Malthus's optimism also 2: 205, 229–30.
111 See Evelyn Forget, "J.-B. Say and Adam Smith: An Essay in the Transmission of Ideas," *Canadian Journal of Economics*, 26 (1993), 121–33.
112 See Richard Whatmore, *Republicanism and the French Revolution: An Intellectual History of Jean-Baptiste Say's Political Economy* (Oxford: Oxford University Press, 2000), 123–5, 148–53, 183. For more on his criticism of British society see 157, 170, 194–6, 217. For more on his criticism of luxury see 165–7.

113 Ibid., 153.
114 *STPE*, 112.
115 Say, *Letters to Mr. Malthus*, 50, 64.
116 Ibid., 69–70.
117 *STPE*, 429n.
118 Ibid., 429–32.
119 See Anna Plassart, "'Un Impérialiste Libéral'? Jean-Baptiste Say on Colonies and the Extra-European World," *French Historical Studies*, 32 (2009), 223–50.
120 *STPE*, 305.
121 Ibid., 376–81.
122 Ibid., xli, note.
123 Ibid., 189–98, and also 246, 322.
124 Ibid., 300n.
125 Ibid., 467–8n.
126 Ibid., 339. For further criticism of Sismondi, see Say, *Letters to Mr. Malthus*, 5–8, 18, 48, 67–8, 71–4. For Sismondi see the Epilogue below.
127 Ibid., 371–81.
128 John Ramsay McCulloch, *The Principles of Political Economy, With Some Inquiries Respecting Their Application* (Edinburgh: Adam and Charles Black, 1864), 7–8, 118.
129 Ibid., 165–86. On McCulloch see Schabas, *Natural Origins of Economics*, 120–3; O'Brien, *The Classical Economists Revisited*, 260–3.
130 See the different views in John Aldrich, "The Discovery of Comparative Advantage," *Journal of the History of Economic Thought*, 26 (2004), 379–99; Roy J. Ruffin, "Debunking a Myth: Torrens on Comparative Advantage," *History of Political Economy*, 37 (2005), 711–22; Douglas A. Irwin, *Against the Tide: An Intellectual History of Free Trade* (Princeton: Princeton University Press, 1996), 89–90, 101. For an overview of Torrens's career see S. A. Meenai, "Robert Torrens–1780–1864," *Economica*, New Series 23 (1956), 49–61.
131 Robert Torrens, *An Essay on the Production of Wealth*, Introduction by Joseph Dorfman (London: Longman, Hurst, Rees, Orme and Brown, 1821; reprint New York: Augustus M. Kelley, 1965), 72–3, and also 164–5, 186–7.
132 Ibid., 75–9.
133 Ibid., 83–7.
134 Ibid., 90–1.
135 Ibid., 103–5.
136 Ibid., 108–10.
137 Ibid., 186–7.
138 Ibid., 192, 206–7.
139 Ibid., 147–9, 154–5.
140 Ibid., 79–81.
141 Ibid., 230.
142 See Semmel, *The Rise of Free Trade Imperialism*, 60–4, 78–9, 188, 192–8; Milgate and Stimson, *After Adam Smith*, 201–4.
143 Torrens, *An Essay on the Production of Wealth*, 246–8, 282–8.
144 See Collini, Winch, and Burrow, *That Noble Science of Politics*, 23–61; Milgate and Stimson, *After Adam Smith*, 97–120; Jane Rendall, "Adaptations: History, Gender, and Political Economy in the Work of Dugald Stewart," *History of European Ideas*, 38 (2012), 143–61; Knud Haakonssen, "From Moral Philosophy to Political Economy: The Contribution of Dugald Stewart," in *Philosophers of the Scottish Enlightenment*, ed. V. Hope (Edinburgh: Edinburgh University Press, 1984), 211–32; Hisashi Shinohara, "Dugald Stewart at the Final Stage of the Scottish Enlightenment: Natural Jurisprudence, Political Economy and the Science of Politics," in Sakamoto and Tanaka, *The Rise of Political Economy in the Scottish Enlightenment*, 179–93.

145 See Pietro Corsi, "The Heritage of Dugald Stewart: Oxford Philosophy and the Method of Political Economy," *Nuncius*, 2 (1987), 89–144. Also see Harro Maas, "'A Hard Battle to Fight': Natural Theology and the Dismal Science, 1820–50," *History of Political Economy*, 40 (annual supplement) (2008), 143–67.

146 *LPE*, 1: 64–5; and also 1: 31–3 on population in general. See also Rendall, "Adaptations: History, Gender, and Political Economy in the Work of Dugald Stewart."

147 *LPE*, 2: 255, 275–82, 458–9. On improvement of the condition of the poor see 2: 282–349.

148 Ibid., 2: 323.

149 On Stewart's belief in the progress of humanity, see Rendall, "Adaptations: History, Gender, and Political Economy in the Work of Dugald Stewart."

150 *LPE*, 1: 62–3.

151 Ibid., 1: 104.

152 Ibid., 1: 72–3.

153 Ibid., 1: 309–10.

154 Ibid., 1: 112.

155 Ibid., 1: 202–3.

156 Ibid., 2: 421.

157 Ibid., 1: 198–211. For Stewart's belief in Providence and criticism of atheists, see for example 2: 460–1.

158 On the methodological debate between the Oxford and Cambridge groups see Maas, "'A Hard Battle to Fight'."

159 See Salim Rashid, "Richard Whately and Christian Political Economy at Oxford and Dublin," *Journal of the History of Ideas*, 38 (1977), 147–55; and Waterman, *Revolution, Economics and Religion*, 204–16, who comments on Whately's desire for reconciling political economy and theology, but also notes that he was the least Malthusian of all those who contributed to Christian political economy. Also see Winch, *Riches and Poverty*, 359.

160 See Rashid, "Richard Whately and Christian Political Economy at Oxford and Dublin," 152.

161 Richard Whately, *Introductory Lectures on Political Economy* (London: B. Fellowes, 1832), 108–24.

162 Ibid., 124–7.

163 Ibid., 127–8.

164 Ibid., 130–1.

165 Ibid., 132–3.

166 Ibid., 153–4.

167 On Senior's methodology see Christophe Depoortère, "William Nassau Senior and David Ricardo on the Method of Political Economy," *Journal of the History of Economic Thought*, 35 (2013), 19–42; Maas, "'A Hard Battle to Fight'"; Corsi, "The Heritage of Dugald Stewart," 110–13.

168 *OSPE*, 69.

169 Ibid., 72.

170 On Senior's use of the term "natural agents" see Schabas, *Natural Origins of Economics*, 123–4.

171 *OSPE*, 76. On Torrens's concept of division of labor see Torrens, *Essay on the Production of Wealth*, 154–8, and the discussion in chapter 9 below.

172 *OSPE*, 175–6, and also 224.

173 See Winch, *Riches and Poverty*, 373–7, 385–6.

174 *OSPE*, 30–50.

175 Ibid., 40–1.

176 Ibid., 42–3.

177 See Marian Bowley, *Nassau Senior and Classical Economics* (London: George Allen and Unwin, 1937), 117–26, 173–7, 311–15.

178 *OSPE*, 48–9.
179 Ibid., 124–5.
180 For Jones and his methodology see Salim Rashid, "Richard Jones and Baconian Historicism at Cambridge," *Journal of Economic Issues*, 13 (1979), 159–73; Maas, "'A Hard Battle to Fight'"; Winch, *Riches and Poverty*, 376–81; Corsi, "The Heritage of Dugald Stewart," 114–21; Hollander, *Classical Economics*, 326, 334–6, 409–14, 420–2. On the mutual appreciation of Malthus and Jones, see James, *Population Malthus*, 439–43.
181 Richard Jones, *An Essay on the Distribution of Wealth, and on the Sources of Taxation* (London: John Murray, 1831; reprint New York: Augustus M. Kelley, 1964), vii, xix–xxiv, xxviii.
182 Ibid., viii–xiv.
183 Ibid., xvi–xviii.
184 Ibid., xxxiii–xxxviii.
185 Ibid., 234.
186 Ibid., 221.
187 For an appreciative survey see Paul A. Samuelson, "Thünen at Two Hundred," *Journal of Economic Literature*, 21 (1983), 1468–88.
188 Johann Heinrich von Thünen, *Von Thünen's Isolated State: An English Edition of Der Isolierte Staat*, trans. Carla M. Wartenberg, ed. Peter Hall (Oxford: Pergamon Press, 1966), 158.
189 Ibid., 280–1.
190 Ibid., 186.
191 Ibid., 211–14. For more on land rent see also 261, 265–72.
192 Ibid., 246–7.

Chapter 6: John Stuart Mill and the idea of progress

1 On the significance of this work see N. B. de Marchi, "The Success of Mill's *Principles*," *History of Political Economy*, 6 (1974), 119–57.
2 See John M. Robson, *The Improvement of Mankind: The Social and Political Thought of John Stuart Mill* (Toronto and London: University of Toronto Press and Routledge & Kegan Paul, 1968), 21–49.
3 John Stuart Mill, "Civilization," in *Essays on Politics and Society*, ed. J. M. Robson, Introduction by Alexander Brady [Vol. XVIII of *The Collected Works of John Stuart Mill*] (Toronto: University of Toronto Press; and London: Routledge & Kegan Paul, 1977), 119–47.
4 Ibid., 120.
5 *MPPE*, 1: 10–12.
6 Ibid., 1: 12–17.
7 Ibid., 2: 707–8.
8 Ibid., 2: 760–1.
9 Ibid., 2: 921.
10 Ibid., 1: 17–20.
11 See ibid., 20–1. Also see Schabas, *Natural Origins of Economics*, 125–33; Boianovsky, "Humboldt and the Economists on Natural Resources," 79–82. On the political implications of Mill's concepts of nature, see Gal Gerson, "From the State of Nature to Evolution in John Stuart Mill," *Australian Journal of Politics and History*, 48 (2002), 305–21.
12 *MPPE*, 2: 594, and see also 2: 686, 711.
13 Ibid., 2: 714–15.
14 Ibid., 1: 100–2. On the importance of maritime transportation see also 1: 130.
15 Ibid., 1: 102–3.

16 Ibid., 1: 106–7.
17 Ibid., 2: 710–11.
18 Scholars have been divided in their assessment of Mill's views on cultural progress, and specifically on his colonialism. See Inder S. Marwah, "Complicating Barbarism and Civilization: Mill's Complex Sociology of Human Development," *History of Political Thought*, 32 (2011), 345–66; John Robson, "Civilization and Culture as Moral Concepts," in *The Cambridge Companion to Mill*, ed. John Skorupski (Cambridge, 1998), 338–71; and for more critical interpretations see Pitts, *Turn to Empire*, 133–62; Uday Singh Mehta, *Liberalism and Empire: A Study in Nineteenth-Century British Liberal Thought* (Chicago and London: University of Chicago Press, 1999), 77–114; Don Habibi, "The Moral Dimensions of J. S. Mill's Colonialism," *Journal of Social Philosophy*, 30 (1999), 125–46; Beate Jahn, "Barbarian Thoughts: Imperialism in the Philosophy of John Stuart Mill," *Review of International Studies*, 31 (2005), 599–618; Duncan Bell, "John Stuart Mill on Colonies," *Political Theory*, 38 (2010), 34–64.
19 *MPPE*, 1: 112–15. And see also 1: 403, for more on the need for security, which influenced the tendency to invest capital rather than to consume it, as this occurred in various stages of social development. Such observations clearly implied Mill's stadial outlook on historical development.
20 Ibid., 1: 164–5.
21 See Winch, *Riches and Poverty*, 359.
22 *MPPE*, 1: 283–96.
23 Ibid., 1: 327.
24 Ibid., 1: 340–6.
25 Ibid., 2: 730–2.
26 Ibid., 1: 154–9.
27 Ibid., 1: 346–54.
28 Ibid., 1: 357–60.
29 Ibid., 1: 352–3.
30 Ibid., 1: 367.
31 Ibid., 1: 367–79, and see also 2: 765–6.
32 Ibid., 1: 190–5.
33 Ibid., 2: 744–6, 749, 751. See also 2: 962–7, for Mill's claim that colonization, in the state of civilization prevalent in his time, was the best use of capital that an old and wealthy country could engage in. In Great Britain, with its control of unoccupied colonies, the need for government control advocating such a policy was clear. Moving people from over-crowded to unsettled regions was in the best interest of all humanity.
34 Ibid., 2: 709.
35 Ibid., 1: 74–5.
36 Ibid., 1: 187–90.
37 Ibid., 2: 752–3.
38 Ibid., 2: 753–5, 758.
39 Ibid., 2: 756–7. See chapter 10 for the aesthetic appreciation of nature, which Mill here claimed as a further significant reason for limiting population in order to improve culture and the common quality of life.
40 Ibid., 1: 199. And see 2: 455–6, for the need for political economy to distinguish between things which were determined by natural laws, and those determined by social arrangements.
41 Ibid., 2: 464–5, and see also 2: 488–96.
42 See Kula, *History of Environmental Economic Thought*, 43–4. For Smith's view of resources such as mines, see *WN*, 1: 178–95, 282–4.
43 *MPPE*, 2: 711–14.
44 Ibid., 2: 695–8.
45 Ibid., 2: 719–32, 740.
46 Ibid., 2: 724–7.

47 Ibid., 2: 729–30.
48 Ibid., 2: 491–2, and also 2: 498, 519. For Mill's support for Ricardo's theory of rent, see also 1: 416–29.
49 Ibid., 2: 495–6.
50 Ibid., 2: 705–6, and see also 2: 876–7, for the accumulative nature of progress throughout history.
51 Ibid., 2: 706.

Chapter 7: Managing nature in the Enlightenment

1 See Jonsson, *Enlightenment's Frontier*, passim.
2 See Schabas, *Natural Origins of Economics*, 2, 16–17, 119, 124, 142–58. For a somewhat similar interpretation of Mill, claiming that natural theology played a role in the classical economic view of a natural moral economy, which gave way to a more adversarial conception of nature from Mill onwards, see Earl Gammon, "Nature as Adversary: The Rise of Modern Economic Conceptions of Nature," *Economy and Society*, 39 (2010), 218–46.
3 On Hume and natural resources see Schabas, *Natural Origins of Economics*, 58–78; Boianovsky, "Humboldt and the Economists on Natural Resources," 61–3.
4 Hume, "Of the Jealousy of Trade," in *Essays, Moral, Political, and Literary*, 327–31, at 329.
5 Hume, "Of Taxes," in *Essays, Moral, Political, and Literary*, 342–8, at 343–4.
6 Hume, "Of the Jealousy of Trade," 330–1.
7 Hume, "Of the Rise and Progress of the Arts and Sciences," in *Essays, Moral, Political, and Literary*, 111–37, at 119–23.
8 Hume, "Of Refinement in the Arts," [originally titled *Of Luxury*] in *Essays, Moral, Political, and Literary*, 268–80, at 277–8.
9 Hume, "Of Commerce," 260–2. Also see Alan Macfarlane, "David Hume and the Political Economy of Agrarian Civilization," *History of European Ideas*, 27 (2001), 79–91.
10 Hume, "Of Interest," in *Essays, Moral, Political, and Literary*, 295–307, at 299.
11 Hume, "Of the Populousness of Ancient Nations," in *Essays, Moral, Political, and Literary*, 377–464, at 419–20.
12 Hume, "Of Commerce," 260–2.
13 Verri, *Reflections on Political Economy*, 9–11.
14 Ibid., 23–4, 75–6.
15 Ibid., 30–6.
16 Ibid., 47–8. Verri also noted that a state should refrain from imposing taxes on forms of growth through industry, such as taxes on those who through hard work had enhanced the value of their land. See ibid., 95, and also 99–103 for a discussion of various aspects of the taxation of landed property.
17 Ibid., 79–80.
18 Ibid., 80–1.
19 Ibid., 81–3.
20 Ibid., 115–16.
21 Ibid., 83–4.
22 Ibid., 29–30.
23 See Schabas, *Natural Origins of Economics*, 79–101; and Jonsson, *Enlightenment's Frontier*, 121–46, also 49, 168, 174 and passim.
24 *WN*, 1: 245.
25 Ibid., 1: 163.
26 Thünen was highly appreciative of Smith, claiming he had learned political economy from him. Nevertheless, he thought that Smith had misapprehended the nature of land

rent due to too great an influence of the Physiocratic doctrine, and too little an acquaintance with the practical side of agriculture. Thünen was more appreciative of Ricardo's theory of rent than of Smith's or Say's. He claimed that rent was not just a function of fertility of soil, but also of the location of the farm. See Thünen, *Von Thünen's Isolated State*, 21–2, 147–8, 225.

27 *WN*, 1: 178–82.

28 Ibid., 1: 32–6; 2: 681–2.

29 Ibid., 1: 163. For more on the importance of water carriage, canals and harbors for economic development, see also 1: 224, 372, 405, 424; 2: 681. On the need for government investment in public works such as canal and harbor construction, see 2: 724–5, 757–8.

30 Ibid., 1: 321.

31 Ibid., 1: 234–55.

32 Ibid., 1: 380, 395.

33 For Smith on agriculture see, e.g., O'Brien, *The Classical Economists Revisited*, 249–53; Evensky, *Adam Smith's Moral Philosophy*, 132–4, 179–80; Winch, *Riches and Poverty*, 83–5; Schabas, *Natural Origins of Economics*, 93–5; Hont, *Jealousy of Trade*, 307–10; as well as the more technical discussion in Hollander, *The Economics of Adam Smith*, 95–9, 208–41, 285–93 and passim.

34 *WN*, 1: 332. And see 1: 334 on the price of rent in this context.

35 Ibid., 207.

36 Ibid., 1: 180–2.

37 Ibid., 1: 192–3.

38 See Millar, *The Origin of the Distinction of Ranks*, 380–2. Millar supported farmers, claiming that due to the limited effect of division of labor on their occupation, they had more mental capacities than manufacturing laborers, and thus were less prone to political abuse and subjection than the latter. A commercial society therefore required more emphasis on education to counter this tendency. See ibid., 262, 267, 335, 369, 377.

39 *WN*, 1: 378.

40 Ibid., 1: 363–4.

41 Ibid., 1: 67, 83.

42 Ibid., 1: 72, 78.

43 Ibid., 1: 162–3.

44 Ibid., 1: 169. For more on the connection between the ownership, cultivation and improvement of land, and its profitability for both proprietors and farmers, see 1: 162–77, and see also 178–95 for other resources such as mines.

45 Ibid., 1: 358, 377–8.

46 Ibid., 1: 376–8.

47 Ibid., 1: 141–5, but see also 119.

48 Ibid., 2: 676–8.

49 Ibid., 1: 260.

50 Ibid., 2: 686.

51 Ibid., 2: 627–8.

52 Ibid., 1: 408–12.

53 Ibid., 2: 609, 686. See also 2: 675, for more on how, in contrast with the Physiocratic perspective, the labor of merchants, artificers and manufacturers was not unproductive, even if it was less productive than agricultural labor.

54 Ibid., 2: 663–88, 830.

55 Ibid., 2: 674.

56 Ibid., 1: 16–17.

57 Ibid., 1: 133–4.

58 Ibid., 1: 255–6, and see generally also 429–51.

59 Ibid., 1: 381–96.

60 Ibid., 1: 385–6, 423.

61 Ibid., 2: 822–4.
62 Ibid., 1: 83–6.
63 Ibid., 1: 265–7.
64 Ibid., 1: 70–1.
65 Ibid., 1: 561–2.
66 Ibid., 1: 425.
67 Ibid., 1: 366–7. And see also 378–9 and 422–4, on the accessibility of lands in America, which supported their cultivation, thus leading to progress. The situation of Scotland before the union provided another comparable example. It demonstrated how improvements in the cultivation of land went hand in hand with a rising stock of cattle necessary for manure. Progress in both fields was interdependent, and was therefore slow and gradual, and based on a long course of frugality and industry. The union with England had enabled a rise in the price of cattle, and thus improvement in land cultivation in the Scottish low country. See ibid., 1: 239–40.
68 Ibid., 1: 282–4.
69 Ibid., 1: 94–6.
70 Ibid., 1: 251, 256–9 (quotation at 258).
71 Ibid., 1: 426–7.
72 Ibid., 1: 459–61.
73 Ibid., 1: 245. See also 1: 252–3, on economic improvement and the price of fish, and 264–5, on how rent rose in tandem with progress and rising prices.
74 Ibid., 1: 374–5.
75 Ibid., 2: 828–40, 854–8, 892–3, 927–8. The same applied to the taxation of stock. "Stock cultivates land; stock employs labour." See 2: 849.
76 Ibid., 2: 856–7, and also 1: 394–5.
77 See Rothschild, *Economic Sentiments*, 72–86.
78 Corn, or any other product which formed the staple diet of a society, maintained more than any other produce a constant value in relation to the amount of labor invested in its production. It was less influenced by changes in modes of cultivation, and therefore was the best determinant of the value of other products at various stages of a society's development. See *WN*, 1: 206, 216.
79 Ibid., 1: 506–15.
80 Ibid., 1: 515–17.
81 Ibid., 1: 526–7.
82 Ibid., 1: 517–18.
83 Ibid., 1: 524–43; 2: 875.
84 Ibid., 2: 724–5.
85 See for example Richard A. Smith, "The Eco-Suicidal Economics of Adam Smith," *Capitalism Nature Socialism*, 18 (2007), 22–43; Gilbert F. LaFreniere, *The Decline of Nature: Environmental History and the Western Worldview* (Palo Alto: Academica Press, 2008), 194–6, 341–67. On the other hand, some scholars have seen Smith's philosophy as capable of providing an environmental outlook. See e.g. Patrick R. Frierson, "Adam Smith and the Possibility of Sympathy with Nature," *Pacific Philosophical Quarterly*, 87 (2006), 442–80.

Chapter 8: Ricardo and Malthus on the utilization of nature

1 *RPPE*, 327–35. See also *WN*, 1: 162–3, 182.
2 David Ricardo, *Notes on Malthus's Principles of Political Economy* [Vol. II of *The Works and Correspondence of David Ricardo*], ed. Piero Sraffa, with the collaboration of M. H. Dobb (Cambridge: Cambridge University Press, 1951), 217.
3 *RPPE*, 67–75. Ricardo cited Say in this context. See *STPE*, 359–60, 362–3.
4 *RPPE*, 75.

5 Ricardo, *Notes on Malthus*, 20–2.
6 *RPPE*, 76–7n. See also *WN*, 1: 363–4.
7 See Schabas, *Natural Origins of Economics*, 102–5, 113–20.
8 *RPPE*, 293. See also *WN*, 1: 181–2.
9 Ricardo, *Notes on Malthus*, 210–12.
10 *RPPE*, 285–7. Ricardo also claimed here that Say's criticism of Smith on this point was unjustified. See *STPE*, 75–6, and also 286.
11 Ricardo, *Notes on Malthus*, 128.
12 *RPPE*, 263.
13 Ricardo, *Notes on Malthus*, 211.
14 *OSPE*, 105–8, 116–18, 135–9.
15 *RPPE*, 77.
16 Ibid., 67–9.
17 Ibid., 79–83.
18 Ricardo, *Notes on Malthus*, 112–13, 118, and see also 198–200. Ricardo also claimed that poor rates were a tax which rose together with improvements in the land, and the price of agricultural produce which rose in consequence tended to fall on the consumer. See *RPPE*, 257–62.
19 Ricardo, *Notes on Malthus*, 117–19. But see *RPPE*, 335–7, for a clear exposition of Ricardo's claim that the landlords' interest was almost always opposed to that of the manufacturers and the consumers.
20 *RPPE*, 85–7.
21 Ricardo, *Notes on Malthus*, 104; and see also *STPE*, 359–63.
22 *RPPE*, 398–406, 412.
23 Ricardo, *Notes on Malthus*, 164–5.
24 Ibid., 182, 185–7.
25 Ibid., 276–7, 293.
26 Malthus, *Principles of Political Economy*, 1: 96–104.
27 Ricardo, *Notes on Malthus*, 103–223.
28 Ibid., 71–3.
29 Malthus, *Principles of Political Economy*, 1: 150–5, 160–82, 298–301, 303–13.
30 Ricardo, *Notes on Malthus*, 161.
31 Malthus, *Principles of Political Economy*, 1: 183–91, and also 2: 175–6.
32 Ibid., 1: 316–26.
33 Ibid., 1: 331–2, and see also 1: 334–5; 2: 244, on how profits could never exceed what the cultivation of land for feeding population enabled.
34 Ibid., 1: 337.
35 Ibid., 1: 238n.
36 See Ricardo, *Notes on Malthus*, 211, 223, 283, 362–3; Davis, *Ricardo's Macroeconomics*, 23–9; Irwin, *Against the Tide*, 93–4.
37 *RPPE*, 93–5, and see also 306.
38 *EPP*, 1: 20–1.
39 Malthus, *Principles of Political Economy*, 1: 284–6.
40 *EPP*, 1: 84.
41 Ibid., 2: 296–7.
42 Ibid., 1: 134 and passim (290 for the quotation).
43 Ibid., 2: 197.
44 Malthus, *Principles of Political Economy*, 1: 27, 36–41. For more criticism of the Physiocrats see also 1: 136, 191, 204, 423, 441.
45 Ibid., 1: 134–50. Malthus perhaps preceded Ricardo in commenting about the rent which came from surplus agricultural produce, though in contrast with Ricardo he saw this as providentially ordained. See Winch, *Riches and Poverty*, 349.
46 Malthus, *Principles of Political Economy*, 1: 233–4.
47 *EPP*, 1: 400–9.

48 Ibid., 2: 70. Compare *WN*, 1: 411–27; 2: 647–54. Malthus noted that natural physical reality (decreasing fertility of cultivated land) meant that in agricultural production, due to diminishing effectiveness, labor became more and more expensive, while profits continually diminished. In manufactures and commerce, on the other hand, what reduced profits was diminishing exchangeable value, since in these fields the decrease in the effectiveness of labor was less than in agriculture. See Malthus, *Principles of Political Economy*, 1: 298–301; 2: 228.
49 Yet he criticized Steuart for claiming that populousness preceded agriculture, when in fact the opposite was true and agriculture preceded a rise in population, although both were mutually interdependent. Malthus claimed that this did not negate his earlier assertion regarding the oscillation between increases in population and in food, since even in this context food preceded population. See *EPP*, 1: 439–40, and also the editorial comment at 2: 339.
50 Ibid., 1: 145.
51 Ibid., 1: 301–5. Regarding the inexorable law of nature, which unmercifully removed those who lacked sufficient food, due to the irresponsible growth of human population, see also the well-known remarks which Malthus eventually omitted from the text, at 2: 127–8.
52 Ibid., 1: 293–4.
53 Manufactures and commerce were important to the life of civilized nations, but they were ornaments to the political structure, not its foundation. See ibid., 1: 430. Malthus was therefore willing, in an almost quasi-mercantilist manner, to forsake the otherwise important principal of a free market, since he regarded the maintenance of agricultural surplus as even more important.
54 Ibid., 1: 358, 361.
55 Ibid., 2: 63.
56 Ibid., 1: 362.
57 For opposing views on whether Malthus changed his mind and retreated from his view of the need for Corn Laws, see J. M. Pullen, "Malthus on Agricultural Protection: An Alternative View," *History of Political Economy*, 27 (1995), 517–29; Samuel Hollander, "More on Malthus and Agricultural Protection," *History of Political Economy*, 27 (1995), 531–7.
58 *EPP*, 1: 410–31.
59 See Winch, *Riches and Poverty*, 332–8; Irwin, *Against the Tide*, 94–7.
60 Malthus, *Principles of Political Economy*, 1: 223.
61 *EPP*, 2: 62–76.
62 Ibid., 1: 429–30n.
63 Ibid., 1: 436.
64 Malthus, *Principles of Political Economy*, 1: 427–40.
65 *EPP*, 1: 442–5.
66 Malthus, *Principles of Political Economy*, 1: 81–2.
67 Ibid., 1: 217–25.
68 Ibid., 1: 200–2.
69 Ibid., 1: 204–17. For more on the importance of agricultural improvements see also 1: 263–4, 313–14.
70 Ricardo, *Notes on Malthus*, 185.
71 Malthus, *Principles of Political Economy*, 1: 226–9, 237–9.
72 Ricardo, *Notes on Malthus*, 210–12.
73 Ibid., 336.
74 *EPP*, 2: 115–21.
75 Ibid., 2: 209.
76 Ibid., 2: 140, 142–3, and passim. Malthus's views on the proper policy toward the poor were the main subject of Book IV of the *Essay on the Principle of Population*, at ibid., 2: 87–203.

77 Ibid., 2: 148–55. On the importance of education see also 2: 200.
78 Malthus, *Principles of Political Economy*, 1: 249–52.
79 Ibid., 1: 473–4.
80 Ibid., 1: 511–12.
81 *EPP*, 2: 180–1.
82 Malthus, *Principles of Political Economy*, 1: 360–6.
83 Ibid., 1: 370–2.
84 Ibid., 1: 375–6.
85 *EPP*, 2: 211.

Chapter 9: Jean-Baptiste Say and other contemporaries

1 *STPE*, xl–xli, 75–6, 120, and 245n for the quotation. Compare *WN*, 1: 47–56 and passim.
2 *STPE*, 63–79, and also 318 for further criticism of the Physiocrats.
3 Ibid., 137–8, 381–6.
4 Ibid., 323.
5 Ibid., 246, and the accompanying note at 341–2.
6 Ibid., 64, and see also 127.
7 Ibid., 65.
8 Say, *Letters to Mr. Malthus*, 17, 64, 76–7.
9 *STPE*, 68.
10 Ibid., 93n.
11 Ibid., 80–1.
12 Ibid., 74–5, and see also 86.
13 Ibid., 88. See also 90–1n, where Say criticized Sismondi for not recognizing the advantages of machines, but only the evils they produced, mainly unemployment, which according to Say was only temporary.
14 Ibid., 359–60. And see also Ricardo's support of this passage in Ricardo, *Notes on Malthus*, 104.
15 *STPE*, 362–3, 366–7.
16 Both Senior and Mill regarded water, specifically when scarce, as an item of wealth. This, in contrast with Say's opinion that water was an item of natural wealth freely provided by nature, which did not have exchangeable value and could therefore not become private property. See Nicola Tynan, "Mill and Senior on London's Water Supply: Agency, Increasing Returns, and Natural Monopoly," *Journal of the History of Economic Thought*, 29 (2007), 49–65, at 59–60. On Senior and Mill see below.
17 *STPE*, 286, 293.
18 Ibid., 303–4.
19 Ibid., 472–3.
20 Ibid., 432–3.
21 Ibid., 298–300.
22 Ibid., 321.
23 Ibid., 301n.
24 Ibid., 364–5.
25 Ibid., 175–6.
26 Ibid., 145–6.
27 Whatmore, *Republicanism and the French Revolution*, 143.
28 *STPE*, 201.
29 Ibid., 175–6.
30 Ibid., 357.
31 On Bastiat see, e.g., Milgate and Stimson, *After Adam Smith*, 212–13.
32 Frédéric Bastiat, *Economic Harmonies*, trans. W. Hayden Boyers, ed. George B. de Huszar, Introduction by Dean Russell (Irvington-on-Hudson, NY: Foundation for Economic Education, 1964), 49–54 (quotation at 54), 100–3.

33 Ibid., 236–9.
34 Ibid., 239–83.
35 Ibid., 412–42.
36 Ibid., 268.
37 McCulloch, *Principles of Political Economy*, 5–20. McCulloch openly acknowledged Locke's originality on this point, and quoted him at length to this effect. See ibid., 8–11.
38 See Schabas, *Natural Origins of Economics*, 120–3.
39 See *WN*, 1: 363–4.
40 McCulloch, *Principles of Political Economy*, 118–22.
41 Torrens, *An Essay on the Production of Wealth*, 79–81.
42 Ibid., 4–5.
43 Ibid., 68–9.
44 Ibid., 66–8.
45 Ibid., 70–1.
46 Ibid., 72–3.
47 See Hollander, *Classical Economics*, 412.
48 Torrens, *An Essay on the Production of Wealth*, 118–46.
49 Ibid., 164–70.
50 Ibid., 196–7.
51 Ibid., 248–59, 272–4.
52 Ibid., 276–81, 288–9.
53 See O'Brien, *The Classical Economists Revisited*, 218.
54 Torrens, *An Essay on the Production of Wealth*, 154–8.
55 See *OSPE*, 76.
56 Torrens, *An Essay on the Production of Wealth*, 228–9.
57 *LPE*, 1: 46–7.
58 Ibid., 1: 424–5.
59 Ibid., 1: 403–4.
60 Ibid., 2: 344, 398–9.
61 Ibid., 1: 38–41.
62 Ibid., 1: 152–83.
63 Ibid., 1: 254–5.
64 Ibid., 1: 255–308, and for Stewart's view of the Physiocrats see also 1: 198–211, and regarding land taxes according to the Physiocrats, 2: 237–8. For Stewart's view of the Physiocrats vis-à-vis Smith, see Hont, *Jealousy of Trade*, 384–7; Milgate and Stimson, *After Adam Smith*, 108–9; Semmel, *The Rise of Free Trade Imperialism*, 54–5.
65 *LPE*, 1: 327, and 1: 11–12, on agriculture in general. See also Hont, *Jealousy of Trade*, 315–19.
66 *LPE*, 2: 117–18, 121, 195–6.
67 Ibid., 2: 141.
68 Ibid., 1: 138.
69 Ibid., 1: 141–52, and also 197–8.
70 Ibid., 1: 238–42, 250–2. Stewart was probably referring to *WN*, 1: 87–8, although at 1: 166 Smith addresses a similar point.
71 *LPE*, 2: 52–3, and also 2: 48–99, especially 59–60, 88–89. Compare *WN*, 1: 396, 461, 524–43.
72 *LPE*, 2: 103.
73 Ibid., 2: 106. Similarly, Stewart also regarded the exportation of grain as encouraging the cultivation and improvement of land. In fact, he viewed all limits to trade in grain as improper limits to the cultivation of natural resources. See ibid., 2: 110, and for his position on the exportation of grain in general, while discussing Smith's views on the subject, 2: 100–20.
74 Ibid., 2: 40–7.
75 Ibid., 2: 391–3.

76 Ibid., 2: 210.
77 Ibid., 2: 399, and 2: 397–401, for more regarding Stewart's optimism on the direction of historical development.
78 *OSPE*, 37.
79 Ibid., 86. The more a nation progressed, the more it concentrated on enhancing its manufactures. See ibid., 109.
80 Ibid., 6–8. For Senior's view of water, specifically when scarce, as an item of wealth and as subject to private appropriation, see Tynan, "Mill and Senior on London's Water Supply."
81 *OSPE*, 24.
82 Ibid., 58.
83 Ibid., 89–92.
84 See Schabas, *Natural Origins of Economics*, 123–4. For Senior's rent theory see also Bowley, *Nassau Senior and Classical Economics*, 126–34.
85 *OSPE*, 81–6. See also 119–28, for more consequences of this issue.
86 Ibid., 83.
87 Ibid.
88 Ibid., 119.
89 For criticism of the Physiocrats see ibid., 136–7.
90 See Bowley, *Nassau Senior and Classical Economics*, 125.
91 *OSPE*, 225.
92 See Waterman, *Revolution, Economics and Religion*, 217–54; Winch, *Riches and Poverty*, 359, 381–5; Semmel, *The Rise of Free Trade Imperialism*, 79–82.
93 Chalmers also accepted the Malthusian and Ricardian connection between the level of wages in such a model, and the size of population. See Thomas Chalmers, *An Inquiry into the Extent and Stability of National Resources* (Edinburgh: John Moir, 1808), 1–13.
94 Ibid., 4.
95 Ibid., 23–6.
96 Ibid., 39–40.
97 Ibid., 51–64.
98 Ibid., 322–31 (quotation at 322–3).
99 Jones, *An Essay on the Distribution of Wealth*, xxxi–xxxii.
100 Ibid., xxxiii–xxxix.
101 For a rather critical review of Jones's discussion of rents, see William L. Miller, "Richard Jones's Contribution to the Theory of Rent," *History of Political Economy*, 9 (1977), 346–65.
102 Jones, *An Essay on the Distribution of Wealth*, 10–11, 105, 153–4,178–89, 234–5, 277–82, 300–5.
103 Ibid., 243.
104 See Rashid, "Richard Jones and Baconian Historicism at Cambridge,"169. On Mill see chapter 10 below.
105 Jones, *An Essay on the Distribution of Wealth*, 49–50, 70–1.
106 Ibid., 101–4.
107 Ibid., 120–3.
108 Ibid., 138–42.
109 Ibid., 145–8.
110 Ibid., 157–9, 170–1.
111 Ibid., 177–8.
112 Ibid., 154, 161–4, 176.
113 Ibid., 196–217.
114 Ibid., 286–98.
115 Ibid., 221.
116 Ibid., 228–30, also 222–3.
117 Ibid., 273–4.

118 Ibid., 201–2.
119 Ibid., 210–13, 216.
120 Ibid., 240–2.
121 Ibid., 141.
122 Ibid., 106–7, 159–61, 321–3.
123 Ibid., 177. And see also 190–1, 255, on the rising efficiency of utilizing natural resources which accompanied progress.

Chapter 10: John Stuart Mill's attitude toward nature

1 See Schabas, *Natural Origins of Economics*, 128–31.
2 *MPPE*, 1: 3.
3 Ibid., 2: 971.
4 Ibid., 1: 7–8.
5 Ibid., 1: 25–6. See also 1: 100, on how capital was the product of labor, and was also significant as a type of indirect labor.
6 Ibid., 1: 26–8.
7 See Schabas, *Natural Origins of Economics*, 127.
8 *MPPE*, 1: 28–9.
9 Mill regarded water, specifically when scarce, as an item of wealth and as subject to appropriation, preferably governmental, due to its greater efficiency compared with private ownership. See Tynan, "Mill and Senior on London's Water Supply."
10 *MPPE*, 1: 29–30, and see also 2: 487.
11 Ibid., 1: 44.
12 Ibid., 1: 74.
13 Ibid., 1: 92–3.
14 Ibid., 1: 153–4.
15 Ibid., 1: 120–2.
16 Ibid., 1: 173.
17 Ibid., 1: 173–7.
18 Ibid., 1: 177–85, and also 187–8.
19 Ibid., 1: 185.
20 Ibid., 1: 417.
21 Ibid., 1: 424.
22 Ibid., 1: 416–29, and see also 2: 491–2.
23 Ibid., 1: 226–9.
24 See e.g. Milgate and Stimson, *After Adam Smith*, 204–10, 237–57.
25 *MPPE*, 1: 230–2.
26 On Cairnes see Schabas, *Natural Origins of Economics*, 135; Boianovsky, "Humboldt and the Economists on Natural Resources," 77–9.
27 J. E. Cairnes, "Political Economy and Land," *Fortnightly Review* (1870), 41–63, esp. 41–9.
28 *MPPE*, 1: 277.
29 Ibid., 1: 283–96.
30 Ibid., 1: 146–8.
31 Ibid., 1: 329.
32 See Rashid, "Richard Jones and Baconian Historicism at Cambridge," 169.
33 *MPPE*, 1: 326. See also 2: 988–1002, for Mill's criticism of the Irish cottier system, and for the establishment of peasant proprietors on wastelands, which both enabled finding living space for surplus population, as well as improved the wastelands themselves through cultivation. It may be that Mill had a condescending view of the cultural abilities of the Irish, as noted in Bell, "John Stuart Mill on Colonies." Nevertheless, as this quotation proves, he regarded the Irish poor as both capable of progress, and, even if not, as fully entitled to just remuneration for their agricultural labor.

34 For Mill's views on the pros and cons of both the free market and the socialist economic systems, see e.g. *MPPE*, 2: 985–7.
35 Ibid., 2: 767–9.
36 Ibid., 2: 769–96.
37 See John Stuart Mill, "Nature," in *Essays on Ethics, Religion and Society*, ed. J. M. Robson, Introduction by F. E. L. Priestley [Vol. X of *The Collected Works of John Stuart Mill*] (Toronto: University of Toronto Press; and London: Routledge & Kegan Paul, 1969), 373–402. For discussions see James Eli Adams, "Philosophical Forgetfulness: John Stuart Mill's 'Nature'," *Journal of the History of Ideas*, 53 (1992), 437–54; Schabas, *Natural Origins of Economics*, 128–31; Robson, *The Improvement of Mankind*, 149–51.
38 Mill, "Nature," 375–8.
39 Ibid., 381.
40 Ibid., 381–3.
41 Ibid., 383–7.
42 Ibid., 388–91, 399.
43 Ibid., 391–3, 398.
44 Ibid., 393–7, and also 402.
45 Here again I disagree with Margaret Schabas's generally impressive discussion. She claims that in "Nature," Mill emphasized that humanity conquered nature, and did not obey it. This in contrast with *Principles of Political Economy*, where Mill privileged physical nature to a greater extent as something harnessed by labor, and as affecting production independently of human institutions. See Schabas, *Natural Origins of Economics*, 128–31. The interpretation presented here, on this as on other aspects of Mill's consideration of nature, is different.
46 *MPPE*, 2: 756.
47 For the above passage, and Mill's stationary state in general, see Evensky, *Adam Smith's Moral Philosophy*, 308–12. Also see Kula, *History of Environmental Economic Thought*, 44; Hollander, *Classical Economics*, 238–40.
48 See Robson, *The Improvement of Mankind*, 26, 69–70, 121–2.
49 See John Parham, "What is (Ecological) 'Nature'? John Stuart Mill and the Victorian Perspective," in *Culture, Creativity and Environment: New Environmentalist Criticism*, ed. Fiona Becket and Terry Gifford (Amsterdam and New York: Rodopi, 2007), 37–54; Martin O'Connor, "John Stuart Mill's Utilitarianism and the Social Ethics of Sustainable Development," *European Journal of the History of Economic Thought*, 4 (1997), 478–506; Steiguer, *The Origins of Modern Environmental Thought*, 46, 88, 144, 149–62, 167, 192, 215.
50 A similar outlook was developed by Mill's acquaintance Alexis de Tocqueville, whose *Democracy in America* was very much admired by Mill. Indeed, on this as on other topics Tocqueville may have influenced Mill, although his view of nature was not developed from a political-economic perspective, and is therefore not discussed here. For a detailed discussion see, however, Nathaniel Wolloch, "The Liberal Origins of the Modern View of Nature," *The Tocqueville Review*, 34 (2013), 107–31.
51 See Norbert Elias, *The Civilizing Process: The History of Manners and State Formation and Civilization*, trans. Edmund Jephcott (Oxford and Cambridge, MA: Blackwell, 1994), 496–7. See also Nathaniel Wolloch, "The Civilizing Process, Nature, and Stadial Theory," *Eighteenth-Century Studies*, 44 (2011), 245–59.
52 See Thomas, *Man and the Natural World*, 181–91, 300–3 (303 for the quotation).
53 See D. G. Charlton, *New Images of the Natural in France: A Study in European Cultural History 1750–1800* (Cambridge: Cambridge University Press, 1984), 30–4, 199–220. For similar interpretations see also Roy Porter, "The Urban and the Rustic in Enlightenment London," in Teich, Porter, and Gustafsson, *Nature and Society in Historical Context*, 176–94; and Harriet Ritvo, *The Animal Estate: The English and Other Creatures in the Victorian Age* (Cambridge, MA: Harvard University Press, 1987), 1–6 and passim.

54 See T. C. Smout, *Exploring Environmental History: Selected Essays* (Edinburgh: Edinburgh University Press, 2009), 21–51; Jonsson, *Enlightenment's Frontier*, 50–3 and passim.
55 See Leo Marx, *The Machine in the Garden: Technology and the Pastoral Ideal in America* (New York: Oxford University Press, 1970); Roderick Nash, *Wilderness and the American Mind* (New Haven and London: Yale University Press, 1973).
56 See, e.g., Harman, *The Culture of Nature in Britain*, passim. Different perspectives can also be gleaned from important studies such as Donald Worster, *Nature's Economy: A History of Ecological Ideas* (Cambridge: Cambridge University Press, 1994); or Pierre Hadot, *The Veil of Isis: An Essay on the History of the Idea of Nature*, trans. Michael Chase (Cambridge, MA, and London: Harvard University Press, 2006).
57 See Winch, *Riches and Poverty*, 394–5, 405–22.
58 See Denise Phillips, *Acolytes of Nature: Defining Natural Science in Germany, 1770–1850* (Chicago and London: University of Chicago Press, 2012), 202–53.
59 *MPPE*, 2: 971.
60 Aquinas, *Political Writings*, 51–2.
61 Botero, *Reason of State*, 150.
62 Mun, "Discovrse of Trade," 24–6.
63 Wallace, *Various Prospects*, 129–63.
64 Poivre, *Travels of a Philosopher*, 151–2. Poivre, despite being a Frenchman, here seems to allude to the English style of gardens popular in the eighteenth century. These gardens presented a particular case of the attempt to reconcile pristine nature with the control of nature, evincing in effect a carefully planned sense of wilderness, on which see Charlton, *New Images of the Natural in France*, 30–4, who notes that English gardens evinced a "wish to have the best of both worlds, of the natural and the cultivated at the same time."
65 See Spengler, *French Predecessors of Malthus*, 327.
66 See Necker, *A Treatise on the Administration of the Finances of France*, 1: 218–19. Also see 3: 102, for a similar reference to horses and "parks, or barren gardens."
67 See Verri, *Reflections on Political Economy*, 77–9.
68 *WN*, 2: 824.
69 *STPE*, 442.
70 See *EPP*, 1: 159; and Malthus, *The Travel Diaries*, 45, 65, 68, 70–1, 77, 88, 93, 96, 109–10, 124–8, 133–4, 138, 263–4.
71 See Robert M. Solow, "On the Intergenerational Allocation of Natural Resources," *Scandinavian Journal of Economics*, 88 (1986), 141–9, at 142.
72 For Xenophon's influence on Ruskin, see Henderson, *John Ruskin's Political Economy*, 64–85; and Garnett, "Political and Domestic Economy in Victorian Social Thought." See also Robson, *The Improvement of Mankind*, x, for the claim that Ruskin, in regarding Mill's political economy as abstract and inhuman, failed to understand that for Mill economics was subordinate to sociology and ethics.
73 See John Ruskin, *Unto This Last: Four Essays on the First Principles of Political Economy* (London: George Allen, 1895), 165–8. Ruskin objected to the idea that population growth was unconducive to wealth. People themselves, so long as they were happy, constituted true wealth, and in such a state the more people there were, the better. Furthermore, over-population might exist locally due to misgovernment, but globally this would not occur for ages to come. See ibid., 64–5, 99. This idea, that global finiteness of natural resources was reserved for the remote future, was, as we have seen, common among classical political economists, not least Malthus and Mill. Yet Ruskin does not seem to have realized that his position was close to theirs on this point.
74 Ibid., 156–65 (quotation at 162).
75 *MPPE*, 2: 801.

Epilogue: From socialism to modernity

1 For a short introduction see Thomas Sowell, "Sismondi: A Neglected Pioneer," *History of Political Economy*, 4 (1972), 62–88; and also the translator's introduction to J.-C.-L. Simonde de Sismondi, *New Principles of Political Economy: Of Wealth in Its Relation to Population*, trans. Richard Hyse (New Brunswick and London: Transaction Publishers, 1991).
2 Ibid., 61–4, 69–70 (62 for the quotation).
3 Ibid., 137–41, 143–7.
4 Ibid., 582n.
5 See Mao-Lan Tuan, *Simonde de Sismondi as an Economist* (New York: AMS Press, 1968), 46–53, 127–34.
6 On which see ibid., 83–96.
7 Sismondi, *New Principles of Political Economy*, 511–14, 517–21.
8 See Malthus, *Principles of Political Economy*, 1: 420n. Also see Kula, *History of Environmental Economic Thought*, 51–2.
9 Sismondi, *New Principles of Political Economy*, 525–30.
10 Ibid., 533–7.
11 Ibid., 541–4, 547–52, 555–65, 569–73, 577–86.
12 Ibid., 584–6.
13 However, for an example of an interpretation of Marxism as supporting environmental concerns, see John Bellamy Foster, *Marx's Ecology: Materialism and Nature* (New York: Monthly Review Press, 2000).
14 See William Leiss, *The Domination of Nature* (Boston: Beacon Press, 1974), 122–3, and passim.
15 See *Marx and Engels on Ecology*, ed. Howard L. Parsons (Westport and London: Greenwood Press, 1977). Also see Kula, *History of Environmental Economic Thought*, 53–9; Boianovsky, "Humboldt and the Economists on Natural Resources," 87–8.
16 See in this context Hollander, *Classical Economics*, 359–61.
17 For an overview see Ted Benton, "Engels and the Politics of Nature," in *Engels Today: A Centenary Appreciation*, ed. Christopher J. Arthur (Basingstoke: Macmillan, 1996), 67–93.
18 Frederick Engels, *Dialectics of Nature*, trans. Clemens Dutt (Moscow: Foreign Languages Publishing House, 1954), 238–9.
19 Ibid., 304–6.
20 Ibid., 228–46.
21 Ibid., 231–2. Despite his repeated mention of Darwin in this context, it seems Engels was here influenced by Lamarck's theory of acquired characteristics.
22 See Samuel Hollander, *Friedrich Engels and Marxian Political Economy* (Cambridge: Cambridge University Press, 2011), 35–42, 48–51.
23 Engels, *Dialectics of Nature*, 239–40.
24 Ibid., 241–2.
25 Ibid., 242–4.
26 Ibid., 244–6.
27 Ibid., 47–9.
28 See Max Horkheimer and Theodor W. Adorno, *Dialectic of Enlightenment*, trans. John Cumming (New York: Herder and Herder, 1972), 223–4. See also Helen Denham, "The Cunning of Unreason and Nature's Revolt: Max Horkheimer and William Leiss on the Domination of Nature," *Environment and History*, 3 (1997), 149–75; Kevin DeLuca, "The Frankfurt School and the Domination of Nature: New Grounds for Radical Environmentalism," in *Rethinking the Frankfurt School: Alternative Legacies of Cultural Critique*, eds. Jeffrey T. Nealon and Caren Irr (Albany: State University of New York Press, 2002), 153–67; Alison Stone, "Adorno and the Disenchantment of Nature," *Philosophy & Social Criticism*, 32 (2006), 231–53.

29 See Carolyn Merchant, *The Death of Nature: Women, Ecology, and the Scientific Revolution* (San Francisco: Harper San Francisco, 1980). For a different critical study of early modern attitudes toward nature, centering on artistic sources, see Robert N. Watson, *Back to Nature: The Green and the Real in the Late Renaissance* (Philadelphia: University of Pennsylvania Press, 2006).
30 Eugen von Böhm-Bawerk, *The Positive Theory of Capital*, trans. William Smart (London and New York: Macmillan, 1891), 7–13.
31 Ibid., 15–16, also 20–2.
32 Ibid., 78–81.
33 Ibid., 80.
34 Ibid., 92–3, 95–6, 99.
35 Ibid., 81n.
36 See Antoine Missemer, "William Stanley Jevons' *The Coal Question* (1865), Beyond the Rebound Effect," *Ecological Economics*, 82 (2012), 97–103.
37 See *WN*, 1: 99: "The progressive state is in reality the chearful [*sic*] and the hearty state to all the different orders of the society. The stationary is dull; the declining, melancholy."
38 William Stanley Jevons, *The Coal Question; An Inquiry Concerning the Progress of the Nation, and the Probable Exhaustion of Our Coal-Mines* (London: Macmillan, 1866), v–xxvi.
39 Ibid., 142–4.
40 Ibid., 164–8.
41 Ibid., 169–78.
42 See Missemer, "William Stanley Jevons' *The Coal Question*"; and Blake Alcott, "Jevons' Paradox," *Ecological Economics*, 54 (2005), 9–21.
43 Jevons, *The Coal Question*, 196–8, 204–5.
44 Ibid., 374.
45 See Collini, Winch, and Burrow, *That Noble Science of Politics*, 309–37.
46 See Camille Limoges and Claude Ménard, "Organization and the Division of Labour: Biological Metaphors at Work in Alfred Marshall's *Principles of Economics*," in Mirowski, *Natural Images in Economic Thought*, 336–59.
47 Alfred Marshall, *Principles of Economics, Ninth (Variorum) Edition*, annotations by C. W. Guillebaud, 2 vols. (London: Macmillan for the Royal Economic Society, 1961), 1: 55–6.
48 Ibid., 1: 59.
49 Ibid., 1: 61.
50 Ibid., 1: 62–3.
51 Ibid., 1: 86–91. Marshall did occasionally use stadial concepts. See 1: 220–1. He also outlined a version of the traditional claim regarding the inverse relation between natural surroundings and cultural progress. See 1: 723–5.
52 See ibid., 1: 144–9. Also see Kula, *History of Environmental Economic Thought*, 67–8.
53 Marshall, *Principles of Economics*, 1: 138–9.
54 Ibid., 1: 173–203.
55 Ibid., 1: 690–1.
56 Ibid., 1: 721–2.
57 Ibid., 1: 223–4.
58 Ibid., 1: 321–2.
59 Ibid., 1: 504.
60 See in particular Kula, *History of Environmental Economic Thought*. Also see Steiguer, *The Origins of Modern Environmental Thought*, 43–52, 78–98, 122–35, 149–84; Matt Price, "Economics, Ecology, and the Value of Nature," in *The Moral Authority of Nature*, eds. Lorraine Daston and Fernando Vidal (Chicago and London: University of Chicago Press, 2004), 182–204; Emma Rothschild, "Maintaining (Environmental) Capital Intact," *Modern Intellectual History*, 8 (2011), 193–212. For more general

discussions see, e.g., Philip Mirowski, "The Realms of the Natural," in Mirowski, *Natural Images in Economic Thought*, 451–83; Bo Gustafsson, "Nature and Economy," in Teich, Porter, and Gustafsson, *Nature and Society in Historical Context*, 347–63.

61 John Maynard Keynes, *The General Theory of Employment, Interest and Money* (London and Basingstoke: Macmillan, 1973), xxiii.

62 Ibid., 161–3.

63 See Kula, *History of Environmental Economic Thought*, 89–92.

64 John Maynard Keynes, "Economic Possibilities for Our Grandchildren," in *Essays in Persuasion* (London: Rupert Hart-Davis, 1951), 358–73.

65 Ibid.

66 Keynes, *General Theory of Employment, Interest and Money*, 329–31.

67 See Robert U. Ayres, Jeroen C.J.M. van den Bergh, and John M. Gowdy, "Strong versus Weak Sustainability: Economics, Natural Sciences, and 'Consilience'," *Environmental Ethics*, 23 (2001), 155–68; Jeroen C.J.M. van den Bergh, "Ecological Economics: Themes, Approaches, and Differences with Environmental Economics," *Regional Environmental Change*, 2 (2001), 13–23; Giuseppe Munda, "Environmental Economics, Ecological Economics, and the Concept of Sustainable Development," *Environmental Values*, 6 (1997), 213–33.

68 See the famous and controversial, though to my mind convincing, discussion in William Cronon, "The Trouble with Wilderness; or, Getting Back to the Wrong Nature," in *Uncommon Ground: Rethinking the Human Place in Nature*, ed. William Cronon (New York and London: W. W. Norton, 1996), 69–90. A more detailed consideration of this difficult open issue is beyond the scope of our discussion.

69 See Solow, "On the Intergenerational Allocation of Natural Resources"; Robert M. Solow, "The Economics of Resources or the Resources of Economics," *American Economic Review*, 64 (1974), 1–14; idem, "Does Growth Have a Future? Does Growth Theory Have a Future? Are These Questions Related?" *History of Political Economy*, 41 (annual supplement) (2009), 27–34.

70 See Craufurd D. Goodwin, "Ecologist Meets Economics: Aldo Leopold, 1887–1948," *Journal of the History of Economic Thought*, 30 (2008), 429–52.

71 See Kenneth E. Boulding, "The Economics of the Coming Spaceship Earth," in *Environmental Quality in a Growing Economy*, ed. Henry Jarrett (Baltimore: John Hopkins University Press, 1965), 3–14. See also Steiguer, *The Origins of Modern Environmental Thought*, 88–98; and Kula, *History of Environmental Economic Thought*, 129–33. The finiteness of natural resources, and the limits to growth it implied, was subsequently the topic of the work of the group known as the Club of Rome, on which see ibid., 136–46; and Steiguer, *The Origins of Modern Environmental Thought*, 163–74.

72 See Price, "Economics, Ecology, and the Value of Nature"; Steiguer, *The Origins of Modern Environmental Thought*, 132–4; H. Spencer Banzhaf, "Consumer Sovereignty in the History of Environmental Economics," *History of Political Economy*, 43 (2011), 339–45.

73 See Amartya Sen, "Why We Should Preserve the Spotted Owl," *London Review of Books*, 26 (5 February, 2004), 10–11; idem, "Sustainable Development and Our Responsibilities," *Notizie di Politeia*, 26 (2010), 129–37.

74 See Amartya Sen, *The Idea of Justice* (London: Penguin Books, 2010), 248–9.

75 Robert William Fogel, *The Escape from Hunger and Premature Death, 1700–2100: Europe, America, and the Third World* (Cambridge: Cambridge University Press, 2004), xv, 20–2, 33, 129–30n, and passim.

76 Ibid., 21.

77 Ibid., 27.

78 Ibid., 54, 57.

79 Ibid., 79.

80 Ibid., 83.

Bibliography

Primary sources

Aquinas, St. Thomas, *Political Writings*, ed. and trans. R. W. Dyson (Cambridge: Cambridge University Press, 2002).

Aristotle, *The Politics*, trans. Benjamin Jowett, revised by Jonathan Barnes, ed. Stephen Everson (Cambridge: Cambridge University Press, 1988).

Bacon, Francis, *The New Organon*, eds. and trans. Lisa Jardine and Michael Silverthorne (Cambridge: Cambridge University Press, 2000).

Bastiat, Frédéric, *Economic Harmonies*, trans. W. Hayden Boyers, ed. George B. de Huszar, Introduction by Dean Russell (Irvington-on-Hudson, NY: Foundation for Economic Education, 1964).

Beccaria, Cesare, *A Discourse on Public Economy and Commerce*, trans. anon. (n.p., 1769; reprint New York: Burt Franklin, 1970).

Böhm-Bawerk, Eugen von, *The Positive Theory of Capital*, trans. William Smart (London and New York: Macmillan, 1891).

Boisguillebert [Boisguilbert], Pierre Le Pesant, sieur de, "Le detail de la France," in *Économistes financiers du XVIIIe siècle*, ed. Eugène Daire (Geneva: Slatkine Reprints, 1971 [1851]), 163–247.

——— "Traité de la nature, culture, commerce et intérêt des grains," in *Économistes financiers du XVIIIe siècle*, ed. Eugène Daire (Geneva: Slatkine Reprints, 1971 [1851]), 323–71.

Botero, Giovanni, *The Reason of State & The Greatness of Cities*, trans. [respectively] P. J. and D. P. Waley, and Robert Peterson (1606) (London: Routledge and Kegan Paul, 1956).

Boulding, Kenneth E., "The Economics of the Coming Spaceship Earth," in *Environmental Quality in a Growing Economy*, ed. Henry Jarrett (Baltimore: John Hopkins University Press, 1965), 3–14.

Buffon, Georges-Louis Leclerc, Comte de, "Septième et dernière Époque, lorsque la Puissance de l'Homme a secondé celle de la Nature," in *Histoire naturelle, générale et particulière*, Supplément, vol. 5 (Paris: Imprimerie Royale, 1778), 225–54.

——— "Sur la conservation & le rétablissement des forêts," in *Histoire naturelle, générale et particulière*, Supplément, vol. 2 (Paris: Imprimerie Royale, 1775), 249–71.

——— "Sur la culture & l'exploitation des forêts," in *Histoire naturelle, générale et particulière*, Supplément, vol. 2 (Paris: Imprimerie Royale, 1775), 271–90.

Cairnes, J. E., "Political Economy and Land," *Fortnightly Review* (1870), 41–63.

Cantillon, Richard, *Essai sur la Nature du Commerce en Général*, ed. and trans. Henry Higgs (London: Frank Cass, 1959).

Chalmers, Thomas, *An Inquiry into the Extent and Stability of National Resources* (Edinburgh: John Moir, 1808).

Condorcet, Antoine-Nicolas de, *The Life of M. Turgot*, trans. anon. (London: J. Johnson, 1787).

——— "Réflexions sur le commerce des blés (1776)," in *Oeuvres de Condorcet*, eds. A. Condorcet O'Connor and M. F. Arago (Paris: Firmin Didot Frères, 1847–1849), 11: 99–252.
——— *Sketch for a Historical Picture of the Progress of the Human Mind*, trans. June Barraclough (London: Weidenfeld and Nicolson, 1955).
Copernicus, Nicholas, *Minor Works*, trans. Edward Rosen, with Erna Hilfstein (Baltimore and London: Johns Hopkins University Press, 1985).
Court, Pieter de la, *The True Interest and Political Maxims, Of the Republic of Holland*, trans. John Campbell (London: J. Nourse, 1746).
The De Moneta of Nicholas Oresme and English Mint Documents, trans. and ed. Charles Johnson (Edinburgh: Thomas Nelson and Sons, 1956).
Early English Tracts on Commerce, ed. J. R. McCulloch (Cambridge: Cambridge University Press, 1970 [1856]).
Engels, Frederick, *Dialectics of Nature*, trans. Clemens Dutt (Moscow: Foreign Languages Publishing House, 1954).
Fogel, Robert William, *The Escape from Hunger and Premature Death, 1700–2100: Europe, America, and the Third World* (Cambridge: Cambridge University Press, 2004).
Franklin, Benjamin, *The Autobiography and Other Writings on Politics, Economics, and Virtue*, ed. Alan Houston (Cambridge: Cambridge University Press, 2004).
Galiani, Ferdinand, *Dialogues sur le commerce des blés* ([Paris]: Fayard, 1984).
Hales, John, *A Discourse of the Common Weal of this Realm of England*, ed. Elizabeth Lamond (New York: Burt Franklin, 1971 [1893]).
Horkheimer, Max, and Theodor W. Adorno, *Dialectic of Enlightenment*, trans. John Cumming (New York: Herder and Herder, 1972).
Hume, David, *Essays, Moral, Political, and Literary*, ed. Eugene F. Miller (Indianapolis: Liberty Classics, 1987).
Jevons, William Stanley, *The Coal Question; An Inquiry Concerning the Progress of the Nation, and the Probable Exhaustion of Our Coal-Mines* (London: Macmillan, 1866).
John Duns Scotus, *Political and Economic Philosophy*, ed. and trans. Allan B. Wolter (St. Bonaventure, NY: Franciscan Institute, 2001).
Jones, Richard, *An Essay on the Distribution of Wealth, and on the Sources of Taxation* (London: John Murray, 1831; reprint New York: Augustus M. Kelley, 1964).
Keynes, John Maynard, "Economic Possibilities for Our Grandchildren," in *Essays in Persuasion* (London: Rupert Hart-Davis, 1951), 358–73.
——— *The General Theory of Employment, Interest and Money* (London and Basingstoke: Macmillan, 1973).
Locke, John, "Understanding" (1677), in *Political Essays*, ed. Mark Goldie (Cambridge: Cambridge University Press, 1997), 260–5.
——— *The Works of John Locke, in Nine Volumes*, twelfth edition, vol. 4 (London: C. and J. Rivington et al., 1824).
Malthus, T. R., *An Essay on the Principle of Population*, ed. Patricia James, 2 vols. (Cambridge: Cambridge University Press, 1989).
——— *Principles of Political Economy, Variorum Edition*, ed. John Pullen, 2. vols. (Cambridge: Cambridge University Press, 1989).
——— *The Travel Diaries of Thomas Robert Malthus*, ed. Patricia James (Cambridge: Cambridge University Press, 1966).
Marshall, Alfred, *Principles of Economics, Ninth (Variorum) Edition*, annotations by C. W. Guillebaud, 2 vols. (London: Macmillan for the Royal Economic Society, 1961).
Marx and Engels on Ecology, ed. Howard L. Parsons (Westport and London: Greenwood Press, 1977).
McCulloch, John Ramsay, *The Principles of Political Economy, With Some Inquiries Respecting Their Application* (Edinburgh: Adam and Charles Black, 1864).
Meek, Ronald L., *The Economics of Physiocracy: Essays and Translations* (Cambridge, MA: Harvard University Press, 1963).
Melon, Jean-François, *A Political Essay Upon Commerce*, trans. David Bindon (Dublin: Philip Crampton, 1738).

Merchant, Carolyn, *The Death of Nature: Women, Ecology, and the Scientific Revolution* (San Francisco: Harper San Francisco, 1980).

Mill, John Stuart, "Civilization," in *Essays on Politics and Society*, ed. J. M. Robson, Introduction by Alexander Brady [Vol. XVIII of *The Collected Works of John Stuart Mill*] (Toronto: University of Toronto Press; and London: Routledge & Kegan Paul, 1977), 119–47.

——— "Nature," in *Essays on Ethics, Religion and Society*, ed. J. M. Robson, Introduction by F. E. L. Priestley [Vol. X of *The Collected Works of John Stuart Mill*] (Toronto: University of Toronto Press; and London: Routledge & Kegan Paul, 1969), 373–402.

——— *Principles of Political Economy, with Some of Their Applications to Social Philosophy*, ed. J. M. Robson, Introduction by V. W. Bladen, 2 vols. [Vols. II–III of *Collected Works of John Stuart Mill*] (Toronto: University of Toronto Press, and London: Routledge & Kegan Paul, 1965).

Millar, John, *The Origin of the Distinction of Ranks and other Writings*, in William C. Lehmann, *John Millar of Glasgow 1735–1801* (Cambridge: Cambridge University Press, 1960; reprint New York: Arno Press, 1979).

Mirabeau, Victor de Riqueti, Marquis de, *L'ami des hommes, ou Traité de la population*, 2 vols. (Avignon, 1756–1760; reprint Aalen: Scientia Verlag, 1970).

Montchrestien, Antoine de, *Traicté de l'œconomie politique*, ed. François Billacois (Geneva: Librairie Droz, 1999).

Necker, Jacques, *Sur la législation et le commerce des grains* (Paris: Pissot, 1776).

——— *A Treatise on the Administration of the Finances of France*, trans. Thomas Mortimer, 3 vols. (London: Logographic Press, 1785).

Petty, William, *Several Essays in Political Arithmetick* (London, D. Browne et al., 1755; reprint London: Routledge and Thoemmes Press, and Tokyo: Kinokuniya, 1992).

Poivre, Pierre, *Travels of a Philosopher: Or, Observations on the Manners and Arts of Various Nations in Africa and Asia*, trans. anon. (Dublin: P. and W. Wilson et al., 1770).

Ricardo, David, *Notes on Malthus's Principles of Political Economy* (Vol. II of *The Works and Correspondence of David Ricardo*], ed. Piero Sraffa, with the collaboration of M. H. Dobb (Cambridge: Cambridge University Press, 1951).

——— *On the Principles of Political Economy and Taxation* [Vol. I of *The Works and Correspondence of David Ricardo*], ed. Piero Sraffa, with the collaboration of M. H. Dobb (Cambridge: Cambridge University Press, 1951).

Ruskin, John, *Unto This Last: Four Essays on the First Principles of Political Economy* (London: George Allen, 1895).

Say, Jean-Baptiste, *Letters to Mr. Malthus, On Several Subjects of Political Economy, and on the Cause of the Stagnation of Commerce. To Which is Added a Catechism of Political Economy, or Familiar Conversations on the Manner in which Wealth is Produced, Distributed, and Consumed in Society*, trans. John Richter (London: Sherwood, Neely, and Jones, 1821).

——— *A Treatise on Political Economy, Or the Production, Distribution and Consumption of Wealth*, trans. C. R. Prinsep, Introduction translated by Clement C. Biddle (Philadelphia: Claxton, Remsen & Haffelfinger, 1880; reprint New York: Augustus M. Kelley, 1971).

Sen, Amartya, *The Idea of Justice* (London: Penguin Books, 2010).

——— "Sustainable Development and Our Responsibilities," *Notizie di Politeia*, 26 (2010), 129–37.

——— "Why We Should Preserve the Spotted Owl," *London Review of Books*, 26 (5 February, 2004), 10–11.

Senior, Nassau W., *An Outline of the Science of Political Economy* (London: W. Clowes and Sons, 1836; reprint New York: Augustus M. Kelley, 1965).

Sismondi, J.-C.-L. Simonde de, *New Principles of Political Economy: Of Wealth in Its Relation to Population*, trans. Richard Hyse (New Brunswick and London: Transaction Publishers, 1991).

Smith, Adam, *An Inquiry into the Nature and Causes of the Wealth of Nations*, ed. R. H. Campbell, A. S. Skinner, and W. B. Todd, 2 vols. (Oxford: Clarendon Press, 1976).

——— *Lectures on Jurisprudence*, ed. R. L. Meek, D. D. Raphael, and P. G. Stein (Oxford: Clarendon Press, 1978).

Solow, Robert M., "Does Growth Have a Future? Does Growth Theory Have a Future? Are These Questions Related?" *History of Political Economy*, 41 (annual supplement) (2009), 27–34.

——— "The Economics of Resources or the Resources of Economics," *American Economic Review*, 64 (1974), 1–14.

——— "On the Intergenerational Allocation of Natural Resources," *Scandinavian Journal of Economics*, 88 (1986), 141–9.

Steuart, James, *An Inquiry into the Principles of Political Oeconomy*, 3 vols. (Dublin: James Williams and Richard Moncrieffe, 1770; reprint London: Thoemmes Press, and Tokyo: Kinokuniya Company, 1992).

Stewart, Dugald, "Account of the Life and Writings of Adam Smith, LL.D.," in Adam Smith, *Essays on Philosophical Subjects*, eds. W. P. D. Wightman and J. C. Bryce (Oxford: Clarendon Press, 1980) 269–351.

——— *Lectures on Political Economy*, ed. Sir William Hamilton, 2 vols. [Vols. VIII–IX of *The Collected Works of Dugald Stewart*] (Edinburgh: Thomas Constable, and London: Hamilton, Adams, and Co., 1855–1856; reprint Bristol: Thoemmes Press, 1994).

Thünen, Johann Heinrich von, *Von Thünen's Isolated State: An English Edition of Der Isolierte Staat*, trans. Carla M. Wartenberg, ed. Peter Hall (Oxford: Pergamon Press, 1966).

Torrens, Robert, *An Essay on the Production of Wealth*, Introduction by Joseph Dorfman (London: Longman, Hurst, Rees, Orme, and Brown, 1821; reprint New York: Augustus M. Kelley, 1965).

Tucker, Josiah, *An Essay on the Advantages and Disadvantages which Respectively Attend France and Great Britain, with Regard to Trade* (Glasgow: no printer, 1756).

Turgot on Progress, Sociology and Economics, ed. and trans. Ronald L. Meek (Cambridge: Cambridge University Press, 1973).

Uztáriz, Jerónimo de, *The Theory and Practice of Commerce and Maritime Affairs*, trans. John Kippax (Dublin: George Faulkner, 1752).

Verri, Pietro, *Reflections on Political Economy*, trans. Barbara McGilvray and Peter D. Groenewegen, ed. Peter D. Groenewegen (Fairfield, NJ: Augustus M. Kelley, 1993).

Wallace, Robert, *A Dissertation on the Numbers of Mankind in Antient and Modern Times* (Edinburgh: G. Hamilton and J. Balfour, 1753; reprint London: Routledge/Thoemmes Press, and Tokyo: Kinokuniya, 1992).

——— *Various Prospects of Mankind, Nature, and Providence* (London: A. Millar, 1761).

Whately, Richard, *Introductory Lectures on Political Economy* (London: B. Fellowes, 1832).

Xenophon, "Oeconomicus," in *Memorabilia and Oeconomicus*, trans. E. C. Marchant (Loeb Classical Library; London: William Heinemann, and Cambridge, MA: Harvard University Press, 1923), 363–525.

——— "Ways and Means," in *Scripta Minora*, trans. E. C. Marchant (Loeb Classical Library; London: William Heinemann, and Cambridge, MA: Harvard University Press, 1925), 193–231.

Secondary literature

Adams, James Eli, "Philosophical Forgetfulness: John Stuart Mill's 'Nature'," *Journal of the History of Ideas*, 53 (1992), 437–54.

Alcott, Blake, "Jevons' Paradox," *Ecological Economics*, 54 (2005), 9–21.

Aldrich, John, "The Discovery of Comparative Advantage," *Journal of the History of Economic Thought*, 26 (2004), 379–99.

Aldridge, Alfred Owen, "Franklin as Demographer," *Journal of Economic History*, 9 (1949), 25–44.

Amoh, Yasuo, "The Ancient-Modern Controversy in the Scottish Enlightenment," in *The Rise of Political Economy in the Scottish Enlightenment*, eds. Tatsuya Sakamoto and Hideo Tanaka (London and New York: Routledge, 2003), 69–85.

Appleby, Joyce Oldham, *Economic Thought and Ideology in Seventeenth-Century England* (Princeton: Princeton University Press, 1978).

Appuhn, Karl, *A Forest on the Sea: Environmental Expertise in Renaissance Venice* (Baltimore: Johns Hopkins University Press, 2009).

Arneil, Barbara, *John Locke and America: The Defence of English Colonialism* (Oxford: Clarendon Press, 1996).

Aspromourgos, Tony, "The Life of William Petty in Relation to His Economics: A Tercentenary Interpretation," *History of Political Economy*, 20 (1988), 337–56.

Ayres, Robert U., Jeroen C.J.M. van den Bergh, and John M. Gowdy, "Strong versus Weak Sustainability: Economics, Natural Sciences, and 'Consilience'," *Environmental Ethics*, 23 (2001), 155–68.

Baker, Keith Michael, *Condorcet: From Natural Philosophy to Social Mathematics* (Chicago and London: University of Chicago Press, 1975).

Banzhaf, H. Spencer, "Consumer Sovereignty in the History of Environmental Economics," *History of Political Economy*, 43 (2011), 339–45.

——— "Productive Nature and the Net Product: Quesnay's Economies Animal and Political," *History of Political Economy*, 32 (2000), 517–51.

Barton, Gregory Allen, *Empire Forestry and the Origins of Environmentalism* (Cambridge: Cambridge University Press, 2002).

Becker, Christian, Malte Faber, Kirsten Hertel, and Reiner Manstetten, "Malthus vs. Wordsworth: Perspectives on Humankind, Nature and Economy. A Contribution to the History and the Foundations of Ecological Economics," *Ecological Economics*, 53 (2005), 299–310.

Bell, Duncan, "John Stuart Mill on Colonies," *Political Theory*, 38 (2010), 34–64.

Benton, Ted, "Engels and the Politics of Nature," in *Engels Today: A Centenary Appreciation*, ed. Christopher J. Arthur (Basingstoke: Macmillan, 1996), 67–93.

Bergh, Jeroen C.J.M. van den, "Ecological Economics: Themes, Approaches, and Differences with Environmental Economics," *Regional Environmental Change*, 2 (2001), 13–23.

Berry, Christopher J., *Social Theory of the Scottish Enlightenment* (Edinburgh: Edinburgh University Press, 2001).

Blum, Carol, *Strength in Numbers: Population, Reproduction, and Power in Eighteenth-Century France* (Baltimore and London: Johns Hopkins University Press, 2002).

Boianovsky, Mauro, "Humboldt and the Economists on Natural Resources, Institutions and Underdevelopment (1752–1859)," *European Journal of the History of Economic Thought*, 20 (2013), 58–88.

Bonar, James, *Theories of Population from Raleigh to Arthur Young* (London: Frank Cass, 1966).

Bowley, Marian, *Nassau Senior and Classical Economics* (London: George Allen and Unwin, 1937).

Brewer, Anthony, "Cantillon and the Land Theory of Value," *History of Political Economy*, 20 (1988), 1–14.

——— "The Concept of an Agricultural Surplus, from Petty to Smith," *Journal of the History of Economic Thought*, 33 (2011), 487–505.

——— "The Concept of Growth in Eighteenth-Century Economics," *History of Political Economy*, 27 (1995), 609–38.

Bruni, Luigino, and Pier Luigi Porta, "*Economia civile* and *pubblica felicità* in the Italian Enlightenment," *History of Political Economy*, 35, Supplement (2003), 361–85.

Charlton, D. G., *New Images of the Natural in France: A Study in European Cultural History 1750–1800* (Cambridge, 1984).

Christensen, Paul P., "Fire, Motion, and Productivity: The Proto-Energetics of Nature and Economy in François Quesnay," in *Natural Images in Economic Thought: "Markets*

Read in Tooth and Claw", ed. Philip Mirowski (Cambridge: Cambridge University Press, 1994), 249–88.

Christofides, L. N., "On Share Contracts and Other Economic Contributions of Xenophon," *Scottish Journal of Political Economy*, 39 (1992), 111–22.

Collini, Stefan, Donald Winch, and John Burrow, *That Noble Science of Politics: A Study in Nineteenth-Century Intellectual History* (Cambridge: Cambridge University Press, 1983).

Corsi, Pietro, "The Heritage of Dugald Stewart: Oxford Philosophy and the Method of Political Economy," *Nuncius*, 2 (1987), 89–144.

Cremaschi, Sergio, and Marcelo Dascal, "Malthus and Ricardo: Two Styles for Economic Theory," *Science in Context*, 11 (1998), 229–54.

Cronon, William, "The Trouble with Wilderness; or, Getting Back to the Wrong Nature," in *Uncommon Ground: Rethinking the Human Place in Nature*, ed. William Cronon (New York and London: W. W. Norton, 1996), 69–90.

Davis, Timothy, *Ricardo's Macroeconomics: Money, Trade Cycles, and Growth* (Cambridge: Cambridge University Press, 2005).

DeLuca, Kevin, "The Frankfurt School and the Domination of Nature: New Grounds for Radical Environmentalism," in *Rethinking the Frankfurt School: Alternative Legacies of Cultural Critique*, eds. Jeffrey T. Nealon and Caren Irr (Albany: State University of New York Press, 2002), 153–67.

Denham, Helen, "The Cunning of Unreason and Nature's Revolt: Max Horkheimer and William Leiss on the Domination of Nature," *Environment and History*, 3 (1997), 149–75.

Depoortère, Christophe, "William Nassau Senior and David Ricardo on the Method of Political Economy," *Journal of the History of Economic Thought*, 35 (2013), 19–42.

Dixon, William, "Ricardo: Economic Thought and Social Order," *Journal of the History of Economic Thought*, 30 (2008), 235–53.

Elias, Norbert, *The Civilizing Process: The History of Manners and State Formation and Civilization*, trans. Edmund Jephcott (Oxford and Cambridge, MA: Blackwell, 1994).

Emerson, Roger L., "Conjectural History and Scottish Philosophers," *Historical Papers/ Communications Historiques*, 19 (1984), 63–90.

Evensky, Jerry, *Adam Smith's Moral Philosophy: A Historical and Contemporary Perspective on Markets, Law, Ethics, and Culture* (Cambridge: Cambridge University Press, 2005).

Faccarello, Gilbert, *The Foundations of* Laissez-faire*: The Economics of Pierre de Boisguilbert*, trans. Carolyn Shread (London and New York: Routledge, 1999).

——— "'Nil Repente!': Galiani and Necker on Economic Reforms," *European Journal of the History of Economic Thought*, 1 (1994), 519–50.

Finkelstein, Andrea, *Harmony and the Balance: An Intellectual History of Seventeenth-Century English Economic Thought* (Ann Arbor: University of Michigan Press, 2000).

Fitzmaurice, Andrew, "The Commercial Ideology of Colonization in Jacobean England: Robert Johnson, Giovanni Botero, and the Pursuit of Greatness," *William and Mary Quarterly*, 64 (2007), 791–820.

——— "The Genealogy of *Terra Nullius*," *Australian Historical Studies*, 38 (2007), 1–15.

Forget, Evelyn, "J.-B. Say and Adam Smith: An Essay in the Transmission of Ideas," *Canadian Journal of Economics*, 26 (1993), 121–33.

Foster, John Bellamy, *Marx's Ecology: Materialism and Nature* (New York: Monthly Review Press, 2000).

Frierson, Patrick R., "Adam Smith and the Possibility of Sympathy with Nature," *Pacific Philosophical Quarterly*, 87 (2006), 442–80.

Gammon, Earl, "Nature as Adversary: The Rise of Modern Economic Conceptions of Nature," *Economy and Society*, 39 (2010), 218–46.

Garnett, Jane, "Political and Domestic Economy in Victorian Social Thought: Ruskin and Xenophon," in *Economy, Polity, and Society: British Intellectual History 1750–1950*, eds. Stefan Collini, Richard Whatmore, and Brian Young (Cambridge: Cambridge University Press, 2000), 205–23.

Garrett, Aaron, "Anthropology: the 'Original' of Human Nature," in *The Cambridge Companion to the Scottish Enlightenment*, ed. Alexander Broadie (Cambridge: Cambridge University Press, 2003), 79–93.

Gerson, Gal, "From the State of Nature to Evolution in John Stuart Mill," *Australian Journal of Politics and History*, 48 (2002), 305–21.

Gislain, Jean-Jacques, "James Steuart: Economy and Population," in *The Economics of James Steuart*, ed. Ramón Tortajada (London and New York: Routledge, 1999), 169–85.

Glacken, Clarence J., *Traces on the Rhodian Shore: Nature and Culture in Western Thought from Ancient Times to the End of the Eighteenth Century* (Berkeley: University of California Press, 1967).

Goodwin, Craufurd D., "Ecologist Meets Economics: Aldo Leopold, 1887–1948," *Journal of the History of Economic Thought*, 30 (2008), 429–52.

Gordon, Barry, *Economic Analysis Before Adam Smith: Hesiod to Lessius* (London and Basingstoke: Macmillan, 1975).

Griswold, Charles L., Jr., *Adam Smith and the Virtues of Enlightenment* (Cambridge: Cambridge University Press, 1999).

Groenewegen, Peter, "Turgot's Place in the History of Economic Thought: A Bicentenary Estimate," *History of Political Economy*, 15 (1983), 585–616.

Grove, Richard H., *Green Imperialism: Colonial Expansion, Tropical Island Edens and the Origins of Environmentalism, 1600–1860* (Cambridge: Cambridge University Press, 1995).

Gustafsson, Bo, "Nature and Economy," in *Nature and Society in Historical Context*, eds. Mikuláš Teich, Roy Porter, and Bo Gustafsson (Cambridge: Cambridge University Press, 1997), 347–63.

Haakonssen, Knud, "From Moral Philosophy to Political Economy: The Contribution of Dugald Stewart," in *Philosophers of the Scottish Enlightenment*, ed. V. Hope (Edinburgh: Edinburgh University Press, 1984), 211–32.

Habibi, Don, "The Moral Dimensions of J. S. Mill's Colonialism," *Journal of Social Philosophy*, 30 (1999), 125–46.

Hadot, Pierre, *The Veil of Isis: An Essay on the History of the Idea of Nature*, trans. Michael Chase (Cambridge, MA, and London: Harvard University Press, 2006).

Harman, P. M., *The Culture of Nature in Britain 1680–1860* (New Haven and London: Yale University Press, 2009).

Harris, Robert D., *Necker: Reform Statesman of the Ancien Régime* (Berkeley: University of California Press, 1979).

Harrison, Peter, *The Bible, Protestantism, and the Rise of Natural Science* (Cambridge: Cambridge University Press, 1998).

Hartwick, John M., "Robert Wallace and Malthus and the Ratios," *History of Political Economy*, 20 (1988), 357–79.

Headley, John M., "Geography and Empire in the Late Renaissance: Botero's Assignment, Western Universalism, and the Civilizing Process," *Renaissance Quarterly*, 53 (2000), 1119–55.

Heckscher, Eli F., *Mercantilism*, trans. Mendel Shapiro, ed. E. F. Söderlund, 2 vols. (London: George Allen & Unwin, and New York: Macmillan, 1962).

Heilbroner, Robert L., "The Paradox of Progress: Decline and Decay in *The Wealth of Nations*," *Journal of the History of Ideas*, 34 (1973), 243–62.

Henderson, Willie, *John Ruskin's Political Economy* (London and New York: Routledge, 2000).

Herlitz, Lars, "Art and Nature in Pre-Classical Economics of the Seventeenth and Eighteenth Centuries," in *Nature and Society in Historical Context*, eds. Mikuláš Teich, Roy Porter, and Bo Gustafsson (Cambridge: Cambridge University Press, 1997), 163–75.

Hollander, Samuel, *Classical Economics* (Oxford and New York: Basil Blackwell, 1987).

——— *The Economics of Adam Smith* (London: Heinemann Educational Books, 1973).

——— *Friedrich Engels and Marxian Political Economy* (Cambridge: Cambridge University Press, 2011).

——— "More on Malthus and Agricultural Protection," *History of Political Economy*, 27 (1995), 531–7.

Hont, Istvan, *Jealousy of Trade: International Competition and the Nation-State in Historical Perspective* (Cambridge, MA, and London: Harvard University Press, 2005).

Höpfl, H. M., "From Savage to Scotsman: Conjectural History in the Scottish Enlightenment," *Journal of British Studies*, 17 (1978), 19–40.

Hutchison, Terence, *Before Adam Smith: The Emergence of Political Economy, 1662–1776* (Oxford and Cambridge, MA: Basil Blackwell,1988).

Irwin, Douglas A., *Against the Tide: An Intellectual History of Free Trade* (Princeton: Princeton University Press, 1996).

Jahn, Beate, "Barbarian Thoughts: Imperialism in the Philosophy of John Stuart Mill," *Review of International Studies*, 31 (2005), 599–618.

James, Patricia, *Population Malthus: His Life and Times* (London: Routledge & Kegan Paul, 1979).

Johnson, E. A. J., *Predecessors of Adam Smith: The Growth of British Economic Thought* (New York: Augustus M. Kelley, 1965).

Johnstone, Paul H., "The Rural Socrates," *Journal of the History of Ideas*, 5 (1944), 151–75.

Jonsson, Fredrik Albritton, *Enlightenment's Frontier: The Scottish Highlands and the Origins of Environmentalism* (New Haven and London: Yale University Press, 2013).

——— "Natural History and Improvement: The Case of Tobacco," in *Mercantilism Reimagined: Political Economy in Early Modern Britain and Its Empire*, eds. Philip J. Stern and Carl Wennerlind (Oxford: Oxford University Press, 2014), 117–33.

Kaplan, Steven L., *Bread, Politics and Political Economy in the Reign of Louis XV*, 2 vols. (The Hague: Martinus Nijhoff, 1976).

Kaye, Joel, *Economy and Nature in the Fourteenth Century: Money, Market Exchange, and the Emergence of Scientific Thought* (Cambridge: Cambridge University Press, 1998).

Kula, E., *History of Environmental Economic Thought* (London and New York: Routledge, 1998).

Kwass, Michael, "Consumption and the World of Ideas: Consumer Revolution and the Moral Economy of the Marquis de Mirabeau," *Eighteenth-Century Studies*, 37 (2004), 187–213.

LaFreniere, Gilbert F., *The Decline of Nature: Environmental History and the Western Worldview* (Palo Alto: Academica Press, 2008).

Langholm, Odd, "The Medieval Schoolmen (1200–1400)," in *Ancient and Medieval Economic Ideas and Concepts of Social Justice*, eds. S. Todd Lowry and Barry Gordon (Leiden: Brill, 1998), 439–501.

Leiss, William, *The Domination of Nature* (Boston: Beacon Press, 1974).

Leshem, Dotan, "Oikonomia Redefined," *Journal of the History of Economic Thought*, 35 (2013), 43–61.

Limoges, Camille, and Claude Ménard, "Organization and the Division of Labour: Biological Metaphors at Work in Alfred Marshall's *Principles of Economics*," in *Natural Images in Economic Thought: "Markets Read in Tooth and Claw"*, ed. Philip Mirowski (Cambridge: Cambridge University Press, 1994), 336–59.

Lovejoy, Arthur O., *The Great Chain of Being: A Study of the History of an Idea* (New York: Harper and Row, 1960).

Lowry, S. Todd, "The Agricultural Foundation of the Seventeenth-Century English Oeconomy," *History of Political Economy*, 35, Supplement (2003), 74–100.

——— "The Classical Greek Theory of Natural Resource Economics," *Land Economics*, 41 (1965), 203–8.

——— "The Economic and Jurisprudential Ideas of the Ancient Greeks: Our Heritage from Hellenic Thought," in *Ancient and Medieval Economic Ideas and Concepts of Social Justice*, eds. S. Todd Lowry and Barry Gordon (Leiden: Brill, 1998), 11–37.

Luehrs, Robert B., "Population and Utopia in the Thought of Robert Wallace," *Eighteenth-Century Studies*, 20 (1987), 313–35.

Maas, Harro, "'A Hard Battle to Fight': Natural Theology and the Dismal Science, 1820–50," *History of Political Economy*, 40 (annual supplement) (2008), 143–67.

Macfarlane, Alan, "David Hume and the Political Economy of Agrarian Civilization," *History of European Ideas*, 27 (2001), 79–91.

Magnusson, Lars, *The Political Economy of Mercantilism* (Abingdon and New York: Routledge, 2015).

Maifreda, Germano, *From* Oikonomia *to Political Economy: Constructing Economic Knowledge from the Renaissance to the Scientific Revolution*, trans. Loretta Valtz Mannucci (Farnham and Burlington: Ashgate, 2012).

Marchi, N. B. de, "The Success of Mill's *Principles*," *History of Political Economy*, 6 (1974), 119–57.

Marouby, Christian, "Adam Smith and the Anthropology of the Enlightenment: The 'Ethnographic' Sources of Economic Progress," in *The Anthropology of the Enlightenment*, eds. Larry Wolff and Marco Cipolloni (Stanford: Stanford University Press, 2007), 85–102.

Marwah, Inder S., "Complicating Barbarism and Civilization: Mill's Complex Sociology of Human Development," *History of Political Thought*, 32 (2011), 345–66.

Marx, Leo, *The Machine in the Garden: Technology and the Pastoral Ideal in America* (New York: Oxford University Press, 1970).

Maverick, Lewis A., "Pierre Poivre: Eighteenth Century Explorer of Southeast Asia," *Pacific Historical Review*, 10 (1941), 165–77.

McCormick, Ted, "Population: Modes of Seventeenth-Century Demographic Thought," in *Mercantilism Reimagined: Political Economy in Early Modern Britain and Its Empire*, eds. Philip J. Stern and Carl Wennerlind (Oxford: Oxford University Press, 2014), 25–45.

——— *William Petty and the Ambitions of Political Arithmetic* (Oxford: Oxford University Press, 2009).

Meek, Ronald L., *Social Science and the Ignoble Savage* (Cambridge: Cambridge University Press, 1976).

Meenai, S. A., "Robert Torrens–1780–1864," *Economica*, New Series 23 (1956), 49–61.

Mehta, Uday Singh, *Liberalism and Empire: A Study in Nineteenth-Century British Liberal Thought* (Chicago and London: University of Chicago Press, 1999).

Meikle, Scott, *Aristotle's Economic Thought* (Oxford: Clarendon Press, 1995).

Milgate, Murray, and Shannon C. Stimson, *After Adam Smith: A Century of Transformations in Politics and Political Economy* (Princeton and Oxford: Princeton University Press, 2009).

Miller, William L., "Richard Jones's Contribution to the Theory of Rent," *History of Political Economy*, 9 (1977), 346–65.

Mirowski, Philip, "The Realms of the Natural," in *Natural Images in Economic Thought: "Markets Read in Tooth and Claw"*, ed. Philip Mirowski (Cambridge: Cambridge University Press, 1994), 451–83.

Missemer, Antoine, "William Stanley Jevons' *The Coal Question* (1865), Beyond the Rebound Effect," *Ecological Economics*, 82 (2012), 97–103.

Mokyr, Joel, "The Intellectual Origins of Modern Economic Growth," *Journal of Economic History*, 65 (2005), 285–351.

Moore, Stanley, "Ricardo and the State of Nature," *Scottish Journal of Political Economy*, 13 (1966), 317–31.

Mossner, Ernest C., *The Forgotten Hume (Le Bon David)* (New York: Columbia University Press, 1943).

Muldrew, Craig, "Afterword: Mercantilism to Macroeconomics," in *Mercantilism Reimagined: Political Economy in Early Modern Britain and Its Empire*, eds. Philip J. Stern and Carl Wennerlind (Oxford: Oxford University Press, 2014), 371–83.

Munda, Giuseppe, "Environmental Economics, Ecological Economics, and the Concept of Sustainable Development," *Environmental Values*, 6 (1997), 213–33.

Nagai, Yoshio, "Robert Wallace and the Irish and Scottish Enlightenment," in *The Rise of Political Economy in the Scottish Enlightenment*, eds. Tatsuya Sakamoto and Hideo Tanaka (London and New York: Routledge, 2003), 55–68.

Nash, Roderick, *Wilderness and the American Mind* (New Haven and London: Yale University Press, 1973).

Oakley, Francis, "Lovejoy's Unexplored Option," *Journal of the History of Ideas*, 48 (1987), 231–45.

O'Brien, D. P., *The Classical Economists Revisited* (Princeton and Oxford: Princeton University Press, 2004).

O'Connor, Martin, "John Stuart Mill's Utilitarianism and the Social Ethics of Sustainable Development," *European Journal of the History of Economic Thought*, 4 (1997), 478–506.

Omori, Ikuo, "The 'Scottish Triangle' in the Shaping of Political Economy: David Hume, Sir James Steuart, and Adam Smith," in *The Rise of Political Economy in the Scottish Enlightenment*, eds. Tatsuya Sakamoto and Hideo Tanaka (London and New York: Routledge, 2003), 103–18.

Otteson, James R., *Adam Smith's Marketplace of Life* (Cambridge: Cambridge University Press, 2002).

Pagden, Anthony, *Lords of All the World: Ideologies of Empire in Spain, Britain and France c. 1500-c. 1800* (New Haven and London: Yale University Press, 1995).

Palmeri, Frank, "Conjectural History and the Origins of Sociology," *Studies in Eighteenth Century Culture*, 37 (2008), 1–21.

Parham, John, "What is (Ecological) 'Nature'? John Stuart Mill and the Victorian Perspective," in *Culture, Creativity and Environment: New Environmentalist Criticism*, eds. Fiona Becket and Terry Gifford (Amsterdam and New York: Rodopi, 2007), 37–54.

Phillips, Denise, *Acolytes of Nature: Defining Natural Science in Germany, 1770–1850* (Chicago and London: University of Chicago Press, 2012).

Pinot, Virgile, "Les physiocrates et la Chine au XVIIIe siècle," *Revue d'histoire modern et contemporaine*, 8 (1906/1907), 200–14.

Pitts, Jennifer, *A Turn to Empire: The Rise of Imperial Liberalism in Britain and France* (Princeton: Princeton University Press, 2005).

Plassart, Anna, "'Un Impérialiste Libéral'? Jean-Baptiste Say on Colonies and the Extra-European World," *French Historical Studies*, 32 (2009), 223–50.

Pocock, J. G. A., *Barbarism and Religion*, vol. 4: *Barbarians, Savages and Empires* (Cambridge: Cambridge University Press, 2005).

——— *Barbarism and Religion*, vol. 2: *Narratives of Civil Government* (Cambridge: Cambridge University Press, 1999).

——— *Virtue, Commerce, and History: Essays on Political Thought and History, Chiefly in the Eighteenth Century* (Cambridge: Cambridge University Press, 1985).

Porta, Pier Luigi, and Roberto Scazzieri, "Pietro Verri's Political Economy: Commercial Society, Civil Society, and the Science of the Legislator," *History of Political Economy*, 34 (2002), 83–110.

Porter, Roy, "The Urban and the Rustic in Enlightenment London," in *Nature and Society in Historical Context*, eds. Mikuláš Teich, Roy Porter, and Bo Gustafsson (Cambridge: Cambridge University Press, 1997), 176–94.

Praag, Philip van, "Un populationniste hollandais: Pieter de la Court (1618–1685)," *Population (French Edition)*, 18 (1963), 349–58.

Price, Matt, "Economics, Ecology, and the Value of Nature," in *The Moral Authority of Nature*, eds. Lorraine Daston and Fernando Vidal (Chicago and London: University of Chicago Press, 2004), 182–204.

Pullen, J. M., "Malthus on Agricultural Protection: An Alternative View," *History of Political Economy*, 27 (1995), 517–29.

——— "Malthus' Theological Ideas and Their Influence on His Principle of Population," *History of Political Economy*, 13 (1981), 39–54.

Rashid, Salim, "Richard Jones and Baconian Historicism at Cambridge," *Journal of Economic Issues*, 13 (1979), 159–73.

——— "Richard Whately and Christian Political Economy at Oxford and Dublin," *Journal of the History of Ideas*, 38 (1977), 147–55.

Rendall, Jane, "Adaptations: History, Gender, and Political Economy in the Work of Dugald Stewart," *History of European Ideas*, 38 (2012), 143–61.

Reynard, Pierre Claude, "Public Order and Privilege: Eighteenth-Century French Roots of Environmental Regulation," *Technology and Culture*, 43 (2002), 1–28.

Richards, John F., *The Unending Frontier: An Environmental History of the Early Modern World* (Berkeley: University of California Press, 2005).

Riskin, Jessica, "The 'Spirit of System' and the Fortunes of Physiocracy," *History of Political Economy*, 35, Supplement (2003), 42–73.

Ritvo, Harriet, *The Animal Estate: The English and Other Creatures in the Victorian Age* (Cambridge, MA: Harvard University Press, 1987).

Robbins, Caroline, *The Eighteenth-Century Commonwealthman: Studies in the Transmission, Development, and Circumstance of English Liberal Thought from the Restoration of Charles II Until the War with the Thirteen Colonies* (Indianapolis: Liberty Fund, 2004 [1959]).

Robertson, John, *The Case for the Enlightenment: Scotland and Naples 1680–1760* (Cambridge: Cambridge University Press, 2005).

Robson, John M., "Civilization and Culture as Moral Concepts," in *The Cambridge Companion to Mill*, ed. John Skorupski (Cambridge, 1998), 338–71.

——— *The Improvement of Mankind: The Social and Political Thought of John Stuart Mill* (Toronto and London: University of Toronto Press and Routledge & Kegan Paul, 1968).

Roncaglia, Alessandro, *Petty: The Origins of Political Economy*, trans. Isabella Cherubini (Armonk, NY: M. E. Sharpe, 1985).

Rothschild, Emma, *Economic Sentiments: Adam Smith, Condorcet, and the Enlightenment* (Cambridge, MA, and London: Harvard University Press, 2001).

——— "Maintaining (Environmental) Capital Intact," *Modern Intellectual History*, 8 (2011), 193–212.

Ruffin, Roy J., "Debunking a Myth: Torrens on Comparative Advantage," *History of Political Economy*, 37 (2005), 711–22.

Sakamoto, Tatsuya, "Hume's Political Economy as a System of Manners," in *The Rise of Political Economy in the Scottish Enlightenment*, eds. Tatsuya Sakamoto and Hideo Tanaka (London and New York: Routledge, 2003), 86–102.

Samuelson, Paul A., "Thünen at Two Hundred," *Journal of Economic Literature*, 21 (1983), 1468–88.

Schabas, Margaret, *The Natural Origins of Economics* (Chicago and London: University of Chicago Press, 2005).

Schaffer, Simon, "The Earth's Fertility as a Social Fact in Early Modern Britain," in *Nature and Society in Historical Context*, eds. Mikuláš Teich, Roy Porter, and Bo Gustafsson (Cambridge: Cambridge University Press, 1997), 124–47.

Schumpeter, Joseph A., *History of Economic Analysis*, ed. Elizabeth Boody Schumpeter (New York: Oxford University Press, 1954).

Scully, Edgar, "La philosophie politique de saint Thomas d'Aquin: économie politique?," *Laval théologique et philosophique*, 38 (1982), 49–59.

Sebastiani, Silvia, *The Scottish Enlightenment: Race, Gender, and the Limits of Progress*, trans. Jeremy Carden (New York: Palgrave Macmillan, 2013).

Semmel, Bernard, "The Hume-Tucker Debate and Pitt's Trade Proposals," *Economic Journal*, 75 (1965), 759–70.

——— *The Rise of Free Trade Imperialism: Classical Political Economy, the Empire of Free Trade and Imperialism, 1750–1850* (Cambridge: Cambridge University Press, 1970).

Shelton, George, *Dean Tucker and Eighteenth-Century Economic and Political Thought* (London and Basingstoke: Macmillan, 1981).

Shinohara, Hisashi, "Dugald Stewart at the Final Stage of the Scottish Enlightenment: Natural Jurisprudence, Political Economy and the Science of Politics," in *The Rise of Political Economy in the Scottish Enlightenment*, eds. Tatsuya Sakamoto and Hideo Tanaka (London and New York: Routledge, 2003), 179–93.

Skinner, Andrew S., "The Shaping of Political Economy in the Enlightenment," *Scottish Journal of Political Economy*, 37 (1990), 145–65.

——— "Sir James Steuart: Author of a System," *Scottish Journal of Political Economy*, 28 (1981), 20–42.

Smith, Richard A., "The Eco-Suicidal Economics of Adam Smith," *Capitalism Nature Socialism*, 18 (2007), 22–43.

Smith, Robert S., "Spanish Mercantilism: A Hardy Perennial," *Southern Economic Journal*, 38 (1971), 1–11.

Smout, T. C., *Exploring Environmental History: Selected Essays* (Edinburgh: Edinburgh University Press, 2009).

——— "A New Look at the Scottish Improvers," *Scottish Historical Review*, 91 (2012), 125–49.

Sowell, Thomas, "Sismondi: A Neglected Pioneer," *History of Political Economy*, 4 (1972), 62–88.

Spadafora, David, *The Idea of Progress in Eighteenth-Century Britain* (New Haven and London: Yale University Press, 1990).

Spary, E. C., "'Peaches Which the Patriarchs Lacked": Natural History, Natural Resources, and the Natural Economy in France," *History of Political Economy*, 35, Supplement (2003), 14–41.

Spengler, Joseph J., *French Predecessors of Malthus: A Study in Eighteenth-Century Wage and Population Theory* (New York: Octagon Books, 1965).

Stangeland, Charles Emil, *Pre-Malthusian Doctrines of Population: A Study in the History of Economic Theory* (New York: AMS Press, 1967).

Steiguer, J. Edward de, *The Origins of Modern Environmental Thought* (Tucson: University of Arizona Press, 2006).

Stern, Philip J., and Carl Wennerlind, "Introduction," in *Mercantilism Reimagined: Political Economy in Early Modern Britain and Its Empire*, eds. Philip J. Stern and Carl Wennerlind (Oxford: Oxford University Press, 2014), 3–22.

Stoll, Mark, "'Sagacious' Bernard Palissy: Pinchot, Marsh, and the Connecticut Origins of American Conservation," *Environmental History*, 16 (2011), 4–37.

Stone, Alison, "Adorno and the Disenchantment of Nature," *Philosophy & Social Criticism*, 32 (2006), 231–53.

Thomas, Keith, *Man and the Natural World: Changing Attitudes in England 1500–1800* (Harmondsworth: Penguin Books, 1984).

Thornton, Mark, "Cantillon, Hume, and the Rise of Antimercantilism," *History of Political Economy*, 39 (2007), 453–80.

Tijn, Th. van, "Dutch Economic Thought in the Seventeenth Century," in *Economic Thought in the Netherlands: 1650–1950*, eds. J. van Daal and A. Heertje (Aldershot: Avebury, 1992), 7–28.

Totman, Conrad, *The Green Archipelago: Forestry in Pre-Industrial Japan* (Athens: Ohio University Press, 1998).

Tuan, Mao-Lan, *Simonde de Sismondi as an Economist* (New York: AMS Press, 1968).

Tuck, Richard, *Philosophy and Government 1572–1651* (Cambridge: Cambridge University Press, 1993).

Tynan, Nicola, "Mill and Senior on London's Water Supply: Agency, Increasing Returns, and Natural Monopoly," *Journal of the History of Economic Thought*, 29 (2007), 49–65.

Vardi, Liana, *The Physiocrats and the World of the Enlightenment* (Cambridge: Cambridge University Press, 2012).

Venturi, Franco, *Italy and the Enlightenment: Studies in a Cosmopolitan Century*, trans. Susan Corsi, ed. Stuart Woolf (London: Longman, 1972).

Warde, Paul, *Ecology, Economy and State Formation in Early Modern Germany* (Cambridge: Cambridge University Press, 2006).

——— "The Invention of Sustainability," *Modern Intellectual History*, 8 (2011), 153–70.

Waterman, A. M. C., *Revolution, Economics and Religion: Christian Political Economy, 1798–1833* (Cambridge: Cambridge University Press, 1991).

Watson, Robert N., *Back to Nature: The Green and the Real in the Late Renaissance* (Philadelphia: University of Pennsylvania Press, 2006).

Weinstein, Jack Russell, *Adam Smith's Pluralism: Rationality, Education, and the Moral Sentiments* (New Haven and London: Yale University Press, 2013).

Wells, David, "Resurrecting the Dismal Parson: Malthus, Ecology, and Political Thought," *Political Studies*, 30 (1982), 1–15.

Wennerlind, Carl, "Money: Hartlibian Political Economy and the New Culture of Credit," in *Mercantilism Reimagined: Political Economy in Early Modern Britain and Its Empire*, eds. Philip J. Stern and Carl Wennerlind (Oxford: Oxford University Press, 2014), 74–93.

Weststeijn, Arthur, *Commercial Republicanism in the Dutch Golden Age: The Political Thought of Johan & Pieter de la Court* (Leiden and Boston: Brill, 2012).

Weulersse, Georges, *Le mouvement physiocratique en France (de 1756 a 1770)*, 2 vols. (Paris: Félix Alcan, 1910).

Whatmore, Richard, *Republicanism and the French Revolution: An Intellectual History of Jean-Baptiste Say's Political Economy* (Oxford: Oxford University Press, 2000).

White, Lynn, Jr., "The Historical Roots of our Ecological Crisis," *Science*, 155 (10 March 1967), 1203–7.

Williams, Michael, *Deforesting the Earth: From Prehistory to Global Crisis* (Chicago and London: University of Chicago Press, 2003).

Winch, Donald, *Riches and Poverty: An Intellectual History of Political Economy in Britain, 1750–1834* (Cambridge: Cambridge University Press, 1996).

Wolloch, Nathaniel, "The Civilizing Process, Nature, and Stadial Theory," *Eighteenth-Century Studies*, 44 (2011), 245–59.

——— *History and Nature in the Enlightenment: Praise of the Mastery of Nature in Eighteenth-Century Historical Literature* (Farnham and Burlington: Ashgate, 2011).

——— "The Liberal Origins of the Modern View of Nature," *The Tocqueville Review*, 34 (2013), 107–31.

Worster, Donald, *Nature's Economy: A History of Ecological Ideas* (Cambridge: Cambridge University Press, 1994).

Wrigley, E. A., "The Limits to Growth: Malthus and the Classical Economists," *Population and Development Review*, 14, Supplement (1988), 30–48.

Young, B. W., "Christianity, Commerce and the Cannon: Josiah Tucker and Richard Woodward on Political Economy," *History of European Ideas*, 22 (1996), 385–400.

Young, Robert M., *Darwin's Metaphor: Nature's Place in Victorian Culture* (Cambridge: Cambridge University Press, 1985).

Index